MW00999687

THE GARTER SNAKES

Animal Natural History Series
Victor H. Hutchison, General Editor

THE GARTER SNAKES

Evolution and Ecology

By Douglas A. Rossman,
Neil B. Ford, and
Richard A. Seigel

University of Oklahoma Press
Norman and London

Library of Congress Cataloging-in-Publication Data

Rossman, Douglas Athon, 1936–
    The garter snakes : evolution and ecology / by Douglas A. Rossman,
Neil B. Ford, and Richard A. Seigel.
      p. cm. — (Animal natural history series ; v. 2)
    Includes bibliographical references and index.
    ISBN 0-8061-2820-8 (alk. paper)
    1. Garter snakes. I. Ford, Neil B. II. Seigel, Richad A.
III. Title. IV. Series.
QL666.0636R67 1966
597.96—dc20   95-37746
                                                CIP

The Garter Snakes: Evolution and Ecology is Volume 2 in the Animal Natural History Series.

Text design by Cathy Carney Imboden. Text typeface is Trump Mediaeval.

The paper in this book meets the guidelines for permanence and durability of the Committee on Production Guidelines for Book Longevity of the Council on Library Resources, Inc. ∞

1 2 3 4 5 6 7 8 9 10

DEDICATIONS

Douglas A. Rossman
To Roger Conant, my mentor and friend, who introduced me to the wonderful world of thamnophiine systematics and thereby changed the path of my professional life forever, and in memory of my parents, the late Vernon and Josephine Rossman, whose love and encouragement allowed me the opportunity to discover my niche in the world.

Neil B. Ford
To my parents, Charles and Emily Ford, who, although they have no idea how they did it, obviously instilled a preadolescent fascination for snakes into their son. I hope my son is lucky enough to have a similar obsession. To Joan and David, who lived through the three years of preparation and work this book required. To Charles C. Carpenter, who, through his example, taught me how much fun it is to be a scientist studying reptiles.

Richard A. Seigel
To Henry S. Fitch, pioneer in the study of garter snakes and snake ecology, who serves as a continuing inspiration to all snake biologists, and to Virginia Fitch, who, along with Henry, helped make my schooling in the ways of snakes so much fun. I also want to express my appreciation to my parents, for all their encouragement through the years, and to Nadia and Ben, for all their support and love.

CONTENTS

Contents

COLOR PLATES

Color Plates

Thamnophis elegans vagrans;
Thamnophis elegans vagrans
  ("nigrescens" morph);
Thamnophis elegans
  vascotanneri;
Thamnophis eques eques

5. *Thamnophis eques megalops;*
   Thamnophis eques megalops;
   Thamnophis eques virgatenuis;
   Thamnophis errans;
   Thamnophis exsul (spotted
     morph);
   Thamnophis exsul (unspotted
     morph)

6. *Thamnophis fulvus;*
   Thamnophis gigas (striped
     morph);
   Thamnophis gigas (spotted
     morph);
   Thamnophis godmani;
   Thamnophis hammondii (two-
     striped morph);
   Thamnophis hammondii
     (stripeless morph)

7. *Thamnophis marcianus*
     marcianus;
   Thamnophis marcianus
     bovallii;
   Thamnophis marcianus
     praecularis;
   Thamnophis melanogaster
     canescens ("plain" morph);

Thamnophis melanogaster
  canescens (spotted morph);
Thamnophis melanogaster
  canescens (striped morph)

8. *Thamnophis melanogaster*
     canescens (ventral view);
   Thamnophis melanogaster
     chihuahuaensis;
   Thamnophis melanogaster
     chihuahuaensis (ventral
     view);
   Thamnophis mendax;
   Thamnophis nigronuchalis;
   Thamnophis ordinoides (red-
     striped morph)

9. *Thamnophis ordinoides*
     (yellow-striped morph);
   Thamnophis postremus;
   Thamnophis proximus
     proximus;
   Thamnophis proximus
     diabolicus;
   Thamnophis proximus orarius;
   Thamnophis proximus
     rubrilineatus

10. *Thamnophis proximus*
      rutiloris;
    Thamnophis pulchrilatus;
    Thamnophis radix (light
      morph);
    Thamnophis radix (dark
      morph);

Color Plates

Thamnophis radix (red morph);
Thamnophis rufipunctatus
  (red-spotted morph)

11. *Thamnophis rufipunctatus*
      (dark-spotted morph);
    Thamnophis sauritus sauritus;
    Thamnophis sauritus nitae;
    Thamnophis sauritus sackenii;
    Thamnophis sauritus
      septentrionalis;
    Thamnophis scalaris

12. *Thamnophis scaliger;*
    Thamnophis sirtalis sirtalis
      (light morph);
    Thamnophis sirtalis sirtalis
      (dark morph);
    Thamnophis sirtalis annectens;
    Thamnophis sirtalis concinnus;
    Thamnophis sirtalis dorsalis

13. *Thamnophis sirtalis fitchi;*
    Thamnophis sirtalis fitchi;
    Thamnophis sirtalis infernalis;
    Thamnophis sirtalis
      pallidulus;
    Thamnophis sirtalis parietalis;
    Thamnophis sirtalis
      pickeringii

14. *Thamnophis sirtalis*
      semifasciatus;
    Thamnophis sirtalis similis;
    Thamnophis sumichrasti
      (spotted morph);
    Thamnophis sumichrasti
      (blotched morph);
    Thamnophis validus validus;
    Thamnophis validus celaeno

15. *Thamnophis rufipunctatus*
      habitat, New Mexico;
    Thamnophis sirtalis eating
      Bufo americanus;
    Thamnophis couchii
      containing *Salmo gairdnerii;*
    Salmo gairdnerii regurgitated
      by *Thamnophis couchii*

Color Plates

FIGURES

Figures

MAPS

Maps

ACKNOWLEDGMENTS

A book such as this one cannot be written without the help and cooperation of numerous friends and colleagues, and it is our pleasure to acknowledge their assistance here. For critically reading portions of the manuscript, we thank Jeff Boundy, Gordon M. Burghardt, Henry S. Fitch, Patrick T. Gregory, Robert Hansen, Mary T. Mendonca, and several anonymous reviewers. Errors in interpretation or omission remain our responsibility. For providing photographs, we thank J. Allsteadt, B. Bartholomew, R. M. Blaney, J. Boundy, J. Brode, G. M. Burghardt, J. A. Campbell, J. D. Camper, J. T. Collins, S. L. Collins, R. Conant, W. E. Duellman, H. Fisher, A. Ford, R. Gonzales, L. L. Grismer, B. Hankla, R. Hansen, J. Harding, M. Hoggren, J. Iverson, W. W. Lamar, W. P. Leonard, E. A. Liner, R. T. Mason, F. Mendoza-Quijano, S. J. Minton, W. B. Montgomery, C. W. Myers, M. Rodmer, E. Schaeffer, C. Schwalbe, N. Scott, G. R. Stewart, J. Villa, and R. G. Webb. The maps and line drawings were done by J. Boundy.

For providing references, unpublished data, and assistance in other ways, we thank L. Allen, B. Bowers, G. M. Burghardt, M. B. Charland, J. C. Gillingham, R. Hansen, D. Holtzman, D. Lancaster, C. McCallister, J. Nesmith, G. Schneider, J. Sites, H. M. Smith, and V. Wallach. Pam Hattala heroically typed large portions of the text. Additional support for production of this manuscript was provided by the Department of Biological Sciences, Southeastern Louisiana University; the support of Gary Childers is especially acknowledged.

Acknowledgments

THE GARTER SNAKES

INTRODUCTION

Snakes are enjoying something of a renaissance. People have always been interested in them—look at the numbers who spend time at the reptile house at any zoo, for example—but recently there seems to be a dramatic increase in popular interest in snakes, not only in terms of scientific study but in terms of the numbers of people keeping snakes as pets and enjoying them as part of our natural heritage. In the last few years alone, new journals on keeping snakes and other reptiles as pets have appeared, attendance at meetings devoted to reptile husbandry has increased, and at least four major scientific texts on snakes have been published. The present authors hope that this text, addressed to professionals and hobbyists alike, will contribute to this resurgent interest and will in its own way encourage the movement to protect all reptiles and amphibians, but particularly the garter snakes, in their natural environment, the wild.

As a group, garter snakes are perhaps the most common and widespread of the snakes of North America. Because of their abundance, relative ease of capture, and (usually) docile nature, garter snakes have often been chosen as the subjects of ecological and behavioral studies by biologists. In fact, the genus *Thamnophis* likely qualifies as the best-studied genus of snakes, and arguably, we know more about the common garter snake,

Thamnophis sirtalis, than about any other snake in the world. The literature abounds with papers documenting the natural history of garter snakes in the wild and with information based on work in the laboratory, where garter snakes are used for studies on physiology, cell biology, genetics, and behavior.

This familiarity with garter snakes is evident among nonscientists as well. In much of North America, the snakes most often encountered by the general public are garter snakes. The distinctive stripes of garter snakes allow most people to recognize them as nonpoisonous. Although that does not always prevent their being killed by misguided "snake haters," individuals are often curious enough to watch a garter snake in the wild or even keep one as a pet.

This curiosity is the common ground of scientists and lay persons alike. Indeed, for many herpetologists as well as lay people the first snake they ever encountered was a garter snake. One of the authors (NBF) distinctly remembers as a child catching a fat ribbon snake (thinking it was pregnant) and then watching in amazement as it regurgitated a huge frog. The fascination with how an animal without legs can move so easily, catch and eat prey whole, and locate and attract mates is present in both scientists and nonscientists alike; indeed, the only difference between them is that the scientist tries to find out the answers to her/his questions by observation and experimentation.

What scientists have learned about garter snakes reflects what we know about snakes as a group, primarily because garter snakes have been considered good "models" for studies on subjects such as behavior, thermal ecology, and reproduction. However, readers should not get the impression that we now have "all the answers," either about garter snakes or about snakes in general. Although some species such as the common garter snake, *Thamnophis sirtalis*, are very well studied, we have huge gaps in our understanding of the ecology and behavior of most other species. In fact, as is usually true in science, the more we learn about a species the more questions arise. This book will hopefully indicate those areas and species that badly need more study. As is noted in the text, although some information is available for many members of the group, much of our knowledge is restricted to a few intensely studied species. As this book will illustrate, there is need for much more research on some lesser-known species, particularly those in the southern United States and in Mexico.

The organization of this book departs somewhat from the traditional treatment seen in many books on snakes or other large groups. Instead of making the species accounts the centerpiece of the text, we have tried to provide comprehensive summaries of several major areas of garter snake biology, especially taxonomy and evolutionary relationships, ecology, behavior, and captive care of garter snakes. We hope that these chapters will be of interest to both the scientist and the nonscientist alike. Finally, we present a species-by-species summary of systematics and natural history.

A point should be made about the intended audience for this book. Because garter snakes are of interest to a wide group of persons, we have attempted to write as broadly as possible. We feel that the usefulness of the individual parts will outweigh the possibility that some readers may not find all parts of the book equally interesting. In fact, readers may be surprised by what they learn from the areas of study that they are less interested in (the authors did!)

Finally, it will be noted by the observant reader that the species accounts are not uniformly data-rich. That simply reflects the degree to which the various taxa have been studied. Data on a number of major taxonomic characters have been gathered from all taxa (where they are lacking in the literature), but the sample sizes and geographic representation for many of them are often rather modest. Thus, this book represents a "State of the Union" message, not the "Final Word"—and should be read accordingly.

Some general comments on the taxonomic portions of this book also seem in order. The author responsible for this part of the book (DAR) has tried to walk a fine line between providing sufficient data to make this material useful to the professional herpetologist without, at the same time, overwhelming—and boring— the rest of our readership. Hopefully he has not succeeded only in frustrating both groups.

This book presents the first key to all the species and subspecies of *Thamnophis* since Ruthven's in 1908. It is a long key, partly because there are so many taxa, partly because of the assumption that the user has no locality data for the specimen being keyed, and partly because identification of a morphologically variable species can involve multiple routes. Some readers may be unhappy about the occasional use of dentitional characters, but the decision made in preparing this key was that it is better to have a key that is more time-consuming but accurate than one that is simpler but inaccurate. This is not to say that the present key is infallible—it is not—but it should prove to be the best one published to date.

We have presented definitions of a broader array of the taxonomic characters used more or less successfully to distinguish among the garter snakes than have been published previously, and it is hoped that the cautionary comments accompanying a number of them may save future snake taxonomists from having to extricate themselves from some of the pitfalls Rossman visited during his wanderings in the maze known as *Thamnophis* systematics.

In a few instances (i.e., *T. scaliger, T. postremus, T. pulchrilatus*), species have been recognized on the basis of information presented at national herpetological conferences (and reported in their abstracts) but not yet formally published in a journal. This is not considered to be very good form, but Rossman felt it was important that the taxonomy in this book reflect the actual situations in nature as best he understands them at this point in time. To those who disagree with his decision, he offers his apologies.

A final point concerns authorship. Although we have attempted to produce a unified text, each author has his own specific area of interest and expertise. Thus, although the species accounts are truly a joint effort, each summary chapter is the product of a specific author, and we have reflected that in the listed authorship of the chapters in the table of contents.

Section One

TAXONOMY AND EVOLUTION

Chapter 1

TAXONOMY AND RELATIONSHIPS OF GARTER SNAKES

HISTORICAL REVIEW

In as wide-ranging and highly speciose a group as the garter snakes—a group in which scale variations, pattern polymorphism, and sexual dimorphism (all of which are described in the individual species accounts) run rampant—it is small wonder that Ruthven (1908) opened his classic monograph on *Thamnophis* by stating that "this genus has long stood in the minds of herpetologists as a synonym for chaos. . . ." One should bear in mind, however, that Ruthven's comment was at least in part the reaction of one more inclined toward "lumping" taxa than toward what he saw as the excessive "splitting" indulged in by some of his predecessors, most notably Cope (who, in his final publication in 1900, recognized 25 species of *Thamnophis* and an additional 21 subspecies (as opposed to the 12 species with an additional 7 subspecies subsequently recognized by Ruthven). Ironically, despite Ruthven's major contribution of systematically and graphically presenting geographic variation in meristic characters, as well as his thoughtful and lengthy discussions of character variation and the origin and evolution of the four species groups he recognized, it is now clear that Ruthven did, in fact, seriously underestimate the number of garter snake species that actually exist. In this book, 30 species of *Thamnophis* are recognized, and future taxonomic studies are more likely to increase that number than to reduce it.

Many significant publications on garter snake systematics have appeared since Ruthven's monograph, although none has dealt with all the species in the genus. These papers are cited throughout this book, but two warrant special mention at this point. Fitch (1940) presented an exhaustive study of variation in what he called the *ordinoides* artenkreis (which included the six species we now recognize as *T. atratus, T. couchii, T. elegans, T. gigas, T. hammondii,* and *T. ordinoides*) that established standards of data presentation few, if any, subsequent studies have matched—and none have surpassed. Particularly noteworthy was Fitch's willingness to use nontraditional characters, which he handled in a highly objective—often quantified—manner.

The other landmark paper was by Smith (1942), who presented a complete list of all scientific names that had ever been applied to a species of garter snakes, as well as a key to all the garter snake species and subspecies occurring in Mexico and Central America, which included most of the taxa in the genus.

Although an occasional early au-thor would mention what he thought to be the closest relative of a particular species of garter snake, the first graphic representation of the relationships of a significant number of species was by Cope (1892b), which has been reproduced here as Fig. 1-1. Although Cope did not state what characters his hypothetical tree was based upon, they clearly involved external morphology—and position of the lateral stripe was obviously important. *Thamnophis sirtalis* was considered to be the base stock from which the other taxa arose.

Brown (1904), who considered Cope to be a "splitter," published the hypothetical tree that is reproduced here as Fig. 1-2. His tree is difficult to compare with that of Cope because it does not include any of the many species that do not enter the United States. Brown, like Cope, based his "phylogeny" on external morphology and considered *T. sirtalis* (specifically the subspecies *parietalis*) to represent the hypothetical ancestor, but Brown also envisioned a secondary radiation centering on *T. radix.*

Ruthven (1908) divided the genus into four species groups (Radix, Sauritus, Elegans, Sirtalis) on the basis of such external morphological features as position of the lateral stripe, number of dorsal scale rows, and number

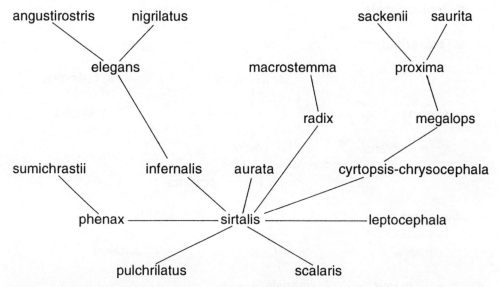

Fig. 1-1. Hypothetical family tree of the garter snake species presented in Cope (1892b) and reprinted unchanged in Cope (1900). Not all taxa recognized by Cope appear in the tree. To put the taxa in a modern perspective, note the following name equivalents: *leptocephala* = *ordinoides*; *megalops* = *eques megalops*; *sackenii* = *sauritus sackenii*; *macrostemma* = *eques*; *aurata* = *cyrtopsis*; *infernalis* = *atratus*; *nigrilatus* = *marcianus*; *phenax* = *sumichrasti*; *angustirostris* = identity uncertain.

of supralabials. Ruthven postulated that the major trend in each of the groups was toward a reduction in body size and a concomitant reduction in the number of scales. Since the "maximum scutellation" in each species group occurs in northern Mexico (in Ruthven's opinion), he concluded that northern Mexico was the probable "center of origin" for the genus. Ruthven did not indicate which species he considered to most closely resemble the hypothetical ancestor, merely stating that the species we now know as *rufipunctatus, eques, cyrtopsis,* and *proximus* seem more closely related to each other than are any other four taxa in the different species groups. Ruthven did not present a hypothetical phylogeny for the genus

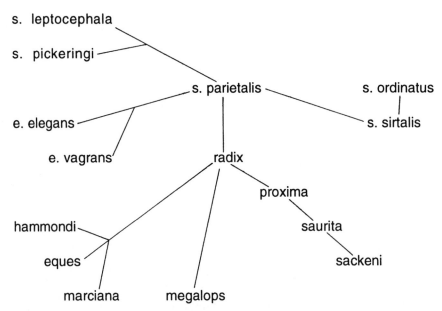

Fig. 1-2. Hypothetical family tree of the garter snake species and subspecies presented in Brown (1904). He did not include any taxa having ranges exclusively outside the United States. To put the taxa in a modern perspective, note the following name equivalents: *s. leptocephala = ordinoides; s. ordinatus = s. sirtalis; eques = cyrtopsis; megalops = eques megalops; sackeni = sauritus sackenii*.

as a whole, but he did so for each of the species groups (reproduced here as Figs. 1-3, 1-4, 1-5, and 1-6).

The first garter snake phylogeny based on biochemical data was that presented by Lawson and Dessauer (1979, Fig. 4), which was limited to portraying relationships among the members of Fitch's (1940) *ordinoides* artenkreis mentioned earlier in this section (see Fig. 1-7). Their phenogram, based on allozyme data, pointed toward the species-level distinctness of *T. elegans, T. couchii, T. hammondii, T. gigas,* and *T. atratus* that was subsequently confirmed by morphological studies (Rossman, 1979; Rossman and Stewart, 1987). The only discordant note in the phenogram was the placement of *T. ordi-*

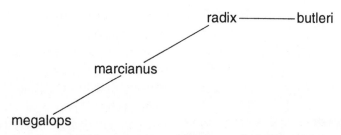

Fig. 1-3. "Phylogenetic development of the Radix group" as presented in Ruthven (1908). Note that *megalops* is now considered to be a subspecies of *T. eques.*

noides as the barely distinguishable sister-taxon to *T. a. atratus.* Lawson (pers. comm.) later stated that this position for *T. ordinoides* was in error.

Dowling et al. (1983) did not produce a phylogeny per se, but they did point out that, on the basis of a micro-complement fixation analysis of albumin, *Thamnophis proximus* and *T. sauritus* are more distantly related to *T. elegans* and *T. sirtalis* than are *Nerodia harteri* and *N. sipedon* (the immunological distance for *N. taxispilota* was found to be comparable to that for the two ribbon snake species), a situation that would render the genus *Thamnophis* paraphyletic.

In referring to the findings of Dowling et al. (1983), Dowling and Maxson (1990) concluded that *"Nerodia* is seen as an aquatic specialization of the generalized terrestrial members of *Thamnophis,"* apparently the first time any workers had suggested that *Thamnophis* was ancestral to *Nerodia.* The statement by Malnate (1960) that *Thamnophis* is "a terrestrial group unquestionably derived from *Natrix* [= *Nerodia*]" succinctly stated what had been the prevailing view prior to 1990. It remains to be seen which view is correct.

The trees presented by de Queiroz and Lawson (Figs. 1-8 and 1-9), based on the respective analyses of mitochondrial DNA sequences and allozymes, represent the most inclusive and objective attempts to date to produce a phylogeny of the garter snakes. Unfortunately, as de Queiroz and Lawson themselves are quick to point out, the two different analyses "give substantially different estimates of garter snake phylogeny." The authors

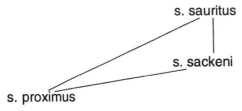

s. sauritus

s. sackeni

s. proximus

Fig. 1-4. "Phylogenetic development of the Sauritus group" as presented in Ruthven (1908), but modified to reflect the fact that he considered all three taxa to be conspecific. The western ribbon snake, *T. proximus*, is now considered to be a separate species. Note that Ruthven thought *T. s. sauritus* had a polyphyletic origin.

attempted to resolve this difficulty by analyzing the combined data sets (Fig. 1-10), but they acknowledged potential problems with this methodology as well and called for further analyses based on other kinds of characters in order to see how the results compare with their work. A cladistic analysis based on a broad suite of morphological characters is presently under way (Rossman, Boundy, and Good, in progress).

SPECIES AND SUBSPECIES

The past 40 years have seen a great deal of ferment in our concepts of the species and subspecies categories. It is not my intention to discuss the controversies here, but the interested reader may wish to refer to Brown and Wilson (1954), Collins (1991), Cracraft (1992), Frost and Hillis (1990), Frost et al. (1992), Mayr (1969), McKitrick and Zink (1988), Simpson (1961), Smith (1990), Van Devender et al. (1992), Wiley (1978, 1981), and Wilson and Brown (1953). Suffice it to say, the 30 species of *Thamnophis* recognized as valid in this book would qualify as species under either the "biological species concept" or the "evolutionary species concept."

The subspecies category has been challenged largely because the discordant variation, which seems to be the rule rather than the exception, causes taxonomists to apply trinomials to clusters of character-states rather than to cohesive populations of animals. Although reflecting natural phenomena, such subspecies are limited constructs, not phylogenetic units. Consequently, it would not be at all surprising to see the eventual demise of the subspecies as a taxonomic category. There is strong resistance to such a move at present, however, so it would not be appropriate in a book such as this one to move beyond the point where the herpeto-

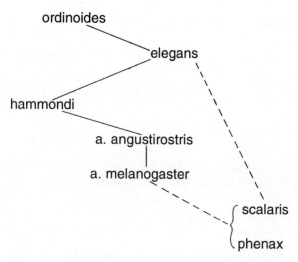

ordinoides

elegans

hammondi

a. angustirostris

a. melanogaster

scalaris

phenax

Fig. 1-5. "Phylogenetic development of the Elegans group" as presented in Ruthven (1908), but modified to reflect the fact that he considered *angustirostris* and *melanogaster* to be conspecific. Ruthven's *elegans* also included what is now known as *atratus* and *couchii*, his *scalaris* also included *scaliger*, his *angustirostris* was what is now known as *rufipunctatus*, and his *phenax* was what is now known as *sumichrasti*.

logical community as a whole seems ready to go. For this reason, I have included the subspecies in the book as a category of convenience, useful in delimiting certain geographically variable features—essentially the same position I adopted more than three decades ago (Rossman, 1963).

I would be less than candid, however, not to admit having suffered a great deal of disillusionment about garter snake subspecies while trying to prepare workable infraspecific keys to such taxa as *T. elegans, T. eques, T. melanogaster,* and *T. sirtalis.* Frankly, there are a number of subspe-

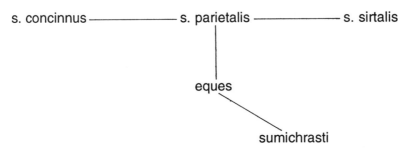

Fig. 1-6. "Phylogenetic development of the Sirtalis group" as presented in Ruthven (1908), but modified to reflect the fact that he
considered *concinnus, parietalis,* and *sirtalis* to be conspecific.
Ruthven's *eques* was what is now known as *cyrtopsis,* and it also
included *pulchrilatus.* His *sumichrasti* included *chrysocephalus*
and *godmani.*

cies that I do not think are diagno-
sable. Several of these I have rejected
in the species accounts, giving expla-
nations; the others were left in the
book only because I presently lack the
data necessary to prove that they are
invalid.

TAXONOMIC CHARACTERS

Over the past century and a half, a
number of morphological characters
have been used either to distinguish
between garter snake taxa or to estab-
lish relationships. Within the past 30
years, improved biochemical techniques have allowed molecular characters to be used for similar purposes.
Below is a selected list of morphological characters that have proven to be
useful in garter snake systematics and
that appear elsewhere in this book.
The meristic and mensural characters
are accompanied by comments on
how each is counted or measured.
See Fig. 1-11 for a drawing of how
various head measurements were
made. For most of the morphological
characters, some examples and cautionary notes—where warranted—
are given.

(1) *Anal plate*—whether the plate is
single or divided into two halves, the
right almost invariably overlapping
the left. Dundee (1989) correctly
pointed out that since this scute lies
anteroventral to the vent, not the

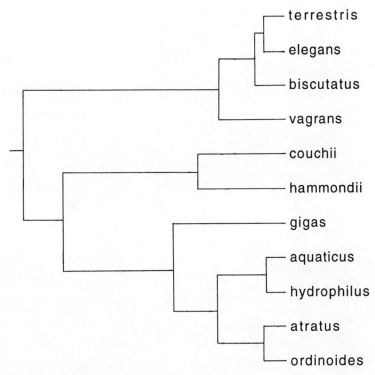

Fig. 1-7. "Genetic affinities of members of the *elegans-couchii-ordinoides* complex" as presented in Lawson and Dessauer (1979), and based on Nei genetic distances for 31 protein loci. The upper four taxa (*terrestris, elegans, biscutatus, vagrans*) are conspecific, as are *aquaticus, hydrophilus,* and *atratus*. The apparently very close affinity between *atratus* and *ordinoides* was subsequently declared to be erroneous (Lawson, pers. comm.)

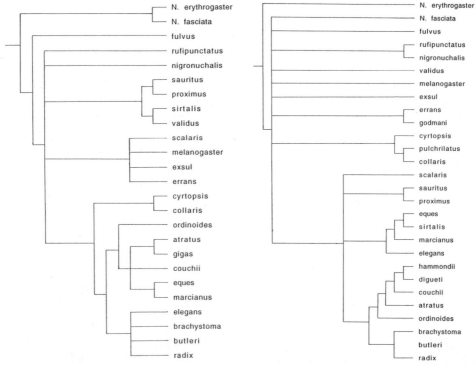

Fig. 1-8. Strict consensus tree of garter snake phylogeny based on the mitochondrial DNA sequence analysis presented in de Queiroz and Lawson (1994).

Fig. 1-9. Strict consensus tree of garter snake phylogeny based on the allozyme analysis presented in de Queiroz and Lawson (1994). Compare with Fig. 1-8 to see both the concordant and discordant branching sequences.

anus, the term *anal plate* is a misnomer. He substituted the term *cloacal scute,* but that has not yet found support among snake systematists so I choose to retain—for now—the more familiar traditional term. The presence of a single anal plate has tra-

ditionally been considered the primary external characteristic fairly consistently distinguishing species of *Thamnophis* from *Nerodia* (which have a divided plate), despite the fact that the alternate character-state does occur—in fairly low frequencies

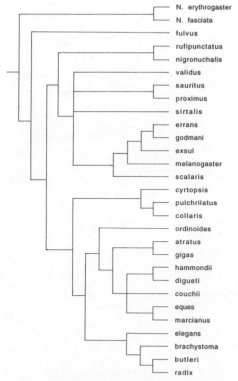

Fig. 1-10. Strict consensus tree of garter snake phylogeny based on analysis of the combined DNA sequences and allozyme data sets presented in de Queiroz and Lawson (1994).

N. erythrogaster
N. fasciata
fulvus
rufipunctatus
nigronuchalis
validus
sauritus
proximus
sirtalis
errans
godmani
exsul
melanogaster
scalaris
cyrtopsis
pulchrilatus
collaris
ordinoides
atratus
gigas
hammondii
digueti
couchii
eques
marcianus
elegans
brachystoma
butleri
radix

(<10%) and/or concentrated in localized populations—in *Nerodia erythrogaster, Thamnophis elegans,* and *T. rufipunctatus* (Conant, 1961; Lowe, 1955; Tanner, 1950, 1959; Thompson, 1957). The recent transfer of *Ner-* *odia valida* to *Thamnophis* by Lawson (1987) on biochemical grounds created the anomalous situation of a *Thamnophis* species characteristically possessing a divided anal plate. The jury is still out on that transfer, however, so it remains to be seen if *Thamnophis* will once again be distinguishable from *Nerodia* on the basis of the anal plate condition.

(2) *Ventrals*—total number, beginning with the first scale that contacts the first dorsal scale row on *both* sides of the venter and not including the anal plate. Prior to establishment of this standardized method by Dowling (1951), ventral counts usually were begun with the first ventral that was wider than long—or some approximation thereof—a method that produces counts averaging 2 or 3 scales more than those obtained by the "Dowling count." The species accounts in this book, by necessity, include counts generated by both methods, and the reader should keep in mind that ventral counts published before 1951 (and probably for at least several years thereafter) were not recorded by the Dowling method.

Ventral counts closely approximate the number of trunk vertebrae and may be rather variable within a spe-

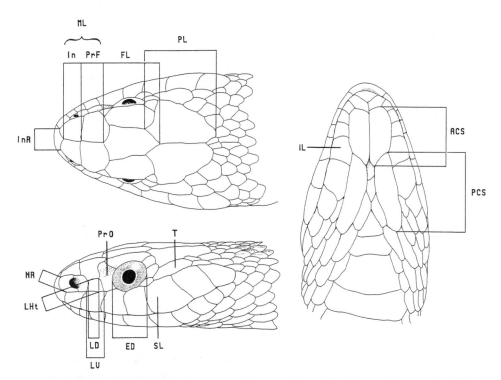

Fig. 1-11. Mensural features in garter snakes used to calculate various ratios found to have taxonomic significance in certain cases:

InR	internasorostral contact	NR	nasorostral contact
Prf	prefrontal length	In	internasal length
FL	frontal length	PL	parietal length
ACS	anterior chin-shield length	ML	muzzle length
PCS	posterior chin-shield length.	LD	loreal length dorsally
LH	loreal height	LV	loreal length ventrally
ED	eye diameter		

Other labelled features include an infralabial (IL), a preocular (PrO), a supralabial (SL), and an anterior temporal (T).

cies, especially those that extend across a broad geographic area. The largest number (187) occurs in a male *T. couchii*, the smallest (127) in a female *T. validus*; the greatest range of variation within a species (40) occurs in *T. elegans* and *T. sirtalis* females. Sexual dimorphism occurs in all species except *T. chrysocephalus* and *T. pulchrilatus*, males in most local populations having somewhat more ventrals than females—except for *T. scalaris*, in which the females have the higher average number. Despite their great variability, ventral counts can be useful in helping to distinguish between superficially similar sympatric or parapatric species (e.g., *T. couchii* and *T. atratus, T. couchii* and *T. gigas;* Rossman and Stewart, 1987). It should be noted, however, that geographically proximate populations within a single subspecies also may have significantly different ventral counts (e.g., *T. s. sauritus* from the Apalachicola River basin in the central Florida Panhandle have a mean ventral count more than 9 scales less than those from the western Florida Panhandle and adjacent Mobile Bay region; Rossman, 1963).

(3) *Subcaudals*—total number on one side, beginning with the first scale behind the vent that contacts a subcaudal from the other side; the terminal spine is not included. Care must be taken not to confuse an incomplete tail having a healed tip with one that is complete or lacks only the terminal spine.

Subcaudal counts closely approximate the number of caudal vertebrae and are subject to individual, sexual, and geographic variation. The fewest subcaudals recorded for a garter snake are 40 (a female *T. scaliger*), the most 136 (a male *T. sauritus*); the greatest range of variation (42) occurs in *T. proximus* females. Sexual dimorphism apparently occurs in all species, the males having the greater number of scales in all but a few local populations of certain species (e.g., *T. proximus* from the vicinity of Galveston Bay, Texas; Rossman, 1963). As with the ventral counts, subcaudal numbers can help to distinguish between superficially similar sympatric or parapatric species (e.g., *T. couchii* and *T. hammondii, T. atratus* and *T. gigas;* Rossman and Stewart, 1987). And again, as with the ventrals, geographically proximate populations within a single subspecies may have significantly different subcaudal counts (e.g., *T. s. sauritus* from southeastern Mississippi have mean counts 7 scales less in males and 9 scales less in females than those from the western Florida Panhandle and adjacent Mobile Bay region; Rossman, 1963.)

(4) *Labials*—number of supralabials on each side; number of infralabials on each side (including the last one in which >50% of the scale lies anterior to a vertical plane extending from the posterior margin of the last supralabial); number of supralabials entering the orbit. Most species have a fairly consistent number of supralabials, but individual and geographic variation does occur and is pronounced in some cases (e.g., *T. postremus* has 7 or 8 scales in fairly similar frequencies; *T. sauritus sauritus* and *T. s. septentrionalis* predominantly have 7, *T. s. nitae* and *T. s. sackenii* have 8).

Infralabial numbers also show varying degrees of intraspecific variation, but in some instances can be useful in helping to distinguish between sympatric or parapatric species that are superficially similar in appearance (e.g., *T. couchii* and *T. atratus, T. couchii* and *T. gigas, T. couchii* and *T. hammondii;* Rossman and Stewart, 1987)—if one remembers that some individuals in each species may have a number more characteristic of the other species. Such a situation neither invalidates the general usefulness of the character nor, of and by itself, nec-

essarily reflects hybridization. Only a typological mind-set demands character invariability.

Most garter snake species typically have two supralabials entering the orbit; *T. rufipunctatus* usually has only one, although there is some minor geographic variation in this feature (Rossman, 1993).

(5) *Preoculars*—number on each side. Most species of *Thamnophis* characteristically have only a single preocular, but the number can be both individually and geographically variable (e.g., *T. couchii,* Rossman and Stewart, 1987; *T. elegans* and *T. ordinoides,* Fitch 1940). In a few species (*T. hammondii, T. melanogaster, T. nigronuchalis, T. rufipunctatus*), two preoculars predominate.

(6) *Dorsal scale rows*—number around body, counting alternately at the level of the tenth ventral scute, at midbody, and at the level of the penultimate ventral. The largest number usually occurs on the neck (but many specimens of *T. elegans* and *T. radix* have it at, or slightly anterior to, midbody), the first reduction occurring at or shortly beyond midbody, and subsequent reductions—if any—thereafter. A uniform count throughout the body is known from

80% of *T. exsul,* > 76% of *T. brachystoma,* > 40% of *T. godmani,* and 20% of *T. scalaris* from Veracruz. The dorsal scale row formula can be remarkably constant within a species (e.g., 19-19-17 in > 96% of *T. proximus* and *T. sauritus;* Rossman, 1963) or rather variable (e.g., *T. scalaris* and *T. scaliger;* Rossman, 1992b).

Taken in conjunction with other characters, dorsal scale row number can be useful in helping to distinguish between superficially similar sympatric or parapatric species (e.g., *T. couchii* and *T. atratus, T. atratus* and *T. gigas;* Rossman and Stewart, 1987). Some authors have stressed the presence of an extra pair of rows for a short distance on the body (< 10% of body length) as being an important taxonomic character-state for subspecies recognition in *T. elegans* (Fitch 1940, 1980a) and *T. sirtalis* (Tanner, 1988). I consider this to be an example of local variation too trivial to be given serious consideration for taxonomic purposes.

(7) *Maxillary teeth*—total number, including empty sockets. Freeing the upper lip along one side and temporarily folding it up against the side of the head permits the drying and teasing away of the tissue surrounding the teeth, which allows one to make an accurate count. Special care must be taken to locate the anteriormost tooth, which is somewhat smaller than the one adjacent to it and—because of the often strongly curved anterior end of the maxilla—sometimes lies anteromedial to that tooth. When the count has been recorded, the lip can be pressed back into place.

Maxillary tooth counts are variable, within limits, in garter snake species. Where series are large enough to overcome the possible effects of sampling error, males usually average about one more tooth than females— an unexplained phenomenon first demonstrated in *Thamnophis* by Rossman (1979) and otherwise reported in snakes only by Thorpe (1975), who stated that it occurred in *Natrix natrix* but presented no data.

Maxillary tooth numbers often can be used to help distinguish between superficially similar sympatric or parapatric species (e.g., *T. atratus* and *T. elegans*—Rossman, 1979; *T. cyrtopsis* and *T. pulchrilatus,* Rossman, 1992a; *T. chrysocephalus* and *T. godmani,* previously unpubl. data). In a few species the number of maxillary teeth varies geographically (e.g., *T. sauritus,* Rossman, 1963; *T. elegans,* Rossman, 1979; *T. marcianus,* Rossman, 1971; *T. cyrtopsis,* Rossman, 1992a). In these instances the change does not appear to be clinal but occurs dramatically over relatively short distances.

Most species of *Thamnophis* have the posterior 2 or 3 maxillary teeth enlarged, but the extent of the enlargement is variable, and in *T. rufipunctatus* the posterior teeth are actually substantially shorter than those in the middle of the tooth row. A detailed examination of this character in all thamnophiine species is currently under way.

(8) *Visceral topography*—relative lengths and/or positions of heart, gall bladder, liver, pancreas, and kidneys (N. J. Rossman et al., 1982). Most species of *Thamnophis* cannot be distinguished on the basis of these characters, but *T. proximus* and *T. sauritus* differ from their congeners in most topographic features in that their organs lie in a more posterior position than those of other species. In the cases of the posterior end of the heart and the anterior end of the liver, the ribbon snakes share the phenomenon of posterior displacement with *T. melanogaster* and *T. rufipunctatus*, but in all other positional characters they stand alone within the genus.

(9) *Relative tail length*—tail length/ total length (T/TL) expressed as a percentage. Care must be taken to include only specimens having a complete tail. Absolute values range from a low of 15.5% in female *T. scaliger* to a high of 38.8% in both sexes of *T. sauritus*. Generally speaking, and not surprisingly, the longer the tail the greater the range of individual variation (the maximum, in female *T. sauritus*, is 10.0%). Relative tail length is positively, but not absolutely, correlated with subcaudal number (e.g., parapatric female *T. couchii* and *T. atratus* have identical mean subcaudal numbers, but the T/TL in the latter species is 2.2% greater; Rossman and Stewart, 1987). In some instances, relative tail length can be used to help distinguish between superficially similar sympatric or parapatric species (e.g., *T. couchii* and *T. atratus, T. couchii* and *T. hammondii, T. atratus* and *T. gigas*; Rossman and Stewart, 1987). Geographic variation in this character also occurs in many wideranging species (e.g., *T. couchii, T. cyrtopsis, T. proximus, T. sauritus*).

(10) *Relative head length*—head length/snout-vent length (HL/SVL) expressed as a percentage. Head length is recorded as straightline measurement from the anteriormost tip of the rostral scale to the angle of the jaw. The head and body increase in length disproportionately before

reaching a growth plateau (see Fig. 1-12), so it is important to compare adults only. Sexual dimorphism appears to be present in about one-third of the species; in those cases the females tend to have a slightly longer head than do the males.

The proportionately longest head (5.7%) occurs in female *T. godmani* and in *T. mendax* (no sexual dimorphism apparent), the shortest (3.9%) in *T. proximus* and *T. sauritus* (neither showing sexual dimorphism). Paradoxically, since the former two species have relatively low ventral counts and the ribbon snakes relatively high ones, what the HL/SVL values actually may be reflecting in these cases is relative body length rather than relative head length. Clearly, interpretation of this character is ambiguous. Relatively little geographic variation has been demonstrated, but *T. cyrtopsis cyrtopsis* does have a significantly lower HL/SVL than *T. cyrtopsis collaris* (Rossman, 1992a).

(11) *Relative eye size*—eye diameter/frontal length (ED/FL) expressed as a percentage. Eye diameter is measured horizontally, frontal length along the midline of the scale. Because the muzzle may be slightly flexed either posterodorsally or ante- roventrally when a specimen is fixed in preservative, the anterior end of the frontal may be completely covered or completely exposed, respectively, by the adjacent prefrontal scales. Seemingly intrapopulational differences in frontal length between individuals of the same size and sex usually are due to this artifact of preservation. Frontal length—rather than head length—is used as a constant for comparing the dimensions of many other head scales because head length has been shown to exhibit marked allometric growth in at least some thamnophiine species, whereas the length of the frontal bone has not (see Rossman, 1980, for *Nerodia rhombifer*).

The proportionately smallest eye occurs in *T. brachystoma* (59.0%) and *T. scaliger* (59.5%), the largest in *T. sumichrasti* (76.4%) and *T. fulvus* (74.7%). Close relatives are not necessarily similar to each other in regard to relative eye size, the most dramatic example being *T. mendax* (64.7%) and *T. sumichrasti* (76.4%).

(12) *Relative parietal length*—frontal length/parietal length (FL/PL) expressed as a percentage. Parietal length is measured from the posterior tip of one parietal to its junction anteriorly with the frontal and supraocular. The basic assumption here—cor-

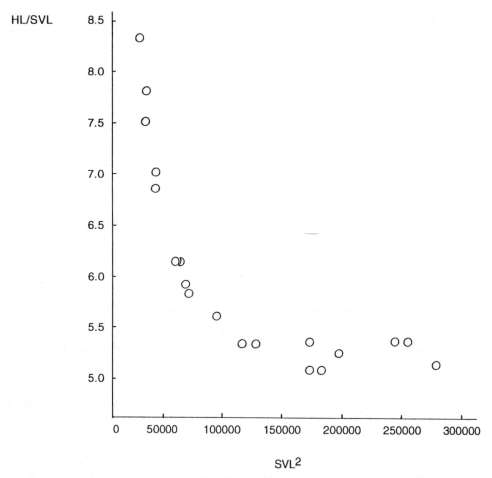

Fig. 1-12. Allometric growth in relative head size of male *T. nigronuchalis*. The ratio HL/SVL is expressed as a percentage. Snout-vent length values have been squared to provide near-equal variance in deriving the regression equation reflected in this plot.

rectly or incorrectly—is that frontal length is the constant.

The relatively longest parietals occur in *T. gigas* (65.3%) in the southern populations), the shortest in *T. scalaris* (85.0% in the eastern populations) and *T. scaliger* (83.9%). Relative parietal length has been used in some cases to help distinguish between superficially similar sympatric or parapatric species (e.g., *T. atratus* and *T. couchii*, *T. couchii* and *T. gigas*, *T. couchii* and *T. hammondii*, *T. atratus* and *T. gigas*; Rossman and Stewart, 1987).

(13) *Relative muzzle length*—muzzle length/frontal length (ML/FL) expressed as a percentage. Muzzle length is the combined length of the prefrontals and internasals measured along their median sutures from the anterior end of the frontal to the posterior tip of the rostral. The relatively shortest muzzles occur in *T. scaliger* (55.5%) and *T. brachystoma* (58.5%), the longest in *T. gigas* (females average > 95%, males about 85%). Relative muzzle length can be used in conjunction with other characters to distinguish between some superficially similar sympatric or parapatric species (e.g., *T. proximus* and *T. saurituus*—Rossman, 1963; *T. atratus* and *T. couchii*, female *T. couchii* and *T. gigas*, female *T. atratus* and *T. gigas*—

Rossman and Stewart, 1987; *T. scalaris* and *T. scaliger*—Rossman and Lara-Gongora, 1991).

(14) *Relative width of the muzzle tip*—width of contact between combined internasals and rostral/width of contact between nasal and rostral (InR/NR) expressed as a percentage. The proportionately narrowest muzzle tip occurs in the northern populations of *T. couchii* (44.2% in females, 64.6% in males), the broadest in *T. errans* (151.5%) and *T. exsul* (147.9%). In general, values well below 100% are found in aquatic/semi-aquatic species, values well above 100% in terrestrial taxa. Marked exceptions are habitat generalists such as *T. marcianus* (averaging 80% or less) and the geographically variable *T. cyrtopsis* (with population means ranging from 81% to nearly 114%). Yet again, relative muzzle tip width can contribute to distinguishing between some superficially similar sympatric or parapatric species (e.g., *T. atratus* and *T. elegans*—Rossman, 1979; *T. cyrtopsis* and *T. pulchrilatus*—Rossman, 1992a; *T. atratus* and *T. couchii*—unpubl. data).

(15) *Relative length of the prefrontals and internasals*—prefrontal length/internasal length (Prf/In) ex-

pressed as a percentage. Prefrontal length is measured on the shortest prefrontal along the median prefrontal suture from the anterior end of the frontal to the posterior end of the longest internasal. Internasal length is measured on the longest internasal along the median internasal suture from the posterior edge of the scale to the posterior tip of the rostral.

The proportionately shortest prefrontals (or longest internasals, depending on your viewpoint) occur in the northern populations of *T. couchii* (67.7%), the longest in female *T. exsul* (143.3%)—the latter being the only species exhibiting sexual dimorphism in this feature (but the sample size is *very* small). Geographic variation is present in several species (e.g., *T. couchii*—Rossman and Stewart, 1987; *T. marcianus*—Rossman, 1971). The relationship between the prefrontals and internasals may help to distinguish between some superficially similar sympatric or parapatric species (e.g., *T. atratus* and *T. couchii*, *T. couchii* and *T. gigas*; Rossman and Stewart, 1987).

(16) *Relative length of loreal dorsally*—dorsal loreal length/ventral loreal length (LD/LV) expressed as a percentage. Dorsal and ventral loreal lengths are measured along the dorsal

and ventral sutures, respectively, from the junction with the nasal to the junction with the preocular. The higher the value, the more square the appearance of the loreal scale; the lower the value, the more triangular. Apparently the latter condition reflects a more acutely depressed muzzle. Loreal shape, taken in conjunction with other characters, may help to distinguish between some superficially similar sympatric or parapatric species (e.g., *T. atratus* and *T. couchii*, *T. atratus* and *T. gigas*, *T. couchii* and *T. gigas*, *T. couchii* and *T. hammondii*—Rossman and Stewart, 1987; *T. scalaris* and *T. scaliger*—Rossman and Lara-Gongora, 1991).

(17) *Relative height of loreal*—loreal height/ventral loreal length (LHt/LV) expressed as a percentage. Loreal height is measured vertically from the junction of the loreal, preocular, and prefrontal to the ventral border of the scale. This relationship reflects to some degree the relative height (or length) of the muzzle. *Thamnophis fulvus* is the only species examined in which LHt/LV averages greater than 100%, although other garter snake species approach it. At the other extreme, *T. rufipunctatus* has a long, low loreal (56.0%), one of the features that help distin-

guish it (Rossman, 1993) from its superficially similar sister-species, *T. nigronuchalis* (76.4%).

(18) *Relative lengths of the chin shields*—anterior chin-shield length/posterior chin-shield length (ACS/PCS) expressed as a percentage. In the literature, the chin shields are sometimes referred to as *genials*. The higher the value, the shorter the posterior chin shields (or the longer the anterior ones); the lower the value, the longer the posterior shields. The proportionately shortest posterior chin shields occur in the northern population of *T. couchii* (104.9%) and *T. elegans* (98.2%), the longest in *T. sauritus* (74.0%) and the northern subspecies of *T. marcianus* (73.7%). Geographic variation occurs in some species (e.g., *T. couchii* and *T. marcianus*). Relative chin-shield length can be used to help distinguish between some superficially similar sympatric or parapatric species (e.g., *T. atratus* and *T. elegans*—Rossman, 1979; *T. atratus* and *T. couchii, T. atratus* and *T. gigas*, Sacramento Valley *T. couchii* and *T. gigas*—Rossman and Stewart, 1987).

(19) *Relative width of dorsal scale row 1*—width of dorsal scale row 1/width of vertebral row (DSR 1/VR) expressed as an absolute value rather than as a percentage. Width of the first dorsal scale row is measured as the maximum vertical width measured at midbody; maximum width of the vertebral row is measured at the same point on the body. Most species of garter snake have dorsal scale row 1 substantially enlarged (means range from 2.3 to 3.0), but there are three notable exceptions—*T. validus* (1.7), *T. proximus* (1.6 in males, 1.7 in females), and *T. sauritus* (1.2 in males, 1.5 in females). The first species falls within the range (1.7 to 2.3) for the water snakes (*Nerodia*) with which it had long been associated, and it raises some questions about the validity of the removal of *validus* from that group by Lawson (1987). The two ribbon snake species show even less differentiation of row 1 than do the water snakes, and this character—combined with the visceral topographic data, the very short head (or greatly elongated body), and the greatly elongated tail—serves to set aside the ribbon snakes from all the other garter snakes. Statistically significant sexual dimorphism has been demonstrated in twelve species (Rossman, 1995a); in all cases the females have a proportionately wider row 1.

(20) *Lateral stripe position*—which dorsal scale rows are involved in the

light lateral stripe. Care should be taken to determine the stripe position *anterior* to the point of dorsal scale row reduction, because the position may change thereafter. This character has long been used by herpetologists as a primary means of identifying species of *Thamnophis* as well as for grouping presumably related taxa (e.g., members of Ruthven's Radix and Sauritus groups have the stripe on rows 3 and 4, members of the Elegans and Sirtalis groups on rows 2 and 3). As with most generalizations, there are exceptions that do not quite fit (e.g., *T. butleri* has the stripe on rows 2, 3, and 4; *T. marcianus* on row 3 only; *T. chrysocephalus* on row 2 only; *T. postremus* and some *T. cyrtopsis* and *T. sirtalis* on rows 1, 2, and 3; and *T. godmani* on rows 1 and 2, 2 only, 2 and 3, or 1, 2, and 3). The chances of "keying out" an isolated individual are complicated even further by those species in which the stripe occasionally may be so indistinct that its position is difficult, if not impossible, to determine. And there are, of course, those species that never have a lateral stripe (*T. mendax*, *T. nigronuchalis*, *T. postremus*, *T. rufipunctatus*, *T. sumichrasti*). Finally, in some species there is geographic variation in lateral stripe position (e.g., in the Great Lakes region some *T. radix* and *T. sauritus* have the stripe on rows 2, 3, and 4, at least on the neck—this condition also characterizes *T. sirtalis annectens* [Brown, 1950] and occurs in at least some specimens of *T. sirtalis parietalis* [Tanner, 1988]).

(21) *Vertebral stripe*—presence or absence; if present, how many dorsal scale rows (or portions thereof) are involved in the vertebral stripe; color in life. This stripe is sometimes referred to in the literature as the *dorsal stripe*. Most species of *Thamnophis* consistently have a discernible light vertebral stripe running the full length of the body, but in some species the stripe may be distinctly present only on the anterior end of the body (*T. couchii*, *T. fulvus*), faint or absent in some (often most) populations or individuals, or invariably absent (*T. hammondii*, *T. nigronuchalis*, *T. rufipunctatus*, *T. sumichrasti*).

(22) *Dorsolateral pattern*—presence or absence of spots or blotches; relative size of spots. Some garter snakes (*T. brachystoma*, *T. proximus*, *T. sauritus*) rarely have dark markings in the dorsolateral area, but most striped species have two alternating rows of black spots between the vertebral stripes. More frequently, the upper

and lower spots fuse on the anterior end of the body and extend ventrally to encroach upon (*T. cyrtopsis ocellatus*) or interrupt the lateral stripe (e.g., *T. sirtalis semifasciatus*, the "vicinus" morph of *T. cyrtopsis collaris*, and many specimens of *T. chrysocephalus* and *T. marcianus*). Finally, in a few species, black-bordered brown blotches may extend from the vertebral stripe to the lateral stripes (*T. scalaris, T. scaliger*) or completely across the back (*T. mendax*, blotched phase of *T. sumichrasti*).

(23) *Nuchal blotches*—divided or undivided; size. When there is only a single blotch immediately behind the head, it is often referred to in the literature as a *nuchal collar*. The nuchal blotches are usually separated by the vertebral stripe, but they are characteristically fused in a few taxa (*T. cyrtopsis collaris, T. nigronuchalis*) and occasionally fused in many others. The contrast between the large nuchal blotches of *T. couchii* and the small ones of *T. hammondii* is one of the features that helps to distinguish them where they are parapatric (Rossman and Stewart, 1987).

(24) *Supralabial pattern*—presence and relative prominence of black bars bordering sutures; presence or absence of brown pigmentation on posterior scales. Although a certain amount of individual variation exists in the relative prominence of the black bars that border at least some of the supralabial sutures in most garter snakes (*T. proximus* and *T. sauritus* are the only species that consistently lack such barring), the degree of development can be used to help differentiate between superficially similar sympatric or parapatric species (e.g., *T. butleri* and *T. radix, T. cyrtopsis* and *T. pulchrilatus, T. nigronuchalis* and *T. rufipunctatus*).

Most garter snake species have all of their supralabial scales basically the same color (disregarding the barring). However, in a few instances (*T. cyrtopsis, T. marcianus*, and *T. scaliger*) one or more of the supralabials have the same pigmentation as the top of the head, a feature that helps to distinguish each of them from its closest relative.

Because these relatively subtle (to human eyes) but consistent interspecific differences in "facial" patterns (from a snake's eye view) obviously did not evolve for the benefit of snake taxonomists, one can only speculate as to what they might mean to the snakes. Since odor trails do not provide foolproof species discrimination—especially among close

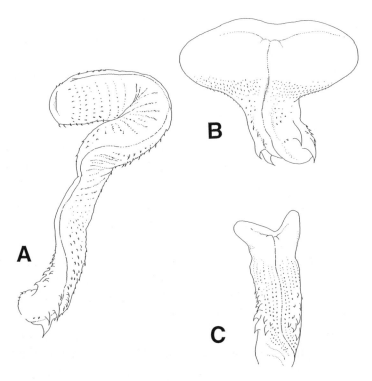

Fig. 1-13. Three morphotypes of everted garter snake hemipenes: (A) *Thamnophis scalaris* (AMNH 94714); (B) *T. godmani* (LSUMZ 11131); (C) *T. sirtalis* (LSUMZ 16487).

relatives (Ford, 1986)—one wonders if the different facial patterns don't provide the snakes with secondary visual reenforcers to help maintain species integrity if the primary scent cues fail to do the job. The general assumption that snakes rely entirely on odor for mate selection has never been adequately tested; in the case of the gar-

ter snakes, at least, it surely needs to be.

(25) *Tongue color*—red with black tips or all black (or perhaps dark gray). The majority of garter snakes have a red tongue with black tips, but the tongue is entirely black in a substantial minority (*chrysocephalus, errans,*

exsul, fulvus, godmani, mendax, nigronuchalis, rufipunctatus, scalaris, scaliger, sumichrasti). The significance of this dichotomy is unknown, but the latter group does include a number of pairs of presumed sister-species (i.e., mendax-sumichrasti, nigronuchalis-rufipunctatus, errans-godmani, scalaris-scaliger).

(26) *Hemipenis length* (inverted)— of moderate length or extremely long. A careful longitudinal incision in the subcaudals on the underside of the tail of a male garter snake ought to reveal one of the paired hemipenes. Carefully sliding a blunt probe beneath the structure and gently but firmly lifting it should provide confirmation of its identity: A band of ordinary muscle tissue will usually tear; a hemipenis will not (unless jerked). Another longitudinal incision, this time along the organ from the base to the apex (its limits determined by gently sliding a blunt probe posteriorly until it meets resistance) will allow the length of the hemipenis to be recorded relative to the number of subcaudals it lies above.

Most species of *Thamnophis* for which inverted hemipenis lengths have been reported (such data are lacking for many) have an organ that extends for an average 8 to 14 subcaudals. In *T. scalaris,* however, the average hemipenis length is 28 subcaudals (Rossman and Lara-Gongora, 1991). The significance of the dramatically longer organ in *T. scalaris* is unknown.

(27) *Hemipenis shape* (everted)— very slender or relatively stout; markedly expanded distally or not markedly expanded distally. The fully everted organ of *T. scalaris* is not only extremely long but very slender, and it is not expanded distally (Fig. 1-13). All other *Thamnophis* have a relatively stout hemipenis, which usually is expanded distally (as it is in the related genus *Nerodia*). However, the expansion is essentially lacking in a few species (brachystoma, marcianus, proximus, sauritus, sirtalis). Data are lacking for *T. errans; T. butleri* and *T. pulchrilatus* appear to have an intermediate condition. Of particular interest are the presence of an expanded distal region in *T. radix,* its reduction in *T. butleri,* and its absence in *T. brachystoma,* the latter two being the presumably derived sister-species of *T. radix.* It would appear that the presence of an expanded distal region represents the primitive character-state for the genus.

Taxonomy and
Relationships

33

Chapter 2

CHRONOLOGICAL LIST
OF THE NEW GENUS, SPECIES, AND SUBSPECIES
NAMES PROPOSED FOR GARTER SNAKES

NEW GENUS NAMES

Year	Name/Author	Type-Species (or Rationale for Change)
1843	*Thamnophis* Fitzinger	*sauritus*
1853	*Eutainia* Baird and Girard	*sauritus*
1854	*Eutaenia* Baird	Emendation of *Eutainia* Baird and Girard
1861b	*Prymnomiodon* Cope	*chalceus = sauritus*
1875	*Chilopoma* Cope *in* Yarrow	*rufipunctatus*
1883a	*Atomarchus* Cope	*multimaculatus = rufipunctatus*
1885b	*Stypocemus* Cope	Substitute name for *Chilopoma* Cope, incorrectly thought to be preoccupied by *Cheilopoma* Murray, 1867

NEW SPECIES AND SUBSPECIES NAMES

Year	Original Name/Author/Genus*	Present Status
1758	*sirtalis* Linnaeus [*Coluber*]	*sirtalis sirtalis*
1766	*ordinatus* Linnaeus [*Coluber*]	*sirtalis sirtalis*
1766	*saurita* Linnaeus [*Coluber*]	*sauritus sauritus*
1788	*taenia* Schoepf [*Coluber*]	*sirtalis sirtalis*
1803	*ibibe* Daudin [*Coluber*]	*sirtalis sirtalis*
1818	*trivittata* Rafinesque [*Coluber*]	nomen dubium
1820	*kentuckensis* Rafinesque [*Coluber*]	nomen dubium
1820	*similis* Rafinesque [*Coluber*]	nomen dubium
1823	*parietalis* Say *in* James [*Coluber*]	*sirtalis parietalis*
1823	*proximus* Say *in* James [*Coluber*]	*proximus proximus*
1830	*trivittatus* Deppe [*Tropidonotus* (*Coluber*)]	nomen nudum
1830	*melanogaster* Deppe [*Tropidonotus* (*Coluber*)]	nomen nudum
1834	*eques* Reuss [*Coluber*]	*eques eques*
1835	*infernalis* Blainville [*Coluber*]	*sirtalis infernalis*
1837	*bipunctatus* Schlegel [*Tropidonotus*]	*sirtalis sirtalis*
1839	*subcarinata* Gray *in* Richardson [*Coluber* (*Natrix*)]	*eques eques*
1852	*ordinoides* Baird and Girard [*Tropidonotus*]	*ordinoides*
1852	*concinnus* Hallowell [*Tropidonotus*]	*sirtalis concinnus*
1853	*faireyi* Baird and Girard [*Eutainia*]	*proximus proximus*
1853	*pickeringii* Baird and Girard [*Eutainia*]	*sirtalis pickeringii*
1853	*leptocephala* Baird and Girard [*Eutainia*]	*ordinoides*
1853	*dorsalis* Baird and Girard [*Eutainia*]	*sirtalis dorsalis*
1853	*radix* Baird and Girard [*Eutainia*]	*radix*
1853	*elegans* Baird and Girard [*Eutainia*]	*elegans elegans*
1853	*vagrans* Baird and Girard [*Eutainia*]	*elegans vagrans*
1853	*marciana* Baird and Girard [*Eutainia*]	*marcianus marcianus*
1853	*trivittatus* Hallowell [*Tropidonotus*]	*elegans elegans*
1854	*jauresi* Duméril, Bibron, and Duméril [*Tropidonotus*]	*sirtalis sirtalis*
1859	*couchii* Kennicott [*Eutaenia*]	*couchii*
1859	*ornata* Baird [*Eutaenia*]	*sirtalis dorsalis*

continued

Year	Original Name/Author/Genus*	Present Status
1859	*sackenii* Kennicott [*Eutaenia*]	*sauritus sackenii*
1860	*atrata* Kennicott *in* Cooper [*Eutaenia*]	*atratus atratus*
1860	*cooperi* Kennicott *in* Cooper [*Eutaenia*]	*ordinoides*
1860	*haydenii* Kennicott [*Eutaenia*]	*radix*
1860	*megalops* Kennicott [*Eutaenia*]	*eques megalops*
1860	*macrostemma* Kennicott [*Eutaenia*]	*eques eques*
1860	*hammondii* Kennicott [*Eutaenia*]	*hammondii*
1860	*angustirostris* Kennicott [*Eutaenia*]	nomen dubium
1860	*cyrtopsis* Kennicott [*Eutaenia*]	*cyrtopsis cyrtopsis*
1860	*valida* Kennicott [*Regina*]	*validus validus*
1860	*celaeno* Cope [*Tropidonotus*]	*validus celaeno*
1860	*tephropleura* Cope [*Tropidonotus*]	*validus celaeno*
1861a	*scalaris* Cope	*scalaris*
1861b	*chalceus* Cope [*Prymnomiodon*]	*sauritus sackenii*
1861c	*cyrtopsis cyclides* Cope	*cyrtopsis cyrtopsis*
1863	*collaris* Jan [*Tropidonotus (Eutainia)*]	*cyrtopsis collaris*
1863	*scaliger* Jan [*Tropidonotus (Eutainia)*]	*scaliger*
1863	*glaphyros* Jan [*Tropidonotus (Eutainia)*]	*radix*
1863	*kennicotti* Jan [*Tropidonotus (Eutainia)*]	*radix*
1863	*mesomelanus* Jan [*Tropidonotus (Regina)*]	See *melanogaster* account
1864	*melanogaster* Peters [*Tropidonotus*]	*melanogaster melanogaster*
1865	*baronis mulleri* Troschel *in* Müller [*Tropidonotus*]	Not a binomial name
1866	*flavilabris* Cope [*Eutaenia*]	*eques eques*
1866	*sumichrasti* Cope [*Eutaenia*]	*sumichrasti*
1868	*phenax* Cope [*Eutaenia*]	*sumichrasti*
1875	*rufipunctatum* Cope *in* Yarrow [*Chilopoma*]	*rufipunctatus*
1875	*sirtalis obscura* Cope *in* Yarrow [*Eutaenia*]	*sirtalis sirtalis*
1875	*sirtalis tetrataenia* Cope *in* Yarrow [*Eutaenia*]	*sirtalis infernalis*
1878	*radix twiningi* Coues and Yarrow [*Eutaenia*]	*radix*
1878	*imperialis* Coues and Yarrow [*Eutaenia*]	nomen nudum
1879	*quadriserialis* Fischer [*Tropidonotus*]	*validus validus*

Year	Original Name/Author/Genus*	Present Status
1880	*cyrtopsis ocellata* Cope [*Eutaenia*]	*cyrtopsis ocellatus*
1883a	*multimaculatus* Cope [*Atomarchus*]	*rufipunctatus*
1883b	*biscutata* Cope [*Eutaenia*]	*elegans elegans* × *elegans vagrans*
1883	*vagrans plutonia* Yarrow [*Eutaenia*]	*elegans vagrans*
1883	*henshawi* Yarrow [*Eutaenia*]	*elegans vagrans*
1885a	*insigniarum* Cope [*Eutaenia*]	*eques eques*
1885a	*chrysocephala* Cope [*Eutaenia*]	*chrysocephalus*
1885a	*pulchrilatus* Cope [*Eutaenia*]	*pulchrilatus*
1885b	*rutiloris* Cope [*Eutaenia*]	*proximus rutiloris*
1889	*nigrolateris* Brown [*Eutaenia*]	*marcianus marcianus*
1889	*butleri* Cope [*Eutaenia*]	*butleri*
1889	*sirtalis graminea* Cope [*Eutaenia*]	*sirtalis sirtalis*
1889	*radix melanotaenia* Cope [*Eutaenia*]	*radix*
1889	*sirtalis melanota* Higley [*Eutaenia*]	*sirtalis sirtalis* × *sirtalis semifasciatus*
1892	*praeocularis* Bocourt [*Eutaenia*]	*marcianus praeocularis*
1892a	*brachystoma* Cope [*Eutaenia*]	*brachystoma*
1892b	*elegans brunnea* Cope [*Eutaenia*]	*elegans elegans* × *elegans vagrans*
1892b	*elegans lineolata* Cope [*Eutaenia*]	*elegans elegans*
1892b	*infernalis vidua* Cope [*Eutaenia*]	*atratus atratus*
1892b	*aurata* Cope [*Eutaenia*]	*cyrtopsis cyrtopsis*
1892b	*sirtalis semifasciata* Cope [*Eutaenia*]	*sirtalis semifasciatus*
1892b	*nigrilatus* Cope [*Eutaenia*]	Emendation of *nigrolateris* Brown
1892b	*sirtalis trilineata* Cope [*Eutaenia*]	*sirtalis pickeringii*
1893	*cyrtopsis fulvus* Bocourt [*Eutaenia*]	*fulvus*
1893	*baronis-mülleri* Boulenger [*Tropidonotus*]	*melanogaster melanogaster*
1894	*godmani* Günther [*Tropidonotus*]	*godmani*
1899	*leptocephalus olympia* Meek	*ordinoides*

continued

New Species and
Subspecies Names

Year	Original Name/Author/Genus*	Present Status
1899	*rubristriata* Meek	*ordinoides*
1899	*sirtalis pallidula* Allen	*sirtalis pallidulus*
1899	*digueti* Mocquard [*Tropidonotus*]	*hammondii*
1899	*stejnegeri* McClain	*eques megalops*
1903	*obalskii* Mocquard [*Tropidonotus*]	*sirtalis pallidulus*
1923	*ordinoides hueyi* Van Denburgh and Slevin	*elegans hueyi*
1936	*ordinoides hydrophila* Fitch	*atratus hydrophilus*
1937	*arabdotus* Andrews	*marcianus praeocularis*
1938	*ruthveni* Hartweg and Oliver	*marcianus marcianus*
1940	*halophilus* Taylor	*sumichrasti*
1940	*eburatus* Taylor	*chrysocephalus*
1940	*bovallii* Dunn	*marcianus bovallii*
1940	*rozellae* Smith	*marcianus marcianus × marcianus praeocularis*
1940	*ordinoides gigas* Fitch	*gigas*
1942	*vicinus* Smith	*cyrtopsis collaris*
1942	*eques postremus* Smith	*postremus*
1942	*sumichrasti cerebrosus* Smith	nomen dubium
1942	*ordinoides errans* Smith	*errans*
1942	*melanogaster canescens* Smith	*melanogaster canescens*
1947	*elegans nigrescens* Johnson	*elegans vagrans*
1950	*melanogaster linearis* Smith, Nixon, and Smith	*melanogaster linearis*
1950	*sumichrasti salvini* Smith, Nixon, and Smith	*cyrtopsis collaris*
1950	*sirtalis annectens* Brown	*sirtalis annectens*
1951a	*elegans aquaticus* Fox	*atratus atratus × atratus hydrophilus*
1951a	*elegans terrestris* Fox	*elegans terrestris*
1951b	*sirtalis fitchi* Fox	*sirtalis fitchi*
1953	*valida isabelleae* Conant [*Natrix*]	*validus isabelleae*
1955	*mendax* Walker	*mendax*

Year	Original Name/Author/Genus*	Present Status
1957	*nigronuchalis* Thompson	*nigronuchalis*
1959	*melanogaster chihuahuaensis* Tanner	*melanogaster chihuahuaensis*
1961	*valida thamnophisoides* Conant [*Natrix*]	*validus thamnophisoides*
1963	*proximus orarius* Rossman	*proximus orarius*
1963	*proximus rubrilineatus* Rossman	*proximus rubrilineatus*
1963	*proximus diabolicus* Rossman	*proximus diabolicus*
1963	*proximus alpinus* Rossman	*proximus alpinus*
1963	*sauritus septentrionalis* Rossman	*sauritus septentrionalis*
1963	*sauritus nitae* Rossman	*sauritus nitae*
1963	*eques virgatenuis* Conant	*eques virgatenuis*
1965b	*sirtalis similis* Rossman	*sirtalis similis*
1969	*exsul* Rossman	*exsul*
1986	*rufipunctatus unilabialis* Tanner	*rufipunctatus*
1988	*sirtalis lowei* Tanner	*sirtalis dorsalis*
1989	*elegans arizonae* Tanner and Lowe	*elegans arizonae*
1989	*elegans vascotanneri* Tanner and Lowe	*elegans vascotanneri*

*Genus given only if other than *Thamnophis*.

Chapter 3

KEY TO THE SPECIES AND SUBSPECIES OF *THAMNOPHIS*

The following key is typical of the dichotomous variety and should be used as such. Some characters (various aspects of color pattern) will work best with live or fresh material, others (most meristic and mensural features) with preserved specimens. Mensural features used to calculate ratios of taxonomic significance are illustrated in Fig. 1-11. The most reliable results will be obtained when series are available. Some characters (tooth counts, head scale measurements) may require a greater investment of time than users of keys are accustomed to giving, but it is hoped that the increased reliability of identifications will prove ample compensation for the users' efforts. Because of the high degree of variability in some key characters, species may "key out" in a number of different couplets. Always use the species accounts and photographs to confirm identifications reached in the key. The first 59 couplets should provide a species identification. Keys to the subspecies of those species in which they are recognized (designated ssp. in the species key) follow in alphabetical order.

SPECIES OF *THAMNOPHIS*

1. Anal plate divided .... *T. validus* (ssp.) (p. 276)
    Anal plate undivided 2
2. Lateral stripe involving 4th dorsal scale row anteriorly[1] 3
    Lateral stripe, if present, usually[2] not involving 4th dorsal scale row
        anteriorly 11
3. Maxillary teeth[3]≤ 4
    Maxillary teeth usually <27 6
4. A maximum[4] of 19 dorsal scale rows; no vertical bars on any supralabial
        suture 5
    A maximum of >19 dorsal scale rows; vertical bars present on at least
        some supralabial sutures .... *T. eques* (ssp.) (p. 171)
5. Paired parietal spots almost always present, fused, bright, and relatively
        large; brown pigment usually not extending onto ventrals to form
        dark ventrolateral stripe on each side or, if present, usually covering
        less than 2/5 of each scute .... *T. proximus* (ssp.) (p. 225)
    Parietal spots often lacking; when present small and rarely fused or
        bright; brown pigment always extending onto ventrals and usually
        covering 2/5 or more of each scute .... *T. sauritus* (ssp.) (p. 248)
6. Lateral stripe involving 2nd dorsal scale row anteriorly 7
    Lateral stripe not involving 2nd dorsal scale row anteriorly 10
7. A maximum of 17 dorsal scale rows anteriorly ....
    .... *T. brachystoma* (p. 137)
    A maximum of >17 dorsal scale rows anteriorly 8
8. Lateral stripe involving most of 2nd dorsal scale row at midbody; InR/NR
        averaging > 120% .... *T. sirtalis* (ssp.) (p. 259)
    Lateral stripe involving no more than upper margin of 2nd dorsal scale
        row at midbody; InR/NR averaging < 105% 9

---

1. At, or behind, the level of the 10th ventral scute.
2. "Usually" in this key refers to at least 90% of the specimens examined.
3. Counting empty sockets as well as attached teeth.
4. Counting across the back at the level of the 10th ventral scale. In most species the highest count
will be obtained at this point, but in a few it will occur between the neck and midbody.

9. A maximum of 19 scale rows; supralabial barring weakly developed or absent; ventrals usually ≤ 145 in males, ≤ 142 in females .... *T. butleri* (p. 141)

   Usually a maximum of 21 dorsal scale rows; supralabial barring usually well developed; ventrals usually ≥ 145 in males, > 142 in females .... *T. radix* (p. 235)

10. Light keels present on dark scales of dorsum .... *T. eques* (ssp.) (p. 171)
    No light keels on dark scales of dorsum .... *T. radix* (p. 235)

11. A maximum of 17 dorsal scale rows 12
    A maximum of > 17 dorsal scale rows 22

12. Preoculars usually 1 on at least one side 13
    Preoculars usually 2 on at least one side .... *T. melanogaster* (ssp.) (p. 207)

13. Supralabials usually 6 or 7 on at least one side; maxillary teeth < 25 14
    Supralabials usually 8 on at least one side; maxillary teeth > 25 .... *T. chrysocephalus* (p. 147)

14. Supralabials usually 6 on at least one side 15
    Supralabials usually 7 on at least one side 16

15. Dorsal scale rows reducing to 15 anterior to vent; ML/FL averaging > 72% .... *T. ordinoides* (p. 218)
    Dorsal scale rows usually not reducing to 15 anterior to vent; ML/FL averaging < 60% .... *T. brachystoma* (p. 137)

16. Infralabials usually 8 on at least one side 17
    Infralabials usually 9 or 10 on at least one side 18

17. Dorsal scale rows reducing to 15 anterior to vent; InR/NR averaging < 120%; vertebral stripe often brightly colored; nuchal blotches not conspicuous .... *T. ordinoides* (p. 218)
    Dorsal scale rows only infrequently reducing to 15 anterior to vent; InR/NR averaging > 140%; vertebral stripe not brightly colored, often indistinct; nuchal blotches usually conspicuous .... *T. exsul* (p. 181)

18. Vertebral stripe often brightly colored; nuchal blotches not conspicuous .... *T. ordinoides* (p. 218)

Vertebral stripe not brightly colored, often indistinct or absent; nuchal blotches usually conspicuous 19

19. Lateral stripe absent; maxillary teeth > 20 .... *T. mendax* (p. 213)
Lateral stripe often faint, but usually present; maxillary teeth ≤ 20 ....
.... 20

20. Top of head unpatterened; two rows of relatively small black spots between vertebral and lateral spots .... *T. godmani* (p. 190)
Top of head usually with light lines along some sutures; one or two rows of large, black-edged brown spots or blotches between vertebral and lateral stripes 21

21. Subcaudals[5] < 60 in males, < 50 in females; posterior supralabials same color as temporals .... *T. scaliger* (p. 257)
Subcaudals > 60 in males, > 50 in females; posterior supralabials same color as other supralabials .... *T. scalaris* (p. 254)

22. A maximum of 19 dorsal scale rows 23
A maximum of > 19 dorsal scale rows 52

23. Supralabials usually 7 on at least one side 24
Supralabials usually 8 on at least one side 38

24. One or two rows of large, black-edged brown spots or blotches between vertebral and lateral stripes 25
Dorsolateral spots, if present, black and moderate in size 26

25. Subcaudals < 60 in males, < 50 in females; posterior supralabials same color as temporals .... *T. scaliger* (p. 257)
Subcaudals > 60 in males, > 50 in females; posterior supralabials same color as other supralabials .... *T. scalaris* (p. 254)

26. Dorsal scale rows reducing to 15 anterior to vent 27
Dorsal scale rows reducing to 17 anterior to vent 28

27. InR/NR averaging > 110%; Prf/In averaging > 115% ....
.... *T. ordinoides* (p. 218)
InR/NR averaging < 85%; Prf/In averaging < 100% ....
.... *T. atratus* (ssp.) (p. 131)

28. Vertebral stripe largely confined to vertebral row or absent 29

---

5. This character works only for animals having a complete tail.

Vertebral stripe involving vertebral row and at least 1/2 width of scales in paravertebral rows 36

29. Ventrals ≤ 151 in males, ≤ 143 in females 30
    Ventrals ≥ 150 in males, ≥ 146 in females 31

30. Lateral stripe present; InR/NR averaging > 120%; Prf/In averaging > 120% .... *T. sirtalis* (ssp.) (p. 259)
    Lateral stripe absent; InR/NR averaging < 95%; Prf/In averaging < 90% .... *T. postremus* (p. 223)

31. Large dark spots present below lateral stripe or area black 32
    If dark spots present below lateral stripe, then not large 33

32. Prf/In averaging > 120%; ACS/PCS averaging ≤ 75% .... *T. sirtalis* (ssp.) (p. 259)
    Prf/In averaging ≤ 90%; ACS/PCS averaging > 86% .... *T. pulchrilatus* (p. 232)

33. Tongue all black .... *T. errans* (p. 178)
    Tongue red with black tips 34

34. InR/NR averaging > 125%; Prf/In averaging > 120% .... *T. sirtalis* (ssp.) (p. 259)
    InR/NR averaging < 115%; Prf/In averaging < 100% 35

35. InR/NR averaging ≤ 90%; ACS/PCS averaging ≤ 81% .... *T. atratus* (ssp.) (p. 131)
    InR/NR averaging ≥ 99%; ACS/PCS averaging ≥ 81% .... *T. elegans* (ssp.) (p. 162)

36. InR/NR averaging > 125%; Prf/In averaging > 120% .... *T. sirtalis* (ssp.) (p. 259)
    InR/NR averaging < 115%; Prf/In averaging < 100% 37

37. InR/NR averaging ≤ 90%; ACS/PCS averaging ≤ 81% .... *T. atratus* (ssp.) (p. 131)
    InR/NR averaging ≥ 99%; ACS/PCS averaging ≥ 81% .... *T. elegans* (ssp.) (p. 162)

38. Dorsal scale rows reducing to 15 anterior to vent 39
    Dorsal scale rows reducing to 17 anterior to vent 40

39. InR/NR averaging > 110%; Prf/In averaging > 115% .... *T. ordinoides* (p. 218)

InR/NR averaging < 85%; Prf/In averaging < 100% ....
.... *T. atratus* (ssp.) (p. 131)

40. Vertebral stripe present, at least anteriorly 41
    Vertebral stripe usually absent 49
41. Preoculars usually 1 on at least one side 42
    Preoculars usually 2 on at least one side 51
42. Posterior supralabials same color as temporals, set off fore and aft by
    black-edged light areas; lateral stripe, if present, confined to 3rd
    dorsal scale row anteriorly .... *T. marcianus* (ssp.) (p. 198)
    Posterior supralabials same color as other supralabials; lateral stripe not
    confined to 3rd dorsal scale row anteriorly 43
43. Tongue all black 44
    Tongue red with black tips 45
44. Vertebral stripe distinct throughout; maxillary teeth < 20 ....
    .... *T. errans* (p. 178)
    Vertebral stripe usually indistinct, especially posteriorly; maxillary teeth
    > 20 .... *T. fulvus* (p. 183)
45. Lateral stripe present 46
    Lateral stripe absent 48
46. Prf/In averaging < 102% 47
    Prf/In averaging > 120% .... *T. sirtalis* (ssp.) (p. 259)
47. FL/PL averaging ≥ 81%; ED/FL averaging ≥ 72% ....
    .... *T. cyrtopsis* (ssp.) (p. 155)
    FL/PL averaging ≤ 74%, ED/FL averaging ≤ 67% ....
    .... *T. atratus* (ssp.) (p. 131)
48. Dorsum light brown with small black spots; maxillary teeth ≥ 27 in
    males, ≥ 25 in females .... *T. postremus* (p. 223)
    Dorsolateral spots, if visible, relatively large; maxillary teeth ≤ 27 in
    males, ≤ 25 in females .... *T. atratus* (ssp.) (p. 131)
49. Preoculars usually 1 on at least one side 50
    Preoculars usually 2 on at least one side ...... *T. melanogaster* (ssp.) (p. 207)
50. Black-edged, brown nuchal blotches elongated and at least partially sepa-
    rated middorsally; a prominent, dark postocular stripe usually
    present .... *T. sumichrasti* (p. 272)

Black nuchal collar divided middorsally or not; no dark postocular stripe present .... *T. cyrtopsis* (ssp.) (p. 155)

51. Posterior supralabials same color as temporals, set off fore and aft by black-edged light areas; lateral stripe, if present, confined to 3rd dorsal scale row anteriorly .... *T. marcianus* (ssp.) (p. 198)

    Posterior supralabials same color as other supralabials; lateral stripe not confined to 3rd dorsal scale row anteriorly ....
    .... *T. melanogaster* (ssp.) (p. 207)

52. No vertebral or lateral stripes present 53

    One, two, or three stripes present 55

53. Venter with several rows of dark spots or an irregular dark reticulum; ACS/PCS averaging > 92% 54

    Venter with very little dark pigment; ACS/PCS averaging < 82% ....
    .... *T. hammondii* (p. 194)

54. A large, undivided nuchal blotch; supralabial bars usually black, often narrow; LHt/LV > 66% .... *T. nigronuchalis* (p. 215)

    Usually two moderately small, separate nuchal blotches; supralabial bars broad, black-edged brown wedges; LHt/LV < 66% ....
    .... *T. rufipunctatus* (p. 241)

55. Posterior supralabials same color as temporals, set off fore and aft by black-edged light areas; lateral stripe, if present, confined to 3rd dorsal scale row anteriorly .... *T. marcianus* (ssp.) (p. 198)

    Posterior supralabials same color as other supralabials; lateral stripe not confined to 3rd dorsal scale row anteriorly 56

56. InR/NR averaging ≥ 99% .... *T. elegans* (ssp.) (p. 162)

    InR/NR averaging ≤ 96% 57

57. Supralabial 6 equal to or longer than supralabial 7 (at midheight) ... 58

    Supralabial 7 longer than supralabial 6 (at midheight) 59

58. Vertebral stripe present and distinct for at least a short distance on neck; black nuchal blotches large; LD/LV averaging < 60% in males, ≤ 52% in females .... *T. couchii* (p. 150)

    Vertebral stripe not present; black nuchal blotches small; LD/LV averaging ≥ 70% in males, ≥ 64% in females ....
    .... *T. hammondii* (p. 194)

59. Subcaudals averaging ≤ 77 in males, ≤ 71 in females; ML/FL averaging 85% in males, 95% in females; LD/LV averaging ≥ 75% in males, ≥ 73% in females .... *T. gigas* (p. 186)
   Subcaudals averaging ≥ 85 in males, ≥ 76 in females; ML/FL averaging ≤ 77% in males, ≤ 79% in females; LD/LV averaging ≤ 69% in males, ≤ 66% in females .... *T. atratus* (ssp.) (p. 131)

SUBSPECIES OF *THAMNOPHIS ATRATUS*

1. Lateral stripe present 2
   Lateral stripe absent 3
2. Dorsal scale rows reducing to 15 anterior to vent .... *T. a. atratus* (p. 131)
   Dorsal scale rows reducing to 17 anterior to vent ....
   .... *T. a. hydrophilus* (p. 131)
3. Dorsal scale rows reducing to 15 anterior to vent; ventrals averaging ≤ 154 in males; ≤ 147 in females .... *T. a. atratus* (p. 131)
   Dorsal scale rows reducing to 17 anterior to vent; ventrals averaging ≥ 164 in males, ≥ 160 in females .... *T. a. hydrophilus* (p. 131)

SUBSPECIES OF *THAMNOPHIS CYRTOPSIS*

1. Nuchal blotches fused to form a collar; maxillary teeth ≥ 26 in males, ≥ 25 in females .... *T. c. collaris* (p. 155)
   Nuchal blotches usually separated by vertebral stripe; maxillary teeth ≤ 27 in males, ≤ 25 in females 2
2. Dorsolateral spots on anterior part of body fused to form large blotches .... *T. c. ocellatus* (p. 155)
   Dorsolateral spots on anterior part of body not fused to form large blotches .... *T. c. cyrtopsis* (p. 155)

SUBSPECIES OF *THAMNOPHIS ELEGANS*

1. Vertebral stripe, if present, interrupted by black crossbars along much of its length .... *T. e. vascotanneri* (p. 162)

Vertebral stripe distinct, at least anteriorly, and interrupted by few or no black crossbars 2

2. Vertebral stripe involving three entire scale rows; no red in pattern .... *T. e. arizonae* (p. 162)

    Vertebral stripe involving less than three entire scale rows, or with red in pattern 3

3. Vertebral stripe largely confined to vertebral row, with uneven edges due to encroachment of upper row of dorsolateral spots .... *T. e. vagrans* (p. 162)

    Vertebral stripe involving at least 1/2 width of each scale in paravertebral rows; edges of stripe even 4

4. Dorsum velvety black (dark gray-brown in San Bernadino Mountains)[6] .... *T. e. elegans* (p. 162)

    Dorsum usually not velvety black (except in southern Coast Ranges)[7] 5

5. No red pigment present on dorsum or venter........ *T. e. hueyi* (p. 162)

    Red pigment present (in varying amounts) on dorsum, venter, or both (except in southern Coast Ranges)[7].............. *T. e. terrestris* (p. 162)

SUBSPECIES OF *THAMNOPHIS EQUES*

1. Dorsum predominantly brown; vertebral stripe not confined to vertebral row 2

    Dorsum predominantly black; vertebral stripe largely confined to vertebral row .... *T. e. virgatenuis* (p. 171)

2. Subcaudals usually ≤ 78 in males, usually ≤ 68 in females............... .... *T. e. eques* (p. 171)

    Subcaudals usually ≥ 79 in males, usually ≥ 69 in females............... .... *T. e. megalops* (p. 171)

---

6. *T. e. elegans* from the San Bernadino Mountains are not morphologically distinguishable from *T. e. hueyi* (Fitch, 1940).

7. *T. e. terrestris* from the southern Coast Ranges are not morphologically distinguishable from *T. e. elegans* (Bellemin and Stewart, 1977).

SUBSPECIES OF *THAMNOPHIS MARCIANUS*

1. Usually a maximum of 21 dorsal scale rows; vertebral stripe not involving more than the vertebral row and 1/2 width of each scale in paravertebral rows; maxillary teeth ≤ 25 .... *T. m. marcianus* (p. 198)
   A maximum of 19 dorsal scale rows; vertebral stripe, if present, involving three entire scale rows; maxillary teeth ≥ 26 2
2. Vertebral stripe always present; black ventral spots small and separate .... *T. m. praeocularis* (p. 198)
   Vertebral stripe usually absent; black ventral spots large and often connected across venter .... *T. m. bovallii* (p. 198)

SUBSPECIES OF *THAMNOPHIS MELANOGASTER*

1. Vertebral stripe present in juveniles and some adults; subcaudals ≤ 64 in males, usually ≤ 54 in females .... *T. m. linearis* (p. 207)
   Vertebral stripe most often lacking; subcaudals ≥ 64 in males, ≥ 54 in females 2
2. Subcaudals ≥ 75 in males, ≥ 68 in females; venter usually without black markings .... *T. m. chihuahuaensis* (p. 207)
   Subcaudals ≤ 75 in males, ≤ 63 in females; venter usually with some black markings 3
3. Venter mostly black; 2nd supralabial frequently touching nasal; postoculars frequently 3 or more .... *T. m. melanogaster* (p. 207)
   Venter rarely with more than a median black stripe; 2nd supralabial infrequently touching nasal; postoculars most often 2 .... *T. m. canescens* (p. 207)

SUBSPECIES OF *THAMNOPHIS PROXIMUS*

1. Dorsum black; vertebral stripe orange; dark ventrolateral stripe lacking .... *T. p. proximus* (p. 225)
   Dorsum olive-gray or some shade of brown; vertebral stripe color variable; ventrolateral stripe development variable 2

Key to Species and
Subspecies

49

2. Dorsum dark brown; vertebral stripe gold; ventrolateral stripe broad (to 1/10 width of scale on each side); T/TL averaging 27.5% in males, 27% in females .... *T. p. alpinus* (p. 225)
   Dorsum olive-gray or brown (not dark); ventrolateral stripe relatively narrow or absent; T/TL usually > 29% in males, > 28% in females 3
3. Vertebral stripe bright red .... *T. p. rubrilineatus* (p. 225)
   Vertebral stripe orange, grayish-tan, or gold 4
4. Vertebral stripe grayish-tan; labials yellow-orange; lateral stripe narrow anteriorly, further reduced posteriorly; ventrals averaging < 161 in males, < 158 in females .... *T. p. rutiloris* (p. 225)
   Vertebral stripe orange or gold; labials greenish-white or greenish-yellow; lateral stripe not narrow, at least anteriorly; ventrals averaging > 162 in males, > 158 in females 5
5. Vertebral stripe orange; dorsum olive-gray; lateral stripe frequently reduced posteriorly; narrow ventrolateral stripe frequently present .... *T. p. diabolicus* (p. 225)
   Vertebral stripe gold; dorsum usually olive-brown; lateral stripe rarely reduced; ventrolateral stripe usually absent .... *T. p. orarius* (p. 225)

SUBSPECIES OF *THAMNOPHIS SAURITUS*

1. Supralabials usually 7, occasionally 8; vertebral stripe some shade of yellow; lateral stripe occupying 1/2 or more of both 3rd and 4th dorsal scale rows 2
   Supralabials usually 8, rarely 7; vertebral stripe tan or lacking; lateral stripe occupying less than 1/2 of either 3rd or 4th dorsal scale row or both 3
2. Dorsum reddish-brown; lateral stripe rarely widened anteriorly; T/TL usually > 34% in males, > 33% in females .... *T. s. sauritus* (p. 248)
   Dorsum dark brown to velvety black; lateral stripe frequently widened anteriorly to involve 4th dorsal scale row; T/TL rarely > 33.5% in males, > 32.5% in females .... *T. s. septentrionalis* (p. 248)
3. Dorsum tan or brown, rarely dark; lateral stripe yellow, occasionally white .... *T. s. sackenii* (p. 248)

Dorsum dark brown to black; lateral stripe light blue or bluish-white, occasionally white .... *T. s. nitae* (p. 248)

SUBSPECIES OF *THAMNOPHIS SIRTALIS*

1. Dorsum usually lacking red pigment (except occasionally on stripes) 2
    Dorsum usually with red pigment forming regular rows of spots, bars, or flecks, or longitudinal stripes 7
2. Ventrolateral black stripe encroaches extensively onto ventrals; vertebral stripe confined to vertebral row; dorsolateral area black ....
    .... *T. s. pickeringii* (p. 259)
    Ventrolateral dark stripe usually brown, extending only slightly if at all onto ventrals; vertebral stripe wider than vertebral row if dorsolateral area black 3
3. Lateral stripe interrupted anteriorly by regular series of vertical black bars .... *T. s. semifasciatus* (p. 259)
    Lateral stripe interrupted by few, if any, black bars 4
4. Vertebral stripe bright yellow or orange, involving at least 1/2 of each paravertebral row; lateral stripe involving 2nd, 3rd, and 4th dorsal scale rows anteriorly .... *T. s. annectens* (p. 259)
    Vertebral stripe (when present) some shade of white, yellow, or tan, usually involving no more than 1/2 of each paravertebral row; lateral stripe usually confined to 2nd and 3rd dorsal scale rows throughout
    5
5. Lateral stripe light blue or bluish-white .... *T. s. similis* (p. 259)
    Lateral stripe not so colored 6
6. Venter green or tinted with yellow; vertebral stripe present or absent
    .... *T. s. sirtalis* (p. 259)
    Venter white or pale gray; vertebral stripe pale tan, usually poorly defined, and often present only anteriorly .... *T. s. pallidulus* (p. 259)
7. Top of head red or reddish-brown 8
    Top of head gray, brown, or black; red present only on temporals, if at all 9
8. Red pigment forms a nearly continuous, broad dorsolateral stripe occasionally interrupted by vertical black bars .... *T. s. infernalis* (p. 259)

Key to Species and
Subspecies

51

Red pigment forms evenly spaced spots or vertical bars ....
.... *T. s. concinnus* (p. 259)

9. Single series of red spots along lower margin of dorsolateral area; top of
   head black; black spotting on margins of ventrals reduced or absent
   .... *T. s. fitchi* (p. 259)

   Double series of red spots present, at least anteriorly; top of head gray,
   brown, or black (if black, then single or double row of black spots
   present on ventral margins) 10

10. Upper row of red markings poorly defined with obscure edges; red mark-
    ings tending to fuse and segregate dark dorsolateral area into series
    of black spots above lateral stripe; upper row of black spots often
    fused, forming broad black border to vertebral stripe ....
    .... *T. s. dorsalis* (p. 259)

    Upper row of red spots, if present, well defined; lower row of red markings
    enclosed within dark dorsolateral area; no distinct black border to
    vertebral stripe .... *T. s. parietalis* (p. 259)

SUBSPECIES OF *THAMNOPHIS VALIDUS*

1. A prominent, pale vertebral stripe present ....
   .... *T. v. thamnophisoides* (p. 276)

   Pale vertebral stripe absent 2

2. Dorsum gray or brown (rarely dark brown), usually with four alternating
   rows of small black spots (averaging 70 in one row); lateral stripe,
   if present, not ragged-edged 3

   Dorsum very dark brown or black (if visible, dorsal spots averaging > 86
   in one row); lateral stripe, if present, pale and ragged-edged ....
   .... *T. v. celaeno* (p. 276)

3. Dorsum usually gray or dull brown; lateral stripe absent; ventrals averaging > 140 (both sexes combined) .... *T. v. validus* (p. 276)

   Dorsum often rich brown; lateral stripe usually present; ventrals averaging < 135 (both sexes combined) .... *T. v. isabelleae* (p. 276)

Section Two

**ECOLOGY, BEHAVIOR,
AND CAPTIVE CARE**

Chapter 4

ECOLOGY AND CONSERVATION OF GARTER SNAKES

Masters of Plasticity

It's a good thing you Yanks have garter snakes, or you wouldn't have anything to study.

—*Rick Shine, ca. 1987*

As we noted in the introduction to this book, garter snakes are without question among the most successful of all North American reptiles, both in terms of distribution and abundance. A quick glance at any field guide will convince you of this; garter snakes are found in every state in the mainland United States, in Canada from the Maritime Provinces west to British Columbia, and through much of Mexico and Central America. In addition, garter and ribbon snakes are frequently the most abundant species of snake at a given site (e.g., Dalrymple et al., 1991a; Fitch, 1993; Seigel, 1984).

Attempting to account for the extraordinary ecological success of these snakes is a daunting challenge. To meet this challenge, one must answer two questions: What do garter snakes do? and (more important), What do garter snakes do differently from other species that makes them so successful? In this chapter, I will attempt to begin to answer these questions, although a final answer must await the collection of more data, especially on poorly known species (e.g., most Mexican forms) and on areas such as population ecology where our database is still relatively meager. Our primary goal is not to attempt a "theoretical" synthesis of garter snake ecology, as has been attempted recently for snakes in general (e.g., Dunham et al., 1988; Seigel and Ford, 1987). Neither do we have the space needed to review *all* aspects of garter snake ecology. Rather, we want to provide an overview of the ecology of these snakes, emphasizing areas that are well known and pointing out topics or species that require additional study.

REPRODUCTIVE ECOLOGY

Introduction and Overview

Several factors combine to make snakes "model organism" for studying reproduction, including the ease of maintaining them in captivity to observe courtship and obtain live offspring (see Chap. 6) and the relative ease of counting developing offspring without the need to kill gravid females. (See Farr and Gregory, 1991; Fitch, 1987; Seigel, 1993.) It is therefore not surprising that there is an enormous literature on garter snake reproductive ecology, ranging from basic data on clutch size (see review by Seigel and Ford, 1987), to experi-

mental studies on neurobiology (see review in Gans and Crews, 1992) and phenotypic plasticity (Ford and Seigel, 1989a). For example, of the 39 references on reproductive biology of colubrid snakes in Seigel and Ford's recent review (1987), over a third (14) were for garter snakes.

A summary of the basic data on the reproductive biology of garter snakes is presented in Table 4-1. We have not attempted to include every reference, because many papers report only very limited data (e.g., clutch size from one or a few females); instead, except in cases where no other data were available, we have focused on relatively large, well-quantified studies.

One clear lesson from Table 4-1 and the material that follows is the general lack of data on garter snakes from southern, subtropical, and tropical localities. Indeed, much of our apparent wealth of knowledge about garter snake reproductive ecology is based on a single species (*sirtalis*) and (even worse) is mainly from populations of *sirtalis* from the northern portion of their range. By way of illustration, 35% of the data in Table 4-1 are for *T. sirtalis*, and 86% of the *sirtalis* studies were from northern localities. Although the studies on northern populations of *T. sirtalis* have been extremely valuable, they tend to give

Table 4-1. Summary of Data on the Reproductive Ecology of Garter Snakes. Except in cases where no other data were available, only studies with sample sizes > 5 are reported; data from long-term captives are also excluded except when no other data are available.

Species	Site	Clutch Size*	N	Offspring SVL (mm)	Offspring Mass (g)	Reproductive Frequency	Source
atratus	California	7.8	5				Hansen and Tremper, *in prep.*
atratus	California	8.4	9	99.1 (M) 100.4 (F)			J. Boundy, pers. comm.
brachystoma	New York	7.2				75.0	Pisani and Bothner, 1970
brachystoma	Pennsylvania	7.6	8	99.1 (M) 100.4 (F)			Swanson, 1952 (in Ernst and Gotte, 1986)
butleri	Michigan	11.0	4				Carpenter, 1952a
butleri	Michigan	11.4	28			67.0	Ford and Killebrew, 1983
butleri	Ontario	8.5	6				Freedman and Catling, 1978
butleri	Wisconsin	11.9	12	113	1.23		N. Ford, pers. obs.
cyrtopsis	Arizona	19.0	4				Jones, 1990
elegans	British Columbia	7.5	22	176			Farr, 1988
elegans	California	6.3	12				Hansen and Tremper, *in prep.*
elegans	California	10.6	10				Hansen and Tremper, *in prep.*
eques	Arizona	13.6	8	165		50.0	Rosen and Schwalbe, 1988
errans	Mexico	7.8	4				Fitch, 1985
errans	Mexico	8.0	3				Webb, 1976
gigas	California	23.1	19	206.4			Hansen and Hansen, 1990
hammondii	California	15.6	7	203–217			Hansen and Tremper, *in prep.*
marcianus	Arizona	15.3	14				Seigel and Ford, pers. obs.
marcianus	Northern Texas	13.2	23				Seigel and Ford, pers. obs.
marcianus	Southern Texas and Northern Mexico	13.2		150	2.3	71.4	Ford and Karges, 1987
melanogaster	Michoacan	12.9	11				Ford and Ball, 1977

continued

Table 4-1. (Continued)

Species	Site	Clutch Size*	N	Offspring SVL (mm)	Offspring Mass (g)	Reproductive Frequency	Source
ordinoides	British Columbia	5.8	16				Brodie, 1989a
ordinoides	Oregon	6.8	20				Brodie, 1989a
ordinoides	Oregon	5.2	11				Brodie, 1989a
ordinoides	Oregon	9.5	10	136 (M) 140 (F)		77.0	Stewart, 1968
ordinoides	Washington	8.8	44			67.0	Hebard, 1951
proximus	Louisiana	12.9	13			88.0	Tinkle, 1957
proximus	Texas	8.4	20			100.0	Clark, 1974
proximus	Missouri					81.0	Seigel, unpubl.
proximus	Mexico	10.0	5		2.2		Conant, 1965
radix	Colorado	11.6	8	137	1.6		N. Ford, pers. obs.
radix	Illinois	17.0	12	131	1.5		N. Ford, pers. obs.
radix	Manitoba	29.5	6				Gregory, 1977a
radix	Missouri	9.0–11.9	47			88.0	Seigel, unpubl.
rufipunctatus	Arizona	11.3	3				Rosen and Schwalbe, 1988
sauritus	Maryland	10.7	7				McCauley, 1945
sauritus	Michigan	6.0	5			41.6	Burt, 1928
sauritus	Michigan	10.0	5			65.0	Carpenter, 1952a
sauritus	Ontario	12.2	9	141.1–165.3			Rossman, 1963
sirtalis	Alberta	13.8	21	175.5	1.7		Gregory and Larsen, 1993
sirtalis	British Columbia	7.6	15	180.7	2.5		Gregory and Larsen, 1993
sirtalis	British Columbia	10.7	26	182.3	2.4		Gregory and Larsen, 1993
sirtalis	British Columbia	9.7	10	201.3	3.0		Gregory and Larsen, 1993
sirtalis	British Columbia	13.0	7	197.8	3.0		Gregory and Larsen, 1993
sirtalis	British Columbia	13.3	15	172.3			Gregory and Larsen, 1993
sirtalis	California			178–202	2.4–3.3		Jayne and Bennett, 1990
sirtalis	California	7.6	29				Kephart, 1981 in Gregory and Larsen, 1993

sirtalis	Kansas	14.5		168	1.9	64.5	Fitch, 1965; Seigel and Fitch, 1985
sirtalis	Lake Erie					75.0	King, 1988
sirtalis	Manitoba	18.8	30	154.4		78.0	Gregory , 1977b; Gregory and Larsen, 1993; Larsen et al., 1993
sirtalis	Manitoba					23.5–88.0	Whittier and Crews, 1990
sirtalis	Maryland	32.5	11				McCauley, 1945
sirtalis	Michigan	16.9	8			28.6	Burt, 1928
sirtalis	Michigan	18.0	20			65.0	Carpenter, 1952a
sirtalis	Minnesota	13.7	35				Dunlap and Lang, 1990
sirtalis	Missouri	11.0–14.3				65.0	Seigel, unpubl.
sirtalis	New Hampshire	12.9	104				Zehr, 1962 *in* Gregory and Larsen, 1993
sirtalis	Alberta	12.5	23	191.4	2.6	36.0	Larsen et al., 1993
sirtalis	Ontario	18.3	25				Gregory and Larsen, 1993
sirtalis	Oregon	11.3	18	185.8 [M] 181.8 [F]		68.0	Stewart, 1968

*A range of clutch sizes indicates variation among years.

the misleading impression that the reproductive ecology of garter snakes needs little additional study—something that is not at all true.

Male Reproductive Cycles

Our understanding of male reproductive cycles in garter snakes is based primarily on a exhaustive series of studies on populations of *T. sirtalis* from Manitoba and other northern sites (e.g., Aleksiuk and Gregory, 1974; Bona-Gallo and Licht, 1983; Crews et al., 1984; Garstka et al., 1982; Gregory, 1977b; Moore and Lindzey, 1992; Weil, 1985; Whittier et al., 1987). However, few other species or geographic areas have been studied in nearly the same detail. Notable exceptions to this pattern include studies on *T. brachystoma* (Pisani and Bothner, 1970), *T. marcianus* (Ford and Cobb, 1992), *T. melanogaster* (Garstka and Crews, 1982), and *T. radix* (Cieslak, 1945).

Based on these studies, the general outline of male reproductive cycles is as follows. Garter snakes studied to date appear to have a *postnuptial* reproductive cycle, i.e., maximal spermatogenetic activity occurs in the later summer and early fall (see Fig. 8-1 in Seigel and Ford, 1987). Males emerge from hibernation with abundant sperm in the vas deferens (Crews and Garstka, 1982). Male *T. sirtalis* in Manitoba are ready to engage in courtship immediately after emergence from hibernation, and actively court females as they emerge a few days later (Gregory, 1977b). Since most males emerge earlier than do females, this leads to a severely biased operational sex ratio, and the formation of mating balls, i.e., groups of males courting a single female (Fig. 4-1). The huge numbers of snakes at the Manitoba snake dens, coupled with the oblivious nature of the males, makes this a truly awesome sight to behold. Fittingly, it is a tradition in southern Manitoba for tourists to come see these mating displays on Mother's Day, which coincides with the peak of the courtship rituals. (See Chap. 5 for details of mating behavior.)

Although most studies indicate that males are ready to mate immediately after emergence from hibernation, this is not always the case. Ford and Cobb (1992) found considerable variation among populations of *T. marcianus* in terms of timing of mating. As in *T. sirtalis* from Manitoba, male *T. marcianus* from southern Arizona mated almost immediately after emergence from hibernation (Ford and Cobb, 1992), and we have

Fig. 4-1. Photo of large aggregations of common garter snakes (*T. sirtalis parietalis*) at snake dens in Manitoba, Canada. Although most dens are smaller than this, these large aggregations are truly spectacular.

observed mating balls in the field in this population in late March, soon after snakes are thought to emerge from hibernation (Seigel and Ford, in prep). Conversely, male *marcianus* from southern Texas refused to mate until at least 24 days postemergence.

Such variation suggests that timing of mating may be an adaptive response to local environmental conditions (Ford and Cobb, 1992). These findings further show the need for studies on the evolution and regulation of mating times in more species and populations of garter snakes.

Environmental and hormonal control of reproductive cycles has been a hot topic for many years (see Gans and Crews, 1992, for review). The extensive work on northern populations of *sirtalis* shows that male reproductive cycles are regulated by rising air temperatures at the end of hibernation (Whittier et al., 1987). In addition, northern populations of *sirtalis* have a "dissociated" relationship between courtship behavior and hormonal cycles, i.e., courtship occurs independently of testosterone levels (Crews, 1984; Moore and Lindzey, 1992).

There are several problems with making overly broad generalizations from the research done on male reproductive cycles so far. For example, there is increasing evidence that mating in *T. sirtalis* in Manitoba occurs regularly in the fall as well as the spring (Mendonca and Crews, 1989; Whittier and Crews, 1986). Fall mating has also been reported in *T. atratus* (Fitch, 1940), *T. ordinoides*

(Hebard, 1951; Stewart, 1968), and *T. sirtalis* (Blanchard and Blanchard, 1941, 1942; Fitch, 1965; Fox, 1956), and is suggested to occur in *T. radix* (Pope, 1944) and *T. elegans* (Farr, 1988; Hansen and Tremper, in prep.). The absence of more records and studies of fall mating may simply reflect the mind-set of recent investigators who assumed that fall mating was unlikely or rare and therefore did little fieldwork during that time of year. This is unfortunate, since fall mating in garter snakes has been known since at least 1940 (see above citations). A further complication is that individual females may mate more than once and store sperm (Blanchard 1943; Gibson and Falls, 1975; Stewart, 1972). Thus much of the apparent paradigm of females mating once and the spring being the major mating period may be erroneous. Finally, other factors besides temperature may control male reproductive cycles. For example, the timing of mating in *T. melanogaster* is apparently initiated by the presence of receptive females and occurs at irregular intervals (Gartska and Crews, 1982, 1985). Again, only additional detailed research on other populations and species, especially in subtropical and tropical locations, will allow us to make broad generaliza-tions. (See Chap. 5 for additional discussion.)

Female Reproductive Cycles

Probably because of the relative ease of determining if females are gravid and when they give birth, the database on female reproductive cycles is much larger than that on males (see reviews in Duvall et al., 1982; Seigel and Ford, 1987; Whittier and Tokarz, 1992). Nevertheless, most of our quantified data are still based primarily on northern species or populations, especially *T. sirtalis* (Bona-Gallo and Licht, 1983; Fitch, 1965; Gartska et al., 1982; Gregory and Larsen, 1993; Whittier et al., 1987), *T. brachystoma* (Pisani and Bothner, 1970), *T. butleri*, (Carpenter, 1952a), *T. elegans* (Farr, 1988), *T. ordinoides* (Hebard, 1951; Steward, 1968), and *T. sauritus* (Carpenter, 1952a). The only southern species or populations of garter snakes that have been studied in sufficient detail are *T. marcianus* in southern Texas and Arizona (Ford and Karges, 1987; Ford and Cobb, 1992; Seigel and Ford, in prep.), *T. proximus* in Texas and Louisiana (Clark, 1974; Tinkle, 1957), and *T. melanogaster* in Mexico (Ford and Ball, 1977; Gartska and Crews, 1982).

The basic female reproductive cycle of garter snakes seems fairly predictable, at least for northern populations. Almost all *Thamnophis* populations studied so far have *prenuptial* or *Type I secondary vitellogenesis* (Aldridge, 1979; Licht, 1984), i.e., females enter hibernation with small, previtellogenic follicles, then undergo secondary vitellogenesis and ovulation following mating in the spring. One possible exception to this pattern is *T. eques* in southern Arizona, where females have been reported to have developing follicles in the fall (Rosen and Schwalbe, 1988). However, this exciting finding requires additional study and verification.

The environmental factors controlling the basic prenuptial cycle is another area of considerable study (see Whittier and Tokarz, 1992, for review), but, as for male reproduction, most of our detailed experimental data come from the Manitoba populations (but see Ford and Cobb, 1992). The Manitoba data suggest that female receptivity is regulated mainly by increasing temperature following hibernation, although the puzzle of fall mating remains unresolved (Whittier and Tokarz, 1992).

Although the prenuptial reproductive cycle appears to hold for all species studied so far, there is still a remarkable degree of plasticity in the timing of reproduction, both within and among species. For example, although the total length of the reproductive cycle in Manitoba lasts only about four months, births can occur anywhere from the end of July to the end of September (Gregory, 1977b). Southern populations can have even more variable cycles; female *T. marcianus* from southern Texas have been found to give birth from as early as late May to as late as early October (Ford and Karges 1987; N. Ford, pers. obs.). The sources of such variation are of considerable interest, since natural selection would seem to favor females who either gave birth early (allowing additional time for offspring feeding and growth prior to hibernation) or who produced offspring when resources or environmental conditions were optimal (which should also produce synchronized cycles; Seigel and Ford, 1987; Shine, 1977). In northern populations, selection might also favor birth immediately before hibernation, allowing neonates to enter dens with large yolk reserves, and be ready to exploit more abundant prey in the spring. Gregory (1977b) suggested the variation in timing of reproduction in Manitoba represented interden or intraden site variation in time of emergence, i.e., females that emerged earlier also mated and gave birth earlier. However, the consequences of such variation in female fitness are unstudied. Variance in the timing of emergence also seems unlikely to explain the large degree of variation in mating periods among populations of *T. marcianus*, and the environmental correlates of reproduction remain largely unstudied in most southern populations of garter snakes. This is clearly an area badly in need of additional study.

Fecundity, Offspring Size, and Reproductive Frequency

Basic data on the fecundity and other life-history traits of garter snakes are summarized in Table 4-1. The quality of the data sets varies from extensive (e.g., *elegans, sirtalis*) to virtually nonexistent (e.g., Mexican species such as *chrysocephalus, exsul, fulvus*, etc.). However, even for reasonably well-studied species, there are important gaps in our knowledge, mainly the absence of data from southern populations and incomplete information on temporal variation (Seigel and Ford, 1987).

Average clutch sizes in *Thamno-* *phis* range from 6.0 in *T. sauritus* from Michigan to 32.5 for *T. sirtalis* from Maryland (Table 4-1). (Note that individual females may produce larger clutches; these figures are the *averages* for populations.) However, these clutch sizes are subject to considerable variation, depending mainly on female size and food availability. The correlation between female size and the number of offspring is widespread in snakes (see Seigel and Ford, 1987 for review), and comparisons between years or localities can be made only after correcting for female size with the appropriate statistical procedure (analysis of covariance or ANOVA on the residuals from the clutch size–body size regression; Seigel and Fitch, 1985). However, even after correcting for female size, clutch sizes are subject to additional variation from female foraging success. For example, Seigel and Fitch (1985) showed that clutch sizes in two populations of *T. sirtalis* from Kansas and Missouri showed significant variation among years. In the Kansas population, the yearly average varied from 11.3 to 23.4, a more than twofold difference. These differences were correlated with local rainfall patterns, which in turn affected food availability. This is an example of phenotypic plasticity, where changes in the local environment affect the phenotypic expression of life-history traits (Bull, 1987). Ford and Seigel (1989a, 1994) have shown that much of the observed variation in clutch sizes in some species of garter snakes results from phenotypic plasticity via changes in prey availability.

Data on offspring size are much less widespread than are data on clutch size (see Table 4-1), making broad conclusions at this time difficult. Well-quantified data on offspring size are available for only 12 species of garter snakes, and some of these data are from a single population (Table 4-1). Based on these limited data, offspring size in garter snakes is smallest in *T. atratus* and largest in *T. gigas* (the latter is perhaps not surprising, considering the large body size of *gigas*). The overall lack of data on offspring size is unfortunate, since such data are needed badly for tests of life-history theory (see Seigel and Ford, 1987, for review). Data on offspring size can be collected fairly easily by maintaining gravid females in captivity for a short period prior to birth. However, it is important that this period be as short as possible, since females kept in captivity for long periods may produce different-sized offspring (King, 1993). In addition, offspring size may also be subject to phenotypic plasticity via

the female's diet in some populations (Seigel and Ford, in prep.), and may be subject to trade-offs between clutch size and female size (King, 1993; Ford and Seigel, 1989b).

Reproductive frequency (the number of clutches or broods produced by females) is an important determinant of lifetime reproductive potential and fitness (Cole, 1954). Unfortunately, data on reproductive frequency are available for only nine species of garter snakes (Table 4-1), and these data are based on overall population values, i.e., the percent of females gravid at some point in time. Such data are not as desirable as information on individual females (Vitt and Seigel, 1985), information still unavailable for most snakes.

The available data on reproductive frequency suggest that most females in a population reproduce each year, although some females may skip years between reproduction. This is especially likely to occur in northern populations (e.g., *T. sauritus* in Michigan [Burt, 1928] and *T. sirtalis* in Manitoba [Whittier and Crews, 1990]). Indeed, recent studies suggest that reproductive frequency may be extremely low in some populations; only 3 of 24 female *T. sirtalis* from the Northwest Territories of Canada were found to be gravid in consecutive years (Larsen et al., 1993). However, the proportion of females gravid in a given year is also subject to considerable fluctuation. In Manitoba, Whittier and Crews (1990) found that only 23.5% of females underwent vitellogenesis in 1983, whereas 88% did so in 1984. In addition, reproductive frequency may vary among age or size classes (King, 1989).

Although reliable data are lacking, no garter snake is definitively known to produce multiple clutches in the wild, although several authors have suggested the possibility for southern populations (e.g., Ford and Karges, 1987; Rossman, 1963). However, these suggestions are based mainly on the presence of extended reproductive seasons. For example, Ford and Karges (1987) suggested that *T. marcianus* might be capable of producing a second clutch in southern Texas and northern Mexico. The fact that *T. marcianus* in southern Texas produces offspring as early as mid-May and as late as early October (see above) certainly indicates the *possibility* of a second clutch, but this cannot be confirmed without following individual females over an entire season (Vitt and Seigel, 1985).

The plasticity to the local environment makes interpretation of geographic differences in fecundity or other reproductive traits difficult. However, some detailed studies of such variation have been attempted (e.g., Fitch, 1985; Gregory and Larsen, 1993). In the most comprehensive review to date, Gregory and Larsen (1993) examined geographic variation in clutch and offspring size among several populations of common garter snakes (*T. sirtalis*). After correction for differences in female body size, Gregory and Larsen found considerable east-west differences in both clutch size and offspring size; snakes from western Canada produced relatively small clutches of relatively large offspring. Other patterns of geographic variation await further research.

FORAGING ECOLOGY

Introduction and Overview

The ability of investigators to identify stomach contents (via regurgitation) without killing or seriously disturbing the individual makes snakes excellent subjects for studies on foraging ecology (Seigel, 1993). However, as reviewed by Arnold (1993), the literature on snake diets has progressed rather slowly from simple lists of prey taken to more sophisticated analyses incorporating variation in prey availability, prey size, predator size, population genetics, and physiology. These studies increasingly show that what we once perceived as the static diet of snakes is merely a slice of a dynamic process that is partially controlled by innate genetic mechanisms, partially by body size and physiological constraints, and partially by proximate environmental factors (e.g., Arnold, 1977, 1980; 1993; Feder and Arnold, 1982; Gregory and Nelson, 1991; Kephart, 1982; Kephart and Arnold, 1982; Macias Garcia and Drummond, 1988a; Mushinsky et al., 1982; Plummer and Goy, 1984; Pough and Groves, 1983; Seigel, 1984; Voris and Moffett, 1981). This has made the study of snake foraging ecology both more complicated (because data must be collected on different size classes, seasons, and years) and more exciting, since we are now addressing some fascinating ecological and evolutionary questions.

Overall Patterns of Diet

Although data on foraging ecology of some species of snakes are limited by small sample sizes, the characteristic abundance of garter and ribbon snakes means that they are (to some degree)

ideally suited for research in this area. This conclusion is reinforced by the numbers of citations available on the diets of *Thamnophis*, most of which are summarized in Table 4-2. However, many earlier studies were conducted over very short time intervals or were based on very limited sample sizes. Because of the current recognition of temporal, ontogenetic, and spatial variation in diet (see below), these limited studies are not discussed unless the data reported are unavailable from other sources. Also, data on foraging behavior are not the emphasis of this chapter; see Chap. 5 for a review of that topic.

As was true of reproductive studies, there are some clear biases in the data available on foraging ecology of garter snakes, mainly stemming from the lack of data on southern and (especially) Mexican forms. Indeed, quantified data on foraging ecology are entirely absent for 10 species of *Thamnophis* (mainly Mexican species), and the majority of our quantitative database comes mainly from Canada and the United States north of about 40° latitude. The absence of quantified data from the majority of the areas where garter and ribbon snakes are found is unfortunate, to say the least.

Ecology and
Conservation

Table 4-2. Summary of Data on the Diet of Garter Snakes. A large X means that the prey type is a major component of the diet (> 10%) for that species, whereas a small + indicates that the prey type is a minor component of the diet (< 10%). This summary is designed to illustrate the variation in diet among species; consequently, the data presented below represent a *combined* sample, i.e., lumping information from different geographic regions and age classes. See the text and the species accounts for a detailed discussion of geographic, ontogenetic, and temporal variation in the foraging ecology of garter snakes.

			Prey Type					
			Amphibian					
Species	Invertebrates*	Fish	Larvae	Amphibians	Reptiles	Birds	Mammals	Sources
atratus		X	X	X				Fitch, 1940, 1941b; Fox, 1951a; Lind and Welsh, 1994
brachystoma	X (EW)							Asplund, 1963; Wozniak and Bothner, 1966
butleri	X (EW)							Catling and Freedman 1980a
couchii		X	X	X				Fitch, 1949
cyrtopsis		+	X	X				Fleharty, 1967; Fouquette, 1954; Jones, 1990
elegans	X (LE, SL, SN, EW)	X	X	X	+	+	X	Arnold, 1977, 1981a; Arnold and Wassersug, 1978; Farr, 1988; Fitch 1940, 1941b, 1949; Fleharty, 1967; Gregory, 1978, 1984b; Kephart, 1982; Kephart and Arnold, 1982; Seigel and Ford, pers. obs.; White and Kolb, 1974
eques	X (EW, LE)	X	X	X				Macias Garcia and Drummond, 1988a; Rosen and Schwalbe, 1988
gigas		X						Hansen and Tremper, *in prep.*

Species	Prey items							References
hammondii	+ (EW)			+	X	X		Fitch, 1940, 1941b; Hansen and Tremper, *in prep.*
marcianus	+ (EW)			+	X	X		Fouquette, 1954; Seigel, pers. obs.
melanogaster	X (LE) crayfish			X	+	X	+	Drummond, 1983; Halloy and Burghardt, 1990
ordinoides	X (EW, SL)			+	X	X	X	Fitch, 1941b; Fox, 1952; Gregory, 1978, 1984b
proximus		+		+	X	X	X	Clark, 1974; Fouquette, 1954
radix	X (EW, LE)	+		+	X	X	X	Dalrymple and Reichenbach, 1981; Hart, 1979; Seigel, 1984
rufipunctatus				X	+	X	+	Fleharty, 1967; Rosen and Schwalbe, 1988; Stebbins, 1985
sauritus				+	X	X	X	Carpenter, 1952a; Rossman, 1963
scalaris			X			X		Fouquette and Rossman, 1963; Lemos-Espinal and Ballinger, 1992
scaliger						X	X	Lara-Gongora, pers. comm.
sirtalis	X (LE, SL, EW)	X	+	+	X	X	X	Carpenter, 1952a; Catling and Freedman, 1980a, Dalrymple and Reichenbach, 1981; Farr, 1988; Fitch, 1941b, 1965, 1982; Fouquette, 1954; Gregory, 1978, 1984b; Gregory and Nelson, 1991; Seigel, 1984, Stewart, 1968; White and Kolb, 1974
validus				X	X	X		Conant, 1969

*EW = earthworms, SL = slugs, SN = snails, LE = leeches.

Table 4-2 shows that, as a group, garter and ribbon snakes consume an impressive diversity of prey types, including a variety of invertebrates (mainly earthworms, leeches, and slugs, but also crabs and gastropods from the intertidal zone [Arnold, 1980]), fish, amphibians and their larvae (both salamanders and frogs), reptiles (mainly other snakes and lizards), birds, and mammals (including such unexpected prey as bats). By comparison, no other single genus of snakes for whom data are available consumes as wide a variety of prey, with the possible exception of *Coluber constrictor* (Mushinsky, 1987). However, there is a wide disparity among species in terms of diet breadth; *T. elegans* and *T. sirtalis* both have very broad diets, consuming as many as eight different major groups of prey, whereas at least two species (*T. brachystoma* and *T. butleri*) are specialists on earthworms in the wild and *T. scalaris* is only known to eat lizards. (See Table 4-2 and the individual species accounts for details.) In addition, except for the specialist species, it may be misleading to speak of the "diet" of a species, since the diet of garter snakes is subject to substantial ontogenetic, temporal, and geographic variation (Arnold, 1980). These patterns are discussed below.

Temporal Variation in Diet

Temporal variation in diet has been studied in detail in at least four species: *Thamnophis elegans* (Kephart and Arnold, 1982), *T. eques* (Macias Garcia and Drummond, 1988a), *T. radix* (Seigel, 1984), and *T. sirtalis* (Gregory and Nelson, 1991; Seigel, 1984). Significant variation in diet among seasons was found in *eques*, *radix*, and one population of *sirtalis*. In Missouri, sympatric populations of both *radix* and *sirtalis* fed primarily on ranid frogs in the summer, whereas both species fed mainly on earthworms in the spring and fall (Fig. 4-2; Seigel, 1984). These changes appeared to be a proximate result of seasonal changes in prey availability, because the switch to ranid frogs in summer corresponded to the transformation of large numbers of *Rana blairi* and *R. catesbeiana* (Seigel, 1984). *Thamnophis eques* from Hidalgo, Mexico, also showed strong seasonal changes in diet (Macias Garcia and Drummond, 1988a). For example, the percentage of stomachs containing the dominant prey (earthworms) varied from 80% in August to 10% in October. As in Missouri, these changes were correlated with changes in the local abundance of the prey. In contrast to these studies, Gregory and

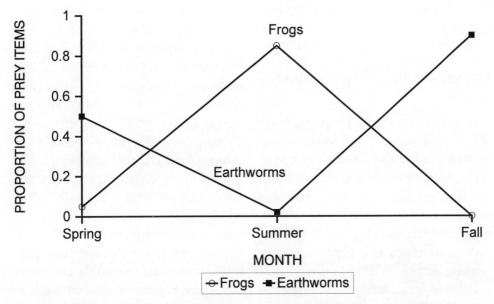

Fig. 4-2. Seasonal variation in the diet of *Thamnophis radix* from northwestern Missouri. Frogs are shown in the solid line, earthworms in the dotted line. Note that diet is mainly a function of time of year. (Data from Seigel, 1984.)

Nelson (1991) did not find any seasonal variation in the diet of *sirtalis* from Vancouver Island. However, they suggested that snakes might shift foraging sites as a result of declining prey availability, and such shifts in foraging sites might lead to seasonal changes in the types of prey taken (P. Gregory, pers. comm.).

To date, only Kephart and Arnold (1982) have studied yearly variation in the diet of garter snakes. They found dramatic differences in diet in California populations of *T. elegans* during seven consecutive summers, with a close relationship between diet and prey availability. As their study site dried progressively during a severe drought, toads (*Bufo boreas*) stopped breeding, and toad metamorphs were dropped from the diet of the snakes. As the authors pointed out, any short-term studies done just before or just after the drought would have reached very different conclusions about the diet of *T. elegans*. These data serve as an excellent cautionary tale about the need for long-term data in reaching conclusions about the foraging ecology of garter snakes.

Ontogenetic and Sexual Variation in Diet

The often-enormous range in body size between birth and maturity in snakes has led to a number of excellent studies examining how diets of snakes vary with changing body size (see review in Arnold, 1993). However, this subject has been studied only a relatively few times in garter snakes, although it has been well studied in water snakes and other natricines. Changes in diet with increasing body size can occur in several ways: larger snakes can switch to different prey types altogether, larger snakes can simply eat larger individuals of the same prey type as the snake grows, or larger snakes can eat a broader variety of prey than do neonates (Arnold, 1993). Most studies on garter snakes seem to show the latter pattern, although exceptions occur. Seigel (1984) found that in populations of *T. radix* and *T. sirtalis*, neonates and juveniles of both species ate earthworms almost exclusively, whereas adults had a much broader diet that included earthworms, tadpoles, frogs, and other vertebrates. Macias Garcia and Drummond

(1988a) found that small *T. eques* fed mainly on earthworms and leeches, whereas larger snakes dropped earthworms from the diet, feeding mainly on leeches, frogs, and fish. Farr (1988) showed that overall diet diversity was lowest among small *T. sirtalis* and *T. elegans* from British Columbia, although very large *T. elegans* (> 500 mm SVL) were also very specialized, feeding entirely on mammals. White and Kolb (1974) suggested similar ontogenetic variation in diet in both *T. elegans* and *T. sirtalis*, but their published tables unfortunately combined data from both species of snakes and thus are difficult to interpret.

By contrast with these patterns of increased diet diversity with larger body sizes, juvenile *T. sirtalis* (200–399 mm SVL) from Kansas actually had broader diets than did adults (Fitch, 1965). Small snakes ate earthworms and a wide variety of small frogs (*Acris, Bufo, Hyla*, and recently transformed *Rana*), whereas larger snakes fed mainly on a more restricted diet of larger frogs (*Rana*) and mammals. Finally, some populations show no changes in diet as snakes get larger; Gregory and Nelson (1991) found relatively little ontogenetic variation in the diet of *T. sirtalis* at fish hatcheries in British Columbia.

Sexual differences in diet have not

been well studied in garter snakes. Farr (1988) found significant differences in the diets of adult *T. sirtalis* and *T. elegans* from British Columbia; in both cases, females had a higher percentage of mammals in their diets than did males. However, these differences may be compounded by sexual differences in body size (P. Gregory, pers. comm.). White and Kolb (1974) suggested that male and female *T. elegans* and *T. sirtalis* had very different diets in California, but as noted above, their data were confounded by combining data from two species. By contrast, Gregory and Nelson (1991) found no statistical differences in diet between the sexes of *T. sirtalis* at fish hatcheries in British Columbia, but this study may not be comparable with the others listed because of the artificially high food supply (P. Gregory, pers. comm.). Additional studies on sexual differences in diet are needed badly.

Geographic Variation in Diet

Because species such as *T. elegans* and *T. sirtalis* have such broad geographic ranges and are found in so many different habitats, it is easy to envision how natural selection or other evolutionary factors (e.g., genetic drift) could result in considerable spatial variation in their foraging ecology. This has led to numerous studies on geographic variation in feeding in these and other species of garter snakes (e.g., Arnold, 1977, 1980, 1981a,b; Fitch, 1965; Gregory, 1978, 1984b; Gregory and Nelson, 1991; Kephart, 1982; Macias Garcia and Drummond, 1988a; White and Kolb, 1974). In a now-classic set of papers, Arnold (1977, 1981a,b) showed that variation in the preference for slugs between coastal and inland populations of *T. elegans* was heritable and the result of a genetic polymorphism. More recent studies have emphasized the fact that diet of wide-ranging species such as *T. elegans* and *T. sirtalis* are site-specific and well correlated with prey availability. For example, Kephart (1982) examined the diet of 22 populations of *T. elegans* and *T. sirtalis* in California and found the microgeographic differences in diet were the result of the availability of prey at each site. Indeed, site was a much better predictor of diet than was species of snake.

POPULATION ECOLOGY

Introduction and Overview

Historically, data on the population ecology and demography of snakes has lagged behind that of other reptiles, especially turtles and lizards (e.g., Turner, 1977). The reasons for this have been discussed many times (e.g., Parker and Plummer, 1987; Seigel, 1993; Turner, 1977) and will not be reviewed here. The bottom line is that we need much more effort directed at understanding the population ecology of snakes in general, and garter snakes are no exception. The basic data on population ecology of garter snakes is reviewed in Table 4-3; these data were drawn primarily from the reviews of Dunham et al. (1988) and Parker and Plummer (1987). The limited nature of the data set is clear: Most of our data are from just a few species from northern locations. Hence, our ability to make broad generalizations concerning the population ecology of garter snakes must await additional data.

Abundance

Actual density estimates are available for 16 populations of 8 species of *Thamnophis* (Table 4-3). The highest densities are reached by *T. radix* from Illinois (845/ha). This is one of the highest density estimates ever recorded for snakes (Parker and Plummer, 1987), but these represent fairly limited "pockets" of snakes. Densi-

ties of many of the other species of garter snakes in Table 4-3 are much lower than that of *T. radix* (range 1.7–320/ha), but these densities are still fairly high in comparison with most other kinds of snakes, which frequently exist at densities of < 1 individual/ha (Parker and Plummer, 1987). This supports the qualitative impression of many field herpetologists that garter snakes are among the most abundant kinds of snakes at a given site.

Growth

Growth rates are best studied by making multiple observations of individuals rather than by making broad generalizations based on seasonal changes in population size structure (see Vitt, 1983, for discussion). Unfortunately, data on individual growth rates in garter snakes are quite limited. The best data sets are from northern populations of either *T. sirtalis* (Carpenter, 1952b, for Michigan; Fitch, 1965, for Kansas; and Gregory 1977b, for Manitoba) or *T. elegans* (Farr, 1988, for British Columbia). The general patterns derived from these data are similar to those of reptiles in general (see Andrews, 1982, for review); i.e., growth is most rapid prior to sexual maturity, then slows when reproductive activity begins. However, individual variation in growth rates is quite pronounced, and not all growth ceases when sexual maturity is reached. Fitch (1965) found that a number of adult females from Kansas continued to grow well after reaching the minimum size at sexual maturity. For example, a 748 mm (SVL) female captured in early 1959 reached 950 mm SVL by June 1960, an increase of 200 mm in about 10 months of activity.

Size and Age at Sexual Maturity

Because of the strong influence of age at maturity on lifetime reproductive potential (Cole, 1954), data on the timing of maturity are of considerable interest. However, although determining the size at sexual maturity is fairly easy (especially for females), determining age at maturity accurately requires recapturing known-aged individuals at frequent intervals. Consequently, data on individual ages at maturity are still uncommon for most species of garter and ribbon snakes (Table 4-3; Dunham et al., 1988; Parker and Plummer, 1987).

Parker and Plummer (1987) classified *Thamnophis* as belonging to the "early-maturing temperate colubrid" group of snakes. Most *Thamnophis*

for which data are available reach sexual maturity during the second or third full season of growth; i.e., individuals born in the late summer of 1994 would presumably mate and/or give birth for the first time in 1996 or 1997 (Dunham et al., 1988; Parker and Plummer, 1987). However, even with our limited data set, there appears to be wide variation among populations and species. Clark (1974) found that two individually marked female *T. proximus* in Texas reached adult size in 12 to 15 months. Conversely, Jayne and Bennett (1990) found that none of the individual *T. sirtalis* marked as neonates in 1985 in northern California had reached maturity by 1988, and suggested a minimum age at maturity of four years in this population. Obviously, we need much better data on age at maturity in snakes; it is hoped that the use of new techniques (such as using PIT-tags [passive-integrated-transponder microchips] on large numbers of neonates) and increased emphasis on long-term studies will provide a more comprehensive data set in the future.

Data on body size at maturity are summarized in Table 4-3. Most garter snakes mature at SVLs of 400 to 500 mm, with males usually maturing at smaller sizes than females. The minimum size at maturity is smallest

Table 4-3. Summary of Data on the Densities and Age and Size at Sexual Maturity of Garter Snakes. Ranges of densities indicates variation among years.

Species	Site	#/ha	Female age at maturity (months)	Male age at maturity (months)	Female SVL* at maturity (mm)	Male SVL* at maturity (mm)	Source
atratus	California				386		J. Boundy, pers. comm.
brachystoma	New York, Pennsylvania	20	24	24	250	220	Pisani and Bothner, 1970; Bothner, 1986
butleri	Michigan	7.2	24		345		Carpenter, 1952a, b
butleri	Ontario	23					Freedman and Catling, 1978
couchii	California		32–44				Hansen and Tremper, in prep.
elegans	British Columbia	2.8			420	400	Farr, 1988
elegans	California		24				Hansen and Tremper, in prep.
eques	Arizona		24–36	24	550		Rosen and Schwalbe, 1988
gigas	California				920		Hansen and Tremper, in prep.
marcianus	Arizona				515		R. Seigel (pers. obs.)
marcianus	Southern Texas				345		N. Ford (pers. obs.)
melanogaster	Mexico	158.5					Gregory et al., 1983
ordinoides	Oregon		24	12	360	390	Stewart, 1968
ordinoides	Washington				330+		Hebard, 1951
proximus	Louisiana		24–36	24	485	410	Tinkle, 1957
proximus	Texas	16–61	24–36	12	515	368	Clark, 1974
radix	Colorado	320					Bauerle, 1972 in Reichenbach and Dalrymple, 1986
radix	Illinois	845					Seibert, 1950
radix	Ohio	52–123					Reichenbach and Dalrymple, 1986
rufipunctatus	Arizona		24	24			Rosen and Schwalbe, 1988
sauritus	Michigan	24.6	24	24	421		Carpenter, 1952a, b
sauritus	Michigan				384–426		Burt, 1928

Subspecies	Locality					Reference
sirtalis	British Columbia	1.7		445		Farr, 1988
sirtalis	California		36+	440		Jayne and Bennett, 1990
sirtalis	Illinois	18.7				Blaesing, 1979
sirtalis	Kansas	3.7–11.0	20	504	387	Fitch, 1965, 1982
sirtalis	Michigan			550+		Burt, 1928
sirtalis	Michigan	24.8	24	426		Carpenter, 1952a, b
sirtalis	Ohio	45–89	24			Reichenbach and Dalrymple, 1986
sirtalis	Ontario	4				Freedman and Catling, 1978
sirtalis	Northwest Territories, Canada			570		Larsen et al., 1993
sirtalis	Oregon			435	360	Stewart, 1968

* SVL = snout-vent length.
+ TL = total length.

in *T. brachystoma* (250 mm SVL for females) and largest in *T. gigas* (920 mm SVL for females). However, variation within and among populations can be marked; female checkered garter snakes from southern Texas matured at 345 mm SVL, whereas females from southern Arizona matured at 515 mm SVL (N. Ford and R. Seigel, pers. obs.). This variation probably reflects both genetic differences among litters and individuals and stochastic variations in prey availability.

Survival

Quantitative studies of survival rates in garter and ribbon snakes are few, and information regarding the survival of neonates and juveniles is especially uncommon. Hence, no general patterns are yet apparent. The best data on individual survival rates comes from Jayne and Bennett's (1990) study of *T. sirtalis* in northern California. Of 250 neonates born in 1985, 79 (28.7%) survived until 1986, and 45 (16.4%) survived until 1987. Of 86 neonates born in 1986, 37 survived until 1987 (43.0%). The survival of yearling snakes was somewhat higher than that of juveniles; 127 of 250 yearling snakes survived from 1986 to 1987 (50.8%). However,

survival of snakes > 2 years old was relatively low; only 37 of 113 snakes survived between 1986 and 1987 (32.7%). Other data sets on *T. sirtalis* show variable results. Using Fitch's (1965) data set from Kansas, Parker and Plummer (1987) calculated first-year survival at 36% and survival of adults at 50%. Gregory (1977b), Larsen and Gregory (1989), and Larsen et al. (1993) calculated the annual survival of adult males at 34% in Manitoba and 67% in the Northwest Territories.

Sources of Mortality

As noted by Parker and Plummer (1987), few studies have determined the exact sources of mortality for snake populations. Garter snakes are subject to predation from a wide variety of sources, but especially hawks, raccoons, minks, foxes, and badgers (Fitch, 1965). Other species of snakes (e.g., *Coluber constrictor* [Fitch, 1965], *Sisturus catenatus* [Seigel, 1986]) are also known to eat garter snakes. Rosen and Schwalbe (1988) suggested that populations of Mexican garter snakes (*T. eques*) in Arizona were declining as a result of predation pressure from introduced bullfrogs (*Rana catesbeiana*).

A second source of mortality is starvation. Although ectotherms are well adapted to deal with periodic episodes of low prey availability (Pough, 1980), lengthy periods without food can sometimes have severe effects on garter snakes, especially on neonates (H. Fitch, P. Gregory, pers. comm.). The severe droughts in California during the 1980s drastically reduced populations of *T. sirtalis* in northern California (C. Peterson, pers. comm.) and populations of *T. hammondii* in southern California (S. Sweet, pers. comm.). Indeed, it was common to find dead and dying garter snakes in northern California where large populations once existed (C. Peterson, pers. comm.). Fitch (1965) suggested that low rainfall in the late summer and early fall might result in high mortality among neonate *T. sirtalis* in Kansas, which are heavily dependent on earthworms for most of their prey. Gregory (pers. comm.) reported finding skeletons of *T. melanogaster* in the rocks surrounding a lake in Mexico.

Abiotic factors are also important sources of mortality for garter snakes, especially in northern areas. Gregory (1977) found low overwinter survival of adult male *T. sirtalis* in communal dens in Manitoba; between a third and almost one-half of all snakes may die during this period. Carpenter (1952b) suggested that winter mortality was a major factor in the survival of young garter snakes in Michigan. However, Larsen and Gregory (1989) found higher annual survival in adult male *T. sirtalis* from Alberta.

THERMAL ECOLOGY

Introduction and Overview

Studies of the thermal ecology of snakes have used one of three major techniques, and garter snakes have been studied using each approach (see Avery, 1982; Lillywhite, 1987; Peterson et al., 1993 for reviews). Until recently, the most widely used technique was the "capture measurement method" (also known as the "grab-and-stab" method), in which a quick-reading thermometer is used to determine cloacal temperatures of individuals immediately after their capture in the field. This method has been used for many species of *Thamnophis*, especially *butleri* (Carpenter, 1956), *cyrtopsis* (Fleharty, 1967; Rosen, 1991), *elegans* (Flehart, 1967; Gregory, 1984a, 1990; Gregory and McIntosh, 1980; Huey et al., 1989; Scott et al., 1982), *eques* (Rosen, 1991), *marcianus* (Rosen, 1991), *ordinoides* (Brattstrom, 1965; Gregory, 1984a; Gregory and McIntosh, 1980;

Stewart, 1965; Vitt, 1974), *radix* (Hart, 1979), *rufipunctatus* (Fleharty, 1967; Rosen, 1991), *sauritus* (Carpenter, 1956; Rosen, 1991), and *sirtalis* (Carpenter, 1956; Gibson and Falls, 1979a,b; Gregory, 1984a, 1990; Gregory and McIntosh 1980; Rosen, 1991; Stewart, 1965). Unsurprisingly, most of these data are from northern localities (with the exception of Fleharty, 1967, and Rosen, 1991).

Interpreting data from the capture measurement technique is difficult, because the data are biased toward actively moving individuals and replication is difficult or impossible (see Peterson et al., 1993, for discussion). This has led to increased use of two other methods, laboratory gradients and radiotelemetry, as alternatives to capture measurements. Laboratory gradients allow replicated observations in a controlled setting, and are especially useful for determining preferred body temperatures and examining physiological effects of such variables as reproductive condition and feeding state. Laboratory gradients have been used for relatively few species of garter snakes, except for *T. elegans* (Gibson et al., unpubl.; Gregory et al., 1982; Scott and Pettus, 1979; Stevenson et al., 1985), *T. ordinoides* (Gregory et al., 1982), and *T. sirtalis* (Gibson et al., 1989; Gregory et al., 1982; Kitchell, 1969; Lysenko and Gillis, 1980; Smucny and Gibson, in press).

The most recently developed method for studying thermal ecology is also the most promising and exciting; this method involves implanting temperature-sensitive radiotransmitters in the body cavity of snakes, while at the same time using physical models to determine operative environmental temperatures (see Peterson et al., 1993, for review). This method allows continuous monitoring of the body temperatures of individual snakes during periods of both activity and inactivity, while avoiding the stress and altered behavior that captive conditions can sometimes entail. This method has been used mainly by C. Peterson and his co-workers on *T. elegans* (Peterson, 1987); examples of the kinds of data this approach can generate are shown in Fig. 4-3.

Field Activity Temperatures: Interspecific, Daily, Seasonal, and Geographic Patterns

Based on data from both capture measurements and implanted transmitters, garter snakes are known to be active over a very broad range of temperatures, usually ranging from 10 to

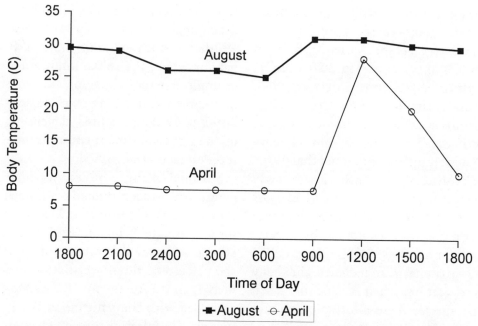

Fig. 4-3. Illustration of the kinds of data obtained from the use of implanted radiotransmitters in snakes. The figure shows seasonal variation in the body temperature of *T. elegans* from California. Compare the relatively constant body temperatures in August with the strong daily variation seen in April. (Redrawn from Peterson, 1987.)

36 C (see individual species accounts as well as Avery [1982] and Lillywhite [1987] for data). Presumably reflecting its long seasonal activity period (see species accounts for details), *T. sirtalis* has the broadest range of active temperature and is apparently able to operate at remarkably low temperatures. For example, some males emerging from hibernation in north-ern Alberta had cloacal temperatures as low as 0.5 C (Larsen and Gregory, 1988). However, there is no general pattern of interspecific differences in activity temperature in garter snakes. Carpenter (1956) found little varia-tion in mean body temperature among sympatric populations of *T. butleri, T. sauritus,* and *T. sirtalis* in Michigan, and Rosen (1991) found

that the mean activity temperature for six species of *Thamnophis* during the active season varied only from 28.0 C in *T. eques* to 30.0 C in *T. sauritus*. By contrast, Stewart (1965) found that body temperatures of *T. sirtalis* were higher than those of *T. ordinoides* in Oregon, but Gregory and McIntosh (1980) found that *T. sirtalis* had significantly lower body temperatures than either *T. elegans* or *T. ordinoides*, although there was little variation explained by species in their analysis. Finally, Hart (1979) reported that *T. radix* had higher body temperatures than *T. sirtalis* when the species were allotropic, but not when they were syntopic.

The daily pattern of body temperatures has been well illustrated using implanted transmitters. In the most common pattern, individuals experience a rapid rise in body temperature for a short period in the morning; body temperature then stabilizes at what is known as a *plateau phase*, often in a narrow range between 28 and 32.5 C (Peterson et al., 1993; see Fig. 4-3). When individuals seek shelter in the late afternoon or evening, body temperatures drop to lower levels, the degree of reduction depending on the shelter used by the snake (Peterson et al., 1993). Varia-

tions on this pattern may also occur, depending on the season, local weather conditions, and the microhabitat where the snake forages. For example, snakes foraging in cold mountain streams may exhibit oscillating body temperatures, depending on the length of time spent in the water (Peterson et al., 1993).

Seasonal changes in activity temperature have been studied using both implanted transmitters and capture measurements. Peterson (1987) found strong seasonal differences in both the pattern of thermoregulation and body temperatures in *T. elegans* equipped with transmitters in Washington. The plateau was most common in the summer, whereas oscillating patterns were prevalent in the spring and the fall. In addition, there was wide seasonal variation in mean body temperature among seasons (Fig. 4-3). However, data from capture measurements have shown contradictory results. Gibson and Falls (1979a) found significant differences among months in the body temperatures of both male and female *T. sirtalis* from Ontario. Conversely, Rosen (1991) found no significant differences in activity temperatures in *T. sauritus* and *T. sirtalis* from Michigan, at least not when data from the hibernacula were excluded. Additional data on seasonal variation in activity temperatures would be welcome, especially for species from more southern areas.

There have been few studies examining geographic variation in thermal ecology in garter snakes, reflecting the bias toward northern species or populations. Rosen (1991) found very little difference in the mean active temperature of *T. sirtalis* from Michigan (mean = 28.3 C) and New Mexico (mean = 27.3 C). However, additional data obviously are needed to confirm this pattern. See Chap. 5 for additional discussion on thermoregulatory behavior.

Thermal Gradient Studies and Selected Body Temperatures

As noted above, thermal gradients allow controlled studies of the thermal preferences of snakes under controlled conditions. This technique has been used for several species of garter snakes (see references given above) to determine the so-called preferred body temperature, more properly termed the *mean selected body temperature* (Pough and Gans, 1982). These studies have produced some interesting results, although much

more needs to be done. First, data from *T. elegans* suggest that its mean selected body temperature closely approximates the body temperature where net energy gain is maximized (Lillywhite, 1987; Stevenson et al., 1985). Second, thermal gradient data support the hypothesis that seasonal variation in body temperature does indeed occur in garter snakes. Scott and Pettus (1979) showed that the mean selected temperature of *T. elegans* after hibernation in the laboratory was over 6 C cooler than that of snakes captured in midsummer. Finally, there is some indication that snakes in thermal gradients may select higher body temperatures than do snakes in the field (Gregory et al., 1982). Whether this reflects constraints on thermoregulation in individuals in the wild or is a "lab artifact" is unknown at this time.

Effects of Sex and Reproductive Condition

Both field and laboratory studies have been used to examine the effect of sex and physiological condition in garter snakes. Fitch (1965) first suggested that gravid *T. sirtalis* selected warmer thermal sites than did nongravid animals, and a long debate has ensued over whether gravid females have higher body temperatures than either nongravid females or males and whether gravid females are more "precise" thermoregulators than are nongravid females or males, reflecting the possible need to maintain constant body temperatures for their developing offspring. These issues are still not fully resolved, primarily because of methodological problems (see Peterson et al., 1993, for review). However, most of the data to date seem to support Fitch's hypothesis. Stewart (1965) found that field-collected gravid females had a higher mean body temperature than did nongravid females, but the differences were "nonsignificant." Gregory and McIntosh (1980) found significant differences in body temperatures between sexes and reproductive condition in *T. elegans, T. ordinoides,* and *T. sirtalis,* with gravid females having the highest temperatures. A later study by Gregory (1984a) with the same species showed that gravid females had higher body temperatures in *ordinoides* and *sirtalis* but not in *elegans.* After combining data from several species and localities, Rosen (1991) reported that gravid female garter snakes had both higher and less variable body temperatures than did nongravid females. Peterson (1987) reported that gravid female *T. elegans* with implanted transmitters had standard deviations in body temperatures that were "quite low." Recently, Charland (in press) found that gravid female *T. elegans* and *T. sirtalis* had significantly higher body temperatures than did nongravid females and that gravid females regulated their temperatures more precisely than did nongravid individuals.

In contrast to these field studies that have supported Fitch's original suggestion, Gibson and Falls (1979a) found no indication that gravid female *T. sirtalis* preferred higher body temperatures in the field. They suggested that the impression of higher body temperatures is due only to the fact that gravid females predominate in midsummer but that nongravid animals are collected in the spring and fall, when temperatures are cooler. However, recent laboratory studies support the hypothesis that gravid females have different thermal patterns than do other individuals. Gravid *T. sirtalis* had a much higher frequency of use of hot shelters than did nongravid females (Gibson, unpubl., in Peterson et al., 1993). L. Crampton and P. Gregory (pers. comm.) also found higher rates of use of the warm end of cages in gravid as compared with nongravid *T. elegans.*

CONSERVATION

Overview and Summary

Because of their general abundance and wide distribution, garter snakes in general would not appear to be severely jeopardized by human activities. To a certain degree, this is true; only two species or subspecies of garter snakes (the giant garter snake, *T. gigas*, and the San Francisco garter snake, *T. sirtalis infernalis* [see *T. sirtalis* account for the use of subspecific names for this form]) are listed on the U.S. Endangered Species List, and relatively few garter snakes are listed as endangered or threatened by state wildlife agencies in the United States or Canada. Table 4-4 summarizes those populations or species listed by state or federal agencies. A close inspection of the table shows that many of the taxa listed are so-called peripheral species that may be rare within a given state and but are quite common in other parts of the range (e.g., *T. proximus*, *T. marcianus*, and *T. radix*).

However, this does not mean that certain species or populations of garter snakes have not been threatened by human activities. The most insidious threat is obviously habitat destruction, which impacts all species,

not just garter snakes (see Dodd, 1987). Such habitat loss was responsible for the federal listing of the giant garter snake, and other aquatic snakes in California may also be in jeopardy (N. Scott., pers. comm.)

Other man-made threats also affect garter snake populations. Garter snakes are frequently killed by cars on highways, and the potential impact of road mortality has been the subject of several studies. For example, Freedman and Catling (1979) suggested that roads were a barrier to dispersal for *T. butleri* in Ontario. Bernardino and Dalrymple (1992) reported that 73% of their sample of snakes found at Everglades National Park in Florida were killed by cars, including large numbers of *T. sauritus* and *T. sirtalis*. Dalrymple and Reichenbach (1984) found that roadkills were an important factor in determining mortality in an endangered population of *T. radix* in Ohio, and Seigel (pers. obs.) has seen large number of garter snakes killed on roads at national wildlife refuges in Missouri (*T. proximus*, *radix*, and *sirtalis*) and in Florida (*T. sauritus* and *sirtalis*). Perhaps the largest number of snakes ever reported killed by cars was the 10,000 red-sided garter snakes (*T. s. parietalis*) killed during the fall of 1992 while returning to den sites in

Table 4-4. Summary of Information on the Conservation Status of Garter Snakes. Data from Allen (1988) unless otherwise noted.

Species	Location	Status	Cause of Decline (if Available) and Comments
T. brachystoma	New York	Declining	Habitat loss (Bothner, 1986; Dodd, 1987)
T. butleri	Indiana	Threatened	
T. eques	Arizona	Endangered	Predation by introduced bullfrogs
T. eques	New Mexico	Endangered	Habitat modification
T. gigas	California	Threatened	Habitat loss; also listed on U.S. Endangered Species List
T. hammondii	California	Candidate Species	Habitat loss (N. Scott, pers. comm.)
T. marcianus	Kansas	Threatened	
T. proximus	Indiana	Special Concern	
T. proximus	Kentucky	Threatened	
T. proximus	New Mexico	Endangered	
T. proximus	Wisconsin	Endangered	
T. radix	Ohio	Endangered	Habitat loss
T. rufipunctatus	Arizona	Threatened	Human interference; competition with introduced fish
T. rufipunctatus	New Mexico	Endangered	
T. sauritus	Florida	Threatened	Lower Keys population only
T. sauritus	Illinois	Endangered	
T. sauritus	Kentucky	Special Concern	
T. sauritus	Maine	Special Concern	
T. sauritus	Wisconsin	Endangered	
T. sirtalis infernalis	California	Endangered	Habitat loss and overcollecting; also listed on U.S. Endangered Species List

Manitoba (Chan, 1993). The long-term impacts of road mortality remain unknown; quantified studies of its effects on population viability are needed badly.

A serious problem with our understanding of the conservation status of garter snakes is that we have virtually no data on the current status of most of the species of *Thamnophis* that are endemic to, or found primarily in, Mexico and Central America. Because some of these species are known from only a few specimens (e.g., *T. exsul, T. mendax*), some garter snakes may be in serious trouble without our knowledge. This clearly shows the need for better data on the ecology and status of southern garter snakes. Indeed, some of the peripheral species or populations listed as endangered or threatened in Table 4-4 may represent genetically distinct forms whose diversity we may wish to preserve, even if they are not given formal taxonomic recognition.

Case Histories

Space constraints preclude a case-by-case review of the threats to the existence of garter snakes. However, we discuss a few well-documented problems below.

Red-Sided Garter Snakes in Canada

The spectacular abundance of red-sided garter snakes (*T. sirtalis parietalis*) in Manitoba (Fig. 4-1) would seem to indicate that such populations are not being harmed by human activities. However, these very concentrations have resulted in some serious problems in recent years.

Garter snakes are popular items in biological supply catalogs. In a 1993 catalog from a large, well-known commercial supplier, live red-sided garter snakes sold for $23.50 each. Such high prices attract dealers who need large quantities and reliable sources; this makes the Manitoba populations vulnerable to exploitation. Under Canadian law, aboriginal peoples are allowed to collect or "pick" red-sided garter snakes during set seasons in the fall when snakes are less concentrated and females have already given birth to that year's brood. However, illegal collections are common in the spring, when snakes are collected more easily and females have yet to reproduce. When one of us (RAS) visited the Manitoba sites in 1989, he was told of major damage done to den sites by the crowbars and pickaxes used in attempts to collect large numbers of snakes in a short period. Because few enforcement personnel are available to patrol these rather large areas, it is easy for a few individuals to collect hundreds or thousands of snakes in a very short time.

This overcollection led authorities to impose a ban on the exportation of garter snakes from Manitoba starting in 1991. However, it is likely that this will lead to higher prices and/or a shift in collecting sites to U.S. locations where protection is not as strong. In addition, the high rate of road mortality (see above) is another source of concern for the long-term fate of this population.

Mexican Garter Snakes

Populations of Mexican garter snakes (*T. eques*) in Arizona and New Mexico have declined substantially in recent years (Rosen and Schwalbe, 1988). In addition to rapid habitat destruction in Arizona, Mexican garter snakes are also jeopardized by interactions with introduced bullfrogs (*Rana catesbeiana*). Rosen and Schwalbe (1988) found that Mexican garter snakes were rare or extirpated at localities where bullfrogs are now abundant and suggested that this was due to predation pressure on neonates and juveniles. Rosen and Schwalbe (1988) also

speculated that checkered garter snakes (*Thamnophis marcianus*) may be replacing *T. eques* because *marcianus* is less affected by bullfrogs and, indeed, commonly eats bullfrog tadpoles and froglets (Seigel, pers. obs.). Mexican garter snakes also were apparently impacted by cattle grazing and the introduction of predatory fish (Rosen and Schwalbe, 1988).

SUMMARY

At the beginning of this chapter, I posed two questions: (1) What do garter snakes do? and (2) What do they do differently from other snakes that may explain their apparent success? This somewhat incomplete review suggests that in terms of their overall life-history and ecological traits, garter snakes do not do anything radically differently from most other snakes. This conclusion is supported by more-quantitative analyses. For example, when Dunham et al. (1988) placed snake life-history patterns on a Prim Network to graphically display variation in life histories of snakes, most garter snakes turned up virtually in the middle of the network, suggesting no extreme ecological patterns. Such an analysis needs to be repeated with a larger sample (especially from southern species), but for now, the available data do not show any dramatic differences between *Thamnophis* and most other snakes.

Perhaps the main difference between garter snakes and other groups of snakes may be their degree of ecological plasticity. As noted above, garter snakes show considerable plasticity in reproduction, feeding, and thermal ecology, and it may be this plasticity that accounts for their widespread distribution and success. This may be especially true of foraging ecology. For example, when dietary data are combined across localities, *T. sirtalis* and *T. elegans* each clearly has the potential to feed on an impressive variety of prey items (see Table 4-2). Although each species may be much more specialized at any given site, populations retain considerable flexibility in prey choice, as evidenced by frequent shifts in prey preferences as body size increases and as prey availability changes seasonally. When combined with equally impressive plasticity in reproductive and thermal ecology, this flexibility may be a major cause for the success and abundance of garter snakes. Obviously, we need much more data to test this suggestion; as stated before, I hope this book will stimulate the kinds of studies we need so badly.

Chapter 5

BEHAVIOR OF
GARTER SNAKES

Snakes may be the most asocial of all reptiles.

          Bayard H. Brattstrom, 1974

GARTER SNAKES AS MODELS FOR STUDIES OF BEHAVIOR

Based primarily on studies of garter snakes, our understanding of the behavior of snakes has increased dramatically in the more than two decades since Brattstrom's (1974) comments on their sociality. *Thamnophis sirtalis* is without a doubt the most commonly used snake in behavioral experiments, although several other species of this genus are also popular subjects in such research.

Much of the behavioral repertoire of garter snakes has also been examined in the field, and aspects of the behaviors correlated to their ecology. In addition, garter snakes have been important animals in laboratory experiments on the physiological mechanisms of behavior. Garter snakes have also been models for the study of the adaptive nature of behavioral traits, and the roles of learning and genetics in evolution are well known.

In terms of behavior, *Thamnophis* may be the most variable genus within the large family Colubridae. However, the genus exhibits several traits that have made it the subject of choice for many ethologists. Although the assumption is not particularly valid—there being some 2000 species of snakes—*Thamnophis* have been considered to be fairly representative of snakes in general. Species of *Thamnophis* grow to an average shape and size for snakes, and many exhibit typical habits, food preferences, and behaviors for terrestrial snakes. Perhaps most importantly, because some species of garter snakes den in aggregations, large numbers have been easy to collect. This availability has meant that the laboratory biologist could obtain specimens from scientific supply companies at low cost, and the field biologist could be assured of obtaining a reasonable amount of data in a short time period. Fortuitously, these snakes are also easily maintained in the laboratory, even under the severe conditions that early researchers assumed were appropriate for them. For these reasons, we have learned more about the behavior of *Thamnophis* than any other group of snakes.

BEHAVIORAL CAPABILITIES

As with all snakes, the behaviors of garter snakes are regulated both by their restricted motor capabilities (i.e., not having legs) and by the changes in their sensory mechanisms that resulted from their evolution from fossorial organisms. The perceptual capabilities of snakes as related to their behavior have recently been reviewed (Ford and Burghardt, 1993), and much of the research cited was based on studies of *Thamnophis*. The sensory mechanisms involved in detecting chemicals, which have been examined extensively, are very important in feeding and predator avoidance. The olfactory system of the nasal cavity is involved in initial detection of important cues (volatile chemicals from prey or predators), but the vomeronasal system is used to specifically identify the organism releasing the odor (see review by Halpern, 1992). The vomeronasal organ consists of sensory epithelia in dome-shaped pits in the roof of the mouth (Halpern, 1983; Fig. 5-1). The tongue picks up nonvolatile chemicals and transfers them to this system through the vomeronasal ducts (Cooper and Burghardt, 1990a). Elevated tongue-flick rates have therefore been used as an assay of the relevance of particular chemical cues to a snake (Cooper and Burghardt, 1990b; Fig. 5-2). Since its first use as a measure of prey preferences in naive garter snakes (Burghardt, 1966), tongue-flick rates have been used to analyze geographical and species variation in prey preferences (Arnold, 1981a, b;

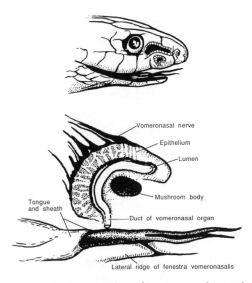

Fig. 5-1. Vomeronasal organ and nasal cavity of a garter snake (above). Enlargement (below) illustrates the principal feature of the vomeronasal organ and relative position of the tongue to the duct of the vomeronasal organ. (From Halpern, 1992.)

Burghardt, 1969, 1970, 1975), ontogenetic changes and the role of learning in feeding (Arnold, 1978; Burghardt, 1978), some aspects of predator avoidance (Arnold and Bennett, 1984; Herzog and Burghardt, 1986; Weldon, 1982), and recognition of conspecifics (Burghardt, 1983; Ford, 1986; Graves and Halpern, 1988).

Vision is also an important sense in garter snakes; it is involved in both initial detection of and orientation to prey (Drummond, 1985; Teather, 1991). Aquatic species, in particular, can see clearly underwater (*T. couchii*, Schaeffel and de Queiroz, 1990; *T. cyrtopsis*, Jones, 1990; *T. atratus*, Lind and Welsh, 1994; *T. melanogaster*, Drummond, 1983). Movement of the female during the breeding season facilitates a male's finding her to begin courtship, and vision is involved in the chase sequence during reproduction (Perry-Richardson et al., 1990). *Thamnophis* also uses vision to recognize predators, and in particular, the eyes of mammalian predators elicit antipredator strikes (Herzog and Bern, 1993).

Anyone who has fed a garter snake by touching it on the side with a food

Fig. 5-2. Setup to test prey preferences of snakes. (Redrawn from Burghardt, 1975.)

item (it will rapidly swing to bite appropriate prey) knows that tactile cues play an important role in this animal's feeding behavior. However, this aspect of feeding needs research because current studies of *Thamnophis* foraging suggest that strikes are only visually or chemically mediated (Drummond, 1983, 1985; Lind and Welsh, 1990). Tactile cues are also important in the signals male garter snakes send to females during courtship, but their role (i.e., species identification) has not been established experimentally.

The legless nature of snakes has intrigued both laypersons and scientists alike for centuries. How these animals accomplish the daily tasks of finding and eating food, avoiding predators, mating, and other critical life-history functions are marvelous examples of the nature of adaptation. Our understanding of the sensory capabilities of *Thamnophis* has made the genus useful as a model to study how various behaviors play roles in their natural history. Biologists have examined aspects of foraging strategies, habitat selection, thermoregulation, orientation and navigation, and antipredator behaviors of garter snakes. Additionally, in many localities two or more species of garter snake occur together, making it possible to examine competition and niche separation in regard to many of these traits (Carpenter, 1952a; Gregory 1984b).

FORAGING BEHAVIOR

Snakes can be classified as either active foragers or sit-and-wait predators (Mushinsky, 1987). As a group, garter snakes are generally considered to be active foragers, but notable variation in foraging behaviors occurs both ontogenetically and among species. Garter snakes may follow trails of skin chemicals left by prey (Kubie and Halpern, 1978), explore casts of earthworm burrows (Gillingham et al., 1990), search drying ponds containing trapped fish or amphibian larva (Fitch, 1941b), actively crawl underwater for fish (Drummond, 1983), or strike aquatic prey from perches above water (Lind and Welsh, 1994). Like other snakes, *Thamnophis* generally localizes prey by searching for appropriate odors using the tongue and the vomeronasal organ (Chiszar et. al., 1981; Cooper et al., 1989; Halpern, 1992). This was termed *cue-induced chemosensory searching* by Burghardt and Chmura (1993). Such cues may allow the animal to hunt or to wait in an appropriate site. Visual or tactile stimuli may be necessary to elicit ac-

Behavior

Fig. 5-3. Elevated walkway to observe foraging behavior in *T. sirtalis* on Beaver Island, Michigan. (Courtesy J. Gillingham.)

tual attacks on the prey (Burghardt and Denny, 1983; Drummond, 1985; Teather, 1991; Ford, pers. obs.).

Gillingham and Rowe (1984) studied the daily activity of *T. sirtalis* on Beaver Island in Michigan from an elevated walkway (Fig. 5-3). Individual snakes left their nocturnal refuges and foraged in a nearby meadow where earthworms were abundant. An individual snake located specific prey by finding freshly deposited castings, then thrust its snout into the tunnel below to capture the worms. Snakes captured an average of 19 worms per day (Gillingham et al., 1990). Ribbon snakes use vision to chase down anuran prey (Wendelken, 1978), and the movements of frog vocal sacs have also been suggested as attracting *T. proximus* (Rossman,

1963). Several species of garter snakes (i.e., *T. atratus*, *T. couchi*, and *T. melanogaster*) that specialize in capturing relatively large aquatic amphibians or fish either utilize a sit-and-wait strategy by coiling around a rock and striking at passing prey or search with an underwater substrate-crawling method (Lind and Welsh, 1994; Drummond, 1983; Fig. 5-4). Species with more generalized prey selection may also adopt these strategies at certain ages or in some environmental situations.

Halloy and Burghardt (1990) found that although neonate *T. sirtalis* and *T. radix* had difficulty eating fish, adults of these species had no difficulty. Older individuals tend to catch the fish by the head (70% of the time in adults) facilitating ingestion. This inclination was particularly evident with large fish, but the species differed in this tendency (i.e., *T. melanogaster* and adult *T. sirtalis* always ate fish headfirst, whereas other species did so only with large fish). Adults of the earthworm specialist *T. butleri* took much longer (a mean of 240 seconds) to eat larger fish, but only the young of other species had trouble with larger fish.

Juvenile *Thamnophis* often shift from smaller to larger prey species as they mature. Earthworms and

Fig. 5-4. The foraging behaviors of Oregon garter snakes, *T. atratus hydrophilus:* (a) basking/resting; (b) peering; oriented toward the water; (c) craning, head extended over the water and tongue flicking; (d) ambush position with head within a few centimeters of the water and tongue flicking; (e) underwater-substrate crawling with body submerged; (f) cruising, moving from place to place; (g) margin wandering, crawling on shore to get from place to place. (Redrawn from Lind and Welsh, 1994.)

leeches, in particular, are common prey for neonates, whereas amphibians, fish, and sometimes mammals may be preferred by adult snakes. (See Chap. 4 for additional discussion.) Lind and Welsh (1994) found the aquatic specialist, *T. atratus hydrophilus,* changed from frequent feeding on small prey to infrequent feeding on large prey as the snake aged. A shift from "sit and wait" to active foraging accompanied the maturation process. These changes in diet may be common in *Thamnophis* and probably reflect the long time required for small snakes to ingest prey (Feder and Arnold, 1982); they also suggest that reducing exposure to predation in diurnally active snakes as they age may be an important selection factor for garter snakes (Lind and Welsh, 1994). Mammalian prey such as voles and deermice pose the additional problem in that they can bite. Such prey are typically taken only by adults of larger species of garter snakes. *Thamnophis elegans,* which commonly takes rodents, uses both salivary toxins and loops of the body to restrain these prey (Gregory et al., 1980; Jansen, 1987).

In addition to ontogenetic shifts, *Thamnophis* often exhibit specialization on prey species that are locally

Behavior

available (Kephart, 1982; Drummond and Burghardt, 1983). This plasticity has been the basis of a multitude of studies of innate food preferences both at the species and population level (Ford and Burghardt, 1993). However, the selection of prey by adults is not always due to local adaptation. Phenotypic variation in diet can exist, especially in generalist species, and types of prey taken by snakes in a particular population may be relative to the availability of the food (Fuchs and Burghardt, 1971). (See Chap. 4 for further discussion.)

The mechanism involved in shifting to alternative food probably involves habituation and other simple forms of learning (Burghardt, 1992) rather than a genetically programmed ontogenetic change. For example, Greenwell et al. (1984) found that an insular population of *T. sirtalis* frequently ate birds, even though neonates had the same innate responses to prey-species odors (not birds) as did mainland populations. However, genetic differences are involved in the ability of *T. sirtalis* to eat the potentially deadly Pacific newt, *Taricha granulosa* (Brodie and Brodie, 1990). The newt produces tetrodotoxin, a potent neurotoxin that would kill most potential predators, but *T. sir-* *talis* from areas where *Taricha* occurs have evolved resistant to the toxin.

Numerous studies have examined the prey taken by garter snakes in the field, and some workers have examined the diets of sympatric species. (See Chap. 4.) However, as the above limited descriptions indicate, the behaviors involved in foraging have been examined in only a few species. Studies of hunting and feeding behaviors of other individual taxa and populations would be useful, particularly for a comparative examination.

HABITAT SELECTION

From studies on sympatric species of garter snakes in northern California (Fitch, 1941b), in Michigan (Carpenter, 1951), on Vancouver Island, British Columbia (Gregory, 1984b), in Ohio (Dalrymple and Reichenbach, 1981, 1984), in Manitoba (Hart, 1979), and other comparative field studies, we know that individual species of *Thamnophis* show distinct preferences for particular habitats. The general finding of all these research projects is that the habitat selection by various species of *Thamnophis* is complex, involving aspects of the canopy coverage (thickness of the forest), availability of thermal sites (sunny spots), and prey availability. Species-specific habitat preferences do likely exist, but how these sites are behaviorally selected has rarely been studied (but see Huey et al., 1989).

THERMOREGULATORY BEHAVIOR

Many behavioral activities of *Thamnophis* depend on physiological processes that are sensitive to the body temperature of the animal (e.g., locomotion, digestion, and crawling speed; Stevenson et al., 1985). Theoretically, snakes should behaviorally maintain body temperature at levels that maximize these functions as they relate to ecological success. However, some activities of garter snakes create variation in body temperature and confuse our understanding of their thermoregulation (Gregory, 1984a). (See also Chap. 4.) Smaller individuals of most species often hide under cover to avoid predation and therefore cannot bask as much as adults do (Gregory, 1984a). Also, foraging snakes or those seeking mates are restricted in basking time and may exhibit lower body temperatures because they are hunting in less thermally optimal habitats (Gregory, 1984a). In addition, a full digestive tract is known to stimulate snakes to prefer higher body temperatures (Gibson et al., 1989), and it has been suggested that gravid females thermoregulate at a higher temperature (see Gibson and Falls, 1979a, for arguments against this position). With all these factors affecting body temperatures it has been difficult to determine if different species of *Thamnophis* exhibit different body temperatures in the wild (but see Rosen, 1991). Additional information on the thermal ecology of garter snakes can be found in Chap. 4.

Even with such a plastic phenomenon, we can still generate a general thermoregulation model for *Thamnophis*. Northern populations hibernate when diurnal temperatures are sufficiently low as to prevent the digestive process (about 12 to 15 C). During this time snakes are aphagic and draw on stored glycogen and protein from liver and muscle; lipids are less important (Costanzo, 1985; Gregory, 1982). Snakes choose underground sites that are appropriate for preventing both freezing and dehydration. These dens may be traditional, and learning their location is important to the individual's survival. Water may be critical in *Thamnophis* hibernation, as submergence is strongly correlated to a lowering of metabolism (Costanzo, 1989b, c).

In the spring, the thermal gradient in the den collapses and temperatures begin rising, stimulating animals to become active, although external air temperatures are important in the actual emergence (Macartney et al., 1989). Snakes begin basking at the den primarily to facilitate courtship, not to feed. Sometimes animals rest with only the head exposed to the sun (Gregory, 1990). Body temperatures vary significantly over the diurnal cycle during this period at the den, but males have higher temperatures at this time (Rosen, 1991). As seasonal temperatures rise and stabilize, animals (mated females first) move to foraging areas.

Foraging may require animals to occupy areas where optimal temperature cannot be achieved; but after feeding, the animals may seek microhabitats with more desirable thermal characteristics. Weather conditions during the spring and fall are known to limit both the activity of T. elegans and its level and precision of thermoregulation (Peterson, 1987). However, during much of the diurnal period of midsummer, most Thamnophis seem able to maintain relatively stable body temperatures (the plateau phase of T. elegans in Peterson, 1987) by moving between appropriate thermal sites (Rosen, 1991; Figs. 5-2 and 5-6). In an elegant field study of T. elegans at Eagle Lake, California, Huey et al. (1989) showed how snakes chose rocks to hide under that would allow them to remain for the longest time within their thermal preference range. In the spring and fall, in localities where temperatures are moderate, Thamnophis are most active during the warmer midday period. In midsummer, snakes often shift to a bimodal activity period of early morning and late afternoon. During this time snakes can regulate their temperature more easily with less variation in body temperature (Gibson and Falls, 1979a). In Peterson's (1987) study, T. elegans rapidly warmed up to the plateau temperature in the morning (0.22 C/min.) and were stable for the diurnal period. Cooling rates were slower, averaging only 0.03 C/min. More southerly species (unless at high altitude) may have the option of using this summertime thermoregulatory pattern for much of the year. In areas with hot and dry midsummers (southern and western areas) garter snakes may become completely inactive or switch to a nocturnal activity cycle (T. marcianus, Ten-

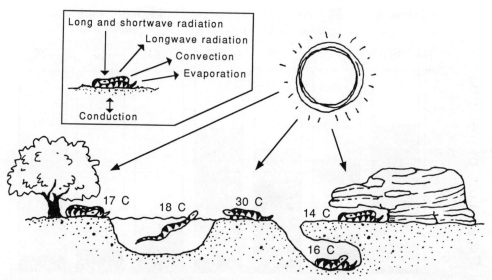

Fig. 5-5. Operative temperatures of the garter snake, *T. elegans,* in various micro-habitats of a meadow in northern California at 0930 on 6 August 1986. (Redrawn from Peterson et al., 1993.)

nant, 1984; *T. hammondii,* Klauber in Fitch, 1940).

Predator avoidance, particularly for juveniles and pregnant females, may also interfere with thermoregulation by requiring individuals to hide under rocks, logs, and other objects during times when basking is needed to obtain preferred body temperatures. Females appear to regulate their temperature more precisely than do males (Gibson and Falls, 1979a). There is some evidence that the pattern of ac-tivity is driven by endogenous circa-dian rhythms (*T. radix,* Heckrotte, 1975; *T. sirtalis,* Justy and Mallory, 1985). Southern and western popula-tions of *Thamnophis* typically have a different bimodal activity pattern. Because of the hotter, and often drier, midsummer, they may become com-pletely inactive or only active in early morning and late afternoon. Although the information is lacking for most species, it is known that a few species may be nocturnal (*T. marcianus,* Ford,

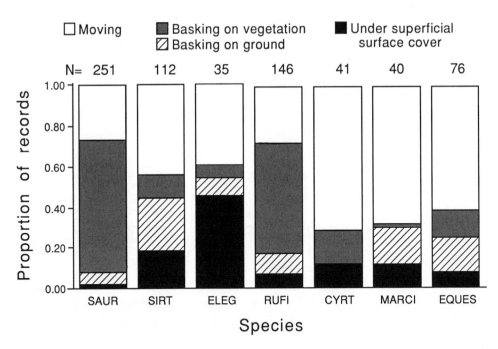

Fig. 5-6. Observed behaviors for garter snakes during the active season (mid-April to mid-September) from southeastern Michigan (SAUR = *T. sauritus*; SIRT = *T. sirtalis*) and Arizona (ELEG = *T. elegans*; RUFI = *T. rufipunctatus*; CYRT = *T. cyrtopsis*; MARCI = *T. marcianus*; and EQUES = *T. eques*). The number of observations for each species is given above each bar. (From Rosen, 1991.)

pers. obs.; *T. hammondii*, Klauber in Fitch, 1940).

Species Variation

Many garter snakes have had their body temperatures measured in an opportunistic fashion in various field studies. (See Chap. 4 for review.)

However, without some knowledge of the previous activities of the snakes and the thermal characteristics of the environment, the values of these observations may be limited (Gregory, 1984a). In a comparative study of six species of *Thamnophis* from three geographic regions, Rosen (1991) found that during the more stable summer period, all species had temperatures higher than the recorded preferred temperatures taken opportunistically, and only slight differences in body temperature existed among species. (*T. rufipunctatus* had somewhat lower temperatures than the other species studied.) There were no differences within species among different localities. Presumably species differences in temperature preferences allow utilization of different habitats (e.g., *T. sirtalis* foraging in forests in British Columbia, and *T. elegans* living at high elevations must be capable of greater activity at lower temperatures than *T. validus* foraging along open streams in Mexico). In actuality, "cold-adapted" species often exhibit thermal preferenda as high or higher than southern species. Laboratory observations of body temperatures of various species of *Thamnophis* average just over 28 C (range 24.5 to 30.7, as reviewed in Rosen, 1991), whereas field data of the plateau-phase (warm-season) body temperatures are usually slightly warmer (Rosen, 1991). Obviously, the limits of environmental conditions affect what the body temperature of individual garter snakes can be in the field, but the consistency among species suggests that there may be some phylogenetic constraints within this genus.

One interesting phenomenon that does occur in colder regions is an increase in melanism, which may allow more rapid warming. Melanistic morphs occur in *T. sirtalis* around Lake Erie (Gibson and Falls, 1979b), in *T. butleri* in Ontario (Catling and Freedman, 1977), and in *T. proximus* in Chiapas, Mexico (Rossman, pers. obs.).

ANTIPREDATOR BEHAVIOR

Garter snakes may be important prey items for numerous vertebrate predators, including hawks, smaller birds such as jays and crows, predatory mammals as small as shrews (which feed on neonate snakes), various ophiophagous snakes, larger carnivorous fish, and even large frogs. The obvious defensive responses of *Thamnophis* (fleeing, striking, and voiding cloacal secretions) are elicited by various sensory cues from the predator (Fig. 5-7). The eyes of models of mammalian predators, for example, stimulate defensive attacks in *T. sirtalis* (Herzog and Bern, 1992), whereas skin odors from king snakes cause rapid flight in *T. elegans* (Weldon, 1982). Moving stimuli and models presented over-

Behavior

101

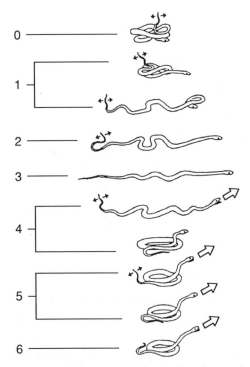

0

1

2

3

4

5

6

Fig. 5-7. The antipredator displays of the garter snake *T. radix*, forming a continuum from defensive (*top*) to offensive (*bottom*). (From Arnold and Bennett, 1984.)

head are more potent than still objects or those at eye level in causing defensive strikes and flight (Hampton and Gillingham, 1989; Herzog et al., 1989; Bowers et al., 1993; Fig. 5-8).

A number of species of *Thamnophis* have been tested for their defensive responses, and differences among them are quite evident. For ex-

ample, *T. melanogaster* is very aggressive, striking more often than *T. butleri*, which rarely bites (Herzog and Burghardt, 1986; Fig. 5-8). *Thamnophis radix* shows high rates of fleeing (Herzog et al., 1992), *T. marcianus* hides its head, and *T. sauritus* waves its tail and reverses direction often when fleeing (Bowers et al., 1993; Fig. 5-8). Individual and litter differences in antipredator responses also occur, even within females of the same population (Arnold and Bennett, 1984; Herzog and Burghardt, 1988). Obviously, this plasticity in responses should correlate to the behaviors of the local predators. However, comparisons of species or populations subject to different predators have not been attempted.

One fascinating series of studies of defensive behavior in garter snakes revolved around a population of *T. ordinoides* that exhibited antipredator behaviors that were correlated with appropriate color patterns (Brodie, 1989b, 1991, 1992, 1993a, b). Striped individuals, which were hard to visually track when they moved in a straight line, tended to move rapidly in one direction when threatened. Unpatterned or spotted individuals tended to reverse directions frequently and were difficult to locate when they stopped. Genetic covari-

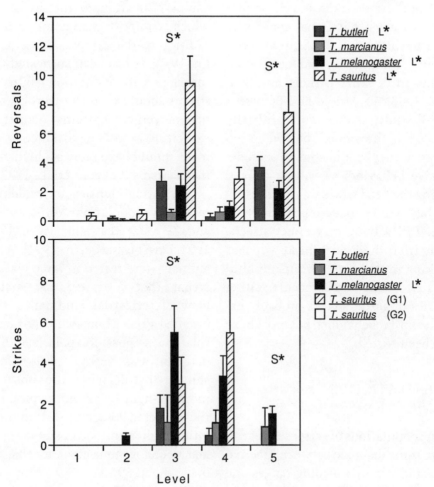

Fig. 5-8. Mean frequency of reversals and strikes for several species of *Thamnophis* at several threat levels: (1) experimenter out of view, (2) experimenter looms over arena, (3) nonmoving hands, (4) moving hands, (5) experimenter touches snake. Significance for a species is indicated by L* and species differences by S*. G1 are for neonates from females collected in Florida. G2 are for offspring from females collected in New York. (Redrawn from Halloy and Burghardt, 1990.)

ance of these patterns and the appropriate escape behavior has apparently occurred (Brodie, 1992). Similar correlation of morphology and locomotion occurs in *T. radix* (Arnold and Bennett, 1988). In Arnold and Bennett's (1988) study, snakes would initially flee when threatened, but when exhausted, they would shift to such defensive behaviors as balling up and hiding the head while waving the tail, or they would strike repeatedly (Fig. 5-7). Tail waving may direct attacks away from the hidden head, whereas striking must be an attempt to bluff because biting rarely occurs. Other species of garter snakes probably exhibit similar behaviors, but most have not been tested.

ORIENTATION AND NAVIGATION

Some populations of garter snakes migrate some distance between hibernacula and summer feeding ranges and many others move from nocturnal refuges to foraging sites (Gillingham et al., 1990). Because delays in movements may be critical, particularly in northern populations, orientation mechanisms may be well developed in *Thamnophis*. Orientation mechanisms can vary from simple use of landmarks, to the ability to select a compass direction, to true navigation, which requires a map component in addition to the compass sense (Griffin, 1952). It has been suggested that the degree of orientation ability in snakes should correlate to their normal movement patterns—i.e., those exhibiting more long-distance movement should have more sophisticated mechanisms (Gregory et al., 1987).

Navigation abilities are evident in migratory populations of *T. sirtalis* and *T. radix* (Lawson, 1989, 1991, 1994; Lawson and Secoy, 1991). When animals were tested in large circular arenas that restricted the snake's view of terrestrial landmarks, they oriented along a homeward axis using solar cues, possibly polarized light (Lawson and Secoy, 1991). Phase shifting by delaying the onset of morning light by six hours produced the predicted 90-degree shift in orientation, indicating both a sun-compass and an endogenous clock mechanism (Lawson, 1989; Fig. 5-9). However, similar tests of nonmigratory *T. sirtalis* demonstrated that they also have advanced navigational abilities, whereas such abilities were absent in *T. ordinoides* (Lawson, 1994). She suggested that species that show little need to migrate any distance (e.g., *T. ordinoides*) may not exhibit navigational skills, but that species with

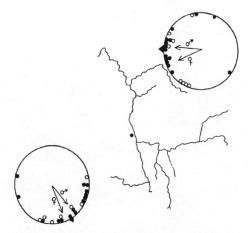

Fig. 5-9. Results of spring tests of *Thamnophis sirtalis* orientation abilities after a 6-hour delayed light/dark shift. Animals were moved 5 km from the den (dot in the map) in opposite directions (where the large circles are) and tested in a 6 m diameter arena for their initial choice of direction. The summer range for the snakes (the direction they should head in the spring) is located at the upper large circle. Note that compensations were made by the snakes both for the time shift and for the different release sites. (From Lawson, 1989.)

some populations that migrate (e.g., *T. sirtalis*) have evolved those abilities, which may still be present in nonmigratory populations.

Pheromone trails are also used for orientation, both to find females for mating (reviewed by Ford, 1986); and to locate dens both by adults (Lawson,

1989) and by neonates (Costanzo, 1989a; Graves and Halpern, 1988; Lawson, 1994). Two studies have indicated that adult females, not males, are the primary source of pheromone trails (Ford and O'bleness, 1986; Lawson, 1994), and Lawson (1994) suggested the females act as "leaders" to both summer ranges and hibernacula. Neonates in some cases spend their first winter isolated from adults and then use adult trails to locate traditional dens the second year. Studies have demonstrated convincingly that the trail produced by a female contains information identifying her species, and males can avoid following heterospecific females (Ford and Schofield, 1984; Ford and O'bleness, 1986). However, neonates may not be as selective as adults, because several studies have suggested that neonates are attracted to pheromones of heterospecifics (Waye and Gregory, 1993; Heller and Halpern, 1982; but see Graves and Halpern, 1988, for contrary data). Female pheromone trails appear to have low volatility and last at least several days (Ford, pers. obs.). Consequently, a concentration gradient of chemicals allowing the determination of direction of the trail would not be present. Trailing snakes can tell the direction of the previous snake because pheromones are depos-

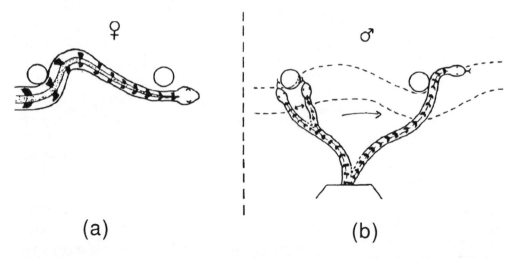

Fig. 5-10. Mechanism by which male garter snakes determine the direction of a female's pheromone trail: (a) Female garter snake laying a trail. Note that she pushes against the anterior surface of the objects. (b) Behavior of the male when he encounters the female's trail. Stipling on the first peg represents the deposition of pheromone, whereas the dashed lines represent the trail on the substrate. The male assays both sides of the peg to determine the direction the female moved. (From Ford and Low, 1984.)

ited not only on the ground but on objects such as rocks that the snake pushes against as it crawls. The direction is determined by which side of the rock has more pheromone (Ford and Low, 1984; Fig. 5-10).

REPRODUCTIVE BEHAVIOR

The mating behavior of several garter snakes has been described in some detail. Davis (1936) offered the first description of courtship in *Thamnophis* from the observations by A. C. Weed of *T. radix* in the field. However, Davis misconstrued caudocephalic waves as orgasmic contractions. Blanchard and Blanchard (1942) documented their careful observations of *T. s. sirtalis* kept in outdoor pits in Michigan. Breder (1946), Gardner (1955), and List (1950) observed the same subspecies mating in the field. *Thamnophis. s. parietalis* has been observed in captivity (Munro, 1948; Fitch, 1965), and its mating behavior has been described in many experiments by several behaviorists, especially David Crews and his students and Mimi Halpern and her colleagues. Pisani (1967) described courtship in *T. brachystoma,* and Finneran (1949) and Noble (1937) observed courtship in *T. butleri.* Ball (1978) detailed the mating of *T. melanogaster.* Although modern techniques have since been used to quantify courtship behavior in several species of snakes, the only *Thamnophis* analyzed so far are *T. marcianus* (Perry-Richardson et al., 1990; Schofield, pers. comm.) and *T. sirtalis* (Bowers, pers. comm.).

In northern species and populations of *Thamnophis,* courtship activity occurs as snakes emerge from hibernation. Large numbers of individuals can be involved, and the behavior is highly visible (Fig. 5-11). These factors have facilitated studies of the environmental and physiological control of sexual behavior, and so most of our knowledge has been detailed in northern populations of *T. sirtalis* (Aleksiuk and Gregory, 1974; Moore and Lindzey, 1992; Whittier and Tokarz, 1992; see Chap. 4 for additional discussion). Although similar patterns are known to occur in other northern *Thamnophis,* southern species that do not hibernate extensively may exhibit their courtship during irregular intervals (*T. melanogaster*— Gartska and Crews, 1985; *T. marcianus*—Karges, 1984; Ford and Karges, 1987; Ford and Cobb, 1992). Still, a description of the basic reproductive pattern of a northern *Thamnophis* is a useful starting point.

Northern Patterns

When den temperatures begin to rise in the spring, male snakes emerge on warm, sunny days to bask; they court females as they emerge (Fig. 5-11). The vas deferens of the males contains spermatozoa that were produced the previous summer, a dissociated cycle noted by Garstka et al., 1982). The males' courtship behavior is regulated not by androgens but rather by environmentally mediated changes in the pineal gland, apparently from the cold of hibernation (Crews et al., 1988; Nelson et al., 1987). Various *Thamnophis* species are reported to mate in the fall (Wright and Wright, 1957), but the significance of this breeding activity is still arguable. (See Chap. 4 for further discussion.) Females emerge from dens in smaller groups and later than males. The female produces a pheromone, released through the skin, that attracts mates.

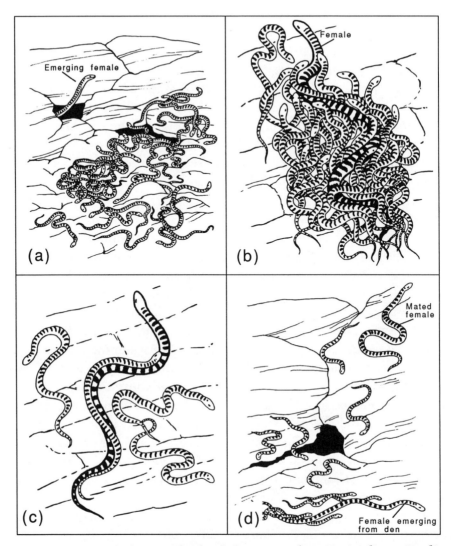

Fig. 5-11. Mating behavior of red-sided garter snakes, *T. sirtalis parietalis*, illustrating the general pattern of many populations of garter snakes in the northern ranges of North America. (*a*) The males emerge first and sun themselves near the den. (*b*) Females emerge later, and several males court one female, forming a "mating ball." (*c*) One male succeeds in mating with the female by inserting one of his hemipenes into her cloaca. The other males are repelled by a pheromone in the male's semen. (*d*) The female leaves the area of the den, but males stay to await the emergence of another unmated female. (Redrawn from Gartska and Crews, 1982.)

Shedding that occurs in many species soon after emergence may enhance the attractiveness of females (Kubie et al., 1978). The female pheromone is a methyl ketone (Mason et al., 1989) and has low volatility. Therefore males find the female by trails rather than by airborne odors (Ford, 1986).

Hormones from the gonads apparently are not involved in the attractiveness of the female nor in her receptivity to the males, because levels of endogenous estrogen (estradiol 17B) are low at this time (Whittier et al., 1987). Interestingly, plasma levels of estrogen are elevated immediately after mating when the females become unreceptive. This hormone may be involved in evacuating the sperm of other males that is stored in the anterior regions of the oviduct (Halpert et al., 1982). Sperm storage from fall matings can occur, and long-term storage (four years) has been reported in *T. hammondii* (Stewart, 1972).

Southern Patterns

Southern populations of *Thamnophis* may hibernate in groups for limited periods, may hibernate singly in shallow refuges and come out on warm winter days, or may not hibernate at all. The environmental cues that elicit reproductive activity for these animals are poorly understood, but some evidence indicates that the male's behavior may be important. Garstka and Crews (1982) showed that *T. melanogaster* females can be stimulated to become receptive by the presence of courting males. More than likely, whenever a female obtains enough lipid stores to reproduce she begins the process.

Courtship Behavior

The courtship behavior of the males when they contact the female follows the same triphasic scheme described by Gillingham (1976) for rat snakes of the genus *Elaphe*. Schofield (pers. comm.) provided data from her analysis of courtship of *T. marcianus*, and Bowers (pers. comm.) provided sequence diagrams for *T. sirtalis* (Fig. 5-12). The following general description comes from these and personal observation of several other species courting.

In Phase I (tactile-chase), the male contacts the female, and she remains passive, flees, or produces a localized head-neck jerk (Perry-Richardson et al., 1990; Fig. 5-13a). This phase is often very active, with the males visually attracted to the female's movements. If the female moves, the male

Behavior

109

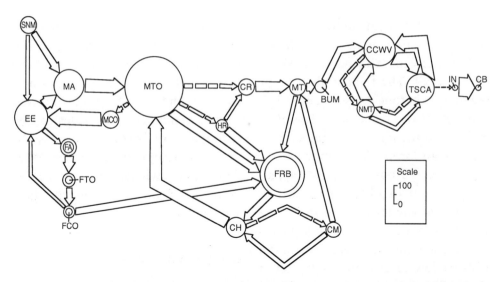

Fig. 5-12. Sequence diagram for courtship behaviors of *T. sirtalis*. The single circles refer to male behaviors and double circles to female behaviors. Diameter of circles corresponds to frequency of occurrence, and width of arrows to the transitional probability that a given behavior immediately follows another behavior. (Dashed lines are not significant.) Scale on right reflects the transitional probability. Behavioral codes are as follows: SNM, stationary mode; EE, exploratory/escape behavior; FA, female approaches male; FTO, female touches male; FCO, female crawls over male; MA, male approaches female; MTO, male touches female; MCO, male crawls over female; FRB, female rejection behaviors (rattles tail, jerks body, or crawls away); CH, chase; CM, chase-mount; CR, chin rub; HR, male's head rests on female; MT, mount; BUM, back up while mounted; CCWV, caudocephalic waves; TSCA, tail-search copulatory attempt; NMT, no movement while mounted; IN, intromission; CB, copulatory behaviors (roll, drag, lie still). (Data and analysis by B. Bowers on 5 males and 11 females from Wisconsin using the ELAG sequential-analysis program by Roger Bakeman of Georgia State University.)

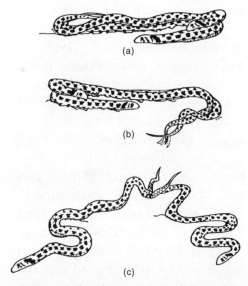

(a)

(b)

(c)

Fig. 5-13. The three stages of courtship behavior in garter snakes, illustrated by *T. marcianus:* (a) Phase I, chase, mount, and dorsal advance; (b), Phase II, tail-search copulatory attempt; (c) Phase III, hemipenal intromission. (Figure from C. Schofield, unpubl.)

chases her and attempts to reestablish contact and mount her dorsum (touch-mount). He then presses his chin on the back of the female and advances while chin-pressing, to within 10 to 30 cm of the female's snout, depending upon the ratio of his size to the female's length. This dorsal crawl may be reversed, the male proceeding to the cloaca, and may be repeated several times. After ob-

taining juxtaposition of the tails, he will loop his body over both sides of the female. The loops can pass as a sinasoidal wave posteriorly down the female's body (Ball, 1978). The male apparently uses tactile signals to align his cloaca next to hers, because he often backs up at this time. Suggestions that males must have longer tails to accomplish this alignment have often been made (Pisani, 1976,) and stub-tailed females create some difficulty for the male. Chases are an important component of this Phase I behavior and may be involved in female mate selection by dislodging less energetic males (Perry-Richardson, 1987).

Once aligned on the female's back, the male begins tactile activities that encompass Phase II (Fig. 5-13b). These behaviors include the cephalocaudal waves mentioned above, ripples or waves that begin posteriorly and move anteriorly (caudocephalic waves), gentle tail shaking, and attempts to lift the female's tail by forceful pushing of his tail (tail-search copulatory attempts). These tactile activities may serve as species-specific signals because their occurrences differ in species. For example, *T. sirtalis* (List, 1950), *T. melanogaster* (Ball, 1978), *T. radix*, *T. butleri*, and *T. proximus* (N. Ford, pers. obs.),

Behavior

111

and *T. elegans* (Riches, 1976) exhibit caudocephalic waves, but one population of *T. marcianus* does not (Perry-Richardson et al., 1990). However, an Arizona population of *T. marcianus* does perform caudocephalic waves (Ford, pers. obs.), and *T. brachystoma* apparently produces these waves after intromission (Pisani, 1967). Whether there are also signals allowing females to assess male fitness is problematic. Male size apparently is not an important cue for the female (Joy and Crews, 1988; N. Ford, pers. obs.), but the speed and vigor of tail searching may be (Perry-Richardson, 1987). Whether females play an active role by lifting the tail or gaping the cloaca is also questionable at this time, but they do appear to evacuate the cloaca by defecation prior to the male's insertion (Ball, 1978; N. Ford, pers. obs.).

Phase III begins when the female accepts hemipenal intromission after several minutes up to several hours of courtship (Fig. 5-13c). Copulation is short relative to other genera of snakes, usually lasting only several minutes in *T. sirtalis* (Fitch, 1965) to an average of 13.5 minutes for *T. melanogaster* (Ball, 1978). The female may be passive or active during this stage; if she moves, she drags the male tailfirst (Ball, 1978; Ford, pers. obs.).

Some females terminate mating by violent axial rotations (Ball, 1978; Perry-Richardson et al., 1990). In some species males leave a pheromonal plug that inhibits other males from courting the female (Devine, 1975, 1984; Fitch, 1965; Ross and Crews, 1978; Whittier et al., 1985). Some species do not exhibit mating plugs—e.g., *T. marcianus* (Ford, pers. obs.)—and multiple paternity is known to occur in *T. sirtalis* (Gibson and Falls, 1975; Schwartz, et al., 1989), so the actual utility of the mating plug is debatable. Mated and other nonreceptive females may bob their heads or shake their tails vigorously when approached by other males (Ball, 1978; Perry-Richardson et al., 1990).

HIBERNATION

Over much of the ranges of most species of *Thamnophis*, winter temperatures could be fatal. Snakes avoid lethal cold by moving underground to sites where the temperatures remain at tolerable levels. In some extreme northern latitudes *Thamnophis sirtalis* may hibernate for up to seven months (Aleksiuk, 1976; Gregory, 1977a, b). Because of the importance of hibernation to snake survival, biologists have studied dens in a number of localities (reviewed by Gregory, 1982).

Macartney et al. (1989) radio-tracked *T. sirtalis* in a northern Alberta den and found that the snakes moved to more-insulated sites within the dens as outside temperatures dropped. Because all possible den sites do not have characteristics that allow the snakes to survive over winter, those that do may be used traditionally (Fitch, 1965). Adult animals may use sun-compass and landmark orientation to return to the dens, whereas juvenile snakes may follow adult pheromone trails to locate dens the first time (Ford, 1986; Lawson, 1989; Lawson and Secoy, 1991).

Water is also critical during garter snake hibernation and a number of authors have noted *Thamnophis* hibernating in wells and other sources of water. Costanzo (1989b, c) found that *T. sirtalis* has a significantly lower metabolic rate (over 50% less) and higher survival when it can submerge in water during hibernation. (See Chap. 6.)

AGGREGATIONS

Another social behavior of *Thamnophis* is the tendency of gravid females to aggregate in midsummer prior to parturition (reported for *T. sirtalis* by Gregory, 1975, and Gordon and Cook, 1980; and for *T. couchii* by Hansen and Tremper, *in prep.*). Increased survival of the individual young may occur if large numbers of neonates are born together because predators may have difficulty catching individual offspring or may be saturated by the "mast" crop. Alternatively, the burden of carrying a litter reduces a female's ability to escape a predator (Seigel et al., 1987), and pregnancy may stimulate shifts to antipredator strategies that do not involve flight—e.g., crypsis (Brodie 1989a). Alternatively, females may simply be aggregating in the only refuges available.

LEARNING

The lack of postnatal care constrains garter snakes to begin life on their own, and thus instinctive behaviors are critical to their initial survival. However, this does not imply that learning is unimportant in the behaviors exhibited by snakes in the wild. For example, although adult *Thamnophis* have different prey than do juveniles and this ontogenetic shift is controlled by the animals' genes,

Behavior

113

many aspects of the changes in foraging are controlled by environmental factors through learning (Halloy and Burghardt, 1990; Lind and Welsh, 1994). It is also likely that learning is involved in defensive and other behaviors of garter snakes. However, due to the perception of many ethologists that snakes are not "good" models for learning experiments, our understanding of the role of learning in the natural history of garter snakes is still quite limited (Ford and Burghardt, 1994).

Although the kinds of prey taken by *Thamnophis* are constrained to some degree by innate preferences, prey availability and habitat utilization significantly affect what is eaten (i.e., a species that forages under leaf litter will not be eating fish). Improvement in foraging time occurs with practice in handling a particular prey (Halloy and Burghardt, 1990). As mentioned earlier, the tendency for *Thamnophis* to eat fish headfirst increases with experience. These changes in prey taken may indicate the development of chemically based search images. Fuchs and Burghardt (1971) found that neonate *Thamnophis sirtalis* responded more readily to specific prey chemicals from the type of food they were fed, and Burghardt (1990) found that *T. radix* could detect much more

dilute extracts of prey after two months of feeding on the same diet. However, Arnold (1978) found that after several weeks of feeding *T. sirtalis* only fish or frogs their responses to frog odors were not modified, but that responses to fish were increased by a diet of fish. Consequently, the relationship between innate preferences and learning cues from available prey is not a simple one.

How learning is involved in the responses of *Thamnophis* to predators has also been examined. Neonate *T. radix* show habituation to shadows (Fuenzalida et al., 1975) and have some ability to learn paths to a refuge (Fuenzalida and Ulrich, 1975). *Thamnophis melanogaster*, an aggressive species, shows declines in defensive striking when stimuli are presented repeatedly (Herzog and Burghardt, 1986; Herzog et al., 1989), and *T. sirtalis* shows short-term habituation to overhead objects (Hampton and Gillingham, 1989). Harassment early in life also causes *T. sirtalis* to have a greater flight tendency weeks later (Herzog, 1990).

Obviously, much more work on the role of learning in behavioral activities of garter snakes is needed. This is an area of research where laboratory studies will be very important, and the results may also be of utility to keeping individual *Thamnophis* in captivity.

GENETICS AND EVOLUTION OF BEHAVIOR

After Burghardt (1970, 1975) demonstrated that neonate garter snakes exhibited both population and individual differences in preferences for prey extracts (Fig. 5-2), several researchers began to examine the evolution of these innate preferences. Arnold (1977, 1981a, b) studied the slug-eating habits of coastal California populations of *T. elegans*, and he suggested that separate groups of genes affect responses to amphibians, slugs and leeches, and the toxic newt, *Taricha*. Crosses of the inland and coastal populations of *T. elegans* indicated that slug refusal is dominant over slug eating, but the trait may be polygenic or exhibit incomplete penetrance (Ayres and Arnold, 1983). One of the difficulties of such genetic behavior studies is that the generation time for garter snakes even in the laboratory is typically two or three years.

Other researchers have examined the genetic basis of antipredator defense in *Thamnophis*. Arnold and Bennett (1984) found that antipredator behaviors of neonate *T. radix* varied individually, ranging from defensive tail waving and fleeing to aggressive striking. However, individual snakes were consistent in the behavior they used, and animals from the same litters were more similar in their antipredator activities than were unrelated animals (Arnold and Bennett, 1984). Garland (1988) and Garland et al. (1990) found a similar basis for stamina and antipredator behaviors of *T. sirtalis*. Brodie (1989b, 1991, 1992, 1993a, b) found genetic coupling of the color pattern of the polymorphic *T. ordinoides* with its antipredator behaviors.

Although a number of researchers have compared the defensive actions of several species of *Thamnophis* and found species differences to be quite evident (Bowers et al., 1993; Herzog and Burghardt, 1986), the adaptive nature of the variation has not been commonly addressed. One of the difficulties in discussing the evolution of antipredator mechanisms in garter snakes is that we have very limited knowledge of the predators of specific species of *Thamnophis*.

FUTURE STUDIES: What Do We Need to Know About Garter Snake Behavior?

We have gained much knowledge of the behavior of garter snakes, particularly about *T. sirtalis*, but garter snakes show an amazing amount of variation in their activities, both within and among species. If we are to really understand why behaviors are occurring, we must examine the factors that cause them to be exhibited only in a particular context, in certain populations of garter snakes, or in specific species. I think studies of the lesser-known species of *Thamnophis* will be especially critical in determining the evolutionary pressures involved in the occurrence of behavioral traits.

Although we still have unanswered questions for all garter snakes in the areas of foraging behavior, antipredator behavior, and reproductive behavior, I think one of the most exciting research areas for snakes in general may be the evaluation of mechanisms involved in learning (Holtzman, pers. comm.). Learning may be a major factor in the plasticity in behaviors exhibited by members of this genus. This is particularly ironic because learning has always been a characteristic which snakes were believed to exhibit poorly (Brattstrom, 1974).

Chapter 6

CARE IN CAPTIVITY

[F]or such a widespread group of snakes, the literature on their captive reproduction is incredibly scanty.
—*Rossi and Rossi, 1995*

INTRODUCTION

Keeping a wild animal in captivity offers the chance to gain considerable personal knowledge of that animal's habits and behaviors by observing how it senses its environment, how it captures and eats its food, and even how it defecates (see Chiszar et al., 1995, for the significance of the latter in snakes). However, as animal rights organizations often proclaim, taking an animal out of the wild carries certain implications. Paramount to many people in such groups is the animal's "welfare," the definition of which is not clear but is seemingly not restricted to the animal's health. Often, the goal of animal rights groups is that *no* animals should be kept in captivity. On the other hand, biologists view animal welfare more in relation to survival of the species, not the individual, and studies may actually require that animals be kept in captivity to learn strategies for their long-term preservation. Both sets of concerns should be weighed when deciding whether to keep an animal in captivity. Also, because some populations and species of garter snakes may be declining, various state and federal governmental organizations now include them as protected species, making it mandatory to check with officials before collecting specimens. Even when snakes are not protected by law, our own ethics should regulate whether we collect and keep animals in captivity.

As a group, garter snakes tend to be both abundant in the wild and, with proper care, easy to keep healthy in captivity. In much of North America garter snakes are found in urban areas and may actually be observed in one's own yard. Collecting a local snake may be preferable in terms of keeping one in captivity, because it can be released after a few days of observation. Snakes purchased at a pet store should not be released in the wild (Pough, 1991). Such animals will likely succumb to predators or starvation, neither being adapted to the local area nor having learned refuges and feeding sites. The possibility of introducing disease into the wild populations is also a real concern.

Garter snakes are usually small enough to keep in a 10-gallon aquarium, are not excessively aggressive, and eat easily obtainable prey. In addition, because scientists have kept garter snakes in lab colonies for many years, through generations of animals, we have accumulated enough knowledge to keep them healthy in captivity. Information specific to maintaining large colonies of snakes is available in Pough (1991) and Ford (1992), and information about keeping snakes in captivity can be obtained from a myriad of new books (e.g., Warwick et al., 1995), some of which are even specific to garter snakes (e.g., Sweeney, 1992). Information from personnel in pet stores may be helpful, but often their knowledge is restricted to mammals and birds. This lack of familiarity with reptiles is also typical of many veterinarians. These deficiencies are changing as unusual pets become more popular. Possibly the best way to learn about snakes is to attend a local reptile or herpetological society meetings. Because of the increasing availability of knowledge of general snake care, and because there is so much variation in the life histories of garter snakes, I will concentrate here on some of the different needs of the members of the genus *Thamnophis*.

HOUSING

Two characteristics are absolutely critical for any container used for keeping a garter snake. First it must be escape-proof, for snakes are magicians of the caliber of Houdini. Lids must be tight and secured. Second, the cage must have good airflow. High humidity from a closed-up cage will prevent garter snakes from being able to dry out and will promote skin disorders. Naturalistic environments within the cage may look appealing, but they usually result in the development of skin blisters on the snake (Rossi and Rossi, 1995). In such settings snakes also spend a lot of time hiding (Warwick and Steedman, 1995). If you really want plants and soil in the terrarium, then at least provide an area where the snake can dry out, e.g., under a small external light (Fig. 6-1). Acidic bedding may also help reduce the occurrence of skin problems. Cages with only bedding, a water bowl, and hiding areas are much easier to clean. Simple tanks with commercial lids work well, as do plastic sweater or blanket boxes with airholes punched in the sides. Remember that commercial terrarium tops are not always escape-proof. Pegboard can be used as the top for an aquarium if aluminum glass framing, into which the pegboard can slide, is cut and glued to the top with silicone. Homemade wooden cages are acceptable if they are well sealed so that they can be easily cleaned, and if they have good airflow—i.e., if pegboard is used as part of the cage.

Some types of beddings are problematic and others must be avoided

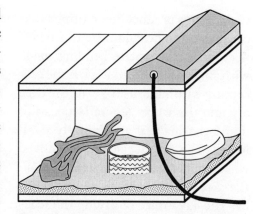

Fig. 6-1. Diagram of general features needed for a cage for garter snakes. Note heavy water bowl and hiding places. Heat source from below is not illustrated.

entirely. Natural soils can be used, but they are hard to clean and can hold so much moisture that humidity in the cage is difficult to control. Rocks or gravel can also harbor moisture, and bacteria buildup may be a problem. Newspaper as flooring is cheap but slick, dusty, and low in absorbency, even in layers. Commercial animal-cage boards designed for use with mammals are expensive, but they are absorbent and can be purchased pretreated with an antibiotic (neomycin) to help control skin irritations. Wood chips work well because they dry out the feces, although the chips can be ingested with wet food.

Care in
Captivity

119

Cedar chips produce toxic fumes that cause neurological damage to snakes. A commercial reptile bedding made with small aspen chips may be the best bedding available, as it keeps the cage dry and the wood generally does not injure the snake if accidentally swallowed. The dry feces can be removed without having to completely clean the cage. Artificial turf is also used and has the advantage of drying the feces and being removable for cleaning. However, it is stiff and has been known to cause skin abrasions on occasion (Burghardt, pers. comm.). Rossi and Rossi (1995) recommend cypress mulch for aquatic snakes, and it may be useful bedding for garter snakes.

Various props are needed in the cage. It should have a water container that is too heavy for the snake to overturn and large enough for the snake to submerge in when it needs to soak prior to shedding. Hiding areas are recommended for garter snakes because they tend to be nervous if exposed. This may make them harder to observe, but some snakes will not eat unless they feel secure. This also suggests that snakes should not be handled frequently, but some arguments have been made for more handling and for habituating the snake to human contact. Large rocks, sticks, or bark look nice and function well as hiding places, but when selecting them, remember they must be cleanable. A cardboard box with a hole cut out can be replaced when it gets fouled, and plastic boxes (food containers or commercial hide boxes) are easy to sanitize. Snakes like the tactile sensation of walls in their hiding places, so use boxes that are only slightly larger than the snake.

One of the factors that greatly improved the success of keeping snakes in captivity was the recognition that thermoregulation was critical to the daily activities of reptiles (see Chaps. 4 and 5 for details). Although some garter snakes occur in very cold climates, the preferred body temperatures for all species are generally around 28 C (see Chap. 5). Snakes also need to be warmer after feeding and when gravid. The best situation therefore is to produce a temperature gradient in the cage from about 72 to 86 F (22 to 30 C). If the room is at least 75 F (24 C), then the container merely needs to have a hot spot. This can be accomplished with commercial reptile heaters (some of the early versions have very hot spots that can cause burns, so it is advisable to check them carefully before use), heat tape (for water pipes), or hot pads placed under part of the tank. Exterior incandescent lights shining on glass can also create small but very hot spots, so use those with care.

HANDLING

Garter snakes tend to be somewhat nervous when first handled, although species and populations vary in their aggressiveness (see chap. 5). Some researchers have attempted to habituate their subjects to handling, while others have studied their garter snakes under conditions of minimal exposure to humans. If held gently with support for the body, most garter snakes do not bite, although most do squirm and sometimes defecate and spray musk. Some species, like *T. marcianus* and *T. cyrtopsis*, tame down and tolerate handling, while others, like *T. proximus*, *T. sauritus*, and *T. melanogaster*, almost always remain nervous and resist handling. For all species, handling probably increases stress and should always be limited before and after feeding. Although not well understood in reptiles, stress can block growth and reproduction and influence immune functions (Guillette et al., 1995).

FEEDING

Garter snakes are one of the easiest snakes to get to eat in captivity, prob-ably because of their extreme dependence on odors to detect prey. Most (the ribbon snakes are the main exceptions) will take earthworms, but unless supplemented with calcium and phosphorus, worms alone are not a good-quality food. Scudder-Davis and Burghardt (1987) found that when these two minerals are added to a diet of worms, good growth can occur. Some bait worms (*Eisenia*, sold as "red wigglers") are toxic, so pieces of the larger night crawlers (*Lumbricus terrestris*) are best for small snakes. If placed in a dish, the food will not pick up floor substrate before it is swallowed. Fish are also satisfactory for almost all species, even those that do not eat them in the wild (e.g., *T. butleri* and *T. brachystoma*). Some fish contain an enzyme that destroys thiamin and causes a deficiency in vitamin B_1. Using dead fish, and denaturing the enzyme by heating the fish first or giving vitamin supplements, takes care of the problem (Rossi and Rossi, 1995). Because fish can carry nematodes, using defrosted frozen prey is best, even if the snakes might feed better on live, moving fish. Although eggs and cysts of parasites can survive freezing, the process seems to prevent parasite transmission.

Garter snakes readily eat amphibians, but many frogs and tadpoles carry parasites, particularly flukes, round-worms, and tapeworms. Again, freezing prey items first and thawing before feeding will reduce the chances of passing parasites to the snake. Feeding amphibians or worms tends to cause the feces to be more liquid. This is not a medical problem, but means the cage must be cleaned frequently. This is one reason why many who keep garter snakes prefer to switch their snakes to eating mice.

Mice produce the best weight gain for amount fed. However, most species of *Thamnophis* do not eat mice readily. By washing a dead newborn or juvenile mouse with soap, rinsing it, and then smearing the mouse with a preferred prey odor, (e.g., that of a frog), you can trick most snakes into eating mice. After several repetitions of this subterfuge, garter snakes usually eat mice without this technique. Some of the aquatic-prey specialists tend to resist switching food preferences. (See Chap. 5.)

The most critical aspect of feeding may be the amount to offer. Garter snakes tend to exhibit individual variability in feeding rates. Some feed consistently, but most eat well one time and then may completely ignore food the next feeding. Therefore it is important to feed them often, preferably twice a week. About 20% of the snake's body weight per week in fish or amphibians should produce a weight gain. A larger quantity of worms may be required, as they contain more water. A diet of mice tends to produce weight gains at only 5 to 10% of body weight each week. The best way to monitor the success of a feeding program is to weigh the snakes on a monthly basis. Even adult snakes should be growing to some degree, so regular gains in weight should occur. Most whole prey have all the vitamins a snake needs, but supplements (particularly of B_1 and calcium) once a month would not hurt.

HYGIENE

Another critical factor for maintaining health in garter snakes is hygiene. Even though recent research suggests that cage odors are important in reducing stress (Chiszar et al., 1995), cages should be cleaned of feces daily. Otherwise, skin infections from fecal bacteria can result. Fresh bedding can be added to replace the soiled bedding. Residual odors are probably sufficient to lend a "personal" nature to the cage. In any case, a short stress period in a clean cage may be preferable to leaving the cage dirty. Depending on the type and amount of food and the type of bedding, the cage will need complete cleaning on a weekly to monthly basis. Organic material in cages can be removed using a detergent. Soap residues must be thoroughly rinsed, as they render disinfectants less effective (Ross and Marzec, 1984). Many authors recommend disinfectants such as Roccal and Nolvasan (Klingenberg, 1993), but others suggest that phenolic disinfectants are more effective against *Pseudomonas* and other gram-negative bacteria that are the likely causes of the few diseases of garter snakes (Ross and Marzec, 1984). Some authors suggest that phenol is toxic to reptiles (Marcus, 1981), but this is debated by others (Ross and Marzec, 1984). A weak bleach solution (10%) is probably a sufficient cleaner in most cases. In any event, cages should be completely rinsed after treatment with any disinfectants. Props and water bowls should be regularly disinfected also.

DISEASES AND TREATMENTS

The best way to deal with diseases in garter snakes is to prevent them from happening in the first place. Most problems can quickly be fatal, and treatments are often prolonged, expensive, and not always successful. Therefore I stress prevention here and will concentrate on what causes diseases. Several good guides offer detailed information on treatment of diseases of snakes (Cooper and Jackson, 1981; Frye, 1991; Hoff et al., 1984; Klingenberg, 1993; Marcus, 1981; Murphy and Collins, 1980; Rossi, 1992), but keep in mind that experimental proof of the effectiveness of most treatments does not exist (Ross and Marzec, 1984).

Some common maladies in captive garter snakes are created by their environmental conditions. As mentioned previously, temperature regulation is important. Without correct body temperatures, snakes often regurgitate food, and pregnant female may produce stillborn young. Cold and fluctuating temperatures can stimulate respiratory infection, which is indicated by wheezing, bubbly mucous secretions from the nose, and elevation of the head. If the problem is detected early, raising the temperature will often correct the situation, but antibiotics may be necessary if the infection is severe (Frye, 1991).

High humidity or a wet cage can cause skin blisters (Rossi, 1992). These subcutaneous pustules may contain mycotic infections (Jacobson, 1980), can lead quickly to septicemia, and often prove fatal to garter snakes.

Other ulcerative sores can occur around the cloaca and between scales if cages are moist and unsanitary. If detected early, this necrotic dermatitis can be treated with polysporin ointment. In severe cases, injections of the aminoglycoside drugs such as amikacin may be needed (Ross and Marzec, 1984). Doses of antibiotics must be calculated correctly, or nephrotoxicity (kidney failure) can occur. Saline injections in combination with antibiotics are often recommended by veterinarians, but the evidence that this prevents kidney failure is not convincing.

Dry conditions can lead to difficulty in shedding. The snake mite, *Ophionyssus natricis*, also can cause shedding problems and decreased appetite. A water bowl large enough for the snake to soak in usually solves a shedding problem, but owners can restrain the animal in a wet cloth bag for 15 to 20 minutes until the skin is soft, and then assist shedding by hand.

Injuries can be treated with topical antiseptics and antibiotics, but mouth injuries can lead to necrotic stomatitis (mouthrot). The bacteria *Aeromonas* and *Pseudomonas* are both associated with this infection of the mouth mucosa (Marcus, 1980). The oral sores interfere with feeding, and the complications of pneumonia and septicemia will kill untreated snakes. The most common form of stomatitis can be treated with polysporin or other polymyxin-containing ointments (Ross and Marzec, 1984). If the situation does not improve rapidly, veterinary treatment with injectable aminoglycoside antibiotics may be necessary.

The snake mite, *Ophionyssus natricis*, is the only ectoparasite that is a common problem in garter snakes. It can be detected as a small moving black dot around the eyes or between the chin shields of the snake. The mites are also easily visible in the water bowl. A small piece (2 sq. cm/10 liter tank) of a dichlorvos insecticide strip will kill the mites within 24 hours. The treatment should be repeated in 10 days when the eggs hatch. Alternatively, a 2% solution of the cattle dip Neguvon can be sprayed in the cage every third day for 9 days.

Some endoparasites can become a problem if live prey is fed to snakes (see section above on feeding). Helminths such as flukes, roundworms, and tapeworms can be detected by fecal exams and treated by feeding the garter snake food injected with a vermicide (Rossi and Rossi, 1995). Often the parasites manifest themselves in cutaneous lumps (sparganosis). Protozoans can cause diarrhea, and metronidazole will cure this situation. The most up-to-date treatments for parasites are given by Klingenberg (1993). For nematodes he suggests Panacur (fenbendazole) at 25 mg/kg orally, once every two weeks for two or three treatments; and for protozoans, Flagyl (metronidazole) at 25 mg/kg orally every two weeks until fecal examinations are negative. Because these parasites require intermediate hosts, most of these difficulties can be prevented by freezing food before feeding. However, be sure that food is completely thawed before giving it to the snake.

CAPTIVE PROPAGATION

Interest in captive propagation has increased as we have seen the decline in wild populations of many species, including snakes. Because garter snakes are one of the easiest snakes for scientists to obtain in quantities, they have served as models to learn about reproduction in snakes. Although other genera may be more commonly bred by the amateur herpetologist, we have developed much of our understanding of the reproductive physiology of North American snakes through laboratory work on *Thamnophis*. A number of laboratory colonies of *T. sirtalis, T. marcianus, T. melanogaster, T. butleri, T. ordi-*

noides, and T. elegans are maintained in various North American universities.

Sexual maturity for *Thamnophis* varies by species, but size may be more important than age (Ford and Seigel, 1994) (see Chap. 4). Females often grow larger than males, and males can be recognized by the presence of hemipenes in the base of the tail. In neonates these can be everted by gentle palpation of the base of the tail (pushing forward toward the cloaca). In adults the hemipenes cause the sides of the base of the tail to be more parallel in males than in females (Fig. 6-2).

The environmental cues that appear to stimulate reproductive behavior for snakes of the northern temperate zones are changes in light cycle and temperature (Whittier et al., 1987). However, fat stores and male courtship activity also may be important (Whittier and Crews, 1986; Whittier and Crews, 1990). For most species of *Thamnophis*, artificially induced hibernation for a minimum of two months (at temperatures of 4 to 10 C for very northern populations, but only 10 to 12 C for southern populations; Holtzman et al., 1989) will place them in condition to reproduce when they are taken out and warmed to normal active body temperatures.

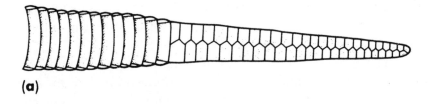

(a)

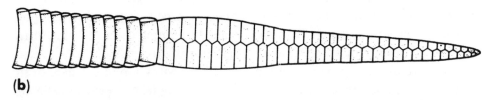

(b)

Fig. 6-2. The tails of (*a*) a female and (*b*) a male garter snake. Note the longer length of the tail and the parallel sides of the area just past the cloaca in the male.

Acclimation does not appear necessary, but the animal's digestive tract should be empty prior to hibernation. With healthy animals, mortality in hibernation is unlikely; however, adequate hydration is critical during hibernation (Costanzo, 1985, 1989b, c), and snakes should have access to large water bowls in which they can submerge. Animals can be individually or communally hibernated, but if sexes are kept separate, mating can be controlled. If the female is receptive and the male interested, courtship should begin within a few minutes to an hour after the animals are paired together.

The timing of courtship after removal from hibernation will vary by species (Ford and Cobb, 1992; Holtzman, et al, 1989), so frequent pairing of individuals is necessary. Microscopic examination of cloacal smears from the female for active spermatozoa is the best way to ensure that mating has actually occurred.

Female garter snakes generally become unreceptive immediately after mating; however, some may mate again several days later. During pregnancy, captive females will continue to feed for some time. Good nutrition is important to the survival of the female after parturition, so she should be well fed during early pregnancy. In the last few weeks before parturition most females will stop eating. They should be kept at their optimal temperature or allowed to thermoregulate; otherwise high incidences of stillbirth will occur. Infrequently, an egg mass or embryo is retained in the uterus after the other young are born. Oxytocin can usually induce its expulsion, but occasionally surgical removal is necessary.

Neonates of several species of *Thamnophis* have been raised in various laboratories in the United States. For example, Gordon Burghardt's laboratory at the University of Tennessee has produced several generations of *T. melanogaster*. Neonates of most species can be started on pieces of nightcrawler (*Lumbricus*) or mosquitofish (*Gambusia*). We have used the tails of frozen bullfrog tadpoles (*Rana catesbeiana*) to start feeding neonate *T. marcianus*, although we later switch them to baby mice for faster growth. Vitamins and minerals, particularly B_1 and calcium, should be dusted on the food periodically. Individuals reach sexual maturity in two to three years if they are fed frequently. Second-generation animals often do much better in captivity.

One problem for captive breeding programs directed toward conservation and recovery of declining populations is whether these laboratory-raised animals or their neonates can be safely and effectively released into the wild (Burghardt and Layne, 1995). At the moment, the conventional wisdom says no, but more work needs to be done in this area.

THE FUTURE

Snakes have always held tremendous interest for humans, but we have lost much of our contact with them in their natural habitat. The growth of the industry involved in captive maintenance of reptiles is a reflection of our need for contact with wild animals. It is heartening to see the improvement in our ability to keep snakes healthy in captivity, but at the same time we should always remember that they really belong in the wild.

Section Three

SPECIES ACCOUNTS

SPECIES ACCOUNTS

Thamnophis atratus
PACIFIC COAST AQUATIC GARTER SNAKE
(Plate 1)

Eutaenia atrata Kennicott *in* Cooper, 1860
    (= *T. a. atratus*)
Eutaenia infernalis vidua Cope, 1892a
    (= *T. a. atratus*)
Thamnophis ordinoides hydrophila Fitch, 1936
    (= *T. a. hydrophilus*)
Thamnophis elegans aquaticus Fox, 1951
    (= *T. a. atratus* × *hydrophilus* intergrades)

Identification

Dorsal scales in a maximum of 19 or 21 rows; supralabials 8 (7th longer than 6th); maxillary teeth 21 to 27; the dorsum gray, brown, dark brown, or black (often with 2 rows of black spots) between the light stripes; the vertebral stripe distinct or indistinct (rarely absent); the lateral stripe—when present—confined to dorsal scale rows 2 and 3.

Content and Distribution

Two subspecies of the Pacific Coast aquatic garter snake are currently recognized: *T. a. atratus*, which ranges from southern Solano Co. and the southern half of the San Francisco Peninsula southward to central Santa Barbara Co., the continuous distribution being interrupted by the Salinas Valley; and *T. a. hydrophilus*, which ranges along the coast from the Gualala River on the Sonoma-Mendocino county line, and on the eastern side of the Coast Ranges from Lake and Yolo counties northward to the Umpqua River Valley in southwestern Oregon (see Map 1). Elevational distribution ranges from 0 to 1920 m (Boundy, pers. comm.)

Description

The following is based on Boundy (in press), Fitch (1940, 1984), Rossman (1979), Rossman and Stewart (1987), and previously unpublished data. *Thamnophis atratus* is a relatively long species of garter snake, reaching a maximum total length of 1016 mm (Boundy, 1990). The color of the dorsum is highly variable; it may be pale gray with two alternating rows of distinct black spots, dark brown with the spots less distinct, or nearly black (and all of these may occur within the same population of *T. a. hydrophilus;*

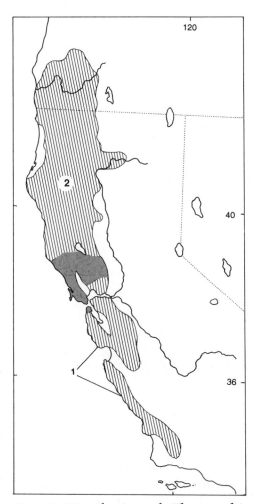

Map 1 Distribution of *Thamnophis atratus* and its subspecies: (1) *T. a. atratus;* (2) *T. a. hydrophilus*. Stippling represents zones of intergradation.

the first color phase is lacking in *T. a. atratus*). The vertebral stripe may be bright yellow or orange and very distinct (both subspecies), indistinct (*T. a. hydrophilus*), or absent (rarely in *T. a. hydrophilus*). The lateral stripe may be bright and distinct (except in some *T. a. atratus*), dull and indistinct (*T. a. hydrophilus*), or lacking altogether (some *T. a. atratus* and some *T. a. hydrophilus*); again, all three stripe conditions may occur within a single population of *T. a. hydrophilus*. The throat is bright yellow in *T. a. atratus*, but not in *T. a. hydrophilus*.

There are 21-21-17, 21-19-17, 19-19-17, or 19-19-15 dorsal scale rows; the occurrence of 21 rows is largely confined to the northern populations of *T. a. hydrophilus* (even there, 21-19-17 is more frequent then 21-21-17), 15 rows to the other subspecies. Ventrals in *T. atratus* range from 145 to 171 in males, 138 to 168 in females; males average 3.0 to 8.6 more ventrals than females. Subcaudals range from 65 to 95 in males, 59 to 84 in females; males average 5.7 to 10.4 more subcaudals than females. Relative tail length ranges from 23.5 to 28.9% in males, 22.1 to 27.4% in females; it averages 1.2 to 2.5% longer in males than in females.

Preoculars usually number 1 to a side (occasionally 2, especially in the Shasta Co., California, population), postoculars 3 (occasionally 4). Maxillary teeth range from 21 to 27, averaging 24.1 in males and 23.2 in females; these data are based on a large series of *T. a. hydrophilus* from Siskiyou Co., California.

The head in *Thamnophis atratus* constitutes 4.9% of SVL—moderate length for a garter snake. The eye is also of moderate size, ED/FL averaging from 63.8 to 66.7%. The tip of the snout is relatively narrow, InR/NR averaging 83.9% in males, 74.1% in females. The muzzle ranges from very long (ML/FL averaging 85.1%) in Shasta Co. to long (74.2%) in the populations in the Coast Ranges west of the Sacramento Valley. The prefrontals are only slightly shorter than the internasals, Prf/In averaging 96.5%. The parietals of *T. atratus* are long, FL/PL averaging 72.1%. The posterior chin shields are of moderate size, ACS/PCS averaging 80.9%.

Taxonomic Comments

As is detailed in the *Thamnophis couchii* account, beginning with Cope (1900) and continuing until just re-

Thamnophis atratus

133

cently, several of the Pacific Coast species of garter snake (including *T. atratus*) were treated either as subspecies or synonyms of the greatly expanded, "catchall" taxa *T. elegans* or *T. ordinoides*. It was only in 1987 that Rossman and Stewart demonstrated that *T. atratus* is a separate species. They also noted that it hybridizes with *T. couchii* in the Pit River system in Shasta Co., California, and with *T. hammondii* at several localities in Santa Barbara and San Luis Obispo counties, California.

Rossman and Stewart (1987) indicated that *T. a. aquaticus* is a weakly differentiated subspecies that apparently represents nothing more than a broad zone of intergradation between *T. a. atratus* and *T. a. hydrophilus*. Boundy (in press) confirmed Rossman and Stewart's conclusion and recommended no longer recognizing *aquaticus* as a separate subspecies.

LIFE HISTORY AND ECOLOGY

Habitat

Thamnophis atratus occurs in dense-canopy oak woodlands, grassy woodland ecotones, and chaparral of the low Transition and high Upper Sono-ran life zones around shallow rocky creeks and swift-flowing streams (Boundy, 1990; Fitch, 1940; Fox, 1951a; Hansen and Tremper, *in prep*). When the species is found near ponds with muddy bottoms, there are generally rocky outcrops in the vicinity. It does seem to require open basking areas along the stream margins. Snakes from the San Francisco Bay Area appear to be somewhat more terrestrial than is *T. hammondii* (Bellemin and Stewart, 1977; Boundy, 1990; Fox, 1951a), although some southern populations apparently are highly aquatic (S. Sweet, pers. comm.).

Activity

In central California this species is active any month of the year, but is most common from April to July, after which it apparently aestivates (Boundy, pers. comm.). Most observations occur in the spring when *T. atratus* is basking and vegetation is low (Hansen and Tremper, *in prep.*). Snakes in the Santa Cruz Mountains appear to be somewhat more active in late summer (Boundy, 1995). This garter snake commonly attempts to escape humans by diving into water and hiding beneath rocks on the bottom (Fitch, 1941b).

Feeding

The foraging behavior of *T. atratus* was studied in detail by Lind and Welsh (1994) in northern California. Foraging mode varied significantly with age; neonates relied mainly on sit-and-wait foraging, whereas adults were mainly active foragers and juveniles used a combination of both behaviors. There was also variation among age classes in terms of habitat use; neonates fed mainly along shallow edgewaters, adults were found in fast-moving water and relatively deep water (0.5 m), and juveniles fed in shallow riffles and edgewaters (Lind and Welsh, 1994).

Although early studies of the diet of *T. atratus* may have accidentally included data on *T. elegans* and *T. couchii*, the primary prey of *T. atratus* appears to consist of the tadpoles of frogs (*Rana*), toads (*Bufo*), small fish (*Cottus* and trout), and aquatic salamanders (*Taricha* and *Dicamptodon*) (Fitch, 1940, 1941b; Fox, 1951a). Plethodontid salamanders (*Aneides lugubris*, *Ensatina*, and *Batrachoseps attenuatus*) have also been taken (J.

Boundy, pers. comm.). Boundy (pers. comm.) observed several *T. atratus* foraging in a stream by anchoring their tails to submerged rocks and lunging at passing minnows. Bellemin and Stewart (1977) suggested that frogs (*Rana aurora* and *Pseudacris regilla*) are more important than fish in the diet of *T. atratus*. Kupferberg (1994) found that large *T. atratus* were capable of eating introduced bullfrog tadpoles in northern California, but suggested that most *T. atratus* were too small to be effective predators on bullfrogs.

Lind and Welsh (1994) reported significant ontogenetic variation in diet, both in terms of feeding frequency and prey type. Neonates had the lowest frequency of full stomachs (18%) and fed primarily on fish and tadpoles. Juveniles also fed mainly on fish and tadpoles, but had a much higher feeding frequency (37%). Adults had an intermediate feeding frequency (20%), but had the broadest diet, feeding on larval and neotenic salamanders and well as fish and tadpoles.

This species differs substantially from other *Thamnophis* in tongue-flick-attack scores used to analyze innate food preferences. It does not re-

Thamnophis atratus

135

spond to worms, leeches, slugs, or mice, but attacks Q-tips scented with extracts from salamanders, frogs, minnows, and goldfish (Burghardt, 1969).

Reproduction

Courtship has been noted from late March to early April (Fitch, 1940). Boundy (pers. comm.) observed mating on 28 March. Fitch (1940) also mentioned the unusual observation of a captive pair courting four days after the female gave birth on 31 August. The offspring are born from late August to mid-October (Burghardt, 1969; Boundy, pers. comm.). Hansen and Tremper (*in prep.*) gave an average clutch size of 7.8 (3 to 12) from five litters from the San Francisco Bay Area, and Boundy (pers. comm.) noted an average clutch size of 8.4 for nine litters. Boundy's neonates ranged from 126 to 166 SVL; one litter from a female from Stanislaus Co. had young measuring 187 to 209 mm in total length (Hansen and Tremper, *in prep.*). Additional data on clutch and offspring size are needed for this species.

Population Biology

Little is known about the population biology of *T. atratus*. Gravid females ranged from 386 to 713 mm SVL (J. Boundy, pers. comm.). The size structure of a population of *T. atratus* from northern California was dominated by small individuals from 150 to 350 mm SVL (Kupferberg, 1994). Based on Boundy's estimates of size at sexual maturity, < 30% of Kupferberg's population would have been composed of adults. D. Rossman (pers. obs.) found a racer (*Coluber constrictor*) attempting to eat an adult *T. atratus*.

Captive Maintenance

Fitch (1940) fed *T. a. hydrophilus* frogs and fish, and *T. a. atratus* lizards and mice. Fox (1951a), however, indicated that *T. a. atratus* would not eat rodents or slugs in the laboratory. Burghardt (1969) found that *T. a. aquaticus* refused worms.

Conservation

This species is not thought to be in jeopardy at this time. The effects of the introduction of bullfrogs (*Rana catesbeiana*) on *T. atratus* is not known at this time (Kupferberg, 1994), but bullfrogs have negatively impacted garter snakes in other areas (see *T. eques* account).

Thamnophis brachystoma
SHORT-HEADED GARTER SNAKE
(Plate 1)

Eutaenia brachystoma Cope, 1892

Identification

Dorsal scales usually in 17 rows throughout (occasionally increasing to 19 at midbody or reducing to 15 anterior to the vent); supralabials usually 6, and infralabials usually 7 or 8; maxillary teeth 17 to 20; the dorsum generally unspotted between the light stripes; the lateral stripe usually confined to rows 2 and 3 (rarely involving row 4).

Content and Distribution

No subspecies of *T. brachystoma* are currently recognized. The short-headed garter snake is known only from northwestern Pennsylvania and adjacent New York (see Map 2) at elevations from 274 to 732 m. An introduced population apparently has been established in Ohio (Novotny, 1990).

Description

The following is based on Barton (1956) and previously unpublished data. *Thamnophis brachystoma* is a short species of garter snake, reaching a maximum total length of 559 mm (Conant, 1958). The dorsum is brown or gray-brown, the stripes yellowish-tan or grayish-tan. The area between the stripes is unspotted, but the stripes frequently have a very narrow black border. The lateral stripes are usually (87% of Barton's sample) confined to dorsal scale rows 2 and 3, but occasionally they may involve the lower edge of row 4.

There are 17-17-17 dorsal scale rows in 76.7% of Barton's series, 17-19-17 in 11.0%, and 17-17-15 in 8.4%. Ventrals range from 134 to 144 in males, 131 to 140 in females; males average 2.7 more ventrals than females. Subcaudals range from 63 to 75 in males, 53 to 64 in females; males average 9.6 more subcaudals than females. Relative tail length ranges from 23.2 to 28.6% in males, 20.3 to 24.5% in females; it averages 3.4% longer in males than in females.

Preoculars number 1 to a side (occasionally 2), postoculars 2 or 3. There normally are 6 supralabials, 7 or 8 infralabials. Maxillary teeth range from 17 to 20, averaging 18.4 in males and 18.2 in females.

The head constitutes 4.3% of SVL

Thamnophis brachystoma

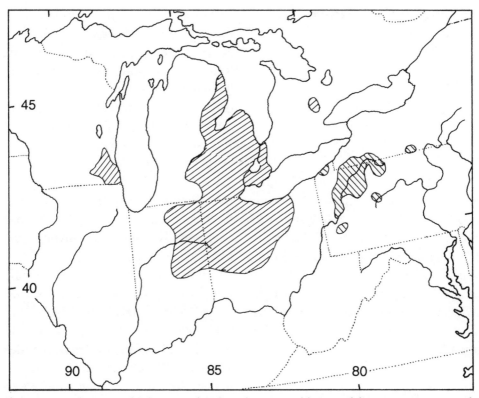

Map 2 Distribution of *Thamnophis brachystoma* (diagonal lines running north-west-southeast) and *T. butleri* (diagonal lines running northeast-southwest).

in adults, which is short for a garter snake. The eye is small, ED/FL averaging 59.0%. The muzzle tip is broad, InR/NR averaging 113.4%. The muzzle is very short, ML/FL averaging 58.5%. The prefrontals are slightly longer than the internasals, Prf/In averaging 106.4%. The parietals of *T. brachystoma* are short, FL/ PL averaging 82.7%. The posterior chin shields are short, ACS/PCS averaging 92.4 percent.

Taxonomic Comments

Within a decade of its description, *T. brachystoma* was relegated to the synonymy of *T. sirtalis* (Brown, 1901).

The short-headed garter snake subsequently was considered to be an eastern population of *T. butleri* (Ruthven, *in* Stone, 1906). Its specific distinctness was not recognized again until A. G. Smith did so in 1945. However, just four years later, Smith (1949) relegated both *brachystoma* and *butleri* to the status of subspecies of *T. radix*. The problem was examined again by Conant (1950), who considered all three taxa to be specifically distinct—a conclusion that was supported by Barton (1956) and has not been challenged since. Barton did point out, however, that the specimens of *T. brachystoma* that most resemble *T. butleri* (in having a maximum of 19 dorsal scale rows, 7 supralabials, and the lateral stripe involving row 4) come from that portion of the range that lies closest to the range of *T. butleri* and therefore, presumably, represents the point of most recent contact.

The short-headed garter snake is the most reduced member of the *radix* species group; *T. radix* occupies the opposite end of the various morphoclines. This reduction can be seen not only in overall adult size, relative head length, and numbers of dorsal scale rows and labials, but also in number of maxillary teeth and the relative diameter of the eye, length of

the parietals, length of the muzzle, and width of the frontal. Many of these characters are undoubtedly correlated.

LIFE HISTORY AND ECOLOGY

Habitat

Thamnophis brachystoma is found within the northern Allegheny Plateau in meadows and old fields with grasses, sedges, low herbaceous growth, and early successional perennials (Bothner, 1986). Like *T. butleri*, it appears to avoid deep woodlands (Bothner, 1976; Ernst and Barbour, 1989; Price, 1978; Wozniak and Bothner, 1966). Typically, individuals are collected under boards, under and around stones or logs, and in clumps of grass, but nearly always in association with creeks, marshes, or streams (Asplund, 1963; Klingener, 1957; Swanson, 1952; Wright and Wright, 1957). Rossman and Richmond (pers. obs.) collected them under rocks on open hillsides adjacent to forests. Two hibernacula in Cattaraugus Co., New York, were on west-facing slopes (Bothner, 1963; Pisani, 1967), and one was located within 20 m of a creek. Known denning associates included *T. sirtalis, Storeria occipitomaculata* (brown snakes), and several species of

Thamnophis brachystoma

139

salamanders (Bothner, 1963; Pisani, 1967). Several introduced colonies exist in urban areas (Bothner, 1976; Conant, 1975).

Feeding

Thamnophis brachystoma is an earthworm specialist; no other prey has been recorded. Average prey mass was about 5% of the snake's body mass (Asplund, 1963). Asplund (1963) found that 55% of his sample had eaten recently, whereas Wozniak and Bothner (1966) found only 25% of their specimens contained prey.

Reproduction

Mating was observed on 17 April near a hibernaculum in New York (Pisani, 1967). One male was observed "chasing" a female for a total distance of about 10 meters over a three-minute period. Pisani and Bothner (1970) found that all mature females examined in April contained motile sperm but found no evidence of fall mating. However, because 25% of the mature females showed no signs of ovulating that year, they concluded that this population had a biennial reproductive cycle. Males produced spermatozoa in the seminiferous tubules of enlarged testes by July and August and stored it over winter in the vas deferens (Pisani and Bothner, 1970). Leydig cell activity (presumably producing testosterone) had peaks both in August and in late March to early April. In the spring, follicles in the 4.0 to 5.0 mm range matured rapidly and were ovulated. Two more potential generations of ova remained. Females store sperm in seminal receptacles, and so the timing of ovulation is not critical to fertilization. It appears to occur in May and early June (Pisani and Bothner, 1970). The distention of the oviduct by the presence of the ova forces sperm out of the seminal receptacles (Fox, 1956). The time of parturition is temperature-dependent; in warmer years it may occur in July but August is more typical.

Data on fecundity are limited. Pisani and Bothner (1970) reported a mean clutch size of 7.2, whereas Swanson (1952, in Ernst and Gotte, 1986) found an average of 7.6. The mean clutch size of nine captive females from New York was 8.8 (Bothner, 1986). Parturition dates for the latter sample were late July and early August. The neonates in Pisani and Bothner's study averaged 99.1 mm SVL for males and 100.4 mm SVL for females.

Population Biology

Both sexes can reach sexual maturity in the second spring following birth—at about 220 mm SVL for males and about 250 mm SVL for females (Pisani and Bothner, 1970), a small size and early age at maturity for garter snakes, especially from northern localities. This species is very abundant in localized habitats. For example, Asplund (1963) suggested his two Pennsylvania populations had at least 200 to 500 individuals. In New York, densities in small areas ranged from 7 to 20/ha (Bothner, 1986).

Captive Maintenance

Asplund (1963) found that this species feeds well in captivity, but not at temperatures < 25 C. As in all snakes that are earthworm specialists, calcium supplements need to be provided. (See Chap. 6.)

Conservation

Dodd (9187) listed this species as one of the few garter snakes in need of conservation and management. Densities of this species are showing declines in areas where *T. sirtalis* is encroaching as abandoned farms become overgrown (Bothner, 1976, 1986).

Thamnophis butleri
BUTLER'S GARTER SNAKE
Plate 1

Eutaenia butleri Cope, 1889

Identification

Dorsal scales in a maximum of 19 rows (reducing to 17 anterior to the vent); supralabials usually 7 or 6 and infralabials usually 8 or 9 on each side of the head; maxillary teeth 19 to 23; dorsum brown to black (two alternating rows of dark spots may be visible in lighter individuals); lateral stripe involving rows 2, 3, and the lower edge of 4 (at least anteriorly); supralabial sutures usually with relatively little black pigment.

Content and Distribution

No subspecies are currently recognized. The continuous range of Butler's garter snake extends from central Ohio and central Indiana northward through eastern Michigan and the extreme southern tip of Ontario at elevations from 152 to 457 m (Wright

Thamnophis butleri

and Wright, 1957). Geographically isolated populations occur in extreme southeastern Wisconsin and the Luther Marsh area in central southern Ontario. (See Map 2.)

Description

The following is based primarily on A. G. Smith (1949) and on previously unpublished data. *Thamnophis butleri* is a moderate-sized garter snake, reaching a maximum total length of 737 mm (Minton, 1972). The dorsum may range from olive-brown or chestnut to black and, at least in the lighter-colored individuals, may have two rows of alternating dark spots between the stripes. The stripes are yellow, the lateral ones always involving rows 2, 3, and the lower edge of 4 (and, rarely, the upper edge of 1)—at least on the anterior part of the body. The venter usually has a row of rounded black spots on each side; occasionally there is also irregular spotting medially.

There are 19-19-17 dorsal scale rows. Ventrals range from 132 to 150 in males, 129 to 151 in females (Minton, 1980, gave a maximum of 154 but did not specify the sex); males average 3.2 to 6.3 more ventrals than do females. Subcaudals range from 57 to 72 in males, 49 to 64 in females (for females the lower extreme is from Ruthven, 1908; the upper extreme from Davis, 1932); males average 6.3 to 9.9 more subcaudals than females. Relative tail length ranges from 21.5 to 28.2% in males, 19.3 to 24.4% in females; it averages 1.6 to 2.9% longer in males than in females.

Preoculars number 1 to a side, postoculars 3 or 2. There normally are 7 or 6 supralabials, 8 or 9 infralabials. Maxillary teeth range from 19 to 23, averaging 21.4 in males and 21.3 in females.

The following data are from the Wisconsin population only. The head constitutes 4.7% of SVL in adults, which is of moderate length for a garter snake. The eye is small, ED/FL averaging 61.4%. The muzzle tip is of moderate width, InR/NR averaging 103.7%. The muzzle is short, ML/FL averaging 64.2%. The prefrontals are longer than the internasals, Prf/In averaging 114.9%. The parietals of *T. butleri* are of moderate length, FL/PL averaging 76.2%. The posterior chin shields are short, ACS/PCS averaging 91.6%.

Taxonomic Comments

A mere four years after its original description, *T. butleri* was considered to be nothing more than a variety of *T. sirtalis* by Boulenger (1893). Almost immediately, Butler's garter snake was restored to the status of a full species by Stejneger (1894). Blanchard (1925) treated *butleri* as a subspecies of *T. radix* in a key to North American snakes, but his action was essentially ignored by subsequent authors until A. G. Smith (1949) reversed his earlier position that *butleri* was a full species (A. G. Smith, 1945) and relegated both *butleri* and *brachystoma* to subspecific status within *T. radix*. Smith's action was immediately countered by Conant (1950), who refuted Smith's alleged evidence of intergradation and treated all three taxa as distinct species. Conant's conclusions have not been challenged seriously since that time, although the possibility of hybridization between *T. butleri* and *T. radix* where their ranges come in contact in southeastern Wisconsin has been suggested by Ford (pers. comm.) and currently is being investigated by D. A. Rossman, Casper, Burghardt, and Good.

It seems clear from both the morphological and biochemical evidence that *T. butleri* is a reduced derivative of *T. radix*, and that it probably was ancestral to *T. brachystoma*.

LIFE HISTORY AND ECOLOGY

Habitat

Butler's garter snake was one of three garter snakes studied extensively near Ann Arbor, Michigan, by Carpenter (1952a). He found that, although Butler's garter snakes were found in the same areas as common garter snakes (*T. sirtalis*) and ribbon snakes (*T. sauritus*), differences in specific habitat preferences were evident. All three species hibernated in dens in grassy pasture, but after hibernation *T. butleri* was confined to thick grass and sedges along the margin of a marsh, where it tended to be found under objects such as rocks, boards, trash, and logs. In contrast to Michigan, Catling and Freedman (1980b) found that *T. butleri* in Ontario was most common in an upland, seasonally dry habitat, and suggested it may be better at withstanding drought than is the common garter snake.

Ford has collected this species in Wisconsin in old house foundations near urban areas. D. A. Rossman collected 23 on 5 April 1955 in an old dump near Waukesha, Wisconsin. Most of the snakes were taken on the south face of a dirt bluff that appeared to be their overwintering site. Others

Thamnophis butleri

143

were basking on piles of bricks or matted grass. In Ohio, Ford has found *T. butleri* to be common in the coastal plains of Lake Erie. It dens in the rocky dikes along with common garter snakes, northern water snakes (*Nerodia sipedon*), and fox snakes (*Elaphe vulpina*).

Activity

The activity period for this species lasts from late March to late September or early October (Wright and Wright, 1957; D. A. Rossman, pers. obs.). Carpenter (1953) found *T. butleri* hibernating in an ant mound at depths of 38 to 80 cm. These snakes emerged over a two-month period from 27 March to 24 May. Carpenter (1956) found a mean cloacal temperature of 26.1 C (range 12.4 to 34.0, N = 24). Soon after hibernation, *T. butleri* moves out to grassy marshes and other foraging sites. It can be very abundant under trash and boards in these areas in the late spring. Seasonal variation in activity is marked; the species is more frequently observed during the day in spring and fall and from sunset until dark only in midsummer (Catling and Freedman, 1980a; Conant, 1938; Logier, 1939).

Carpenter (1952a) reported an average activity range of 3000 m^2 for Butler's garter snake in Michigan. Of 10 *T. butleri* recaptured by Freedman and Catling (1979) in Ontario, only three had moved more than 100 m from the original capture site.

Feeding

As with *T. brachystoma*, most field data indicate that Butler's garter snake has a very restricted diet that consists mainly of earthworms. Carpenter (1952a) documented that *T. butleri* in Michigan begins feeding several weeks after leaving hibernation (by May) and that about 26% have food in the stomach at any given time. This population fed chiefly on earthworms (83%) with leeches as the only other prey taken. Carpenter did find, however, that in the laboratory Butler's garter snake would readily eat toads, red-backed salamanders, small minnows, and some species of small frogs. Insects and spiders were refused and no cannibalism of juveniles was seen. He suggested that amphibians and fish are unavailable to *T. butleri* in the wild because of its habitat preferences. In a study in Ontario, Catling and Freedman (1980a) found that 26 of 27 prey items were earthworms of four species: *Allolobo-*

phora chlorotica, *Aporrectodea trapezoides*, *A. tuberculata*, and *Lumbricus terrestris*. Tests of prey preference by measuring tongue-flick rates of naive young *T. butleri* indicated a strong preference for earthworms, but the snakes also responded to fish and amphibian odors (Burghardt, 1969).

Because this species has not been observed feeding in the wild, whether it captures earthworms by probing earthworm casts in the same fashion as common garter snakes (Gillingham, 1990) is unknown. However, Catling and Freedman (1980a) suggested that Butler's garter snake burrows, and is much faster than the common garter snake in attacking earthworms. They also described an underwater searching for leeches that involves head sweeping similar to the feeding behavior of aquatic *Thamnophis* (Drummond, 1983). The ability of *T. butleri* to handle fish as prey has been compared to both a fish-eating specialist (*T. melanogaster*) and to generalists (*T. sirtalis* and *T. radix*). Butler's garter snakes took significantly longer to ingest fish and were relatively awkward feeders (Halloy and Burghardt, 1990). They tended to drop the fish frequently during the experiment, suggesting that the spe-

cies might not be capable of subduing such prey in the wild.

Reproduction

Courtship has been described by Ruthven (1912) and Finneran (1949), and is apparently quite similar to that of *T. sirtalis* (see Chap. 5). Courtship begins immediately after the snakes exit the hibernacula (Conant, 1938). Males outnumber females at dens and males follow individual females as they leave the site (Finneran, 1949). A pheromone trail is secreted from the females' skin and is species-specific for sympatric *Thamnophis* (i.e., *T. sirtalis*; Ford, 1982). However, *T. butleri* cannot discriminate the pheromone trails of conspecifics from the females of the closely related (but allopatric) *T. radix*.

Near Ann Arbor, Michigan, snakes are gravid by May, and 67% of adult females were gravid in midsummer (Carpenter, 1952a). Mean clutch sizes are remarkably similar throughout much of the range. Examples include 11.0 from Carpenter's (1952a) study site near Ann Arbor, Michigan, 11.4 from southeastern Michigan (Ford and Killebrew, 1983), and 11.9 from Wisconsin (Ford, pers. obs.) The lowest mean clutch size was 8.5 from On-

Thamnophis butleri

145

tario (Freedman and Catling, 1978). As with most garter snakes, larger females have more young (Ford and Killebrew, 1983).

Population Biology

In most localities, *T. butleri* is very common in its preferred habitat. Ford collected 45 adults in two hours in a clumps of grass along the coastline of Lake Erie. Aggregations of up to a half-dozen individuals were also found under boards and other trash. G. S. Casper (pers. obs.) has found this species to be very abundant near Milwaukee, Wisconsin. In marshlands near Toledo, Ohio, Conant (1938) collected 62 in a single day. This species was the most abundant garter snake in Ontario (Catling and Freedman, 1980b). By contrast, Carpenter's 19.4 ha study plot in Michigan was found to hold an estimated 121 Butler's garter snakes (6.2/ha), compared to an estimated 482 common garter snakes and 631 ribbon snakes (Carpenter, 1952a).

Willis et al. (1982) found that 11 to 13% of the *T. butleri* examined exhibited injured tails, suggesting significant predation pressure. However, determining predation rates by using tail-break frequencies has been criticized by Jaksic and Greene (1984). In the field this species generally flees rapidly and rarely exhibits biting or striking.

Captive Maintenance

This species does well in captivity but requires calcium supplements to its diet of earthworms (see Chap. 6). In laboratory experiments *T. butleri* has been found to be much less inclined to strike than is *T. melanogaster* (Herzog and Burghardt, 1986; Herzog et al., 1989, 1992).

Conservation

The species is probably in little danger in most of its range but is considered as "threatened" in Indiana (Allen, 1988). Until the introduction of nonnative earthworms (night crawlers) throughout much of the range of *T. butleri*, this species was probably restricted to marshy habitats where leeches were available. It now is a suburban species, common in moist, grassy areas where trash and rocks occur. Because of its strong association with disturbed habitats, local populations may be decimated quickly by development projects. In addition, Freedman and Catling (1979) found that Butler's garter snakes were reluctant to cross roads, and suggested that populations might become fragmented. Harding (pers. comm.) found that Butler's snake was frequently killed on roads in Michigan, suggesting no reluctance to cross roads.

Comments

A population of Butler's garter snake in Ontario contained a small proportion of melanistic individuals (Catling and Freedman, 1977).

Thamnophis chrysocephalus
GOLDEN-HEADED
GARTER SNAKE
(Plate 2)

Eutaenia chrysocephala Cope, 1885a
Thamnophis eburatus Taylor, 1940

Identification

Dorsal scales usually in a maximum of 17 rows; supralabials usually 8 (occasionally 7); maxillary teeth 26 to 32; the dorsum uniformly black or brown with 4 rows of small, irregular black spots between the lateral stripes; vertebral stripe lacking except occasionally on the neck; the lateral stripe usually confined to dorsal scale row 2; tongue uniformly black.

Content and Distribution

No subspecies are currently recognized. The golden-headed garter snake occurs at relatively high elevations (1219 to 3078 m) in the southern Sierra Madre Oriental in Puebla and Veracruz, the Mesa del Sur in Oaxaca, and the Sierra Madre del Sur in Guerrero (see Map 3).

Description

The following is based primarily on unpublished data. *Thamnophis chrysocephalus* is a moderate-sized species of garter snake, reaching a maximum total length of 692 mm (AMNH 72500).* The dorsum may be brown or uniformly black; if the former, there are two alternating rows of irregular black spots on each side (the latter are more distinct on the neck, and occasionally one or more anterior spots fuse vertically to form bars extending from the paravertebral area to the edge of the ventrals). The venter may be light bluish-gray (in the brown morph) or almost entirely suffused with black pigment (in the black morph). The top of the head is

Thamnophis chrysocephalus

147

brown (often with an orange cast); the supralabials and infralabials are often yellow—as is the skin between the scales in the lowermost 4 or 5 rows on the neck. Supralabial barring is usually reduced or lacking. The vertebral stripe is usually lacking but may be present for a short distance on the neck (however, a faint, discontinuous vertebral stripe does persist in TCWC 9551* from Guerrero). White or gray lateral stripes are usually present, but they may have irregular edges (thus producing a zigzag effect) or be interrupted anteriorly by one or more black bars. The tongue is uniformly black.

There usually are 17-17-15 dorsal scale rows (75% of the 85 specimens examined), but an anterior increase to 19 occurs in 8%, and a posterior reduction to 14 occurs in 14%. Ventrals in *T. chrysocephalus* range from 139 to 154 in males, 135 to 155 in females; there appears to be little, if any, sexual dimorphism, but ventral counts average higher in the Puebla-Veracruz population than in those from either Oaxaca or Guerrero. Subcaudals range from 73 to 87 in males, 69 to 77 in females; males average 4.8 to 7.4 more subcaudals than females. Relative tail length ranges from 24.3 to 27.7% in males, 23.2 to 26.4% in females; it averages 1.0 to 1.5% longer in males than in females. The tail is proportionally shorter in the Puebla-Veracruz population than in those from either Oaxaca or Guerrero.

Preoculars number 1 to a side, postoculars usually 3 (occasionally 4 or 2). There usually are 8 supralabials to side (occasionally 7, rarely 9). Maxillary teeth range from 26 to 32, averaging 29.8 in males and 27.5 in females.

The head in *Thamnophis chrysocephalus* constitutes 4.8% of SVL, which is of moderate length for a garter snake. The eye is large, ED/FL averaging 73.9%. The muzzle tip is of moderate width, InR/NR contact averaging 104.8%. The muzzle is of moderate length, ML/FL averaging 68.5%. The prefrontals are much shorter than the internasals, Prf/In averaging 82.3%. The parietals of *T. chrysocephalus* are short, FL/PL averaging 82.2%. The posterior chin shields are of moderate length, ACS/PCS averaging 88.5%.

Taxonomic Comments

Taylor (1940) described the black morph as a separate species, *T. eburatus*, but H. M. Smith (1942) correctly

---

*AMNH 72500 and TCWC 9551 are museum catalogue numbers designating specific individual specimens. The museum acronyms used in these and other references to specific specimens follow those listed by Leviton et al. (1985).

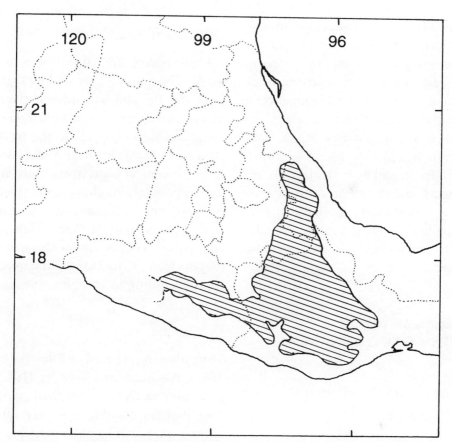

Map 3 Distribution of *Thamnophis chrysocephalus*. Open area at western end of range indicates uncertainty about actual limits.

pointed out that it is a color phase of *T. chrysocephalus*. Nonetheless, the name *eburatus* (type locality: Cerro San Felipe, Oaxaca) remains available for the Oaxaca and Guerrero populations should they prove to be subspecifically distinct from the nominate Puebla-Veracruz population (type locality of *T. chrysocephalus:* Orizaba, Veracruz).

LIFE HISTORY AND ECOLOGY

Virtually nothing is known about the ecology of this relatively rare garter snake. Watkins field notes (in the

Thamnophis chrysocephalus

149

Kansas University collection) include "collected at night, swimming in slow-moving portion of stream," "several meters from a stream in afternoon," "near small aqueduct in pine oak forest," and "crossing dirt road on cloudy, cool day." D. A. Rossman (pers. obs.) has found *T. chrysocephalus* in and near small pools and streams, and he saw an adult foraging on the bottom of a shallow pool. Individuals in the process of shedding were found under rocks near the water.

Thamnophis couchii
SIERRA GARTER SNAKE
(Plate 2)

Eutaenia couchii Kennicott, 1859

Identification

Dorsal scales usually in a maximum of 21 rows; supralabials 8 (6th longer than 7th); maxillary teeth 23 to 27; the dorsum olive-brown to very dark brown or black with two alternating rows of black spots between the light stripes; the vertebral stripe indistinct or absent except on neck; the lateral stripe—when present—confined to dorsal scale rows 2 and 3.

Content and Distribution

No subspecies are currently recognized. The Sierra garter snake ranges from the Pit and Sacramento rivers in north-central California southward along the Sierra Nevada to the western end of the Tehachapi Mountains in south-central California; there are outlier populations along major rivers in west-central Nevada and Owens Valley, California (see Map 4). The Sierra garter snake occurs at elevations ranging from 91 to 2438 m (the upper limit according to Stebbins, 1985).

Description

The following is based on Fitch (1940, 1984), Rossman and Stewart (1987), and previously unpublished data. *Thamnophis couchii* is a very long species of garter snake, reaching a maximum snout-vent length of 957 mm (tail incomplete on largest individual, LSUMZ 55661). The dorsum is olive-brown or grayish-brown, often so dark as to obscure the two alternating rows of black spots that lie between the stripes (most individuals in the population in Plum Creek, Tehama Co., California, are totally melanistic). The vertebral stripe may be yellow and distinct on the neck, but usually it is indistinct or lacking thereafter. The lateral stripe may be bright and distinct or lacking altogether (especially in the streams draining into the Sacramento River in north-central California). Northern *T. couchii* have extensive black mottling or marbling on the labials, chin shields, and venter; the black pigment is reduced in the central portion of the range, and the southern populations lack it altogether. The black nuchal blotches are elongated.

There are 21-21-17 dorsal scale rows in most individuals, but occasionally there are 23 at the neck or 19 at midbody (the latter condition is most common at the southern end of the range). Ventrals in *T. couchii* range from 166 to 187 in males, 161 to 178 in females; males average 2.7 to 5.8 more ventrals than females. Subcaudals range from 79 to 99 in males, 68 to 91 in females; males average 12.3 to 13.6 more subcaudals than females. Relative tail length ranges from 22.1 to 27.5% in males, 20.6 to 25.4% in females; it averages 1.8 to 2.5% longer in males than in females.

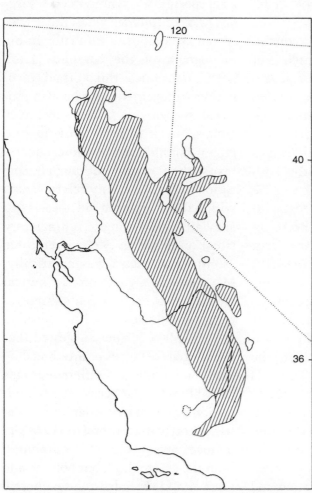

Map 4 Distribution of *Thamnophis couchii*.

Thamnophis couchii

151

Preoculars usually number 1 to a side (occasionally 2, especially in the northern populations), postoculars 3 (occasionally 2, rarely 4). Maxillary teeth range from 23 to 27, averaging 25.6 in males and 24.8 in females.

The head in *Thamnophis couchii* constitutes 4.9% of SVL, which is of moderate length for a garter snake. The eye is of moderate size, ED/FL averaging 64.6% in the northern populations, 68.5% in the southern populations. The tip of the muzzle is narrow, although the degree varies both sexually (the muzzle tip is 7 to 20% narrower in females) and geographically. For example, on a north-to-south axis, InR/NR averages from 64.6 to 87.6% in males, 44.2 to 81.1% in females. The muzzle is long, ML/FL averaging 77.8%. The prefrontals are shorter than the internasals, Prf/In averaging 72.0% in the northern populations and 84.9% in the southern populations. The parietals of *T. couchii* are of moderate length, FL/PL averaging 78.3%. The posterior chin shields are shorter than the anterior ones in the Pit River drainage (ACS/PCS = 104.9%), slightly longer (96.2%) in the Sacramento Valley, and substantially longer (85.4%) in the southern populations.

Taxonomic Comments

Beginning with Cope (1900), and for many years thereafter, the Sierra garter snake was considered to be either a subspecies or a synonym of *T. elegans* or *T. ordinoides* when those taxa served as composite catchalls. In his monograph of the complex, Fitch (1940) continued this formal taxonomic arrangement, but he also proposed recognizing three subspecies groups, one of which (the *hydrophila* group) comprised the more aquatic taxa such as *couchii*. Although Fitch's action helped to clarify relationships within the complex, it did not serve to alleviate the seemingly contradictory situation in which two or even three "subspecies" occurred sympatrically. Mayr (1942) argued on theoretical grounds that each of the subspecies groups should be treated as a separate species. Mayr further suggested that the alleged instances of interbreeding between members of different groups probably reflected occasional hybridization rather than regular intergradation. Shortly thereafter, Fox (1948) did remove one taxon (*T. ordinoides*) from the assemblage, but both he and Fitch (1948) defended the taxonomic treatment of the remaining forms as members of a single species (*T. eleg-*

ans). Savage (1960), without presenting any data, treated *T. elegans* and *T. couchii* as separate species, and Mayr (1963) reiterated his earlier arguments to support such an action. Preliminary supporting data were presented in two grant reports to the American Philosophical Society (Rossman, 1964; Fox and Dessauer, 1965), but it was not until 1979 that detailed morphological (Rossman) and biochemical (Lawson and Dessauer) evidence was published. Subsequently, Rossman and Stewart (1987) demonstrated that *T. couchii* itself was a composite of four distinct species: *atratus, couchii, gigas,* and *hammondii.* They noted that *T. couchii* hybridizes at low frequency with *T. atratus* in the Pit River drainage and with *T. hammondii* at the western end of the Tehachapi crest.

LIFE HISTORY AND ECOLOGY

Habitat

This highly aquatic garter snake appears to occupy a variety of habitats as long as the area is associated with water (Fitch, 1940). *Thamnophis couchii* ranges from low-elevation seasonal creeks up to rapid-flowing mountain rivers, high-elevation meadow ponds, small lakes, and even reservoirs (Hansen and Tremper, *in prep.*). It tends to prefer streams with rocky beds (Fitch, 1940). *Thamnophis couchii* occurs in oak woodlands, grassy valleys, chaparral, and montane conifer forests. In foothill streams, the vegetation associated with this species includes willows, cottonwoods, sycamores, rushes, sedges, and grasses (Hansen and Tremper, *in prep.*). In the Transition Life Zone of the northern Sierra Nevada the forest is predominantly white fir, Douglas fir, incense cedar, and black oak (Fitch, 1940). At higher elevation sites, alders also occur in association with this species.

Activity

This species is more likely than most other garter snakes to be actually found in the water. Individuals were seen to bask in the morning in protected areas, such as tall grass (G. Stewart and D. A. Rossman, pers. obs.). After warming up, individuals moved to the water to forage. The dark dorsal color of *T. couchii* may allow rapid warming, which could be adaptive because the streams it occupies are often cold. At ponds or stream sites this snake may bask along the

Thamnophis couchii

153

water's edge in the spring, but in summer it is often found lying in shallow water or on mats of floating vegetation.

At lower elevations, *T. couchii* may be active for 10 months of the year, but it becomes difficult to find in midsummer when surface water may disappear in ephemeral creeks (Fitch, 1949). High-elevation populations have an active season as short as 3 to 3.5 months (Hansen and Tremper, *in prep.*).

Feeding

Thamnophis couchii feeds in ephemeral habitats on anuran and salamander larvae and newly transformed adult amphibians (Fitch, 1949). In permanent streams it predominantly eats fish, including trout, Sacramento suckers, and mosquitofish. It forages in the slower-moving water of streams or quiet side pools (Hansen and Tremper, *in prep.*). *Thamnophis couchii* is capable of slowly crawling along the bottom of stream (due to its negative buoyancy) and searching for prey among submerged leaf litter, in clumps of aquatic vegetation, and around rocks. This species can take extremely large prey, which it typically drags up to the shore to swallow.

Reproduction

Courtship has not been documented in this species. Clutch size varies from 5 to 38 (Hansen and Tremper, *in prep.*). An aggregation of four gravid females was found under a slab of bark on 7 August along the Tule River at 1249 m (Hansen and Tremper, *in prep.*). Fitch (1949) suggested that the young of *T. couchii* are born in late July, which is somewhat earlier than other garter snakes in the area. Hansen and Tremper (*in prep.*) found offspring born between late July and September in the foothills, and from late August through late September at higher elevations.

Population Biology

Hansen and Tremper (*in prep.*) suggested that at lower elevations this species may become sexually mature at 32 to 44 months of age. Red-tailed hawks have been documented to prey on this species of garter snake (Fitch, 1949).

Captive Maintenance

As with other *Thamnophis* that spend their time in exposed streamside sites, *T. couchii* is bad-tempered, always quick to strike and bite (H. Fitch, pers. comm.). Specimens we kept ate tadpoles and fish readily, but not mice even when scented with fish odors. If live food is placed in a water bowl *T. couchii* utilizes the head-swaying foraging technique typical of aquatic snakes.

Conservation

Populations are not thought to be in serious jeopardy, but some populations may be declining as a result of introduction of nonnative fish into streams in California (Seigel and Ford, pers. obs.).

Thamnophis cyrtopsis
BLACK-NECKED
GARTER SNAKE
(Plates 2 and 3)

Eutaenia cyrtopsis Kennicott, 1860
   (= *T. c. cyrtopsis*)
Thamnophis cyrtopsis cyclides Cope, 1861c
   (= *T. c. cyrtopsis*)
Tropidonotus (Eutainia) collaris Jan, 1863
   (= *T. c. collaris*)
Eutaenia cyrtopsis ocellata Cope, 1880
   (= *T. c. ocellatus*)
Eutaenia aurata Cope, 1892b
   (= *T. c. cyrtopsis*)
Thamnophis vicinus H. M. Smith, 1942
   (= *T. c. collaris*)

Thamnophis sumichrasti salvini H. M. Smith, Nixon, and P. W. Smith, 1950
   (= *T. c. collaris*)

Identification

Dorsal scales in a maximum of 19 rows; supralabials usually 8; maxillary teeth 21–29; the dorsum either spotted or uniformly dark between the light stripes; the lateral stripe (when present) either confined to rows 2 and 3 or involving rows 1 to 3; small dark spots usually present below the lateral stripe; throat cream or white.

Content and Distribution

Three subspecies of the black-necked garter snake are currently recognized: *T. c. cyrtopsis*, which ranges from southeastern Utah and southern Colorado southward through most of Sonora, the Sierra Madre Occidental, and the Mexican Plateau as far east as northern Hidalgo; *T. c. collaris*, which ranges from southern Sonora southeastward through western and southern Mexico to west-central Guatemala; and *T. c. ocellatus* which presumably is confined to the Edwards Plateau of central Texas (see Map 5). Intergrades between *T. c. cyr-*

Thamnophis cyrtopsis

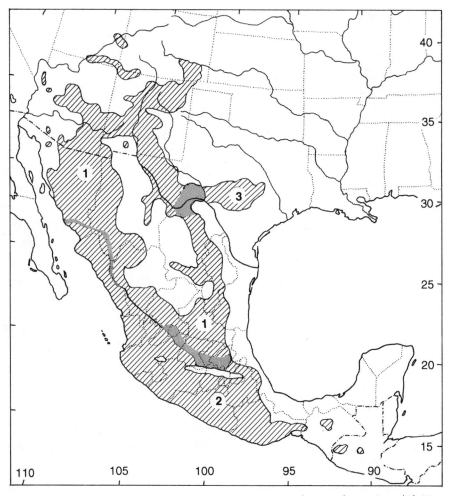

Map 5 Distribution of *Thamnophis cyrtopsis* and its subspecies: (1) *T. c. cyrtopsis*; (2) *T. c. collaris*; (3) *T. c. ocellatus*. Stippling represents zones of intergradation.

topsis and *T. c. collaris* have been reported by Webb (1966), and between *T. c. cyrtopsis* and *T. c. ocellatus* by Milstead (1953). Elevational distribution ranges from 0 to 2700 m (Stebbins, 1985).

Description

The following is based on Milstead (1953), Webb (1966, 1978, 1982), and previously unpublished data. *Thamnophis cyrtopsis* is a relatively long species of garter snake, reaching a maximum total length of 1144 mm (UTA R-4036). The dorsum is gray-brown to very dark brown with two rows of large, alternating black spots (more than 1 scale in length) between the light stripes, which may or may not contrast markedly with the dorsal ground color. The spots may not be readily visible in darker specimens of *T. c. cyrtopsis*, and they are fused into single large blotches on either side of the neck in *T. c. ocellatus* and some specimens of *T. c. collaris* from Michoacán. The lateral stripe is confined to rows 2 and 3 in *T. c. cyrtopsis* and *T. c. ocellatus* (although the stripe is usually scalloped anteriorly in the latter), but in *T. c. collaris* the stripe often involves rows 1 to 3 and may not contrast greatly with the dorsal ground color (apparently being entirely absent in some instances, although this may be difficult to determine with certainty in preserved specimens). The vertebral stripe may be very distinct in all three races or faint to absent in some *T. c. collaris*. The vertebral stripe completely interrupts the nuchal collar in most *T. c. cyrtopsis* and *T. c. ocellatus*, but never does so in *T. c. collaris*. The supralabial sutures are black-barred in all three races, more prominently so in *T. c. cyrtopsis* and *T. c. ocellatus*. Most infralabial sutures usually are also barred in those two subspecies, but in *T. c. collaris* there is either no barring or only the suture between the last two infralabials is barred.

There are 19-19-17 dorsal scale rows. Ventrals in *T. c. cyrtopsis* range from 167 to 179 in males, 163 to 175 in females; in *T. c. collaris* from 148 to 166 in males, 144 to 159 in females; and in *T. c. ocellatus* from 157 to 164 in males, 148 to 165 in females (the values for *ocellatus* are from Milstead [1953], who undoubtedly did not use the Dowling method in making these counts). Males average 3.1 to 3.7 more ventrals than females. Subcaudals in *T. c. cyrtopsis* and *T. c. collaris* range from 86 to 100 in males, 75 to 101 in females; in *T. c. ocellatus* from 73 to 91 in males, 63 to 76 in females. Males average 6.6 to 9.6 more subcaudals

Thamnophis cyrtopsis

than females. Relative tail length in *T. c. cyrtopsis* ranges from 23.3 to 26.8% in males, 22.5 to 26.1% in females; in *T. c. collaris* from 26.4 to 29.6% in males, 25.2 to 30.4% in females (no data are currently available for *T. c. ocellatus*). Relative tail length averages 1.1 to 1.3% longer in males than in females.

Preoculars number 1 to a side, postoculars usually 3 (frequently 4, rarely 2). There normally are 8 supralabials to a side (rarely 7) and 10 infralabials (rarely 9 or 11). Maxillary teeth range from 21 to 29, averaging 24.0 (*T. c. cyrtopsis*), 24.4 (*T. c. ocellatus*), and 27.3 (*T. c. collaris*) in males; 22.9 (*T. c. cyrtopsis*), 22.8 (*T. c. ocellatus*), and 26.2 (*T. c. collaris*) in females.

Head proportion data are not currently available for *T. c. ocellatus*. The head in *T. c. cyrtopsis* constitutes 4.5% of SVL in males, 4.9% in females; in *T. c. collaris* it is 4.9% in males, 5.4% in females. The eye is large, ED/FL averaging 72.9%. Relative muzzle tip width is markedly divergent, InR/NR averaging 113.4% in *T. c. cyrtopsis* and 81.9% in *T. c. collaris*. The muzzle is long, ML/FL averaging 74.9%. The prefrontals are shorter than the internasals, Prf/In averaging 91.4%. The parietals of *T. cyrtopsis* are of moderate length, FL/PL averaging 81.4%. The posterior chin shields are of moderate length, ACS/PCS averaging 79.8%.

Taxonomic Comments

The black-necked garter snake has undergone a very tortuous nomenclatural history. Boulenger (1893) incorrectly associated the species with the name *eques*, an action that was not questioned until H. M. Smith (1951) demonstrated that the holotype of *T. eques* was, in fact, not a black-necked garter snake at all but represented the species that had been known as *T. macrostemma* (and, briefly, *T. subcarinata*; H. M. Smith, 1949) for the first half of the 20th century. The dust had barely settled on the reassociation of the name *T. cyrtopsis* with the black-necked garter snake, when Fitch and Milstead (1961) concluded that the Baird and Girard (1853) name *Eutainia dorsalis* applied to this species and, being older, took precedence. However, Rossman (1962b) and Webb (1966) presented evidence that the name *dorsalis* is more properly associated with the subspecies of *T. sirtalis* living in the Rio Grande valley in New Mexico, so *T. cyrtopsis* continues to be the name of the black-necked garter snake.

The taxonomic history has been no less confusing. After the early period of "lumping" in which only a single wide-ranging taxon was recognized (Boulenger, 1893; Ruthven, 1908), H. M. Smith (1942, 1951) proposed that *T. cyrtopsis* comprised a northern race (*T. c. cyrtopsis*), a southern race (*T. c. cyclides*), and a highly restricted race in the Telpalcatepec Valley of Michoacán (*T. c. postremus*). At the same time, H. M. Smith (1942) characterized another species (which he called *T. sumichrasti*) from the trans-Isthmian lowlands of Mexico and Central America and from the highlands of Chiapas and Guatemala as belonging to the same species group and having shared a common ancestry. He recognized *T. sumichrasti* as having four subspecies (*sumichrasti, praeocularis, cerebrosus, fulvus*). Bogert and Oliver (1945) argued that *T. sumichrasti* undoubtedly was conspecific with the black-necked garter snake, a view followed by Milstead (1953), who also lumped all of the trans-Isthmian forms recognized by Smith (as well as the subsequently described *T. sumichrasti salvini;* H. M. Smith, Nixon, and P. W. Smith, 1950) into his *T. cyrtopsis sumichrasti*. Stuart (1954) did not accept this blanket lumping and recognized the population in the Chiapas-Guatemala highlands as *T. c. fulvus*.

Duellman (1961) resurrected Smith's *T. c. postremus*, but relegated his *T. vicinus* to the synonymy of *T. c. cyclides*. Rossman (1965a) demonstrated that the name *sumichrasti* is properly applied to an entirely different species from the Sierra Madre Oriental of Mexico; later (1971) he showed that the material from the lowlands of trans-Isthmian Mexico and Central America that had been called *T. cyrtopsis sumichrasti* actually represented two subspecies of *T. marcianus*.

Meanwhile, Webb (1966) examined the holotype of *T. cyrtopsis cyclides* and discovered that it had come from Arizona and was a normal representative of the northern *T. c. cyrtopsis;* hence he synonymized the name *cyclides* with the latter and resurrected *T. c. collaris* for the widespread southern subspecies of the black-necked garter snake. At the same time he also revived the name *T. c. pulchrilatus* for a distinctive montane form he believed to intergrade with both *T. c. cyrtopsis* and *T. c. collaris*. Webb followed Duellman (1961) in considering *T. c. vicinus* to be a synonym of *T. c. collaris*, but later (Webb, 1978) he recognized it as a distinct species, although acknowledging its close relationship to *T. c. collaris*.

Rossman (1992a) provided evidence

Thamnophis cyrtopsis

for the full species status of both *T. postremus* and *T. pulchrilatus*, and later (Rossman, 1996) he reexamined the *T. vicinus* question and concluded that *vicinus* was nothing more than a pattern morph of *T. c. collaris*.

Webb (1982) demonstrated that *T. fulvus* is a distinct species and that its range overlaps that of *T. c. collaris* in Chiapas and Guatemala. He suggested a possible relationship between *T. fulvus* and *T. sumichrasti*, a suggestion rejected by Rossman (1992a). Webb (1982) also synonymized *T. sumichrasti salvini* with *T. c. collaris*, and *T. sumichrasti cerebrosus* with *T. marcianus* (the latter action was rejected by Rossman, 1991, who concluded that whatever *cerebrosus* might prove to be—and its identity is still uncertain—it is not *T. marcianus*).

LIFE HISTORY AND ECOLOGY

Habitat

Thamnophis cyrtopsis is strongly associated with streams in canyons, highland plateaus, and mountains (Milstead, 1953; Woodlin, 1950). In Mexico, *T. c. cyrtopsis* is a plateau form that is replaced in highland areas by *T. pulchrilatus* and in lowland and tropical areas by *T. c. collaris* (Webb, 1966). *Thamnophis c. collaris* occurs on the western coast of Mexico, in lowland tropical barrancas in the Sierra Madre, in thorny scrub forest, in tropical deciduous forest, and in upper arid or mixed boreal–tropical cloud forest up to at least 2378 m. In the southwestern United States, *T. c. cyrtopsis* is a canyon species of the desert mountain ranges. *Thamnophis c. ocellatus* is found on rocky hillsides and limestone ledges, and in wooded ravines and cedar brakes of the Texas Hill Country (Milstead, 1953; Tennant, 1984). In desert streams in western Arizona, Jones (1990) found that this species occupied both running water and pools in the spring but favored still water in summer. These snakes used tree roots and vegetative debris as overnight retreats. Jones observed four adults in the desert as far as 0.5 km from aquatic habitats.

Activity

The activity season of the black-necked garter snake is shorter than that of many other south-temperate *Thamnophis*. At most localities, it probably emerges in March or April and enters hibernation sites in September (Wright and Wright, 1957). In the spring snakes are found most often basking along stream banks (Jones, 1990). In the summer this snake becomes more aquatic and is most commonly encountered floating in larger pools. The mean cloacal temperature for snakes in New Mexico was 26.7 C (range 22.0 to 32.0, $N = 47$) (Fleharty, 1967).

Feeding

The diet of the black-necked garter snake has been studied quantitatively at three sites. All showed that *T. cyrtopsis* is mainly an amphibian specialist in aquatic habitats. Of 40 snakes with prey in Fouquette's (1954) study in central Texas, 39 had eaten amphibians and one had eaten a skink (*Scincella*). The amphibians were primarily tadpoles and adult anurans (*Hyla arenicolor, Gastrophryne olivacea, Bufo, Scaphiopus, Rana,* and *Syrrhophus marnocki*). Only two salamanders, both *Plethodon glutinosus*, were eaten. In Jones's (1990) study in Arizona, adult *T. cyrtopsis* shifted from steam banks to pools and used active searching to locate prey in the spring but switched to ambush behavior in the summer. Snakes floated in algae mats and captured *Rana yavapaiensis* and *Hyla arenicolor* as these frogs swam by. The diet was correlated with the abundance and vulnerability of the frogs. Of 29 feeding attempts, 17 successful captures occurred. When frogs were missed, *T. cyrtopsis* pursued them but only 1 of 13 was caught. Newborn snakes fed in landlocked pools on fish and tadpoles, which they caught while floating in algae patches (24 captures of 59 attempts). Fleharty (1967) found that *T. cyrtopsis* fed entirely on amphibians (*Rana catesbeiana*) in New Mexico. Thirty-three percent of his specimens contained recently ingested prey.

Fleharty (1967) indicated that *T. cyrtopsis* has a lower specific gravity than *T. elegans* or *T. rufipunctatus* and suggested that floating semi-submerged may be an important foraging strategy for the species.

Reproduction

Surprisingly little is known about the reproductive biology of this species. Jones (1990) reported four broods born from 29 June to 19 July. Females gave birth in landlocked pools and brood sizes ranged from 14 to 22 (mean = 19).

Captive Maintenance

Fouquette (1954) found that in captivity this species readily ate larval or

Thamnophis cyrtopsis

161

adult amphibians as well as any small fish.

Thamnophis elegans
Western Terrestrial Garter Snake
(Plates 3 and 4)

Eutainia elegans Baird and Girard, 1853
  (=*T. e. elegans*)
Eutainia vagrans Baird and Girard, 1853
  (= *T. e. vagrans*)
Tropidonotus trivittatus Hallowell, 1853
  (= *T. e. elegans*)
Eutaenia biscutata Cope, 1883b
  (= *T. e. elegans* × *vagrans*
    intergrades
Eutaenia vagrans plutonia Yarrow, 1883
  (= *T. e. vagrans*)
Eutaenia henshawi Yarrow, 1883
  (= *T. e. vagrans*)
Eutaenia elegans lineolata Cope, 1892b
  (= *T. e. elegans*)
Eutaenia elegans brunnea Cope, 1892b
  (= *T. e. elegans* × *vagrans*
    intergrades
Thamnophis ordinoides hueyi Van
  Denburgh and Slevin, 1923
    (= *T. e. hueyi*)
Thamnophis elegans nigrescens Johnson,
  1947
    (= *T. e. vagrans*)
Thamnophis elegans terrestris Fox,
  1951a
    (= *T. e. terrestris*)
Thamnophis elegans arizonae Tanner and
  Lowe, 1989
    (= *T. e. arizonae*)

Thamnophis elegans vascotanneri Tanner
  and Lowe, 1989
    (= *T. e. vascotanneri*)

Identification

Dorsal scales usually in a maximum of 19 or 21 rows; supralabials usually 8 (occasionally 7); maxillary teeth 14 to 24; the dorsum uniformly black to brown, red, or gray with 2 alternating rows of black spots between the stripes; vertebral stripe from 3 rows wide to lacking altogether; the lateral stripe distinct or indistinct and confined to dorsal scale rows 2 and 3.

Content and Distribution

Six subspecies of the western terrestrial garter snake are currently recognized: *T. e. elegans*, which ranges from central California (exclusive of the outer Coast Ranges) northward to southwestern Oregon (an isolated population occurs in the San Bernardino Mountains of southern California); *T. e. terrestris*, which occupies the outer Coast Ranges from Curry Co., Oregon, southward to Ventura Co., California; *T. e. vagrans*, which ranges from British Columbia, Alberta, and southwestern Saskatchewan southward to Nevada, central

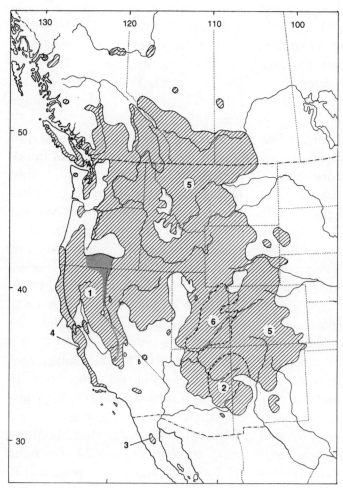

Arizona, and New Mexico; *T. e. arizonae*, which occurs in eastern Arizona (Apache and Navajo counties) and western New Mexico (Catron and McKinley counties); *T. e. vascotanneri*, which occurs in the Colorado and Green river drainages of eastern Utah; and *T. e. hueyi*, which is confined to the Sierra San Pedro Mártir in Baja California (see Map 6). Elevational distribution ranges from 0 to 3990 m (Stebbins, 1985), the second-highest elevation reached by any garter snake.

Map 6 Distribution of *Thamnophis elegans* and its subspecies: (1) *T. e. elegans*; (2) *T. e. arizonae*; (3) *T. e. hueyi*; (4) *T. e. terrestris*; (5) *T. e. vagrans*; (6) *T. e. vascotanneri*. Stippling represents zones of intergradation.

Distribution

The following is based largely on Bellemin and Stewart (1977), Fitch (1940, 1983), Rossman (1979), Tanner and Lowe (1989), and previously unpublished data. *Thamnophis elegans* is a relatively long species of garter

Thamnophis elegans

snake, reaching a maximum total length of 1070 mm (Stebbins, 1985). Between the stripes the dorsum is black in *T. e. elegans,* some southern *T. e. terrestris,* and *T. e. vagrans* from western Washington and adjacent British Columbia; dark olive or gray-brown in *T. e. hueyi* and the San Bernardino Mountains *T. e. elegans;* olive or reddish-brown in northern *T. e. terrestris* (the skin between the scales may also be red); and light grayish-brown or gray in most *T. e. vagrans, T. e. arizonae,* and *T. e. vascotanneri.* Except in those snakes having a black or very dark brown dorsum, two alternating rows of black spots usually are visible, although they vary considerably in how well they are developed. The lateral stripe usually is distinct (but may be indistinct in some *T. e. vagrans, T. e. arizonae,* and *T. e. vascotanneri*) and some shade of yellow (it may contain red pigment in some *T. e. terrestris*). The vertebral stripe may be broad (up to 3 scales wide in *T. e. arizonae*), narrow, or lacking altogether (in most *T. e. vascotanneri*), and some shade of yellow, orange-yellow, tan, or dull white, often indented (*T. e. vagrans, T. e. arizonae*) or even interrupted (*T. e. vascotanneri*) by the upper row of dorsal spots. There often is considerable black flecking irregu-

larly distributed or concentrated medially on the venter in *T. e. vagrans;* red flecking occurs in *T. e. terrestris.*

There usually are 21-21-17 or 19-21-17, rarely 19-19-17, dorsal scale rows. Ventrals in *T. elegans* range from 149 to 185 in males, 137 to 177 in females; males average about 3 to 6 more ventrals than females (more precise data are not available). Subcaudals range from 76 to 101 in males, 64 to 91 in females; males average about 2 to 11 more subcaudals than females (more precise data are not available). Relative tail length ranges from 23.8 to 27.6% in males, 21.9 to 26.5% in females; it averages 1.8% longer in males than in females.

Preoculars usually number 1 to a side (frequently 2), postoculars usually 3 (occasionally 4). There usually are 8 supralabials, occasionally 7 (especially in *T. e. hueyi* and the Alberta population of *T. e. vagrans*). Maxillary teeth range from 14 to 24, averaging 17.7 in male and 16.9 in female *T. e. elegans* from northern California and adjacent Oregon. There is geographic variation in this feature, with the counts in *T. e. elegans* × *vagrans* intergrades from northeastern California and adjacent Oregon and Nevada averaging 21.3 in males, 20.9 in females. Scattered samples of *T. elegans* from Arizona, New Mexico, Colorado, Utah, southern Nevada, and east-central California have modal maxillary tooth counts of 17 to 19; those from northern Nevada, eastern Oregon, Idaho, and Washington have modal counts of 21 or 22.

The head of *Thamnophis elegans* constitutes 4.9% of SVL, a moderate length for a garter snake. The eye is of moderate size, ED/FL averaging 67.2%. The tip of the muzzle is moderately wide to wide, InR/NR averaging from 99 to 112%. The muzzle is long, ML/FL averaging 77.4%. The prefrontals and internasals are essentially subequal, Prf/In averaging 96.2%. The parietals of *T. elegans* are of moderate length, FL/PL averaging 76.5%. The posterior chin shields are variable in length, ACS/PCS averaging from 81 to 102%.

Taxonomic Comments

The convoluted taxonomic history of *T. elegans* as a species distinct from *T. ordinoides, T. atratus, T. couchii, T. gigas,* and *T. hammondii* has been summarized in the *T. atratus* and *T. couchii* accounts and will not be repeated here. Suffice it to say, detailed evidence justifying its recognition was not presented until 1979 (Ross-man, 1979; Lawson and Dessauer, 1979).

The very dark populations of *T. elegans* in the Puget Sound area were described as a distinct subspecies, *T. e. nigrescens,* by Johnson (1947), but that taxon has not been universally accepted. Fitch (1983) recognized *T. e. nigrescens* in his species account for the *Catalogue of American Amphibians and Reptiles,* but neither of the recent field guides covering that area did so (Nussbaum et al., 1983; Stebbins, 1985). Pending a detailed study of geographic variation throughout the entire range of *T. elegans*—and one is needed badly—we elect not to recognize *T. e. nigrescens.*

Rossman (1979) argued that *T. e. biscutatus* apparently represented nothing more than an intergrade population between *T. e. elegans* and *T. e. vagrans.* Fitch (1980a) rejected this conclusion, emphasizing that *biscutatus* differed from both of the other subspecies in average adult size, number of anterior dorsal scale rows, number of preoculars, and degree of swelling of the posterior supralabials. Rossman (1979) had previously addressed the first three characters, pointing out that (1) adult size in many species of garter snakes (including *T. elegans*) apparently reflects local environmental conditions, and very large specimens have been found elsewhere than in the Klamath Basin; (2) an anterior count of 23 dorsal scale rows occurs in few than half of the specimens of *"biscutatus"* that Fitch examined; and (3) 2 preoculars to a side not only occurs in fewer than half of the specimens of *"biscutatus"* that Fitch examined, but there is a higher incidence of this feature in two other populations. These points were not refuted by Fitch (1980a), and his characterization of the posterior supralabials of the taxa in question as "not noticeably swollen, somewhat swollen, or markedly swollen" is too subjective to warrant serious consideration. Moreover, the idea proposed by Fitch (1980a) that *"biscutatus"* has a habitat-mediated head shape strikingly different from that of *T. e. elegans*, the latter being "broad and short" and the former being "longer and narrower," is not supportable. Head length/SVL values for the two are indistinguishable, and if the muzzle tip in *"biscutatus"* is slightly narrower (109% vs. 120% according to Fitch's data), it is essentially the same as he found in *T. e. vagrans* (108%), which has never been characterized as being highly aquatic. There appears to be no justification for reviving *T. e. biscutatus*.

LIFE HISTORY AND ECOLOGY

Habitat

Thamnophis elegans occurs in a large and diverse geographical area of western North America. Although widespread, populations are often restricted due to xeric conditions throughout the area. These snakes inhabit streamsides, springs, and the borders of mountain lakes. In the Great Basin and Rocky Mountain regions, *T. e. vagrans* may be semiaquatic and often is associated with streams and ponds in middle- and high-elevation meadows (Fitch, 1940; Fox, 1951a). In lower valleys, the species may occur in marshes, ditches, streams, ponds, and cultivated pastures. In Oregon and northeastern California, *T. e. elegans* is typically a montane, terrestrial form, except in Modoc and Lassen counties, California, where it may be restricted to the margins of lakes and streams (Fitch, 1940; H. Fitch, pers. comm.). Fox (1951a) suggested that although *T. e. terrestris* is restricted to the humid coastal belt of California, it is not dependent upon permanent water. Although this subspecies can be found in association with streambeds and riparian situations, it prefers open grassland where individuals can feed

Species
Accounts

and bask and where shrubs are available for escape from predators (Fox, 1951a).

Fleharty (1967) compared the ecology of *T. e. vagrans* to two sympatric species of *Thamnophis* occurring at a lake and stream in New Mexico. All three species were found around the lake or along the creeks and river in riparian habitats, but *T. elegans* was usually associated with some type of vegetation, whereas *T. rufipunctatus* and *T. cyrtopsis* occurred more often in rocky areas. A garter snake assemblage including *T. e. vagrans*, *T. ordinoides*, and *T. sirtalis* was studied at eight sites on Vancouver Island (Gregory, 1984b). Although a number of factors are involved, it appears that *T. elegans* is more dominant in habitats with no water and less forest. In addition, the relative abundances of *T. ordinoides* and *T. elegans* were negatively correlated (see species account for *T. ordinoides*).

Activity

In British Columbia, *T. elegans* overwinters in rocky talus slopes, fractured bedrock, and roadbeds in aggregations of approximately 100 individuals (Farr, 1988). At a den excavated in northern Utah, *T. e. vagrans* were located at depths between 1 and 1.6 meters, and cloacal temperatures averaged 5.0 C (Brown et al., 1974). In Utah, males begin exiting dens in March but remain in the immediate vicinity to court females, which exit somewhat later. In south-central Wyoming, individuals emerged from hibernation between 28 March and 14 May, with a median date of 21 April (Graves and Duvall, 1990). Females may move to foraging and basking sites away from the den after mating, but males often do not begin extensive movements for several weeks (Farr 1988). Graves and Duvall (1990) suggested that this occurs because of scramble competition among males for mates. (See Chap. 5). Migrations can be extensive, up to nearly 3 km within a season. One female moved over 2 km in seven days. After the snakes reach the summer activity areas, movements decline again, particularly for gravid females. Gravid females form aggregations of as many as 20 individuals during the latter part of gestation in July and early August. In September, these snakes migrate back to the hibernacula.

In British Columbia, adult home-range size varied from 10 to 100,000 m^2, whereas the home range size in juveniles was only 1000 m^2 (Farr, 1988). This species has a slightly higher active body temperature than

Thamnophis elegans

167

sympatric *T. sirtalis* (Gregory and Mc-Intosh, 1980; see Chap. 5 for the significance of this). Cloacal temperatures during the activity season in British Columbia averaged about 25 C, with slight variation among sexes (Gregory and McIntosh, 1980). Body temperatures for both sexes during the activity season in New Mexico averaged 26.7 C (Fleharty, 1967).

Fleharty (1967) reported the escape behavior of *T. elegans* and indicated that most entered the water from aquatic vegetation but did not dive. A number also hid under logs and in vegetation on shore.

Feeding

The diet of *T. elegans* has been studied extensively in many portions of its range (see Table 4-2). However, taxonomic changes and both micro-geographic and temporal variation in diet make some of these reports difficult to evaluate (see Chap. 4 for a summary). Nevertheless, the overall diet of *T. elegans* is impressive in breadth and, indeed, is among the widest for any species of snake. Only a few detailed examples are discussed here. The riparian *T. e. vagrans* primarily ate fish (*Cottus, Pantosteus,* and *Apocops*), invertebrates (slugs, leeches, and earthworms) and tadpoles, although reptiles, birds, and mice were also eaten (Fitch, 1940). In northwestern California, slugs were the predominant food item of *T. e. terrestris* (Arnold, 1977, 1981a); Fox (1951a) never found frogs in the stomach of this subspecies. In New Mexico, *T. e. vagrans* ate mostly amphibians (Fleharty, 1967), but in British Columbia it ate slugs, fish, and mammals (Farr, 1988; Gregory, 1978). In California, inland populations of *T. e. elegans* and *T. e. vagrans* ate fish and rodents (Fitch, 1941b; White and Kolb, 1974) and leeches and amphibians (Arnold, 1977, 1981a; Kephart, 1982).

The wide geographic variation in diet may reflect differences in local prey availability (Kephart, 1982; White and Kolb, 1974), but some genetic component of prey preference and foraging behavior has been documented (Arnold, 1977, 1981a, b; Ayres and Arnold, 1983; Drummond, 1983; see Chap. 5). Populations of *T. elegans* in coastal northwestern California (where slugs are common) have a genetic predisposition to eat slugs, whereas inland populations (where slugs do not occur) refuse slugs when they are presented as prey items. These differences are chemically mediated, and the response is heritable

(Arnold, 1981a). Crosses between the two morphs indicated that slug-refusal is apparently dominant over slug-preference, but the trait may be polygenic or may exhibit incomplete penetrance (Ayres and Arnold, 1983). The behaviors associated with foraging also appear to be innate. Inland populations exhibit aquatic foraging behaviors and more readily take fish than do coastal populations (Drummond and Burghardt, 1983).

Temporal variation in diet also occurs in this species, further complicating interpretation of geographic variation, especially since many early studies were conducted over a short time period. Kephart and Arnold (1982) found major changes in the diet of California populations of T. elegans during seven consecutive summers and showed a close relationship between diet and prey availability (see Chap. 4 for further discussion).

Ontogenetic shifts in feeding are evident also. In T. e. elegans, first-year young were somewhat aquatic and took aquatic prey, whereas adults were more terrestrial (H. Fitch, pers. comm.). In British Columbia, smaller snakes fed more frequently and tended to eat more slugs than did adults, which fed mainly on mammals (Farr, 1988). In a population we examined in northern California, juvenile snakes ate leeches but all adults ate voles (Ford and Seigel, pers. obs.). Increased body size is probably important for subduing voles (*Microtus*) and shrews (*Sorex*). *Thamnophis elegans* is known to exhibit some constricting behavior (Gregory et al., 1980) and has toxic salivary secretions that may immobilize prey (Jansen, 1987).

Thamnophis elegans often occurs sympatrically with other garter snakes, prompting studies examining the importance of interspecific competition in determining community structure. On Vancouver Island the diet of T. elegans overlaps broadly with T. ordinoides (niche overlap = 0.62), but niche overlap is very limited with T. sirtalis (overlap = 0.08) (Gregory, 1984b). However, Kephart (1982) found that differences in diet between T. elegans and T. sirtalis were mainly due to differences in habitat usage; when both species occurred microsympatrically they tended to eat the same food.

Reproduction

Much of the "anecdotal" data on reproduction for T. elegans (and, indeed, for many snakes) tends to overesti-

Thamnophis elegans

mate litter sizes because the females collected in some studies were not random samples but rather included animals selected for their obvious pregnant condition and therefore were likely to be larger individuals (Fitch, 1985). Here we discuss some of the more representative samples. In 22 females maintained in captivity in British Columbia, the average clutch size was 7.5 and litter size increased with maternal SVL (Farr, 1988). Farr noted no variation in litter size between two consecutive years. Neonates were born in August and averaged 176 mm SVL. Neonate size varied among litters, with larger mothers producing larger offspring. Hansen and Tremper (*in prep.*) gave averages of 6.3 for 12 litters from Sierran populations and 10.6 for 11 litters from eastern and northeastern California. Data on southwestern U.S. and Mexican populations are lacking.

Although most evidence suggests the primary breeding period for this species is the spring, it is interesting to note that fall courtship has been documented in at least two populations. In British Columbia, Farr (1988) recorded courtship occurring in early September; in the Great Basin of California, Hansen and Tremper (*n prep.*) recorded a female containing a sperm plug on 17 September. See Chap. 4 for additional discussion.

Population Biology

Local densities of this species can be extremely high. Farr (1988) estimated that 5520 individuals occurred in a 2000 ha area, an average of 2.8 snakes per hectare. In British Columbia, *T. elegans* reached sexual maturity at about 450 mm SVL in females and about 400 mm in males (Farr, 1988). In central California, sexual maturity may be reached in approximately 24 months (Hansen and Tremper, *in prep.*). Gregory and Prelypchan (1994) found no significant differences in growth rates between the sexes, and suggested that larger body size in females was the result of females growing for a longer period of time rather than at a faster rate.

Captive Maintenance

This species is one of the easier garter snakes to maintain and raise in captivity due to its predisposition to eat mice. Fewer feedings a week are required with mice, and moisture is less of a problem than when fish or amphibians are used as food. Snakes that we have kept became extremely conditioned to feeding and tended to come out of the cage to attack mice. They readily ate fish, but some individuals refused to eat *Rana* tadpoles. Because *T. elegans* is known to eat other snakes, it is advisable to keep this species in individual cages.

This species has been used extensively in genetic experiments and its reproduction in the laboratory is well documented (Arnold 1980). Animals were first artificially hibernated at 5 to 10 C with natural winter photoperiod and high humidity. Prior to breeding, animals were raised to 15 C for one week, then up to 28 C. Copulation occurred within a few weeks of emergence from hibernation.

Conservation

Populations of this snake seem fairly common, and the species does not appear to be in any immediate jeopardy. However, Jennings et al. (1992) suggested that high-elevation populations of *T. elegans* might be subject to declines if populations of frogs continue to disappear.

Comments

The secretion from the Duvernoy's gland of this species is known to cause local swelling in cases of bites to humans (Jansen, 1987). The infrequency of the reports, however, suggests it is not a serious problem in the captive maintenance of the species.

Thamnophis eques
MEXICAN GARTER SNAKE
(Plates 4 and 5)

Coluber eques Reuss, 1834
    (= *T. e. eques*)
Coluber (Natrix) subcarinata Gray *in* Richardson, 1839
    (= *T. e. eques*)
Eutaenia megalops Kennicott, 1860
    (= *T. e. megalops*)
Eutaenia macrostemma Kennicott, 1860
    (= *T. e. eques*)
Eutaenia flavilabris Cope, 1866
    (= *T. e. eques*)
Eutaenia insigniarum Cope, 1885a
    (= *T. e. eques*)
Thamnophis stejnegeri McLain, 1899
    (= *T. e. megalops*)
Thamnophis eques virgatenuis Conant, 1963
    (= *T. e. virgatenuis*)

Identification

Dorsal scales in a maximum of 21 rows; supralabials 8; preoculars 1; maxillary teeth 23 to 28; the dorsum

Thamnophis eques

171

between the light stripes either brown with 2 alternating rows of large dark spots (those in the upper row longitudinally fused in some populations) or almost uniformly black; the vertebral stripe from 1 to 9 scales wide; the lateral stripe confined to rows 3 and 4 anteriorly.

Content and Distribution

Three subspecies of the Mexican garter snake are currently recognized: *T. e. eques*, which ranges from southern Nayarit eastward along the Transverse Volcanic Axis to west-central Veracruz (with an apparently isolated population in central Oaxaca); *T. e. megalops*, which ranges from central Arizona and the lower Gila River in New Mexico southward in the Sierra Madre Occidental to Guanajuato, and thence eastward across the Mexican Plateau to Hidalgo (with an apparently isolated population in central Nuevo León); and *T. e. virgatenuis*, which occurs in three, apparently isolated, high-elevation populations in southwestern Durango and in west-central and northwestern Chihuahua (see Map 7). Elevational distribution ranges from 53 to 2590 meters (Rosen and Schwalbe, 1988; Stebbins, 1985).

Description

The following is based largely on Brumwell (1939), Conant (1963), Ruthven (1908), H. M. Smith (1942), Tanner (1986), and previously unpublished data. *Thamnophis eques* is a relatively long species of garter snake, reaching a maximum total length of 1120 mm (Rosen and Schwalbe, 1988). The dorsum is olive, brown, or black, with two alternating rows of relatively large black spots between the light stripes. The spots in the upper row are fused longitudinally in some populations (see Conant, 1963, Fig. 7A). The spots are scarcely, if at all, visible in those populations having a black dorsum (Conant, 1963, Fig. 7C). The keels of the otherwise black scales are brown. The vertebral stripe is highly variable in width both intra- and interpopulationally. In *T. e. virgatenuis*, the vertebral stripe usually is little, if at all, wider than the vertebral row; in *T. e. megalops*, it may range from a little wider than the vertebral row to involving half or more of each paravertebral row; and in *T. e. eques*, it may range from involving the vertebral row and half of each paravertebral row to involving the vertebral row and as many as 4½ rows on either side of it (the maximum width is from

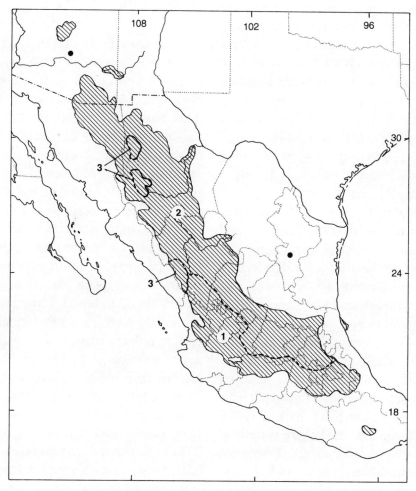

Map 7 Distribution of *Thamnophis eques* and its subspecies: (1) *T. e. eques*; (2) *T. e. megalops*; (3) *T. e. virgatenuis*.

Brumwell, 1939; the broadest stripe reported by any other author involved 3 rows on either side of the vertebral row [Ruthven, 1908]). In the large dark individuals occupying Lakes Chapala and Cuitzeo, the vertebral stripe may be difficult to see, although it is readily apparent in smaller specimens. The lateral stripe is confined to rows 3 and 4 anteriorly (2 and 3 posteriorly) and is usually distinct, but it is difficult to detect in large specimens from Lakes Chapala and Cuitzeo. These dark specimens also are distinctive in having a dark venter that strongly contrasts with a cream-colored throat, anal plate, and subcaudals. In other populations, the venter may be cream-colored, greenish-yellow, bluish-green, or bluish-gray but with no strong contrast to either throat or subcaudals. The supralabials have prominent black bars along all vertical sutures, and there usually is a prominent light crescent between the posterior temporals and the nuchal blotches (these blotches are well developed in some populations, obscure in others). The presence of this posttemporal crescent could cause some confusion in distinguishing between *T. eques* and *T. marcianus*, but the ground color of the temporals does not extend down onto the posterior

supralabials in *T. eques* as it does in *T. marcianus*.

There usually are 21-19-17 dorsal scale rows, rarely 23-21-17 or 19-19-17. Ventrals range from 149 to 176 in males (the lowest value is from H. M. Smith et al., 1950; the 129 ventrals reported by H. M. Smith [1942] surely must have been a typographical error), 149 to 171 in females; males average 4.3 to 9.4 more ventrals than females (in populations having at least five individuals of each sex). Subcaudals range from 65 to 95 in males (the lowest count may reflect an individual with an incomplete tail), 61 to 89 in females (the highest count may have been a typographical error or reflect a missexed individual); males average 9.5 to 14.1 more subcaudals than females (Conant, 1963). Relative tail length ranges from 22 to 27% in males (Conant, 1963, gave range values only as whole numbers), 20 to 25% in females; it averages 0.3 to 3.0% longer in males than in females.

Preoculars number 1 to a side, postoculars usually 3 (occasionally 4). There normally are 8 supralabials (rarely 9 or 7) and 10 infralabials (rarely 11 or 9). Maxillary teeth range from 23 to 28 in females (no counts currently available for males), averaging 25.9.

The head in *Thamnophis eques*

constitutes 4.9% of SVL in males and 5.2% in females, making it moderate-sized and long, respectively, for a garter snake. The eye is of moderate size, ED/FL averaging 69.2%. The muzzle tip is of moderate width, InR/NR averaging 95.0%. The muzzle is of moderate length, ML/FL averaging 70.7%. The prefrontals are shorter than the internasals, Prf/In averaging 86.5%. The parietals of *T. eques* are short, FL/PL averaging 83.0%. The posterior chin shields are of moderate length, ACS/PCS averaging 79.4%.

Taxonomic Comments

The name *eques* was not applied subsequent to its original description (Reuss, 1834) until Boulenger (1893) mistakenly revived it as a senior synonym for the black-necked garter snake (previously, and currently, known as *T. cyrtopsis*). This arrangement was followed in such major systematic works as Cope (1900), Ruthven (1908), Van Denburgh and Slevin (1918), and H. M. Smith (1942), and it was not until 1951 that H. M. Smith demonstrated that the holotype of *T. eques* is actually an example of the Mexican garter snake (known at that time as *T. subcarinata*), not the black-necked garter snake (to which the name *T. cyrtopsis* was restored). Ironically, at the time of the change, the name *T. subcarinata* had been applied to the Mexican garter snake for only two years (H. M. Smith, 1949). For more than half a century prior to that time, the Mexican garter snake had been known as either *T. macrostemma* or *T. megalops*.

Geographic variation in *T. eques* is extensive and some aspects of it currently are being investigated by R. Conant and N. Scott and by E. Liner. The subspecies *T. e. eques* and *T. e. megalops* are distinguished solely on the basis of average differences in subcaudal numbers, and *T. e. virgatenuis* is distinguished from *T. e. megalops* by having a darker ground color and a narrower vertebral stripe. The discontinuous high-elevation distribution of the three populations of *T. e. virgatenuis*, surrounded and separated by lower-elevation populations of *T. e. megalops*, is zoogeographically peculiar and unique among garter snakes.

LIFE HISTORY AND ECOLOGY

Habitat

Thamnophis eques occurs in the upper and lower Sonoran Life Zone

Thamnophis eques

175

(Rosen and Schwalbe, 1988). The species is strongly associated with permanent water with vegetation. Rosen and Schwalbe described three types of habitat for this species in Arizona. They found *T. eques* in source-area wetlands such as stock tanks, cienegas, and cienega streams where the snakes were in aquatic vegetation such as knotgrass, spikerush, bullrush, and cattail. Snakes were also found in low bank vegetation such as deergrass and sacaton; brushy trees such as cottonwoods, willows, and velvet mesquite were also used as refuges by the snakes. *Thamnophis eques* were also found in shallows, on the banks, and in the vegetation of riparian woodlands of large rivers, and, occasionally, in gallery forests of midsize streams where grasses were less dense. In Mexico, D. A. Rossman (pers. obs.) has found them around shallow meadow ponds, in vegetation in rivers, and near cactus and thornbushes around ponds.

Activity

In Arizona, this species had an average body temperature of 27.3 C with a range of 22 to 33 C., which is lower than other south-temperate *Thamnophis* (Rosen, 1991). It apparently is more secretive than other *Thamnophis* and remains in dense vegetation instead of basking in open areas.

Feeding

The prey for this species is generally amphibians and fishes (Van Devender and Lowe, 1977), although invertebrates, lizards, and mammals are sometimes eaten as well. Rosen and Schwalbe (1988) reported that adults and tadpoles of leopard frogs (*Rana chiricahuensis* and *R. yavapaiensis*), young Woodhouse's toads (*Bufo woodhousei*), and newly metamorphosed bullfrogs (*R. catesbeiana*) were eaten, as were small fish such as Gila and roundtail clubs (*Gila robusta* and *G. intermedia*). In Mexico, juvenile *T. eques* were found to feed on earthworms and leeches, whereas adults fed on leeches, fish, and frogs (Macias Garcia and Drummond 1988a). Mexican garter snakes have also eaten fence lizards (*Sceloporus*), racerunners (*Cnemidophorus*), and deermice (*Peromycus maniculatus*) (Rosen and Schwalbe, 1988).

Reproduction

The average clutch size from eight Arizona specimens dissected by Rosen and Schwalbe (1988) was 13.6. Neonates in two clutches averaged 137 and 194 mm SVL. Follicular enlargement begins in the fall, and ovulation occurs in late March or early April with the young born in June or July (Rosen and Schwalbe, 1988). This is a very unusual pattern for garter snakes, which usually do not begin to have enlarged follicles until the spring; these patterns require additional verification and study (see Chap. 4). Females basked on grass tussocks or among rocks during gestation. Rosen and Schwalbe indicated that only 50% of the females bear young each year, although they do not specifically suggest that this species is a biannual breeder.

Population Biology

In southern Arizona, males of this species mature at 2 years of age and females 2 or 3 years of age. Females begin reproduction at 550 to 700 mm SVL (Rosen and Schwalbe, 1988). A mark-recapture study of *T. eques* around an undisturbed 0.1 ha pond indicated a population of 95 snakes, not including young of the year (Rosen and Schwalbe, 1988). Other sites in Arizona also appear to have large populations in very small, restricted habitats. Disturbed habitats, however, are dominated by large, older specimens, thus suggesting greater mortality occurs among the neonates in these situations.

Captive Maintenance

No literature on care of this species in captivity is available.

Conservation

Thamnophis eques is listed as a Category 2 candidate species for federal listing by the U.S. Fish & Wildlife Service and is listed as "endangered" in New Mexico and Arizona. Major threats include habitat modification and predation by introduced bullfrogs (Rosen and Schwalbe, 1988).

Comments

Cope (1900) pointed out that *T. eques* is the species of snake that appears on the Mexican coat of arms, Cortez reputedly having seen one of these garter snakes being seized by an eagle.

Thamnophis eques

177

Thamnophis errans
MEXICAN WANDERING
GARTER SNAKE
(Plate 5)

Thamnophis ordinoides errans H. M.
  Smith, 1942

Identification

Dorsal scales in a maximum of 19 or
21 rows; supralabials usually 7 (occasionally 8); maxillary teeth 16 to 19;
the dorsum uniformly olive-brown or
with 2 alternating rows of indistinct
black spots between the stripes; the
vertebral stripe usually confined to
vertebral row; the lateral stripe confined to dorsal scale rows 2 and 3 (but
only slightly lighter than row 1);
tongue uniformly black.

Content and Distribution

No subspecies are currently recognized. The Mexican wandering garter
snake ranges from northwestern Chihuahua to western Zacatecas (see
Map 8) at elevations from 1860 to
2545 m (Webb, 1976).

Description

The following is based on Webb (1976)
and previously unpublished data.
Thamnophis errans is a moderate-
sized species of garter snake, reaching
a maximum total length of 750 mm
(UTA R-5944). Between the stripes,
the olive-brown or gray-green dorsum
may or may not show a pattern of
indistinct black spots, especially anteriorly. The lateral stripe is cream
to olive-yellow, the vertebral stripe
yellow to yellowish-white or yellowish-green. The vertebral stripe is confined to the vertebral row, except in
some individuals from the lower-
elevation grassland populations near
Yepómera and Santa Clara, Chihuahua, where the stripe involves the inner half of each paravertebral row as
well. The venter is pale yellow to orange, with or without varying
amounts of black pigment (occurring
most frequently in the aforementioned lower-elevation grassland populations). The base of the tongue is
uniformly black.

There usually are 19-19-17 dorsal
scale rows (invariably from southern
Chihuahua southward), but there is
much intra- and interpopulational
variation in the northern one-fourth
of the range, where 19-21-17,
21-19-17, and 21-21-17 rows also frequently occur. Ventrals in *T. errans*
range from 150 to 166 in males, 146
to 160 in females; males average 5.6
to 6.9 more ventrals than females.
Subcaudals range from 78 to 94 in

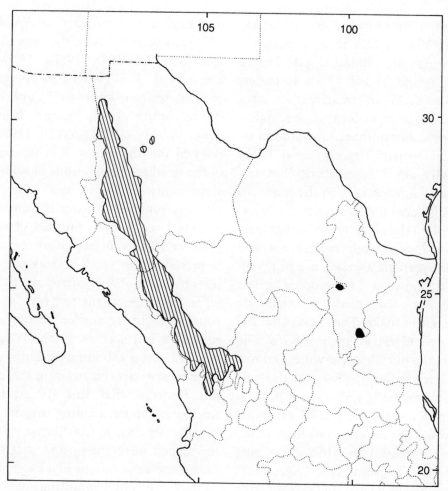

Map 8 Distribution of *Thamnophis errans* (diagonal lines) and *T. exsul* (black blotches).

males, 67 to 83 in females; males average 10.3 to 11.8 more subcaudals than females. Relative tail length ranges from 25.3 to 27.5% in males, 23.4 to 25.2% in females; it averages 2.1% longer in males than in females.

Preoculars number 1 to a side, postoculars usually 3 (rarely 2 or 4). There usually are 7 supralabials (but frequently 8, especially in the northern populations) and 10 infralabials (occasionally 11). Maxillary teeth range from 16 to 19; more tooth counts are needed before realistic averages can be given.

The head of *Thamnophis errans* constitutes 5.4% of SVL, which is long for a garter snake. The eye is of moderate size, ED/FL averaging 68.7%. The tip of the muzzle is the widest known for any species of *Thamnophis*, InR/NR averaging 151.5%. The muzzle is of moderate length, ML/FL averaging 67.6%. The prefrontals are longer than the internasals, Prf/In averaging 111.4%. The pareitals of *T. errans* are of moderate length, FL/PL averaging 78.4%. The posterior chin shields are of moderate length, ACS/PCS averaging 85.6%.

Taxonomic Comments

Since its original description in 1942, the Mexican wandering garter snake (the English name coined by Webb, 1976) has been treated either as a full species (Fitch, 1948, 1980a; H. M. Smith et al., 1950) or as a subspecies of what we now know as *T. elegans* (H. M. Smith, 1942; Tanner, 1959, 1986; Webb, 1976). Webb (1976) pointed out that some (but not all) of the northern populations of *errans* show some similarity to *T. elegans vagrans* from New Mexico in number of dorsal scale rows, number of supralabials, and ventral pattern; he interpreted this as residual evidence of intergradation that occurred at a time when the ranges of the two taxa were contiguous. In arguing for treating *errans* as a full species, Fitch (1980a) stressed that a 280 km distributional gap now separates *errans* from *T. elegans vagrans*; that the alleged intergrades, though tending toward *T. elegans vagrans*, were still easily distinguished from them; and that *errans* possesses a unique black tongue. Actually, the latter condition does occur in several other species of *Thamnophis*, but we know of no instance within this genus in which tongue color varies intraspecifically.

Although Fitch (1980a) considered *T. errans* to be a distinct species, neither he nor any other author questioned its close relationship to *T.*

elegans. Recently, however, de Queiroz and Lawson (1994) performed an electrophoretic analysis of most species of *Thamnophis* and found that the proteins of *T. errans* are almost indistinguishable from those of *T. godmani,* and that these two taxa are not at all closely related to *T. elegans.*

LIFE HISTORY AND ECOLOGY

Virtually nothing is known about the ecology of this species. Fitch (1985) reported a mean of 7.8 offspring from four females (range 6 to 10) and Webb (1976) recorded a mean brood size of 8 from three *T. errans* (range 6 to 10).

Thamnophis exsul
EXILED GARTER SNAKE
(Plate 5)

Thamnophis exsul Rossman, 1969

Identification

Dorsal scales usually in a maximum of 17 rows (often without a posterior reduction to 15); supralabials usually 7 and infralabials usually 8 on at least one side of head; maxillary teeth 19 to 21; the dorsum uniformly putty-brown with 3 indistinct light stripes (the lateral pair on dorsal scale rows 2 and 3) or with 3 or 4 alternating rows of spots or blotches, the light stripes being partially or completely obscured; tongue uniformly black.

Content and Distribution

No subspecies are currently recognized. This, the rarest species of garter snake, is known from only three localities in the Sierra Madre Oriental of southeastern Coahuila and southeastern Nuevo León, Mexico (see Map 8) at elevations between 2650 and 2860 m.

Description

The following is drawn from Rossman et al. (1989) and previously unpublished data. *Thamnophis exsul* is the shortest species of garter snake, reaching a maximum total length of 463 mm (E. A. Liner private collection 4837). The dorsal pattern undergoes a dramatic ontogenetic change, at least in the Nuevo León population. The juveniles are prominently spotted in 4 alternating rows, or in 3 rows when there is a fusion of spots in the upper two rows. A variable

Thamnophis exsul

number of neck spots may be vertically enlarged to reach, or fuse across, the narrow vertebral stripe when one is present. A prominent dark nuchal blotch may or may not be very narrowly divided by the vertebral stripe, and it may or may not be continuous with the dorsal coloration of the head. Most of the spotting is obscured in Nuevo León adults. The lone Coahuila adult retains the spotted juvenile pattern. The tongue is uniformly black.

Nine of the 10 known specimens of *T. exsul* have a maximum of 17 dorsal scale rows (the exception has 19). Two individuals have a posterior reduction to 15 rows, the other 8 do not. The lack of a posterior reduction is unusual for a garter snake, but the condition also occurs commonly in some populations of *T. godmani* and *T. scalaris*. Ventrals range from 152 to 156 in males, 142 to 150 in females; males average 9 more ventrals than females. Subcaudals range from 63 to 65 in males, 52 to 56 in females; males average 9.4 more subcaudals than females. Relative tail length ranges from 21.8 to 22.2% in males, 18.9 to 20.0% in females; it averages 2.6% longer in males than in females.

Preoculars number 1 to a side, postoculars 2 or 3. There are normally 7 supralabials (rarely 6 or 8) and 8 infralabials (rarely 9 or 10) on each side. Maxillary teeth range from 19 to 21, averaging 20.3, the posterior 3 being stouter—though little longer—than those preceding them.

The head constitutes 4.7% of SVL in the three largest adults (> 300 mm SVL), which is of moderate length for a garter snake. The eye is small, ED/FL averaging 62.3%. The muzzle tip is extremely wide, the combined InR/NR averaging 147.9%. The muzzle is long in males, short in females, ML/FL averaging 73.9% and 65.0%, respectively. The prefrontals are longer than the internasals, Prf/In averaging 101.6% in males, 143.3% in females. The marked sexual dimorphism in the two preceding characters may be real or may reflect the limited sample size. The parietals of *T. exsul* are of moderate length, FL/PL averaging 77.1%. The posterior chin shields are of moderate length, ACS/PCS averaging 83.8%.

Taxonomic Comments

Rossman (1969) suggested that—despite marked differences—the Coahuila specimen of *T. exsul* more closely resembled *T. scalaris* than any other garter snake, primarily because of the similarities in body form, the spotted dorsal pattern, and the light streaking on the parietal and frontal scales. Rossman et al. (1989), in redescribing the species on the basis of nine additional specimens from Nuevo León, saw no reason to alter the earlier suggestion of affinities. Rossman (1992b) added a shared habitat preference, but still preferred to leave the question open.

LIFE HISTORY AND ECOLOGY

As is evident from the limited material given below, the ecology of this species is poorly known. *Thamnophis exsul* is found in montane meadows with scrub trees and brush (Rossman et al., 1989). Young were collected in a rotten log on a hillside with scattered rocks and logs amidst mixed pine, oak, and madrone. The general habitat is relatively dry with no apparent standing water or streams nearby, although the holotype was found in a grassy "sump" above the head of a canyon (Rossman, 1969). This species appears to thermoregulate like many other members of the genus. It comes out to bask in the midmorning while the ground is still cool and moist (Rossman et al., 1989).

Thamnophis fulvus MESOAMERICAN HIGHLANDS GARTER SNAKE
(Plate 6)

Eutaenia cyrtopsis var. *fulvus* Bocourt, 1893

Identification

Dorsal scales usually in a maximum of 19 rows; supralabials usually 8 (occasionally 7); maxillary teeth 27 to 31; the dorsum olive-brown with 2 alternating rows of relatively indistinct black spots between the stripes; the vertebral stripe confined to the vertebral row and often indistinct or absent except on neck; the lateral stripe confined to dorsal scale rows 2 and 3 and often indistinct; tongue uniformly black.

Content and Distribution

No subspecies are currently recognized. The Mesoamerican highlands garter snake ranges from central Chiapas, Mexico, through southern Guatemala into southwestern Honduras and adjacent El Salvador (see Map 9) at elevations from 1410 to 3353 m (Stuart, 1948; Webb, 1982).

Thamnophis fulvus

183

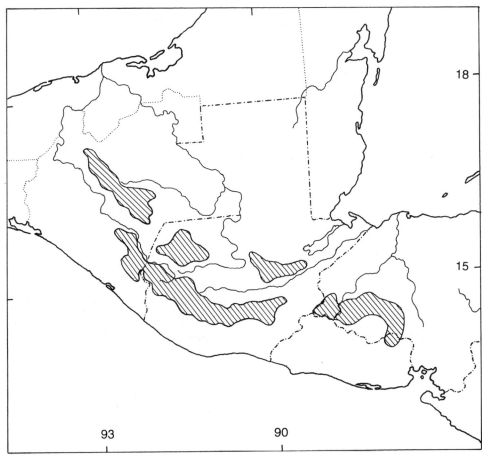

Map 9 Distribution of *Thamnophis fulvus.*

Description

The following is based on Webb (1982), Slevin (1939), and previously unpublished data. *Thamnophis fulvus* is a moderate-sized species of garter snake, reaching a maximum SVL of 652 mm (CM 44006). Between the stripes, the olive-brown dorsum may or may not show two alternating rows of more-or-less distinct black spots, which may be enlarged on the neck to encroach on the vertebral stripe or even fuse across it. The lateral stripe is pale yellow, usually suffused with brown pigment. The vertebral stripe is tan, usually distinct on the neck but indistinct or lacking altogether posteriorly. The ventrals may be unmarked, have two rows of small spots laterally, or have a diffuse dusky midventral stripe. The brown pigment from the lowermost dorsal scale rows extend onto the ventrals for nearly ¼ of their width on each side. Supralabial barring is narrow. In some specimens, there are large, irregular black blotches or vermiculations on the frontal and parietals that often connect to the elongated nuchal blotches. The tongue is uniformly black.

There usually are 19-19-17 (occasionally 19-17-15, rarely 21-19-17 or 19-21-17) dorsal scale rows. Ventrals in *T. fulvus* range from 136 to 154 in males, 132 to 150 in females; males average 3.7 more ventrals than females. Subcaudals range from 63 to 80 in males, 56 to 72 in females; males average 7.7 more subcaudals than females. Relative tail length ranges from 21.4 to 24.1% in males, 20.8 to 22.7% in females; it averages 1.6% longer in males than in females.

Preoculars number 1 to a side (rarely 2), postoculars 3. There usually are 8 supralabials (occasionally 7 or 9), 10 infralabials (occasionally 11, rarely 9). Maxillary teeth range from 27 to 31, averaging 29.8 in males and 28.3 in females.

The head of *Thamnophis fulvus* constitutes 5.2% of SVL, which is long for a garter snake. The eye is large, ED/FL averaging 74.7%. The tip of the muzzle is of moderate width, InR/NR averaging 104.1%. The muzzle is long, ML/FL averaging 74.2%. The prefrontals are much shorter than the infralabials, Prf/In averaging 73.5%. The parietals of *T. fulvus* are of moderate length, FL/PL averaging 74.0%. The posterior chin shields are of moderate length, ACS/PCS averaging 87.2%.

Taxonomic Comments

Originally described (Bocourt, 1893) as a "variety" of *T. cyrtopsis*, the Mesoamerican highlands garter snake was essentially "lost" for the next half-century until it was revived as *T. sumichrasti fulvus* by H. M. Smith (1942), who mistakenly applied the name *sumichrasti* to what he thought was a trans-Isthmian species related to *T. cyrtopsis* but specifically distinct from it. Bogert and Oliver (1945) reconnected *fulvus* (and the other races of Smith's *T. sumichrasti*) to *T. cyrtopsis*, an association that continued even after Rossman (1965a) correctly reapplied the name *sumichrasti* to an

Thamnophis fulvus

entirely different species (see *T. sum-ichrasti* account). Webb (1982) demonstrated that the ranges of *fulvus* and *T. cyrtopsis collaris* overlap extensively in Chiapas and Guatemala with no morphological evidence of intergradation; hence he recognized *T. fulvus* as a distinct species. Webb also suggested that *T. fulvus* may be distantly related to *T. sumichrasti* (in the restricted sense) because they both have a relatively short tail and some similarity in head and nuchal patterns. DNA sequence data (de Queiroz and Lawson, 1994) place *T. fulvus* as the sister species of all other *Thamnophis*; no molecular data are yet available for *T. sumichrasti*.

LIFE HISTORY AND ECOLOGY

Very little is known about the ecology of this species. *Thamnophis fulvus* is mainly found in highland pine-oak forests (Webb, 1982), although it is also found in high bunchgrass plains in the pine-cypress zone (Stuart, 1951). Stuart (1951) found this species most frequently in the vicinity of water; in the pine-cypress zone, most specimens were found near streams (Stuart, 1948, 1951). The few records of reproduction include a female found on 17 May 1940, which contained near-term embryos (Stuart,

1948), and an adult female from Guatemala, which gave birth to a dead but fully formed neonate on 29 or 30 October 1994 and passed infertile eggs for several weeks thereafter. The latter events took place at least 39 months after the female could have had access to a male (D. A. Rossman, pers. obs.). Feeding records include *Hyla spinipollex*, *Plectrohyla cotzicensis*, and tadpoles (Stuart, 1948, 1951). One captive specimen, when agitated, was seen to hide its head in its coils and elevate the tail, which it slowly writhed about while exuding the contents of its cloaca (D. A. Rossman, pers. obs.).

Thamnophis gigas
GIANT GARTER SNAKE
(Plate 6)

Thamnophis ordinoides gigas Fitch, 1940

Identification

Dorsal scales in a maximum of 23 or 21 rows; supralabials 8 (the 6th shorter than the 7th); subcaudals 73 to 81 in males, 65 to 73 in females; lateral stripe, when present, confined to dorsal scale rows 2 and 3; the dorsum either dark brown or olive with 2 alternating rows of small dark spots; vertebral stripe may or may not be visible.

Content and Distribution

No subspecies are currently recognized. The giant garter snake historically ranged throughout the Sacramento and San Joaquin valleys of California from Butte Co. in the north to Kern Co. in the south (see Map 10). The species appears to have been extirpated south of northern Fresno Co. (Hansen and Brode, 1980). Elevational distribution ranges from 0 to 122 m.

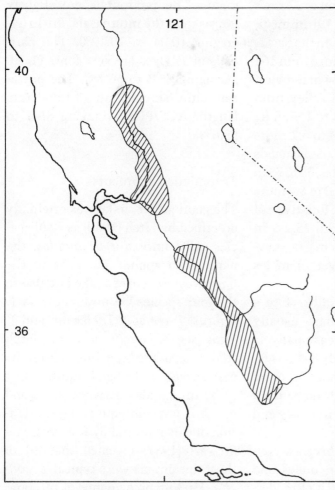

Map 10 Distribution of *Thamnophis gigas.*

Description

The following is based largely on Rossman and Stewart (1987). *Thamnophis gigas* is the longest species of garter snake, reaching a maximum total length of 1626 mm (Stebbins, 1985). In the upper Sacramento Valley, the dorsum of *T. gigas* has a dark-brown ground color that contrasts with the distinct light vertebral and lateral stripes. Farther south, in addition to this pattern morph there occurs one that features two rows of small dark spots (one set immediately be-

Thamnophis gigas

187

low the vertebral stripe, the other immediately above the lateral stripe)—the stripes are usually indistinct and may even be absent.

There is a maximum of either 23 or 21 (rarely 22) dorsal scale rows, with 23 being more frequent in females than in males. There is a reduction to 17 rows (occasionally 18, rarely 19) immediately anterior to the vent. In the Sacramento Valley, ventrals range from 162 to 168 in males, 156 to 164 in females; in the central San Joaquin Valley, from 157 to 161 in males, 150 to 155 in females. Males average 4.3 to 5.2 more ventrals than females. Subcaudals range from 73 to 81 in males, 65 to 73 in females; males average 6.3 to 6.4 more subcaudals than females. Relative tail length ranges from 23.2 to 25.9% in males, 20.4 to 23.4% in females; it averages 2.4 to 2.5% longer in males than in females.

Preoculars usually number 1 to a side, rarely 2. Postoculars usually number 3 to a side, occasionally 2. Supralabials are invariably 8 to a side; infralabials usually number 10 or 11 to a side. Maxillary teeth range from 23 to 27, averaging 26.5 in males and 25.0 in females.

The head in *Thamnophis gigas* constitutes 4.8% of SVL in males and 5.0% in females, making it of moderate length for a garter snake. The eye is of moderate size, ED/FL averaging 64.0 to 64.7%. The muzzle tip is narrow, InR/NR averaging 75.6% in males, 65.1% in females. The muzzle is very long in males, extremely long in females, ML/FL averaging 84.7 to 85.0% in males, 95.4 to 95.9% in females. The prefrontals are slightly longer than the internasals, Prf/In averaging 104.4 to 107.9%. The parietals of *T. gigas* are very long, FL/PL averaging 65.3 to 66.7%. The posterior chin shields are of moderate length, ACS/PCS averaging 86.5 to 88.6%.

Taxonomic Comments

The giant garter snake was originally described by Fitch (1940) as a subspecies of *Thamnophis ordinoides*, the name then applied not only to the northwestern garter snake but also to the four species we now know as *T. atratus*, *T. couchii*, *T. elegans*, and *T. gigas* (see *T. couchii* account). Fitch (1940) considered specimens from the eastern edge of the San Joaquin Valley to be intergrades between *gigas* and *couchii*, but subsequent reexamination of this material by Rossman and Stewart (1987) revealed that all of those specimens were typical *T. couchii*. Finding no evidence of intergradation between the giant garter snake

COLOR PLATES

Plate 1

Thamnophis atratus atratus (one-striped morph), California: Santa Clara Co. Photo by A. Ford.

Thamnophis atratus atratus (three-striped morph), California: Stanislaus Co. Photo by J. Boundy.

Thamnophis atratus hydrophilus (striped morph), California: Shasta Co. Photo by G. R. Stewart.

Thamnophis atratus hydrophilus (spotted morph), California: Siskiyou Co. Photo by D. A. Rossman.

Thamnophis brachystoma, Pennsylvania: Forest Co. Photo by S. A. Minton.

Thamnophis butleri, Ohio: Lucas Co. Photo by S. L. and J. T. Collins.

Plate 2

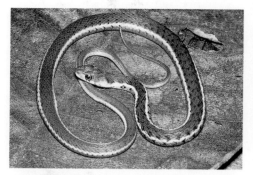

Thamnophis chrysocephalus (light morph), Mexico: Oaxaca. Photo by W. W. Lamar (University of Texas at Arlington slide collection).

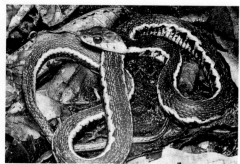

Thamnophis chrysocephalus (dark morph), Mexico: Oaxaca. Photo by W. W. Lamar (University of Texas at Arlington slide collection).

Thamnophis couchii (northern morph), California: Shasta Co. Photo by G. R. Stewart.

Thamnophis couchii (southern morph), California: Kern Co. Photo by R. W. Hansen.

Thamnophis couchii ("plain" morph), California: Tulare Co. Photo by R. Gonzales.

Thamnophis cyrtopsis cyrtopsis, Arizona: Santa Cruz Co. Photo by R. W. Hansen.

Plate 3

Thamnophis cyrtopsis collaris, Mexico: Puebla. Photo by W. W. Lamar (University of Texas at Arlington slide collection).

Thamnophis cyrtopsis ocellatus, Texas: Llano Co. Photo by J. D. Camper.

Thamnophis elegans elegans, California: Fresno Co. Photo by R. W. Hansen.

Thamnophis elegans arizonae, Arizona: Apache Co. Photo by J. Boundy.

Thamnophis elegans hueyi, Mexico: Baja California Norte. Photo by L. L. Grismer.

Thamnophis elegans terrestris (red morph), California: San Mateo Co. Photo by J. Boundy.

Plate 4

Thamnophis elegans terrestris (brown morph), California: Humboldt Co. Photo by J. Boundy.

Thamnophis elegans terrestris (black morph), California: Santa Clara Co. Photo by A. Ford.

Thamnophis elegans vagrans, Utah: Cache Co. Photo by B. Bartholomew.

Thamnophis elegans vagrans ("*nigrescens*" morph), Washington: Pierce Co. Photo by W. P. Leonard.

Thamnophis elegans vascotanneri, Utah: San Juan Co. Photo by J. Boundy.

Thamnophis eques eques, Mexico: Jalisco. Photo by M. Kleiner (FMNH specimen).

Plate 5

Thamnophis eques megalops, Mexico: Queretaro. Photo by S. A. Minton.

Thamnophis eques megalops, Mexico: Nuevo León. Photo by E. A. Liner.

Thamnophis eques virgatenuis, Mexico: Durango. Photo by R. G. Webb.

Thamnophis errans, Mexico: Durango. Photo by R. G. Webb.

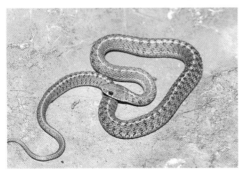

Thamnophis exsul (spotted morph), Mexico: Nuevo León. Photo by E. A. Liner.

Thamnophis exsul (unspotted morph), Mexico: Nuevo León. Photo by E. A. Liner.

Plate 6

Thamnophis fulvus, Guatemala: Jalapa. Photo by J. Boundy.

Thamnophis gigas (striped morph), California: San Joaquin Co. Photo by J. Brode.

Thamnophis gigas (spotted morph), California: Fresno Co. Photo by R. W. Hansen.

Thamnophis godmani, Mexico: Oaxaca. Photo by W. W. Lamar (University of Texas at Arlington slide collection).

Thamnophis hammondii (two-striped morph), California: San Benito Co. Photo by R. W. Hansen.

Thamnophis hammondii (stripeless morph), California: Monterey Co. Photo by J. Boundy.

Plate 7

Thamnophis marcianus marcianus, Arizona: Cochise Co. Photo by R. W. Hansen.

Thamnophis marcianus bovallii, Nicaragua: Managua. Photo by J. Villa.

Thamnophis marcianus praecularis, Guatemala: Izabal. Photo by W. W. Lamar (University of Texas at Arlington slide collection).

Thamnophis melanogaster canescens ("plain" morph), Mexico: Jalisco. Photo by W. W. Lamar (University of Texas at Arlington slide collection).

Thamnophis melanogaster canescens (spotted morph), Mexico: Jalisco. Photo by G. M. Burghardt.

Thamnophis melanogaster canescens (striped morph), Mexico: Jalisco. Photo by G. M. Burghardt.

Plate 8

Thamnophis melanogaster canescens (ventral view), Mexico: Michoacán. Photo by R. M. Blaney.

Thamnophis melanogaster chihuahuaensis, Mexico: Durango. Photo by R. G. Webb.

Thamnophis melanogaster chihuahuaensis (ventral view), Mexico: Durango. Photo by R. G. Webb.

Thamnophis mendax, Mexico: Tamaulipas. Photo by R. M. Blaney.

Thamnophis nigronuchalis, Mexico: Durango. Photo by R. G. Webb.

Thamnophis ordinoides (red-striped morph), Washington: Thurston Co. Photo by W. P. Leonard.

Plate 9

Thamnophis ordinoides (yellow-striped morph), Washington: Pierce Co. Photo by S. L. and J. T. Collins.

Thamnophis postremus, Mexico: Michoacán. Photo by W. E. Duellman (University of Kansas Museum of Natural History slide collection).

Thamnophis proximus proximus, Illinois: Jackson Co. Photo by J. Allsteadt.

Thamnophis proximus diabolicus, Mexico: Coahuila. Photographer unknown.

Thamnophis proximus orarius, Louisiana: Jefferson Parish. Photo by J. Boundy.

Thamnophis proximus rubrilineatus, Texas: Hamilton Co. Photo by S. L. and J. T. Collins.

Plate 10

Thamnophis proximus rutiloris, Mexico: Veracruz. Photographer unknown.

Thamnophis pulchrilatus, Mexico: Jalisco. Photo by C. W. Myers.

Thamnophis radix (light morph), Kansas: Ellsworth Co. Photo by S. L. and J. T. Collins.

Thamnophis radix (dark morph), Wisconsin: Rock Co. Photo by S. L. and J. T. Collins.

Thamnophis radix (red morph), Kansas: Barton Co. Photo by S. L. and J. T. Collins.

Thamnophis rufipunctatus (red-spotted morph), Arizona: Coconino Co. Photo by A. Ford.

Plate 11

Thamnophis rufipunctatus (dark-spotted morph), New Mexico: Grant Co. Photo by W. B. Montgomery.

Thamnophis sauritus sauritus, New Jersey: Burlington Co. Photographer unknown.

Thamnophis sauritus nitae, Florida: Levy Co. Photo by S. L. and J. T. Collins.

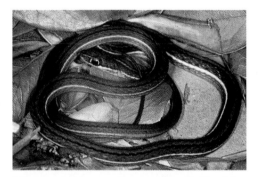

Thamnophis sauritus sackenii, Florida: Dade Co. Photo by M. Hoggren.

Thamnophis sauritus septentrionalis, Michigan: Emmet Co. Photo by S. L. and J. T. Collins.

Thamnophis scalaris, Mexico: Tlaxcala. Photo by S. A. Minton.

Plate 12

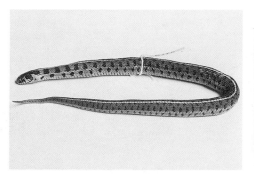

Thamnophis scaliger, Mexico: Distrito Federal. Photo by M. Kleiner (MZFC specimen).

Thamnophis sirtalis sirtalis (light morph), Virginia: Southampton Co. Photo by S. A. Minton.

Thamnophis sirtalis sirtalis (dark morph), Michigan: Schoolcraft Co. Photo by J. H. Harding.

Thamnophis sirtalis annectens, Kansas: Meade Co. Photo by S. L. and J. T. Collins.

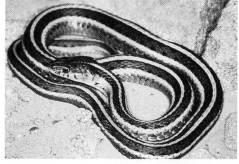

Thamnophis sirtalis concinnus, Oregon: Benton Co. Photo by R. Gonzales.

Thamnophis sirtalis dorsalis, New Mexico: Dona Ana Co. Photo by B. Bartholomew.

Plate 13

Thamnophis sirtalis fitchi, Washington: Okanagon Co. Photo by W. P. Leonard.

Thamnophis sirtalis fitchi, California: Monterey Co. Photo by A. Ford.

Thamnophis sirtalis infernalis, California: San Mateo Co. Photo by C. Schwalbe.

Thamnophis sirtalis pallidulus, Maine: Hancock Co. Photo by S. L. and J. T. Collins.

Thamnophis sirtalis parietalis, Kansas: Sedgwick Co. Photo by S. L. and J. T. Collins.

Thamnophis sirtalis pickeringii, Washington: Pierce Co. Photo by S. L. and J. T. Collins.

Plate 14

Thamnophis sirtalis semifasciatus, Illinois: Cook Co. Photo by E. Schaeffer.

Thamnophis sirtalis similis, Florida: Taylor Co. Photo by E. A. Liner.

Thamnophis sumichrasti (spotted morph), Mexico: Puebla. Photo by I. H. Conant (provided by R. Conant).

Thamnophis sumichrasti (blotched morph), Mexico: Hidalgo. Photo by W. W. Lamar (University of Texas at Arlington slide collection).

Thamnophis validus validus, Mexico: Sinaloa. Photo by N. Scott.

Thamnophis validus celaeno, Mexico: Baja California Sur. Photo by L. L. Grismer.

Plate 15

T. *rufipunctatus* habitat, New Mexico: Grant Co., East Fork, Mogollon Creek, 106° 36′ W, 33° 11′ N. Photo by W. B. Montgomery.

T. *sirtalis* eating *Bufo americanus*, Michigan: Ingham Co. Photo by J. H. Harding.

T. *couchii* containing *Salmo gairdnerii*, California: Tulare Co., South Fork, Kaweah River, South Fork Campground. Photo by R. Gonzales, 27 August 1992.

Salmo gairdnerii regurgitated by T. *couchii*, California: Tulare Co., South Fork, Kaweah River, South Fork Campground. Photo by R. Gonzales, 27 August 1992.

and either *T. couchii* or *T. atratus*, to which it had been shown to have a closer biochemical affinity (Lawson and Dessauer, 1979), Rossman and Stewart (1987) formally recognized *T. gigas* as a full species.

LIFE HISTORY AND ECOLOGY

Habitat

This species is primarily associated with marshes and sloughs (Hansen and Brode, 1980) and only occasionally is found in slow-moving creeks (Hansen and Tremper, *in prep.*). Emergent vegetation such as cattails and tules is apparently important as basking sites for this species (Van Denburgh and Slevin, 1918). Fitch (1940) collected *T. gigas* along overgrown canals with mud bottoms. The species is apparently absent from larger rivers (USFWS, 1991).

This species occupies a niche similar to that of some water snakes (*Nerodia*) in the eastern United States; i.e., it is extremely aquatic, rarely found away from water, and forages in the water for food.

Activity

Thamnophis gigas emerges from overwintering sites in mid- to late March (Hansen and Tremper, *in prep.*). It basks on willow and saltbush or on tules in open water in the spring, whereas in hotter weather ground squirrel and gopher burrows, as well as decaying piles of vegetation, are used for refuges (Hansen and Tremper, *in prep.*). Gravid females may continue basking activity throughout the summer months, and some snakes remain active until October. Fitch (1940) found *T. gigas* to be extremely alert and he had difficulty collecting them. Hansen and Tremper (*in prep.*) indicate the snake will drop into water from arboreal basking sites when observers are as far away as 15 meters.

Feeding

Thamnophis gigas feeds primarily on aquatic prey such as fish and amphibians. Hansen and Tremper (*in prep.*) suggested that the predominant food items for this species now are introduced species such as carp, mosquitofish, and bullfrogs, because historical prey such as the Sacramento blackfish, thick-tailed chub, and red-legged frog are no longer available.

Reproduction

As the largest member of the genus, *T. gigas* has a relatively large mean litter size of 23.1 (Cunningham, 1959; Hansen and Hansen, 1990). Offspring were born from 13 July to 1 September and had a mean SVL of 206.4 mm.

Population Biology

Little is known about the population biology of the giant garter snake. The smallest reproductive female recorded was 920 mm total length (Hansen and Tremper, *in prep.*). Sexual maturity may be reached in three years in males and up to five years in females (USFWS, 1991).

Captive Maintenance

Because they are aggressive in the field, *T. gigas* may be fairly temperamental in captivity.

Conservation

Thamnophis gigas was recently listed as a "threatened" species by the U.S. Fish & Wildlife Service. Major threats include loss of wetlands habitats and introduced fish predators. Hansen and Brode (1980) indicated that this species has been extirpated from the southern portion of its range but that protection of waterfowl habitats may allow *T. gigas* to survive in the Delta and Sacramento Valley regions. This is, however, only a small portion of its original range. A major study of *T. gigas* has recently been initiated by the National Biological Survey (N. Scott, pers. comm.).

Thamnophis godmani
GODMAN'S GARTER SNAKE
(Plate 6)

Tropidonotus godmani Günther, 1894

Identification

Dorsal scales in a maximum of 17 rows; supralabials usually 7 (occasionally 8); maxillary teeth 16 to 20; the dorsum brown with 2 alternating rows of relatively small black spots between the light stripes; the vertebral stripe confined to the vertebral row (distinct, indistinct, or lacking altogether); the lateral stripe variable (on rows 1 and 2, 2 only, 2 and 3, or 1, 2, and 3) but not bright; nuchal collar not interrupted by vertebral stripe; top of the head unpatterned; tongue uniformly black.

Content and Distribution

No subspecies are currently recognized. Godman's garter snake occurs at relatively high elevations (1768 to 3018 m) in the southern Sierra Madre Oriental in Puebla and Veracruz, the Mesa del Sur in Oaxaca, and the Sierra Madre del Sur in Guerrero (see Map 11).

Description

The following is based primarily on unpublished data. *Thamnophis godmani* is a moderate-sized species of garter snake, reaching a maximum SVL of 520 mm (the tail of this specimen is incomplete; TCWC 9550). The dorsum may be some shade of brown with two alternating rows of relatively small black spots, which may or may not be visible. In a few instances, the anteriormost spots (as many as 7) in the lower row are expanded vertically to form narrow bars that interrupt the lateral stripe. The skin between the scales was bright light-yellow in five live specimens from the Puebla-Veracruz state line. In these same specimens, the venter was a rich orange suffused with gray or brown. The top of the head was brown and unpatterned, the supralabials pale grayish-white, gray, grayish-tan, or gray brown (often with prominent black bars along the sutures). The vertebral stripe is usually confined to the vertebral row and, in living specimens, was some shade of tan (light in Puebla-Veracruz, dark at Llano de las Flores, Oaxaca); it may or may not be very distinct, and in some instances may be lacking altogether. The lateral stripe in the living animals was grayish-brown and highly variable in width (occupying rows 1 and 2, 2 only, 2 and 3, or 1, 2, and 3). In some preserved specimens, the lateral stripe may be barely, if at all, distinguishable. The nuchal collar may be indented posteriorly but is never interrupted by the vertebral stripe; the nuchal collar may be largely black, or the black pigment may be confined to its posterior margin. The stalk of the tongue lacks the red coloration characteristic of most garter snake species.

There are usually 17-17-17 or 17-17-15 dorsal scale rows (in about equal numbers), occasionally 17-17-16, and rarely 17-15-15. Ventrals in *T. godmani* range from 135 to 153 in males, 133 to 149 in females; males average 4.2 to 6.7 more ventrals than females. Ventral counts average higher in the Puebla-Veracruz population than in those from either Oaxaca or Guerrero. Subcaudals range from 61 to 84 in males, 51 to 75 in females; males average 6.5 to 7.9 more subcau-

Thamnophis godmani

191

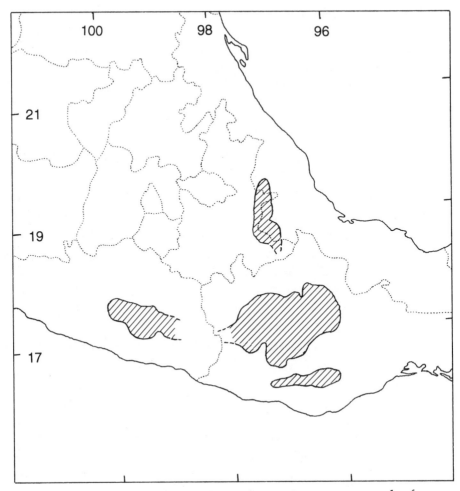

Map 11 Distribution of *Thamnophis godmani*. Open areas at ends of ranges indicate uncertainty about actual limits.

dals than females. Subcaudals counts average higher in the Guerrero population than in those from either Oaxaca or Puebla-Veracruz. Relative tail length ranges form 23.3 to 28.6% in males, 19.9 to 27.2% in females; it averages 1.1 to 2.2 % longer in males than in females. The tail is proportionately longer in the Guerrero population than in those from either Oaxaca or Puebla-Veracruz.

Preoculars invariably number 1 to a side, postoculars usually 3 (rarely 2). There usually are 7 supralabials to a side (occasionally 8), 10 infralabials (frequently 9, occasionally 11). Maxillary teeth range from 16 to 20, averaging 18.7 in males and 17.7 in females.

The head in *Thamnophis godmani* constitutes 5.4% of SVL in males and 5.7% in females—long for a garter snake. The eye is small, ED/FL averaging 62.7%. The tip of the muzzle is very wide, InR/NR averaging 121.8%. The muzzle is short in males (ML/FL averaging 62.1%), but of moderate length in females (ML/FL = 69.3%). The prefrontals are slightly longer than the internasals, Prf/In averaging 109.2%. The parietals of *T. godmani* are of moderate length, FL/PL averaging 77.8%. The posterior chin shields are moderately long, ACS/PCS averaging 81.2%.

Taxonomic Comments

Following its description by Günther in 1894, Godman's garter snake was generally overlooked until Ruthven (1908) synonymized it with *T. cyrtopsis*. There it remained until H. M. Smith (1942) recognized *godmani* as a subspecies of *T. scalaris*. Rossman (in Varkey, 1979) indicated that *T. godmani* is not conspecific with *T. scalaris*, but no evidence was presented. Allozyme data (de Quieroz and Lawson, 1994) showed that *T. godmani* and *T. errans* have identical character states.

LIFE HISTORY AND ECOLOGY

Virtually nothing is known about the ecology and captive maintenance of this species. *Thamnophis godmani* is found in the conifer zone of central Mexican mountains (H. M. Smith, 1942). J. Caldwell (pers. comm.) found them under logs and tar paper at the edge of a llano and in oak and pine-oak forests, and swimming along the edges of ponds and streams. D. A. Rossman (pers. obs.) has seen them in mountain meadows near small streams and under logs, rocks, and an agave leaf. One specimen (390 mm SVL) when captured disgorged a mouse.

Thamnophis godmani

193

Thamnophis hammondii
TWO-STRIPED
GARTER SNAKE
(Plate 6)

Eutaenia hammondii Kennicott,
1860
Tropidonotus digueti Mocquard, 1899

Identification

Dorsal scales in a maximum of 21
rows; supralabials 8; preoculars usually 2 (occasionally 1); maxillary teeth
24 to 30; the dorsum either with 2
rows of small spots or uniformly olive-brown between light stripes; no
vertebral stripe; the lateral stripe confined to rows 2 and 3 (or occasionally
absent).

Content and Distribution

No subspecies are currently recognized. The two-striped garter snake
has a continuous range from Monterey Co., California, southward to
northwestern Baja California, and it
occurs in apparently isolated colonies
in northern Baja California Sur (see
Map 12). It also occurs on Catalina
Island off the California coast (Brown,
1980). Elevational distribution extends from 0 to 2130 m (Stebbins,
1985).

Description

The following is based on Fitch (1940,
1984), Rossman and Stewart (1987),
and previously unpublished data.
Thamnophis hammondii is a relatively long species of garter snake,
reaching a maximum SVL of 840 mm
(the tail of the specimen having the
longest SVL [private collection of J. F.
Copp 62-67] is incomplete). The dorsum is olive-brown or olive-gray
with two alternating rows of small,
black spots (often difficult to see
unless the skin is stretched) on each
side above the lateral stripe, which
is yellow to pale gray (but is often
absent). The vertebral stripe is lacking except for a short section immediately behind the parietal scales that
separates the very short, black nuchal blotches. The light parietal
spots are usually black-bordered,
bright, and fused, but may be absent
in some populations.

There usually are 21-19-17 dorsal
scale rows, occasionally with a posterior reduction to 16. Ventrals range
from 155 to 178 in males, 149 to 172
in females (Fitch, 1940—extrapolated
from Fig. 13); males average 6.9 more
ventrals than females (Rossman and
Stewart, 1987). Subcaudals range
from 66 to 93 in males, 61 to 82 in
females (Fitch, 1940—extrapolated

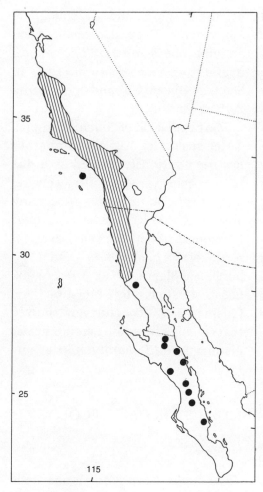

averages 1.4% longer in males than in females.

Preoculars usually number 2 to a side (occasionally 1), postoculars usually 3 (rarely 4). There usually are 8 supralabials and 10 infralabials (rarely 9 or 11). Maxillary teeth range from 24 to 30, averaging 28.7 in males and 26.6 in females.

The head in *Thamnophis hammondii* constitutes 4.8% of SVL in males and 5.0% in females—of moderate length for a garter snake. The eye is large, ED/FL averaging 73.4%. The muzzle tip is narrow, InR/NR averaging 83.4%. The muzzle is moderately long, ML/FL averaging 77.4%. The prefrontals are shorter than the internasals, Prf/In averaging 82.6%. The parietals of *T. hammondii* are long, FL/PL averaging 73.5%. The posterior chin shields are of moderate length, ACS/PCS averaging 80.9%.

Map 12 Distribution of *Thamnophis hammondii*.

Taxonomic Comments

The two-striped garter snake was first associated with *Thamnophis couchii* by Cooper (1870), when he synonymized the two taxa. It remained for Van Denburgh (1897) to resurrect *T. hammondii* as a separate species, an arrangement that was followed by Ruthven (1908). Grinnell and Camp

from Fig. 14); males average 9.3 more subcaudals than females (Rossman and Stewart, 1987). Relative tail length ranges form 22.2 to 25.2% in males, 21.1 to 23.5% in females; it

Thamnophis hammondii

195

(1917) considered *hammondii* to be a subspecies of *T. ordinoides* (not the current concept of the latter, but a catchall for what later proved to be six different species). Fitch (1940) recognized *hammondii* as a distinct species but later (1948), on the basis of examining two alleged intergrades between *hammondii* and *T. elegans couchii* (coming on the heels of Fox's 1948 paper pulling all taxa—except the nominate form—out of *T. ordinoides* and placing them in *T. elegans*), called the two-striped garter snake *T. e. hammondii*. Rossman (1964) and Fox and Dessauer (1965), in a pair of brief grant reports, indicated that the aquatic and terrestrial subspecies groups of *T. elegans* (Fox, 1951a) do not intergrade in nature but behave as two species—the terrestrial *T. elegans* and the aquatic *T. couchii* (which included *hammondii*). Subsequently, Rossman (1979) and Lawson and Dessauer (1979) confirmed and elaborated their initial preliminary reports. Lawson and Dessauer (1979), using biochemical techniques, also revealed that *T. couchii* consists of two distinct subgroups, one of which includes *T. c. couchii* and *T. c. hammondii*. Rossman and Stewart (1987) demonstrated that this complex consists of four separate species, comprising two pairs of sister-species—*T.*

atratus/T. gigas and *T. couchii/T. hammondii*. They also reported examining one *atratus* × *hammondii* hybrid from each of two localities in San Luis Obispo Co., and one in Santa Barbara Co.

The population of *couchii*-complex garter snakes in Baja California Sur has been variously treated as a distinct species (*T. digueti*) closely related to *T. hammondii* (Mocquard, 1899; Fitch, 1940), a subspecies of *T. hammondii* (Stebbins, 1985), or a synonym of *T. hammondii* (Van Denburgh and Slevin, 1918). A recent, exhaustive study by McGuire and Grismer (1993) conclusively showed that *T. digueti* is not taxonomically distinct from *T. hammondii* at any level.

LIFE HISTORY AND ECOLOGY

Habitat

Thamnophis hammondii is one of the most aquatic of the garter snakes and is typically associated with streams, creeks, and pools (Fitch, 1940; Hansen and Tremper, *in prep.*). Ford (pers. obs.) observed several individuals around a small spring-fed cattle trough in the chaparral of Channing Meadow in the Laguna Mountains (San Diego Co., California). *Tham-*

nophis hammondii occurs in oak woodlands and in mixed oak and chaparral (Hansen and Tremper, *in prep.*). The vegetation where this species occurs on San Benito Mountain (San Benito Co.) is sparse pines and cedars, scrub oak and brush (Hansen and Tremper, *in prep.*).

Activity

These snakes may be active from January to November (Hansen and Tremper, *in prep.*). Klauber (1924) suggested that *T. hammondii* may be crepuscular or nocturnal during hot weather.

Feeding

This species eats tadpoles, small anurans, and fish (Fitch, 1940, 1941b; Hansen and Tremper, *in prep.*). Worms and fish eggs also have occasionally been reported in their stomach contents. Presumably *T. hammondii* forages primarily in and under water, but no data on foraging behavior are available.

Reproduction

Courtship has been observed in *T. hammondii* in late March and early April (Cunningham, 1959; Rossi and Rossi, 1995). Clutch size averaged 15.6 (3 to 36) in seven litters; neonates were born in late July and August and averaged 203 to 217 mm in total length (Hansen and Tremper, *in prep.*). An interesting occurrence in this species was that a female isolated from males for 53 months produced a living neonate (Stewart, 1972).

Population Biology

The density and population dynamics of this species are unknown. It appears to be common in isolated pools and streams.

Captive Maintenance

Apparently this species readily feeds in captivity as Klauber (1924) mentioned that a *T. hammondii* ate 30 *Pseudacris regilla* at a single feeding. Tapeworms have been found in wild-caught specimens (Rossi and Rossi, 1995).

Conservation

This species is listed as a "Candidate 2 Species" under the Endangered Species Act. Loss of wetland habitats appears to be the main problem, a common situation in California (N. Scott, pers. comm.).

Thamnophis hammondii

197

Thamnophis marcianus
CHECKERED GARTER SNAKE
Plate 7

Eutainia marcianus Baird and Girard,
1853
  (= *T. m. marcianus*)
Eutaenia nigrolateris Brown, 1889
  (= *T. m marcianus*)
Eutaenia praeocularis Bocourt, 1892
  (= *T. m. praeocularis*)
Thamnophis arabdotus Andrews, 1937
  (= *T. m. praeocularis*)
Thamnophis ruthveni Hartweg and
Oliver, 1938
  (= *T. m. marcianus*)
Thamnophis bovallii Dunn, 1940
  (= *T. m. bovallii*)
Thamnophis rozellae H. M. Smith, 1940
  (= *T. m. marcianus* X
    praeocularis intergrades)

Identification

Dorsal scales in a maximum of 21 or
19 rows; supralabials 8; a distinctive
head pattern (black-bordered brown
area covering supralabials 7 and 8,
bracketed anteriorly by a light area
extending from postoculars to edge of
the lip and posteriorly by a narrow
light crescent; a third light area also
extending from preoculars to edge of
the lip); lateral stripe confined to 3rd
dorsal scale row on neck (rows 2 and
3 thereafter).

Content and Distribution

Three subspecies of the checkered
garter snake are currently recognized:
T. m. marcianus, ranging from southwestern Kansas westward to extreme
southeastern California and southward through northern and eastern
Mexico to northern Veracruz, with an
isolated population at the Isthmus of
Tehuantepec; *T. m. praeocularis*,
ranging from the Yucatán Peninsula
through Belize and northeastern Guatemala to western Honduras; and *T. m.
bovallii*, ranging from southwestern
Nicaragua to northern Costa Rica (see
Map 13). Elevational distribution ranges
from 0 to 1640 m (Stebbins, 1985).

Description

The following is based largely on
Mittleman (1949), Rossman (1971),
and previously unpublished data.
Thamnophis marcianus is a relatively long species of garter snake,
reaching a maximum total length of
1088 mm (Vial, 1957). Two alternating rows of large black spots form a
checkerboard pattern between the
vertebral and lateral stripes. The vertebral stripe is confined to the vertebral row and no more than one-half
of each adjacent paravertebral row in

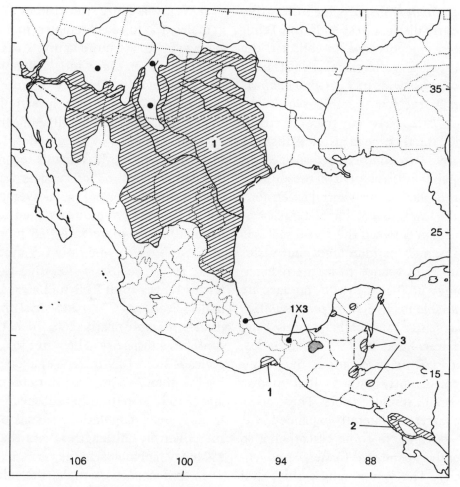

Map 13 Distribution of *Thamnophis marcianus* and its subspecies: (1) *T. m. marcianus*; (2) *T. m. bovallii*; (3) *T. m. praeocularis*. Stippling represents zones of intergradation.

T. m. marcianus, in which the stripe is fairly distinct (less so in the Tehuantepec population). In contrast, the poorly defined vertebral stripe is fully three rows wide in *T. m. praeocularis* and in the few specimens of *T. m. bovallii* that have any trace of a stripe. The lateral stripe is also less distinct in the two southern subspecies, in which it is interrupted on the anterior part of the body by ventral extensions of the lower row of dorsolateral spots. The skin between the dorsal scales is white in *T. m. marcianus*, but varies from light orange to bright reddish-orange in *T. m. bovallii* (no data are available for live *T. m. praeocularis*). The venter is virtually unspotted and cream-colored in *T. m. marcianus*, but in *T. m. praeocularis* the venter is consistently marked with two rows of small, rounded spots. These spots are larger and laterally expanded in *T. m. bovallii*, in some cases being so greatly expanded as to merge midventrally. The venter ranges from dull yellow to bright orange to vermilion in the few *T. m. bovallii* for which color notes in life exist.

There is a maximum of 21 dorsal scale rows in *T. m. marcianus* and 19 in the two southern subspecies. In either case there is a reduction to 17 rows immediately anterior to the vent. Ventrals range from 136 to 173 in males, 134 to 166 in females; males average 5.4 to 7.1 more ventrals than females in *T. m. marcianus*, 2.8 more in *T. m. bovallii*, and only 0.8 more in *T. m. praeocularis* (but the sample size of the later is very small). Subcaudals range from 64 to 82 in males, 56 to 77 in females (Mittleman's record of a female with 83 subcaudals was almost surely an error); males average 7.6 to 9.3 more subcaudals than females in *T. m. marcianus*, 5.8 more in *T. m. bovallii*, and only 0.5 more in *T. m. praeocularis*. Relative tail length ranges from 21.3 to 26.8% in males, averaging 22 to 24% in *T. m. marcianus* and nearly 26% in both southern subspecies. The range in females is from 18.9 to 26.9%, averaging less than 23% in *T. m. marcianus* and 25 to 26% in the other subspecies. In any given population, sexual dimorphism in tail length is less than 2% in favor of males; in the very small *T. m. praeocularis* sample, the relative tail lengths are identical.

Preoculars usually number 1 to a side, but this scale is semidivided or fully divided in a substantial number of *T. m. bovallii* and *T. m. praeocularis*. Postoculars usually number 3 or 4 to a side. There are normally 8 supralabials (rarely 7) and 10 infralabials (rarely 9 or 11) on each side. Maxillary teeth range from 21 to 31, averaging ca. 23 to 24 in *T. m. marcianus*, 27 in *T. m. bovallii*, and 29 in *T. m. praeocularis*.

The head constitutes 5.3% of SVL, which is long for a garter snake. The eye is of moderate size, ED/FL averaging 67.1%. For what is thought to be a predominantly terrestrial garter snake (but see Habitat below), *T. marcianus* has a surprisingly narrow muzzle tip, the combined InR/NR averaging 80.1% in males, 75.0% in females. The muzzle is long, ML/FL averaging 73.6% in males, 76.6% in females. The prefrontals are longer than the internasals (Prf/In averaging 114.0%) in *T. m. marcianus*, shorter (86.8%) in *T. m. bovallii*; no data are available for *T. m. praeocularis*. The parietals of *T. marcianus* are of moderate length, FL/PL averaging 77.1%. The posterior chin shields are long, (ACS/PCS averaging 73.7%) in *T. m. marcianus*, but of moderate length in the two southern subspecies (84.4%).

Taxonomic Comments

The complicated taxonomic history of the lowland garter snakes of Middle America, and their association with *Thamnophis marcianus*, has been discussed in detail by Rossman (1971). The unique head pattern they share clearly establishes *marcianus*, *bovallii*, and *praeocularis* as close relatives. The marked differences between *marcianus* and the latter two taxa in dorsal and ventral pattern, number of dorsal scale rows, relative tail length, and number of maxillary teeth might suggest that one would be justified in recognizing the southern races as part of a species distinct from *marcianus*, were it not for the existence of six specimens from northern Chiapas, Tabasco, and central Veracruz (Rossman, 1971, 1972) that clearly seem to be intermediate between *marcianus* and *praeocularis*. The distinctiveness of *T. m. bovallii* and *T. m. praeocularis* was a factor in the decision not to continue giving taxonomic recognition to the much less well differentiated populations formerly known as *T. m. nigrolateris* and *T. m. ruthveni*.

The relationship of *Thamnophis marcianus* to other species of garter snakes is not clear. Boulenger (1893) treated *marcianus*—along with ⅔ of all the garter snake taxa he recognized—as a variety of *T. sirtalis*. Cope (1900) considered the checkered garter snake to be a subspecies of *T. elegans*. Brown (1904), in producing a hypo-

Thamnophis marcianus

201

thetical family tree of the garter snakes, showed *T. marcianus, T. cyrtopsis*, and *T. hammondii* as sister-species derived from *T. radix*. Ruthven (1908) postulated that *T. marcianus* had evolved from *T. eques* and, in turn, had given rise to *T. radix*. H. M. Smith (1942) opined that at least in terms of body pattern (especially in the neck region), *T. marcianus* showed a much greater similarity to members of the *cyrtopsis* group than to *T. eques*. The affinity of *T. marcianus* to *T. radix* finds some support in H. M. Smith's (1946) report of apparent hybridization between the two species in southwestern Kansas. Webb (1978) suggested a possible relationship between *T. marcianus* and *T. postremus* from the Balsas Basin of Mexico.

The name *Eutaenia angustirostris* Kennicott, 1860, has not been included in the synonymy of *T. marcianus*, as was suggested by Thompson (1957), because Rossman has examined the enigmatic holotype of the former (USNM 959) and finds Thompson's arguments unconvincing (see *T. rufipunctatus* account). Likewise, Rossman (1991) did not accept Webb's (1982) identification of the holotype of *T. sumichrasti cerebrosus* (H. M. Smith, 1942) as a specimen of *T. marcianus* since the animal has a broad muzzle tip and lacks the characteristic *marcianus* head pattern.

LIFE HISTORY AND ECOLOGY

Habitat

Thamnophis marcianus are found primarily in arid grasslands and deserts, although in our experience rarely far from some source of water. Ford and Seigel (pers. obs.) found that populations of *T. m. marcianus* in southeastern Arizona are semi-aquatic, with individuals often occurring in small streams and pools, and rarely seen more than 25 meters from water. In Tucson, specimens were "caught in mud puddles on the desert a mile or more from the river" (Van Denburgh and Slevin, 1918). In Nicaragua and Costa Rica, *T. m. bovallii* has been collected in debris around lakes, near creeks, and in rivers (Shreve and Gans, 1958), and may be highly aquatic (H. Fitch, pers. comm.). Conversely, populations in southern Texas are apparently more terrestrial, sometimes found amidst open brush or around rocks of road embankments (N. Ford, pers. obs.). In southern Texas, checkered garter snakes are also found in backyards and gardens. In fact, these snakes won the unlikely title of King of the Victory Gardens during World War II (Davenport, 1943). Although these anecdotes suggest the general habitat preferences of *T. marcianus*, detailed studies of habitat utilization and seasonal activity are lacking.

Activity

No detailed field studies have followed these snakes through an entire activity season. On the basis of museum records from southern Texas and northern Mexico, *T. marcianus* is active from February until November (Karges, 1983). In southeastern Arizona, we have seen checkered garter snakes active from March until October, and they are primarily diurnal, although some activity does occur at night (Seigel and Ford, pers. obs.). Rosen (1991) found that during the active season in Arizona, checkered garter snakes were more often encountered moving than basking. In southern Texas, as temperatures warm in late spring, they become the most common snakes found on roads at night (N. Ford, pers. obs.).

Feeding

Checkered garter snakes are known to feed on a wide variety of prey, including fish, frogs, tadpoles, lizards, and earthworms. However, amphibians seem to be the favored prey. For example, Fouquette (1954) found that snakes from Texas ate mainly frogs, toads, and salamanders. Woodward and Mitchell (1990) found *T. marcianus* feeding on breeding toads (*Scaphiopus multiplicatus* and *Bufo woodhousei*) in New Mexico. Checkered garter snakes from an aquatic habitat in southeastern Arizona fed primarily on bullfrog tadpoles (*Rana catesbeiana*) and earthworms (Seigel, pers. obs.). This finding shows the ability of garter snakes to adapt to new conditions, because bullfrogs were only introduced into this part of Arizona in the 1950s. Laboratory studies on newborn snakes from southeastern Arizona showed the prey most preferred are earthworms, followed by tadpoles and fish (Rayburn, 1990). Diet also apparently changes with age; juveniles we collected in Arizona ate mainly earthworms, whereas adults ate mainly bullfrog tadpoles (Seigel, pers. obs.).

Little is known about the foraging behavior of *Thamnophis marcianus*. In Arizona, Seigel and Ford have seen snakes actively foraging for prey at night along the shoreline of a man-

Thamnophis marcianus

made pond. In southern Texas, snakes are known to scavenge along the road for toads (Fouquette, 1954). Ford even observed a checkered garter snake attempt to eat a toad that was smashed into the asphalt of a highway (Ford, pers. obs.).

Reproduction

Courtship has rarely been observed in the wild, but Tennant (1984) indicated that mating for this species in central Texas occurs in late March and early April. In Arizona, Ford and Seigel found a female being courted by four males on 25 March. In captivity, females will copulate from 1 to 32 days after emergence from hibernation, depending on the locality where they were collected (Ford and Cobb, 1992). The role of this variability in mating time is not known (see Chap. 4 for discussion). Male courtship activity has been documented for southern Texas snakes and is typical for garter snakes, except for a distinct absence of caudal-cephalic waves and an apparently stronger reliance on tail-search copulatory attempts (Perry-Richardson et al., 1990). However, Arizona *T. marcianus* do exhibit caudal-cephalic waves (Ford, pers. obs.), and this is the first observation of differences in courtship behavior among populations. Mating trials in captivity have indicated that more energetic males (those able to stay with the female during a chase and exhibiting more tail searching) have higher mating success (Perry-Richardson, 1987).

The female reproductive cycle is one of the most intriguing aspects of the biology of this species. In most garter snakes, offspring are born in late summer or early fall—August to September (see Chap. 4). Consequently, we were surprised to find that checkered garter snakes from Arizona and southern Texas give birth as early as mid-May (Ford and Seigel, pers. obs.). There also is some evidence that females from southern Texas and Mexico may give birth to more than two broods per year (Ford and Karges, 1987), although confirmation of this will require a mark-recapture study (see Chap. 4 for discussion).

Clutch size varies widely for this species, with an overall range of 5 to 31 offspring (Ford and Karges, 1987; Karges, 1983). In our field studies, mean clutch size ranged from 9.5 in southern Texas to 15.3 in southeastern Arizona. As in other garter snakes, clutch size is affected by both female size and diet. Consequently, although mean clutch size varies among populations, such geographic variation probably reflects differences in average female size and local prey availability, not adaptation to the habitat (Ford and Seigel, 1989a; see Chap. 4 for discussion).

An interesting trend in *T. marcianus* is geographic variation in offspring size, a phenomenon that is poorly documented in snakes. For example, we found that offspring from southeastern Arizona average 2.8 g, whereas offspring from southern Texas weigh only 1.8 g at birth, a 56% difference (see Chap. 4 for discussion). Data on offspring size variation in snakes are desperately needed and may be easily collected from well-maintained captive animals. This is an area of snake biology where interested amateurs can make an important contribution.

Population Biology

Very little is known about the population biology of *T. marcianus*. Our field data suggest considerable variation in the minimum size at sexual maturity for females, ranging from 345 mm SVL in southern Texas to 515 mm SVL in southeastern Arizona (Ford and Seigel, pers. obs.). Males apparently mature at somewhat smaller sizes than do females, but quantified data are lacking. As in most garter snakes, females are lager than males; mean female SVL in Arizona was 579 mm, whereas mean male SVL was only 477 mm. The sex ratio of a sample of 101 individuals from Arizona was 44 males and 57 females (Seigel, pers. obs.). Specific data on age at maturity are lacking, and no published data on survival or predators are available.

Captive Maintenance

Checkered garter snakes are one of the easiest of the garter snakes to maintain in captivity. They do not appear to resent handling (as do some other species) and are generally docile within minutes of capture. Of several hundred we have kept, only a very few would bite, although those were consistently aggressive and never tamed down. They will musk when annoyed but tend to remain calm when handled gently. Even large specimens can be housed in plastic sweater boxes. Checkered garter snakes will eat a variety of food (earthworms, frogs, toads, and fish), usually after only a few days of acclimation to captive conditions. Some individuals will readily take small mice but most have to be trained to eat this food. In addition, after feeding once or twice in captivity, this species will typically take dead prey, which allows the use of thawed food. Checkered garter snakes are known

Thamnophis marcianus

205

to occasionally eat lizards and snakes, so care in selecting cagemates is warranted. Checkered garter snakes are less susceptible to water blisters than are common garter snakes or ribbon snakes, but they still need to have dry quarters. (See Chap. 6.)

Although checkered garter snakes range in southwestern parts of North America and therefore may not hibernate for more than a few weeks, the best cue to stimulate breeding in this species in captivity still is a period of cold (7 weeks is the shortest hibernation we have tried and it stimulated successful mating). However, the minimum temperatures during the artificial hibernation need only be about 10 C (50 F) (Holtzman et al., 1989). We found that 4 C (40 F) caused some neurological problems after hibernation was terminated. We also found that snakes from an Arizona population of *T. marcianus* bred within a day of leaving hibernation but animals from southern Texas did not start mating until 28 days after emergence (Ford and Cobb, 1992). Therefore it is advisable to pair animals together several times over a period of several weeks. We keep all animals in separate cages but know of breeders who keep males and females together and still have successful matings. Most breeders believe a single male can service several females, but no one has evaluated whether or not this decreases fertility.

Even though field data suggest that snakes decrease feeding when pregnant, in our experience members of this species feed well until about two weeks before parturition. In fact, breeders should keep in mind that pregnancy is a very stressful event, and the healthier the female, the better her chances of survival. We also found that the amount of food the female was given before she became pregnant influenced how many young she produced; therefore large quantities of food are important to produce large litters (we fed up to 30% of the female's body mass twice a week; Ford and Seigel, 1989a, 1994).

Conservation

Possibly because of their distribution in some of the relatively uninhabited southwestern United States, checkered garter snakes appear to be in no jeopardy in this country, and may be increasing their range due to irrigation practices (Stebbins, 1985). Rosen and Schwalbe (1988) found that although introduced bullfrogs had reduced the numbers of *T. eques* in Arizona, the frogs had no apparent effect on *T. marcianus*. The rapid degradation of tropical lowland habitats in Mexico and Central America may be having effects on populations of *T. marcianus* there, but whether they are threatened in any area remains unknown.

Thamnophis melanogaster
MEXICAN BLACK-BELLIED GARTER SNAKE
(Plates 7 and 8)

Tropidonotus (Regina) mesomelanus Jan, 1863
    (Declared, questionably, a *nomen dubium* by H. M. Smith et al., 1950)
Tropidonotus melanogaster Peters, 1864
    (= *T. m. melanogaster*)
Tropidonotus baronis mülleri Troschel *in* Müller, 1865
    (Not a binomial name)
Tropidonotus baronis-mülleri Boulenger, 1893
    (= *T. m. melanogaster*)
Thamnophis melanogaster canescens H. M. Smith, 1942
    (= *T. m. canescens*)
Thamnophis melanogaster linearis H. M. Smith, Nixon, and P. W. Smith, 1950
    (= *T. m. linearis*)
Thamnophis melanogaster chihuahuaensis Tanner, 1959
    (= *T. m. chihuahuaensis*)

Identification

Dorsal scales usually in a maximum of 19 rows (occasionally 17); supralabials usually 8; preoculars usually 2; maxillary teeth 24 to 32; the dorsum dark brown, olive, or tan, with or without 2 alternating rows of dark spots being visible; a light vertebral stripe present in some populations, absent in others; a light lateral stripe, if present, confined to dorsal scale row 2 or also involving adjacent edges of rows 1 and 3.

Content and Distribution

Four subspecies of the Mexican black-bellied garter snake are currently recognized: *T. m. melanogaster*, which is confined to the Valley of Mexico; *T. m. linearis*, which is confined to the Valley of Toluca; *T. m. canescens*, which ranges from southwestern San Luis Potosí southward through Guanajuato to northern Michoacán, thence westward through Jalisco and western Zacatecas to Durango; and *T. m. chihuahuaensis*, an apparently isolated population in the Bavispe and El Fuerte river basins in western Chihuahua and, presumably, adjacent Sonora (see Map 14). Elevational distribution ranges from 1158 to 2545 m (Conant, 1963).

Thamnophis melanogaster

207

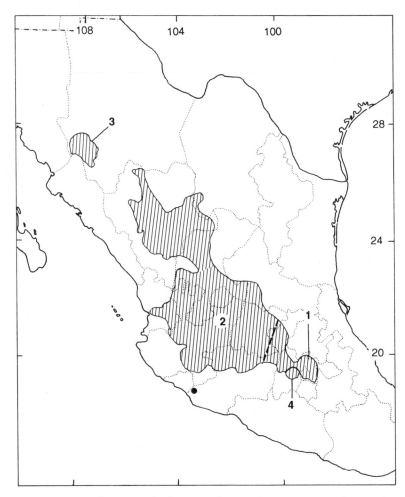

Map 14 Distribution of *Thamnophis melanogaster* and its sub-species: (1) *T. m. melanogaster*; (2) *T. m. canescens*; (3) *T. m. chihuahuaensis*; (4) *T. m. linearis.*

Description

The following is based on Conant (1963), H. M. Smith (1942), H. M. Smith et al. (1950), Tanner (1959), and previously unpublished data. *Thamnophis melanogaster* is a moderate-sized species of garter snake, reaching a maximum total length of 864 mm (Tanner, 1959). The dorsum in most populations is dark brown, either unmarked or with two alternating rows of small dark spots (the lower rows usually more conspicuous) on each side. A vertebral stripe is usually lacking (or, at most, only weakly developed), and lateral stripes usually do not contrast strongly with the dorsal ground color. In *T. m. linearis*, however, the light stripes usually are conspicuous, especially in juveniles and subadults. Ontogenetic pattern changes also occur in *T. m. chihuahuaensis*, which often has spotted juveniles and subadults but unspotted adults. In Lake Cuitzeo, Michoacán, pattern polymorphism runs rampant: Gregory et al. (1983) reported that the dorsal ground color may be brown, green, gray, red, orange, pink, or yellow; the spots may be absent or greatly enlarged; and the light stripes may be present or absent—and all this array of possibilities occurs in varying combinations. The venter may be predominantly black (*T. m. melanogaster*, *T. m. linearis*), have a black midventral stripe (some *T. m. canescens*), or essentially lack black pigment (*T. m. chihuahuaensis*, some *T. m. canescens*).

There are 19-19-17 dorsal scale rows, but 19-17-17 and 17-17-17 occur frequently in Lake Cuitzeo, Michoacán. Ventrals range from 142 to 156 in males, 136 to 150 in females; males average 4.2 to 7.5 more ventrals than females. Subcaudals range from 58 to 84 in males, 49 to 76 in females; males average 7.4 to 10.6 more subcaudals than females. Relative tail length averages (extremes not known) from 23.1 to 25.3% in males, 20.5 to 23.3% in females; it averages 1.5 to 3.1% longer in males than in females.

Preoculars usually number 2 to a side (occasionally 1 or 3), postoculars usually 3 or 2 (rarely 4). There usually are 8 supralabials (rarely 7 or 9) and 10 infralabials (rarely 9 or 11). Maxillary teeth range from 24 to 32, averaging 28.7 in males and 26.6 in females.

All of the succeeding proportional data are based on the Durango highlands population of *T. m. canescens*. The head of *Thamnophis melanogaster* constitutes 5.1% of SVL, which is long for a garter snake. The eye is of

Thamnophis melanogaster

moderate size, ED/FL averaging 66.6%. The tip of the muzzle is narrow, InR/NR averaging 72.4%. The muzzle is short, ML/FL averaging 64.6%. The prefrontals are much shorter than the internasals, Prf/In averaging 74.4%. The parietals of *T. melanogaster* are short, FL/PL averaging 80.9%. The posterior chin shields are moderately long, ACS/PCS averaging 86.6%.

Taxonomic Comments

Although H. M. Smith (1942) designated a lectotype for *Tropidonotus mesomelanus* Jan, 1863, it was not until 1950 (in H. M. Smith et al.) that he explained why he had chosen to set aside that older name in favor of *Tropidonotus melanogaster* Peters, 1864. He argued (in H. M. Smith et al., 1950) that the original citation of *T. mesomelanus* "was accompanied by such an inadequate description that authors even of that date would have been unable to distinguish the species from others then known," and consequently he declared the name a *nomen dubium*. There are problems with this action, however, because a careful reading of Jan (1863) reveals that his original description does, in fact, provide sufficient information to associate *T. mesomelanus* with the Mexican black-bellied garter snake. Jan stated that the species occurs in Mexico and that it has 19 dorsal scale rows, 8 supralabials, 2 preoculars, and 2 postoculars. The generic assignment (*Tropidonotus*) clearly indicates that Jan believed he was dealing with a natricine snake, and the specific epithet characterized a snake with black in the middle (presumably of the ventrals). No other Mexican natricine better, or more typically, fits this description than the black-bellied garter snake. The presence of two preoculars is particularly instructive, since that condition occurs only rarely in other Mexican *Thamnophis*. Many species descriptions from that time period were less informative yet have not been invalidated. Moreover, at least some of the specimens that Jan had before him may still exist (although some were destroyed in World War II). Two of them presumably formed the basis for the figures of *T. mesomelanus* that appeared in Jan and Sordelli (1868) and which unquestionably represent Mexican black-bellied garter snakes. In fact, one of these figures (that of a Vienna Museum specimen), was designated the lectotype of *T. mesomelanus* by H. M. Smith (1942). It would seem that

Smith himself was not really all that dubious about the identity of the name he subsequently declared to be a *nomen dubium*. Although this action seems to have been in error, the fact remains, however, that the senior synonym *mesomelanus* has not been used in place of the junior synonym *melanogaster* since the late-19th century, so nomenclatural stability would not be served by attempting to do so now.

Ruthven (1908) considered the Mexican black-bellied garter snake to be a subspecies of *T. rufipunctatus*. However, the two are broadly sympatric in western Chihuahua and Durango (Conant, 1963), and there is no evidence to suggest that they are even closely related.

Geographic variation in *Thamnophis melanogaster* has not been critically analyzed to date, and most of the existing subspecies are very poorly defined—if not indefinable. Conant (1963) pointed out that the light vertebral stripe supposedly unique to *T. m. linearis* is developed to some degree in 42% of the specimens of *T. m. canescens* he examined from Durango and Zacatecas. Moreover, the dorsal pattern of these animals more nearly resembles that of adult *T. m. chihuahuaensis* than it

does the polymorphic array of patterns in Lake Cuitzeo *T. m. canescens*. There appear to be some clinal differences in scale counts, but it is not at all clear if these are concordant with pattern differences.

LIFE HISTORY AND ECOLOGY

Habitat

This species is most abundant in the streams, lakes, and marshes of the Mexican Plateau, where it is found in association with *T. eques*. The Mexican black-bellied garter snake is very aquatic and apparently fills the "*Nerodia* niche" in the area. Zweifel (in Conant, 1963) indicated he found *T. melanogaster* next to rivers in deciduous woodlands. Rossman (pers. obs.) has found them around shallow meadow ponds.

Activity

Activity appears to depend both on season and elevation. Like *Nerodia*, *T. melanogaster* can be active at night in midsummer. Duellman (1961) found individuals in a hyacinth-choked marsh at Tangamandapio, Michoacán, at night. Conant (1963) collected six in Durango immediately

Thamnophis melanogaster

211

after dark at an air temperature of 22.4 C and a water temperature of 27.8 C. During warm days these snakes were found only under stones or brush. At higher elevations, *T. melanogaster* were seen sunning in brush overhanging streams in late morning (Conant, 1963). Snakes were not active when temperatures were below 19 to 20 C.

This species is quite aggressive and shows high levels of defensive attack from birth (Herzog and Burghardt, 1986). Snakes show individual differences in tendencies to strike, and litter mates are more similar in this regard than are unrelated snakes (Herzog and Burghardt, 1988), suggesting that aggressive behavior is a heritable trait. Realistic models of predators are more effective than just a cotton swab (Herzog et al., 1989), also suggesting that visual ability is acute in this species.

Feeding

This species eats primarily aquatic prey. In a sample from 175 stomachs containing 299 items, Drummond (1983) found 57% of the prey were fish, 20% leeches, 16% tadpoles, 3% earthworms, 2% crabs and 1% anurans. Gregory et al. (1983) found only small fish in 32 individuals examined. Halloy and Burghardt (1990) indicated that crayfish were also used as prey.

Like *T. couchii*, this species uses effective techniques for catching prey underwater, including cruising over the surface and diving underwater. Searching movements underwater are slow, but open-mouth searching, which is common in *Nerodia*, is apparently not used (Drummond, 1983). Vision plays a very important role in these foraging techniques; in laboratory tests these snakes will readily attack fish models even without olfactory cues (Drummond, 1985; see Chap. 5).

Reproduction

Thamnophis melanogaster is the only species of garter snake in Mexico in which the reproductive cycle has been reasonably well studied. In contrast to temperate species, the breeding cycle is more irregular and may be related to individual nutritional status (Gartska and Crews, 1985). Females become attractive and receptive when estradiol levels increase (Gartska and Crews, 1982). The courtship behavior is synchronized in a population by the presence of receptive females and lasts only a week or so (Gartska and Crews, 1985). Thus the nutrition of the females regulates the onset of courtship, possibly through the elevation of estradiol levels and the resultant production of pheromones, but some mechanism in the males regulates the duration of the breeding period. Courtship has been described in this species and resembles that for other *Thamnophis* (Ball, 1978; see Chap. 5).

A captive group of *Thamnophis melanogaster* from Lake Cuitzeo, Michoacán, produced an average clutch size of 12.9 in June and July (Ford and Ball, 1977). The number of offspring increased relative to female length, and the size of the offspring was marginally related to female size.

Population Biology

Gregory et al. (1983) captured 116 individuals (mainly juveniles) in about 3 ha of rock rubble in eight hours of collecting over a four-day period. They estimated the total in a 2 ha area to be 317 (95% confidence limits = 175–1698/ha). As mentioned above, this species shows tremendous color pattern variation (Gregory et al, 1983), which likely relates to preventing predators from developing accurate search images (see Chap. 5).

Thamnophis mendax
TAMAULIPAN MONTANE GARTER SNAKE
(Plate 8)

Thamnophis mendax Walker, 1955

Identification

Dorsal scales in a maximum of 17 rows (reducing to 15 anterior to vent); supralabials usually 7 and infralabials usually 9 on at least one side of head; maxillary teeth 21 to 24; the dorsum, with a series of very broad, black-edged brown blotches separated by narrow interspaces, either with no stripe or with the blotches divided by a light vertebral stripe; a prominent black postocular stripe; tongue uniformly black.

Content and Distribution

No subspecies are currently recognized. This, the second rarest species of garter snake, is known only from the Sierra de Guatemala portion of the Sierra Madre Oriental in southwestern Tamaulipas, Mexico (see Map 15), at elevations between 1050 and 2120 m.

Description

The following is based on Walker

Thamnophis mendax

213

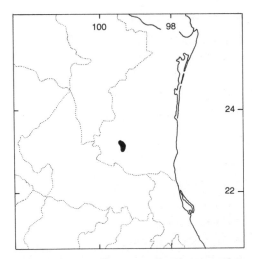

Map 15 Distribution of *Thamnophis mendax.*

(1955) and Rossman (1992b). *Thamnophis mendax* is a moderate-sized species of garter snake, reaching a maximum total length of 710 mm (Walker, 1955), although the next-largest specimen is 115 mm shorter. From 37 to 53 black-edged blotches extend across the dorsum to reach the venter in some specimens. The blotches are 2 ½ to 4 scales in length, separated by slightly lighter interspaces ½ to 1 ½ scales long. Lateral stripes are never present, but a vertebral stripe (confined to the vertebral row) often is. The dark nuchal blotches are shaped like expanded, inverted commas with the "tails" extending

onto the parietals, where they break up into irregular dark spotting. An irregular, broad black postocular stripe extends across the upper portion of the anterior temporal and the lower portion of the lower posterior temporal along the suture between supralabials 6 and 7. The tongue is uniformly black.

Each of the 14 known specimens of *T. mendax* has a maximum of 17 dorsal scale rows, and a posterior reduction of 15 rows. Ventrals range from 141 to 150 in males, 138 to 145 in females; males average 5 more ventrals than females. Subcaudals range from 64 to 69 in males, 56 to 60 in females; males average 8.4 more subcaudals than do females. Relative tail length ranges from 22.3 to 23.9% in males, 20.6 to 22.6% in females; it averages 1.8% longer in males than in females.

Preoculars number 1 to a side, postoculars usually 3. There usually are 7 supralabials (rarely 8) and 9 infralabials (less frequently 8 or 10) on each side. Maxillary teeth range from 21 to 24, averaging 22.0 in each sex.

The head constitutes 5.7% of SVL in adults, which is long for a garter snake. The eye is of moderate size, ED/FL averaging 64.7%. The muzzle tip is very broad, InR/NR averaging 130.2%. The muzzle is of moderate length, ML/FL averaging 65.8% in males, 72.7% in females. The prefrontals are shorter than the internasals, Prf/In averaging 89.3%. The parietals of *T. mendax* are short in males, of moderate size in females, FL/PL averaging 82.0% in males and 76.9% in females. The posterior chin shields are of moderate length, ACS/PCS averaging 83.4%.

Taxonomic Comments

Walker (1955) observed that *T. mendax* appears to be morphologically intermediate between *T. scalaris* and *T. phenax* (now *T. sumichrasti*), but he concluded that *T. mendax* was more closely related to *T. scalaris* and that they might eventually prove to be subspecifically related. Rossman (1992b) agreed that the meristic and mensural data are equivocal, but he argued that the similarities between *T. mendax* and *T. sumichrasti* in head and body patterns strongly suggest they are sister-species.

LIFE HISTORY AND ECOLOGY

Very little is known about this rare species. *Thamnophis mendax* is found along trails through forested mountains in the Humid Pine-Oak, lower Humid Oak–sweet gum, and Upper and Lower Cloud Forest zones (Martin, 1958; Walker, 1955). It appears this species is independent of standing surface water. Two individuals have been recorded with salamanders as prey (*Pseudoeurycea belli* and *P. scandens*) (Martin, 1958).

Thamnophis nigronuchalis
SOUTHERN DURANGO
SPOTTED GARTER SNAKE
(Plate 8)

Thamnophis nigronuchalis Thompson, 1957

Identification

Dorsal scales usually in a maximum of 21 rows; supralabials usually 8; maxillary teeth 24 to 28; two supralabials contacting the orbit; the dorsum brown with 5 or 6 alternating rows of reddish-brown or very dark brown-to-black spots; a single broad, distinct nuchal blotch; vertebral and lateral stripes lacking; supralabial bars usually black and relatively narrow; ventrals predominantly black, at least on posterior half of body; oral peritoneum with black pigment; tongue uniformly black.

Thamnophis nigronuchalis

215

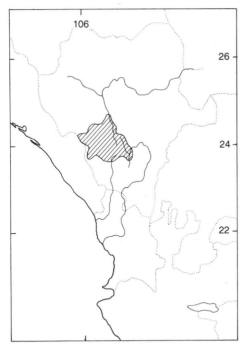

Map 16 Distribution of *Thamnophis nigronuchalis.*

Content and Distribution

No subspecies are currently recognized. All records of the southern Durango spotted garter snake, save one, are from the Rio del Presidio drainage in southwestern Durango (see Map 16). The lone exception is MVZ 59235 from Arroyo Los Mimbres, Durango, which is in the Rio del Tunal drainage. Elevations range from 2195 to 2743 m.

Description

The following is based on Rossman (1995b), Tanner (1986), and Thompson (1957). *Thamnophis nigronuchalis* is a moderate-sized species of garter snake, reaching a maximum total length of 767 mm (MVZ 59235). The dorsum is brown, olive-brown, or gray-brown in living or freshly preserved specimens, and it usually bears 5 or 6 alternating rows of spots (Thompson, 1957, reported as many as 10 rows). These spots, which number about 60 per row from the nuchal blotch to a point above the vent, are either very dark brown or reddish-brown outlined with black. The single, broad nuchal blotch is very dark brown to black and indented medially in several specimens. The throat is cream-colored, but the venter becomes progressively darker posteriorly, a dense black reticulum occupying at least the anterior half of each ventral scute on the posterior ½ to ⅔ of the body. In some individuals, it can be seen that there are two rows of large irregular spots laterally joined by a less well-defined black area medially. The dark bars preceding the supralabial sutures usually are solid black (a few have a brown core) and are narrow and vertically oriented, crescentic, wedge-shaped, or broken into spots. In very large adults the labials and ventrals are covered with a wash of brown pigment. The oral peritoneum is heavily invested with melanophores, a feature this species shares only with *T. rufipunctatus*. The tongue is uniformly black.

There usually are 21-21-17 dorsal scale rows, but an anterior increase to 22 or 23 occurs in 27.5% of the specimens (Tanner, 1986). Ventrals in *T. nigronuchalis* range from 154 to 166 in males, 151 to 158 in females; males average 6.7 more ventrals than females. Subcaudals range from 66 to 78 in males, 62 to 73 in females; males average 5.5 more subcaudals than females. Relative tail length ranges from 21.0 to 24.9% in males, 19.7 to 23.7% in females; it averages 1.5% longer in males than in females.

Preoculars number 2 to a side (rarely 3), postoculars 3 (rarely 2 or 4). Normally there are 8 supralabials to a side (frequently 9, rarely 10) and 10 infralabials (occasionally 9 or 11). Maxillary teeth range from 24 to 28; the sample size was too small to assess possible sexual dimorphism.

The head in *Thamnophis nigronuchalis* constitutes 5.2% of SVL in males and 5.6% in females—long for a garter snake. The eye is of moderate size, ED/FL averaging 67.3%. The tip of the muzzle is narrow, InR/NR averaging 82.1%. The muzzle is long, ML/FL averaging 76.1%. The prefrontals are shorter than the internasals, Prf/In in averaging 81.8%. The parietals of *T. nigronuchalis* are short, FL/PL averaging 80.4%. The posterior chin shields are short, ACS/PCS averaging 92.5%.

Taxonomic Comments

From its description in 1957 until 1985, *Thamnophis nigronuchalis* was recognized as a species distinct from—but clearly related to—its allopatric sister-species, *T. rufipunctatus*. Tanner (1986) concluded that the two taxa are subspecifically related because he believed that *nigronuchalis* differs from the Mexican population of *rufipunctatus* (which he described as *T. r. unilabialis*) only in having a single nuchal blotch, an irregular ventral pattern, and two supralabials contacting the orbit.

Rossman (1995b) reexamined specimens from all three populations, discovered that *nigronuchalis* is much more distinct from its northern relatives than had been realized, and concluded that it deserved reinstatement as a full species. He pointed out that

Thamnophis nigronuchalis

T. nigronuchalis differs from *T. rufi-punctatus* not only in the features Tanner mentioned but also in having a significantly larger eye, shorter but wider muzzle, shorter but higher loreal, and shorter parietals, as well as a different kind of supralabial barring. The two taxa also have fixed allelic differences at the Sod-2 and Fum loci (R. Lawson, pers. comm.).

LIFE HISTORY AND ECOLOGY

Little is known about the ecology of this garter snake. Tanner (1986) suggested that this species is confined to high-elevation basins, where it is often associated with deeper pools of water. D. A. Rossman (pers. obs.) has seen *T. nigronuchalis* swimming on the surface and lying on the bottom of a mountain stream. He also found them basking near the stream on cool days and concealed under logs on the banks.

Thamnophis ordinoides
NORTHWESTERN
GARTER SNAKE
(Plates 8 and 9)

Tropidonotus ordinoides Baird and Girard, 1852
Eutainia leptocephala Baird and Girard, 1853

Eutaenia cooperi Kennicott in Cooper, 1860
Thamnophis leptocephala olympia Meek, 1899
Thamnophis rubristriata Meek, 1899

Identification

Dorsal scales usually in a maximum of 17 rows; supralabials usually 7 on each side of head; maxillary teeth 16 to 20; the dorsum highly variable in color (black, gray, or some shade of brown—occasionally having a bluish or greenish cast); vertebral stripe, if present, red, orange, yellow, white, or blue; lateral stripe often faint or absent, usually confined to dorsal scale rows 2 and 3; venter often with black or red markings.

Content and Distribution

No subspecies are currently recognized. The northwestern garter snake ranges along the Pacific Coast from southwestern British Columbia (including Vancouver Island) to extreme northwestern California (see Map 17) at elevations from 0 to 1370 m (Stebbins, 1985).

Description

The following is based largely on Fitch (1940), Fox (1948), and pre-

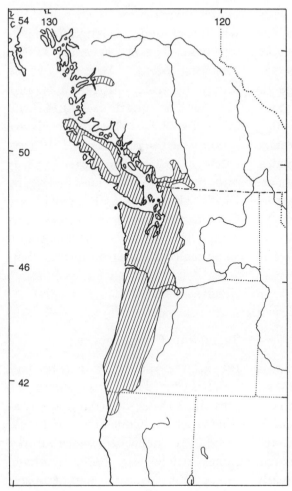

Map 17 Distribution of *Thamnophis ordinoides.*

is exceptionally long. Dorsal coloration is highly variable, various authors reporting ground colors ranging from brown to gray to black (occasionally with a greenish or bluish cast). The vertebral stripe is usually well developed; it is either confined to the vertebral row or it also involves the adjacent edges of the paravertebral rows, but it may be indistinct or lacking altogether. When present, the vertebral stripe is some shade of red, orange, yellow, white, or blue. The lateral stripe is frequently indistinct or absent; when present, it usually is confined to dorsal scale rows 2 and 3 but occasionally may involve the upper edge of row 1 as well. Relatively small dark spots often may be seen adjacent to the vertebral stripe and immediately above the lateral stripe. The venter may range from yellow through some shade of brown to slate gray, often marked with red or black pigment (the latter occurring more commonly in the northern part of the range).

There usually are 17-17-15 dorsal scale rows, rarely reducing to 15 rows at the neck or midbody, rarely reduc-

viously unpublished data. *Thamnophis ordinoides* is a moderate-sized species of garter snake, reaching a maximum total length of 965 mm (Stebbins, 1985), although that record

Thamnophis ordinoides

219

ing to 13 rows in front of the vent, and rarely increasing to 19 rows at midbody. Ventrals in *T. ordinoides* range from 138 to 160 in males, 134 to 159 in females; males average 2.5 more ventrals than do females. Subcaudals range from 61 to 82 in males, 55 to 72 in females; males average 8.5 more subcaudals than do females. These ventral and subcaudal data are based on Fox's (1948) huge series from northwestern California; subcaudal numbers apparently are lower in more-northern populations (Fitch, 1940). Relative tail length in a small series ranges from 22.4 to 27.6% in males, 21.8 to 23.5% in females; it averages 2.6% longer in males than in females.

Preoculars usually number 1 to a side in the southern part of the range, 1 or 2 from extreme northwestern Oregon to the Puget Sound region of Washington, and usually 2 in the northernmost populations. Postoculars usually number 3 (occasionally 2). There usually are 7 supralabials to a side, but 8 also occur (rarely in the north, occasionally in the south), as do 6 (rarely). Infralabials usually number 8 to a side (frequently 9, rarely 7 or 10). Maxillary teeth range from 16 to 20, averaging 19.0 in males and 18.3 in females.

The head of *Thamnophis ordi-noides* constitutes 4.7% of SVL, which is of moderate length for a garter snake. The eye is small, ED/FL averaging 62.4%. The tip of the muzzle is wide, InR/NR averaging 113.1%. The muzzle is long, ML/FL averaging 73.2%. The prefrontals are longer than the internasals, Prf/In averaging 118.2%. The parietals of *T. ordinoides* are long, FL/PL averaging 74.2%. The posterior chin shields are of moderate length, ACS/PCS averaging 82.5%; Fitch (1940) found some regional variation in this character, but no consistent geographic trends.

Taxonomic Comments

Its extreme variability in color pattern has caused the northwestern garter snake to be described repeatedly as a new species; in one instance (Meek, 1899), this happened twice in the same article! In 1908, Ruthven lumped this species in with a cluster of taxa we now recognize as four distinct species (*T. atratus, T. couchii, T. elegans, T. gigas*), and he referred to the whole group as *T. ordinoides*. Although Van Denburgh and Slevin (1918) and Fitch (1940) continued to follow this arrangement (with the former adding in *T. hammondii*, and the latter removing it), Fox (1948) presented convincing evidence that the northwestern garter snake is specifically distinct from the other taxa, whose further taxonomic adventures are related in their respective species accounts.

LIFE HISTORY AND ECOLOGY

Habitat

This species is commonly found in open areas close to thickets in lowlands, meadows, and grassy berms in the coniferous forests of the northwestern United States, frequently associated with the coastal fog belt (Fitch, 1940; Hebard, 1951; Stewart, 1968). Gregory (1984b) has studied this species extensively on Vancouver Island, British Columbia, where *T. ordinoides* is syntopic with *T. sirtalis* and *T. elegans*. Although all three species were often found at the same sites, *T. ordinoides* was found most often near the edges of forests or in less-dense woodlands than was *T. sirtalis*. In general, *T. ordinoides* was less associated with open water than was *T. elegans* (Gregory, 1984b), although it has been seen swimming (Kirk, 1983). The abundance of *T. ordinoides* at a site was negatively correlated with the presence of *T. elegans*, perhaps because of their similar food niches (Gregory, 1984b) or because *T. elegans* can prey on *T. ordinoides*.

Activity

In most of the range of this species, activity begins around den sites in March and early April (Stewart, 1968). Operational body temperatures have been reported to average about 25 C for males and nongravid females (Gregory, 1984a) but about 27 C for gravid animals. These body temperatures are correlated with substrate temperature for individuals found under cover but not for active animals (Gregory, 1984a). Active snakes may be involved in behaviors that limit opportunities for thermoregulation, e.g., foraging or seeking mates, and so body temperatures do not necessarily reflect actual temperature preferences (see Chap. 5). Gravid animals spend more time basking than do males and nongravid animals. In both Washington and Oregon, this species returns to the overwintering site by mid-October (Hebard, 1951; Stewart, 1968).

Lawson (1991) studied the orientation mechanisms of *T. ordinoides* on southern Vancouver Island and found that this species was nonmigratory. Although these snakes used some sun-compass orientation and fol-

Thamnophis ordinoides

lowed other snakes' pheromone trails to locate hibernacula, den sites were so plentiful that these animals showed little fidelity to particular hibernation areas. Individuals often shifted home ranges from year to year (Lawson, 1991).

In an elegant series of studies, Brodie (1989b, 1990, 1992) found that escape behavior in northwestern garter snakes was correlated with color pattern and that behavior and color patterns were genetically correlated. Striped snakes crawled directly away from predators because it is difficult to detect motion or judge the speed of a striped object. On the other hand, spotted or unmarked snakes suddenly changed directions then held still when they encountered potential predators, since a blotched pattern makes it hard for a predator to locate a prey item with this pattern.

Feeding

This species is a specialist on slugs and earthworms (Fitch, 1941b; Fox, 1952; Gregory, 1978; 1984b). Salamanders are taken rarely, although lab tests using tongue-flick scores suggest that T. ordinoides potentially has a wider diet than field data indicate (Burghardt, 1969; Carr and Gregory, 1976), possibly the result of habi-

tat restrictions. Interestingly, *T. ordinoides* has little resistance to the toxin produced by the newt *Taricha granulosa* (Brodie and Brodie, 1990) even though it will eat amphibians in the laboratory.

Reproduction

In both Washington and Oregon, this species exhibited mating activity both in late March to early April and again in late September to early October (Hebard, 1951; Stewart, 1968). Ovulation occurred in late May or early June at both sites (Hebard, 1951; Stewart, 1968). Offspring were born in late August, after about 9 weeks of gestation (Hebard, 1951). Reproductive frequency varied from 66% of females gravid in Washington (Hebard, 1951) to 78% gravid in Oregon (Stewart, 1968). More data on this variable would be welcome.

There is considerable variation in clutch size in this species, with mean clutch sizes ranging from 5.2 to 9.5; interestingly, these extremes both come from Oregon (see summary in Table 4-1). Hebard (1950) indicated that 72 newborn northwestern garter snakes he measured had a mean snout-vent length of 127 mm. Stewart (1968) measured litters from six females and suggested that male neonates were born at a slightly smaller size (136 mm SVL) than were females (140 mm SVL), and he also indicated that larger females had larger offspring. However, conclusions derived from only six animals should be accepted cautiously.

Population Biology

This species matures at a relatively small body size compared with other garter snakes; 280 to 360 mm SVL for females and 225 to 390 mm SVL for males (Fitch, 1940; Fox, 1948; Hebard, 1951; Stewart 1968). Stewart (1968) suggested that males might reach sexual maturity in their first year of growth and females by age 2, but this has not been verified. He also found that the sex ratio among newborn offspring was biased in favor of males.

Captive Maintenance

Although inoffensive in behavior and usually reluctant to bite, this species can be somewhat difficult to maintain in captivity because of its preference for slugs and earthworms. It is easy for snakes to lose weight on this diet if they are not fed quite often (see Chap. 6). Calcium supplements are important for any *Thamnophis* when worms are fed exclusively (Scudder-

Davis and Burghardt, 1987). Rossi and Rossi (1995) mention that a metabolic bone disease occurred in a specimen of this species that was fed earthworms exclusively. Laboratory studies suggest fish and small amphibian larvae would also be consumed by this species (Burghardt, 1969).

Conservation

Populations of this species are not known to be in any immediate jeopardy.

Thamnophis postremus
TEPALCATEPEC VALLEY
GARTER SNAKE
(Plate 9)

Thamnophis eques postremus H. M.
  Smith, 1942

Identification

Dorsal scales in a maximum of 19 rows; supralabials 7 or 8; maxillary teeth 25 to 30; the dorsum tan with 2 rows of small black spots between the light stripes; the lateral stripe involving rows 1 to 3.

Content and Distribution

No subspecies are currently recognized. As its common name implies,

Thamnophis postremus

223

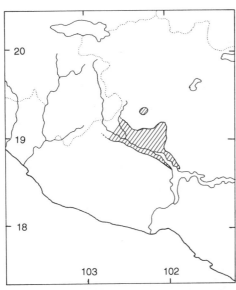

Map 18 Distribution of *Thamnophis postremus*. Open area at western end of range indicates uncertainty about actual limits.

T. postremus is confined to the Tepalcatepec Valley of Michoacán (see Map 18) at elevations from 236 to 1067 m.

Description

The following is based on Webb (1978) and Rossman (1992a). *Thamnophis postremus* is a moderate-sized species of garter snake, reaching a maximum SVL of 595 mm (the tail is incomplete in this specimen, UMMZ 112528). The dorsum is tan with 2 alternating rows of small black spots (not ex-ceeding 1 scale in length) between the light stripes, which do not contrast markedly with the dorsal ground color. The vertebral stripe is confined to the vertebral scale row; the lateral stripes involve rows 1–3. Small, irregular black spots on row 1 extend onto the venter. Black bars along the sutures of the posterior infralabials almost always involve more than one suture. The black nuchal collar is uninterrupted middorsally.

There are 19-19-17 dorsal scale rows. Ventrals range from 142 to 151 in males, 136 to 143 in females; males average 6.3 more ventrals than females. Subcaudals range from 71 to 78 in males, 65 to 73 in females; males average 4.1 more subcaudals than females. Relative tail length ranges from 23.2 to 25.5% in males, 22.3 to 24.8% in females; it averages 0.8% longer in males than in females.

Preoculars number 1 to a side (occasionally 2), postoculars 3 (occasionally 2, rarely 4). There normally are 7 or 8 supralabials, 10 infralabials. Maxillary teeth range from 25 to 30, averaging 28.7 in males and 27.2 in females.

The head constitutes 5.0% of SVL in adult males, 5.5% in adult females—moderate-sized and long, respectively, for a garter snake. The eye is large, ED/FL averaging 73.0%. The muzzle tip is of moderate width, InR/NR averaging 93.5%. The muzzle is long, ML/FL averaging 76.7%. The prefrontals are shorter than the internasals, Prf/In averaging 85.5%. The parietals of *T. postremus* are of moderate length, FL/PL averaging 79.4%. The posterior chin shields are of moderate length, ACS/PCS averaging 79.7%.

Taxonomic Comments

First described as a subspecies of *Thamnophis cyrtopsis* (H. M. Smith 1942), *postremus* was synonymized with *T. cyrtopsis cyclides (= T. c. collaris)* by Milstead (1953). The Tepalcatepec Valley garter snake was again recognized as a subspecies of *T. cyrtopsis* by Duellman (1961). This arrangement was followed by Webb (1966), although later (1978) he expressed the opinion that at the time of his 1966 study he felt that *postremus* was only weakly differentiated from *T. c. collaris*. In his later reexamination of *postremus*, Webb (1978) concluded that not only is *postremus* a well-defined subspecies, but—in the absence of intergradation with *T. c. collaris—postremus* might not even be a population of *T. cyrtopsis*. Webb commented further that he perceived a resemblance between *postremus*

and trans-Isthmian populations of *T. marcianus*. Rossman (1992a) formally elevated *T. postremus* to species status, but he contended that its relationships lie with *T. cyrtopsis collaris* rather than with *T. marcianus*.

LIFE HISTORY AND ECOLOGY

Virtually nothing is known about the ecology of this snake. *Thamnophis postremus* is restricted to the lowland arid tropical scrub forest, which extends up to about 1067 m (Webb, 1978). Duellman (1961) found *T. postremus* to be abundant near temporary pools where frogs were breeding. A 576-mm SVL female produced 25 young on 20 June 1958 (Duellman, 1961). The neonates averaged bout 135 mm SVL and 176 mm total length.

Thamnophis proximus
WESTERN RIBBON SNAKE
(Plates 9 and 10)

Coluber proximus Say *in* James, 1823
    (= *T. p. proximus*)
Eutainia faireyi Baird and Girard, 1853
    (= *T. p. proximus*)
Eutaenia rutiloris Cope, 1885b
    (= *T. p. rutiloris*)
Thamnophis proximus orarius Rossman, 1963
    (= *T. p. orarius*)

Thamnophis proximus rubrilineatus
   Rossman, 1963
      (= *T. p. rubrilineatus*)
Thamnophis proximus diabolicus
   Rossman, 1963
      (= *T. p. diabolicus*)
Thamnophis proximus alpinus Rossman,
   1963
      (= *T. p. alpinus*)

Identification

Dorsal scales in a maximum of 19 rows; supralabials 8 (rarely 7); maxillary teeth 27 to 34; the dorsum uniformly brown, olive-gray, or black between the light stripes; the lateral stripe confined to dorsal scale rows 3 and 4; a dark ventrolateral stripe absent or narrow; labials without dark markings.

Content and Distribution

Six subspecies of the western ribbon snakes are currently recognized: *T. p. proximus*, which ranges from Indiana and southern Wisconsin westward to western Kansas and southward to central Louisiana and eastern Texas; *T. p. alpinus*, a high-elevation race confined to central Chiapas; *T. p. diabolicus*, which ranges from southeastern Colorado southward through the Pecos Valley to Coahuila, Nuevo

León, and west-central Tamaulipas; *T. p. orarius*, which is a coastal form ranging from southeastern Louisiana to northeastern Tamaulipas; *T. p. rubrilineatus*, which is confined to the Edwards Plateau of central Texas; and *T. p. rutiloris*, which ranges from southern Tamaulipas and coastal Guerrero to central Costa Rica (see Map 19). Elevational distribution ranges from 0 to 2438 m.

Description

The following is based on Rossman (1963) and previously unpublished data. *Thamnophis proximus* is a very long species of garter snake, reaching a maximum SVL of 900 mm (the tail is incomplete in this specimen, USNM 761). The dorsum is uniformly olive-gray, olive-brown, dark brown, or black between the lateral stripes, which are some shade of yellow. The dark coloration below the lateral stripes rarely extends very far onto the venter. The vertebral stripe varies in color geographically and may be grayish-tan, gold, orange, or red. The light parietal spots are brightly colored, fused together, and usually rather large.

There are 19-19-17 dorsal scale rows. Ventrals in *T. proximus* range from 142 to 181 in males, 141 to 177

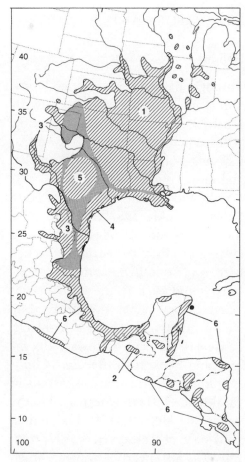

Map 19 Distribution of *Thamnophis proximus* and its subspecies: (1) *T. p. proximus*; (2) *T. p. alpinus*; (3) *T. p. diabolicus*; (4) *T. p. orarius*; (5) *T. p. rubrilineatus*; (6) *T. p. rutiloris*. Stippling represents zones of intergradation. The dot east of the Yucatán Peninsula represents Cozumel Island.

in females. Depending on the population, sexual dimorphism ranges from females averaging 0.3 more ventrals than males to males averaging 6.7 more ventrals than females. Subcaudals range from 91 to 131 in males, 82 to 124 in females; depending on the population, sexual dimorphism ranges from females averaging 0.8 more subcaudals than males to males averaging 15.2 more subcaudals than females. Relative tail length ranges from 26.0 to 33.3% in males and from 25.2 to 33.6% in females; depending on the population, sexual dimorphism ranges from relative tail length averaging 0.4% longer in females than in males to relative tail length averaging 2.2% longer in males than in females.

Preoculars number 1 to a side, postoculars usually 3 (occasionally 4, rarely 2). There usually are 8 supralabials (occasionally 7, rarely 9) and 10 infralabials (rarely 9 or 11). Maxillary teeth range from 27 to 34 with a mean of 30.0; there appears to be neither sexual dimorphism nor geographic variation.

The head in *Thamnophis proximus* constitutes 3.9% of SVL, which is very short for a garter snake. The eye is of moderate size, ED/FL averaging 69.1%. The tip of the muzzle is narrow, InR/NR averaging 79.3%. The

Thamnophis proximus

227

muzzle is long, ML/FL averaging 75.6%. The prefrontals are slightly shorter than the internasals, Prf/In averaging 94.8%. The parietals of *T. proximus* are short, FL/PL averaging 82.3%. The posterior chin shields are long, ACS/PCS averaging 76.1%.

Taxonomic Comments

First described as a distinct species, *Thamnophis proximus* was considered to be a western subspecies of *T. sauritus* by most authors between 1908 (Ruthven) and 1962 when Rossman (1962a) demonstrated that the eastern and western ribbon snakes occur macrosympatrically without intergrading at several points along the common border of their ranges, thus behaving as two species. This conclusion was later confirmed by Gartside et al. (1977). The ribbon snakes seem to have undergone speciation fairly recently (Gartside et al., 1977), with *T. proximus* apparently more closely resembling their common ancestor (Rossman, 1963). In the relative size and position of their visceral organs, *T. proximus* and *T. sauritus* are similar to each other but unlike other garter snakes (N. J. Rossman et al., 1982).

LIFE HISTORY AND ECOLOGY

Habitat

Throughout its extensive range *T. proximus* is strongly associated with brushy habitats in close conjunction with aquatic situations (swamps, marshes, ponds, lakes, rivers, creeks, and desert springs—Rossman, 1963; Wright and Wright, 1957). Near New Orleans, Tinkle (1957) collected most individuals on a ridge through a swamp or along the edges of ditches bordering roads. In the spring, *T. proximus* would bask in the open in elevated areas. When disturbed they would rapidly seek refuge in blackberries (*Rubus* sp.), willows (*Salix nigra*), and buckbrush (*Baccharis halimifolia*) on the ridge and in cattails in the ditches, but rarely retreated to the water (Tinkle, 1957). In Oklahoma, Ford (pers. obs) observed that *T. proximus* was also nearly always in brush very near ponds or small pools, but they would quickly dive into the water when approached. In Indiana, this species has been reported to occupy more open and drier areas than *T. sauritus* (Minton, 1972). In a nature preserve in northeastern Texas, Ford has found this species restricted to a lowland sphagnum bog (Ford et al., 1991).

The ecology of Mexican and Central American populations of *T. proximus* is essentially unstudied. They have been observed in bushes in Belize (Bocourt, 1893) and in rushes in Chiapas and San Luis Potosí, the latter snake being almost two meters above the water (Rossman, 1963). They have also been reported in a brackish mangrove swamp in Yucatán (Ruthven, 1908) and in a high, dry savanna in Belize (Neill and Allen, 1959).

In Kentucky, *T. proximus* hibernates in rocky banks near water, and in Illinois they are known to hibernate in rocky outcrops with copperheads and rattlesnakes (Ernst and Barbour, 1989). Seigel (pers. obs.) has found group hibernacula along spoil banks in a marsh north of New Orleans, whereas Ford (pers. obs.) found a single subadult hibernating underground in a lowland woodland in east Texas.

Activity

In more northern areas in the United States *T. proximus* is probably active from March or April to October or early November. For example, in northern Missouri, Seigel (pers. obs.) recorded activity from 1 April through 12 November. However, in more southern locations such as southern Louisiana and southern Texas, *T. proximus* can be active throughout the year when weather conditions are favorable, and hibernation in southern localities appears to be an intermittent phenomenon (Clark, 1974; Tinkle, 1957; Seigel, pers. obs.). Indeed, Seigel (pers. obs.) has found individuals with fresh prey in their stomachs in December and January, although Clark (1974) did not record feeding during January and February. Activity in midwinter (December and January) may occur only after several warm days (>15 C) in a row (Tinkle, 1957; Seigel, pers. obs.). Rainfall in spring or fall stimulated high activity in this species in both Louisiana and in Texas (Clark, 1974; Tinkle, 1957), presumably because of the increased abundance of anuran prey.

This species appears to be primarily diurnal but may be active at night in areas where nocturnal temperatures permit (Rossman, 1963). Several observations of western ribbon snakes foraging in ponds at night have been reported (Ernst and Barbour, 1989; Wendelken, 1978). In Texas, however, Ford (pers. obs.) has not seen them during his nocturnal road surveys, and Seigel (pers. obs.) rarely has seen

Thamnophis proximus

this species active at night in northwestern Missouri.

Feeding

This species feeds mainly on amphibians. Fouquette (1954) found that 82% of the prey of this snake in Texas were amphibians. Rossman (1963) reported that 17 species of anurans, 2 salamanders, and 4 fish were known as prey of *Thamnophis proximus*. Clark (1974) found that 92% of Texas specimens with prey had eaten amphibians. Clark also found that two individuals had eaten skinks (*Scincella lateralis*) and one had eaten a fish.

Foraging behavior has been observed several times for this species. Wendelken (1978) indicated that *T. proximus* probes for frogs with the anterior body until one moves and then chases it. Fouquette (in Rossman, 1963) described a *T. proximus* localizing a Mexican treefrog (*Smilisca baudinii*) by the movements of the frog's vocal sacs. Seigel (pers. obs.) has seen individuals actively foraging for small leopard frogs along mudflats in Missouri.

Reproduction

Gravid females have been found as early as April (Carpenter, 1958; Neill and Allen, 1959; Tinkle, 1957), and recorded parturition dates range from 25 June to 14 September (Fitch, 1970; Powell, 1982; Rossman, 1963). The percentage of females found gravid ranges from 81% in Missouri (Seigel and Ford, 1987) to 88% in southern Louisiana (Tinkle, 1957) to 100% in southern Texas (Clark, 1974), suggesting that reproduction is likely annual. For a species as long as *T. proximus*, mean clutch size is rather low, ranging from 8.4 to 12.9 (see summary in Table 4-1). Mean neonate SVL varied from 130 to 174 mm among broods from females from Texas (Ford et al., 1990).

Tinkle (1957) suggested that one female in his study area may have been capable of two clutches in one season. It contained large developing follicles, as well as a distended body wall and convoluted oviducts, suggesting recent parturition. However, as indicated in Chap. 4, multiple clutches have never been confirmed for garter snakes (or, indeed, any snakes in the wild).

Population Biology

Clark (1974) reported density estimates of 16 to 61 snakes/ha over a three-year period. Minimum size at maturity apparently varies among populations; the smallest gravid female from Tinkle's (1957) Louisiana population was 485 mm SVL, whereas Clark (1974) reported a minimum size of 515 mm SVL in Texas. Sexual maturity may occur at a smaller size in the Mexican and Central American populations as Rossman (1963) recorded gravid females with SVLs of 355 mm from Belize and 385 mm from Veracruz. On the basis of limited mark-recapture data, Clark (1974) suggested females reach mature size about 12 to 15 months after birth and probably mate for the first time during their second spring. Tinkle (1957) suggested that male *T. proximus* mature at about 2 years of age at 410 mm SVL. On the basis of growth data, Clark (1974) reported a minimum age at maturity for males of less than one year, but this has not been confirmed by other studies.

Captive Maintenance

This species seems to feed and reproduce fairly well in captivity. Conant (1965) maintained a pair collected from Nuevo León, Mexico, for four years, and the female gave birth to five litters, each separated by a little as three months. However, their nervous nature and the habit of "launching" themselves out of a cage as soon as it is opened make them one of the less enjoyable *Thamnophis* to keep. Even so, this species is one of the most common snakes sold in pet stores in the United States. They are active and quite visible in a terrarium but adapt to handling only with difficulty. Rossi and Rossi (1995) report a Texas specimen had whipworms (*Capillaria*) in its stool.

Conservation

Ernst and Barbour (1989) suggested that populations of this species have disappeared because of draining and filling of wetlands. Indeed, western ribbon snakes are listed as "endangered," "threatened," or "species of special concern" in four states in the United States, albeit mainly in areas of peripheral distribution. By contrast, populations of *T. proximus* in northwestern Missouri have remained apparently stable between 1979 and 1994, and the species is quite abundant in the Gulf Coast areas of Louisiana and Texas (Seigel and Ford, pers. obs.). We have no information on population status outside the United States.

Thamnophis proximus

Thamnophis pulchrilatus
YELLOW-THROATED GARTER SNAKE
(Plate 10)

Eutaenia pulchrilatus Cope, 1885a

Identification

Dorsal scales in a maximum of 19 rows; supralabials usually 7; maxillary teeth 17 to 23; the dorsum either spotted or uniformly dark between the light stripes; the lateral stripe confined to rows 2 and 3; large dark spots present below the lateral stripe; throat yellow.

Content and Distribution

No subspecies are currently recognized. The yellow-throated garter snake is an upland species distributed from Durango to Tamaulipas and Nuevo León in an arc that roughly outlines the Mexican Plateau but reaches as far south as Oaxaca (see Map 20) at elevations ranging from 1372 to 2804 m. Were it not for the Tamaulipas locality, the minimum elevation for its occurrence would be 2240 m.

Description

The following is based on Webb (1966, 1978) and Rossman (1992a). *Thamnophis pulchrilatus* is a moderate-sized species of garter snake, reaching a maximum total length of 772 mm (FMNH 37124). The dorsum is black or brown with 2 rows of large, alternating black spots (the black scales having brown keels); the very narrow vertebral stripe is bright yellow, and the lateral stripes are cream or white. A series of large dark spots is present below the lateral stripe but is often difficult to see posterior to the neck in snakes having a black dorsum. The infralabials, chin, and throat are yellow (often rather bright). A light postocular spot occupies the anterior end of the large anterior temporal as well as the two lower postoculars. A broad black bar extends from the lower posterior portion of the anterior temporal ventrally across the suture between supralabials 6 and 7 to the lip. The nuchal collar is not interrupted by the vertebral stripe.

There are 19-19-17 dorsal scale rows. Ventrals range from 154 to 172 in males, 152 to 173 in females; there appears to be little, if any, dimorphism. Subcaudals range from 80 to 94 in males, 68 to 84 in females; males

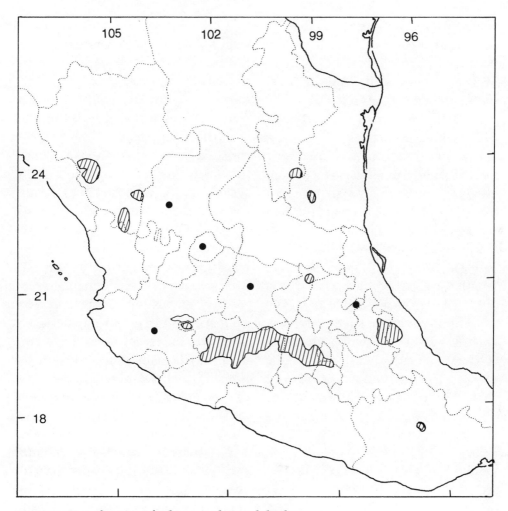

Map 20 Distribution of *Thamnophis pulchrilatus.*

average 10.2 more subcaudals than females. Relative tail length ranges from 24.5 to 26.8% in males, 22.1 to 25.2% in females; it averages 2.1% longer in males than in females.

Preoculars number 1 to a side, postoculars 3 (occasionally 4). There normally are 7 supralabials to a side rarely 8) and 10 infralabials (occasionally 11, rarely 9). Maxillary teeth range from 17 to 23, averaging 19.8 in males and 18.9 in females.

The head constitutes 4.8% of SVL in both sexes, which is of moderate length for a garter snake. The eye is large, ED/FL averaging 71.6%. The muzzle tip is very broad, InR/NR averaging 126.8%. The muzzle is of moderate length, ML/FL averaging 69.8%. The prefrontals are shorter than the internasals, Prf/In averaging 89.9%. The parietals of *T. pulchrilatus* are of moderate length, FL/PL averaging 77.9%. The posterior chin shields are of moderate length, ACS/PCS averaging 86.9%.

Taxonomic Comments

Just eight years after its description by Cope (1885a), *T. pulchrilatus* was synonymized with *T. cyrtopsis* (then known as *eques*) by Boulenger (1893), only to be revived by Cope (1900), who stated that *pulchrilatus* "belongs to a different section of the genus." Cope's opinion notwithstanding, Ruthven (1908) again relegated *pulchrilatus* to the synonymy of *T. cyrtopsis*, insisting that the two taxa were indistinguishable save for the number of supralabials. The yellowthroated garter snake remained unrecognized as a valid taxon until Webb (1966) established it as a subspecies of *T. cyrtopsis*. Webb (1966) noted the apparently sympatric occurrence—without evidence of intergradation—of *pulchrilatus* with *T. cyrtopsis collaris* in Guanajuato and Michoacán, but—believing there was evidence of intergradation between these two taxa elsewhere—he attributed the Guanajuato record to questionable locality data and the Michoacán record to probable elevational differences at the collecting site. In a subsequent publication, Webb (1978) again noted the absence of intergradation in Michoacán. Rossman (1992a) demonstrated that *pulchrilatus* occurs either sympatrically or parapatrically with *T. c. cyrtopsis* in Durango and Tamaulipas, and with *T. c. collaris* in Jalisco, Nayarit, Oaxaca, and Queretaro (in addition to Guanajuato and Michoacán), without intergrading with either subspecies of *T. cyrtopsis*; consequently, he raised *T. pulchrilatus* to species status.

LIFE HISTORY AND ECOLOGY

Except for distribution records, little is known about the ecology of this species. *Thamnophis pulchrilatus* occurs in high-elevation boreal, nontropical, pine-oak and fir forests (Duellman, 1965; Webb, 1966, 1978). Rossman (pers. obs.) found a gravid female beneath a chunk of lava at the edge of a pine forest in Veracruz.

Thamnophis radix
PLAINS GARTER SNAKE
(Plate 10)

Eutainia radix Baird and Girard, 1853
Eutaenia haydenii Kennicott, 1860
Tropidonotus (Eutainia) glaphyros Jan, 1863
Tropidonotus (Eutainia) kennicotti Jan, 1863
Eutaenia radix twiningi Coues and Yarrow, 1878
Eutaenia radix melanotaenia Cope, 1889

Identification

Dorsal scales in a maximum of 21 or 19 rows (frequently only 19 on neck); supralabials usually 7 or 8 and infralabials 9 or 10; maxillary teeth 20 to 27; light lateral stripe usually confined to rows 3 and 4; dark spots between light stripes occasionally obscured by dark ground color; supralabial sutures with black bars and/or wedges.

Content and Distribution

No subspecies are currently recognized. The plains garter snake ranges southeastward from southern Alberta through eastern Montana, Wyoming, and Colorado, to northeastern New Mexico and the Oklahoma panhandle, thence eastward through the Great Plains to southern Wisconsin, northern Illinois, and northwestern Indiana; isolated populations exist in west-central Ohio and in Missouri and adjacent Illinois near St. Louis (see Map 21). Elevations range from 120 to 2290 m (Stebbins, 1985).

Description

The following is based primarily on A. G. Smith (1949), P. W. Smith (1961), and previously unpublished data. *Thamnophis radix* is a relatively long species of garter snake, reaching a maximum total length of 1092 mm (Nero, 1957). The dorsum is usually some shade of olive or brown (occasionally very dark), but in some cases it may be a shade of red. Lighter-colored individuals have two alternating rows of moderately large black spots between the stripes. The stripes are

Thamnophis radix

235

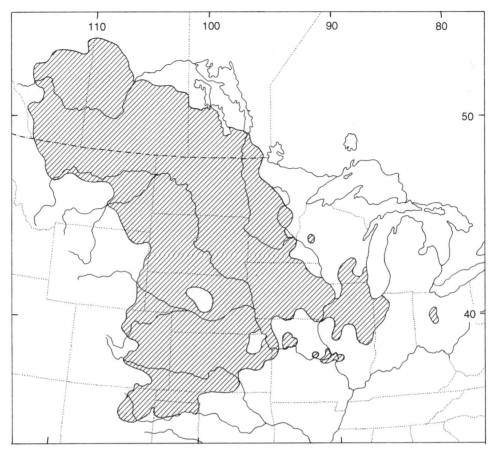

Map 21 Distribution of *Thamnophis radix*.

some shade of yellow or orange, the lateral ones always involving rows 3 and 4 (and sometimes row 2 as well, in southeastern Wisconsin), at least on the anterior end of the body. The venter has a row of rounded black spots on each side and may have varying amounts (often considerable) of black pigment medially.

According to A. G. Smith (1949), there usually are 19-21-19-17 dorsal scale rows in eastern populations (with 19-19-17 a frequent, and 21-21-19-17 a rare, variation) and

21-21-19-17 in western populations (with 19-21-19-17 a frequent variation) of *T. radix*. A maximum of 23 rows on the neck is a rare variation. Ventrals range from 138 to 175 in males, 135 to 174 in females; males average 1.9 to 6.5 more ventrals than females. Subcaudals range from 64 to 88 in males, 54 to 74 in females; males average 5.4 to 11.6 more subcaudals than females. Relative tail length ranges from 20.5 to 27.8% in males, 17.6 to 27.5% in females (both extremes for females are reported by A. G. Smith [1949] and both are suspect—the lowest value we can personally verify is 19.0); relative tail length averages 2.1% to 3.3% longer in males than in females.

Preoculars number 1 to a side (rarely 2), postoculars 3 (rarely 2 or 1). There usually are 7 supralabials (frequently 8, rarely 6) and 9 or 10 infralabials (rarely 8 or 11). Maxillary teeth range from 20 to 27, averaging 24.5 to 24.9 in males and 23.3 to 24.4 in females.

The following data are from the Wisconsin population only. The head constitutes 4.6% of SVL in adults, which is of moderate length for a garter snake. The eye is of moderate size, ED/FL averaging 65.2%. The muzzle tip is of moderate width, InR/NR averaging 93.6%. The muzzle is of moderate length, ML/FL averaging 71.3%. The prefrontals are longer than the internasals, Prf/In averaging 119.6%. The parietals of *T. radix* are long, FL/PL averaging 72.4%. The posterior chin shields are of moderate length, ACS/PCS averaging 82.7%.

Taxonomic Comments

Since its description, the plains garter snake has not been confused with any other species, although A. G. Smith (1949) believed that *T. radix* was conspecific with *T. butleri* and *T. brachystoma*, a position refuted by Conant (1950). The possibility that *T. radix* and *T. butleri* may hybridize where their ranges come in contact in southeastern Wisconsin has been suggested by Ford (pers. comm.) and is currently being investigated by Rossman, Casper, Burghardt, and Good. Hybridization between *T. radix* and *T. marcianus* reportedly occurs in southwestern Kansas (H. M. Smith, 1946), but it has not been confirmed.

Two subspecies, *T. r. radix* and *T. r. haydenii*, have been recognized since A. G. Smith first distinguished between them in 1949 on the basis of average differences in the numbers of anterior dorsal scale rows and ven-

Thamnophis radix

237

trals. Unfortunately, Smith's own data on ventral numbers (as well as those published subsequently by Conant [1951] and P. W. Smith [1961]) contradict his diagnosis of *T. r. radix*—it would not apply to males. Apparently, the variability in dorsal scale row numbers also is such that this character fails to support the recognition of subspecies, at least as diagnosed by A. G. Smith (P. Ostermeier and J. Lynch, pers. comm.).

LIFE HISTORY AND ECOLOGY

Habitat

The plains garter snake ranges throughout the wet prairie regions of central North America and includes two isolated populations in the relict prairies of central Ohio. *Thamnophis radix* occurs in meadows and prairies adjacent to marshes or near streams, roadside ditches, ponds, and marshy areas (Gregory, 1977a; Jordan, 1967). The streams where it occurs tend to be deep and sluggish, with few riffles. In the Chicago region, the species is common in abandoned farmsteads and trash heaps near second-growth woods in vacant lots (Smith, 1961; Wright and Wright, 1957). Debris in grassy areas can attract large numbers

of *T. radix*. In Ohio they are associated with original prairie plants—prairie dock, sawtooth sunflower, white wild-indigo, prairie cordgrass, big bluestem, and prairie lily—although they survive in cultivated fields, even being found under shocks of oats during threshing (Conant et al., 1945). The species occasionally is found in areas of aspen forest in Manitoba (Gregory, 1977a). The plains garter snake is known to use crayfish burrows as hibernacula and daily refuges in Ohio (Dalrymple and Reichenbach, 1984; Reichenbach and Dalrymple, 1986).

Activity

Early April to late October is the general activity season for *T. radix* throughout much of its range (Wright and Wright, 1957), although the exact dates depend on locality and weather conditions. In northwestern Missouri, this species became active in early April (usually a few days later than sympatric *T. sirtalis* and *T. proximus*) and was seen active as late as 12 November (Seigel, pers. obs.). In Manitoba members of this species occupied dens in communal hibernacula which they exited in late April (Gregory, 1977a). Surprisingly, the majority of these animals were females and the snakes were not noted to court there. In summer, the animals moved out to foraging areas.

Several detailed studies have shown that daily activity times in *T. radix* shift seasonally. In Ohio, plains garter snakes were active during midday from March to May, became bimodally active in June to August when temperatures exceeded 34 C (crayfish burrows were used as retreats), and then returned to midday activity in September and November (Dalrymple and Reichenbach, 1984; Reichenbach and Dalrymple, 1986). In Minnesota in midsummer, *T. radix* exhibited a bimodal diurnal activity cycle, being found between 1100 and 1200 and 1500 and 1600 (Jordan, 1967). Hart (1979) also found a bimodal activity pattern in Manitoba during midsummer. Activity patterns may also depend on sex and reproductive condition; for example, gravid females spent more time out basking than did nongravid females in Ohio (Reichenbach and Dalrymple, 1986; see Chap. 5).

Feeding

Thamnophis radix has been the subject of several detailed studies of foraging ecology. The species consumes an impressive variety of prey types. Hart (1979) compared the diets of *T. radix* and *T. sirtalis* in Manitoba and found no significant differences. Both species fed mainly on wood frogs (*Rana sylvatica*), chorus frogs (*Pseudacris triseriata*), tadpoles, and leeches; results very similar to an earlier study in Manitoba (Gregory 1977a). Seigel (1984) showed that the diet of *T. radix* in Missouri showed strong seasonal variation; snakes ate mainly earthworms in the spring and fall, but mainly ranid frogs in summer. Seigel (1984) also recorded leeches, slugs, fish, salamanders, toads, shrews, and mice as prey in Missouri. In Minnesota, earthworms were the predominant prey (Jordan, 1967). In Ohio, adults consume primarily earthworms and frogs with occasional toads and leeches (Dalrymple and Reichenbach, 1981). Ballinger et al. (1979) reported plains garter snakes foraging on salamander and anuran larvae (*Ambystoma tigrinum, Scaphiopus bombifrons, Pseudacris triseriata*, and *Rana pipiens*). On one occasion, they observed 30 to 40 plains garter snakes actively feeding on tiger salamander larvae: "once a salamander was caught it was carried to the shore and eaten, after which the snake would return to the pond."

Thamnophis radix

This must have been quite a spectacle!

Reproduction

One of the earliest detailed descriptions of garter snake courtship was given for this species (Davis, 1936; see Chap. 5). Spring mating is probably most common, although fall mating may also occur (see Chap. 4). In general, courtship takes place near the hibernation site in April or May. Seigel (pers. obs.) has seen small mating balls (4 to 6 males per female) in northwestern Missouri in mid-April. Parturition occurs from late July through early September (Wright and Wright, 1957).

Geographic variation in clutch size is marked in the plains garter snakes. The largest clutch sizes are from Manitoba, with a mean of 29.5 from six females. Seigel and Fitch (1985) showed that annual mean clutch sizes in *T. radix* from northwestern Missouri ranged from 9.0 to 11.9, but, unlike other species of snakes they studied, the differences among years were not significant. From laboratory births of a population from near Chicago, clutch size averaged 17.0 ($N = 12$, range = 3 to 36), with an average offspring SVL of 131 mm and average body mass of 1.46 g (Ford, pers. obs.).

For a sample of eight females from Boulder, Colorado, mean clutch size was 11.6 (5 to 20) with average offspring SVL of 137 mm SVL and body mass of 1.59 g (Ford, pers. obs.). Taken together, these data might suggest the possibility of considerable geographic variation in clutch size, but effects of female size and diet must be considered before any conclusions can be made (Ford and Seigel, 1989a; see Chap. 4).

Population Biology

Plains garter snakes reach the highest densities of any *Thamnophis* for which data are available, 845 individuals/ha (Seibert, 1950). Although Seibert's data were from a disturbed site, other density estimates have also been very high, from 52 to 123 per ha in Ohio (Reichenbach and Dalrymple, 1986) to 320/ha in Colorado (Bauerle, 1972 *in* Reichenbach and Dalrymple, 1986). In Ohio, mortality rates were calculated at 8 to 12% a month for newborns and 1.4 to 2.9% for adults (Reichenbach and Dalrymple, 1986). Roadkills and mowing of grasslands in wildlife areas were substantial sources of mortality in Ohio (Dalrymple and Reichenbach, 1984). Crows are known to kill *T. radix* at den sites in Manitoba (Gregory, 1977a).

Although this species is sympatric with *T. sirtalis* in much of its range, there is high overlap in habitat use, activity patterns, thermal biology, evaporative water loss, and diet (Dalrymple and Reichenbach, 1981; Hart, 1979; Seigel, 1984). It is possible that food and other resources are not limited for these species and competition is not occurring. Dalrymple and Reichenbach (1981) and Reichenbach and Dalrymple (1986) suggested that in Ohio food was probably not a limiting resource for either common or plains garter snakes.

Captive Maintenance

Newborn *T. radix* eat earthworms, fish, and frogs (but reject grasshoppers) in the laboratory (Reichenbach and Dalrymple, 1986). Although adult snakes also readily eat worms, the quantity needed to maintain their body weight can be prohibitive (to say nothing about the production of watery feces). Scudder-Davis and Burghardt (1987) raised neonates on different diets and documented no difference in their growth rate when fed worms or fish *ad libitum*. However, fish have more calories per wet mass and therefore require less feeding than do worms. Worms are also lower in calcium and phosphorus than are fish (Scudder-Davis and Burghardt, 1987).

This species is one of the more sedate members of the genus. With gentle training they will tolerate handling. *Thamnophis radix* is one of the more common species showing up in pet stores.

Conservation

This species is considered "endangered" in Ohio as a consequence of limited habitat availability (Dalrymple and Reichenbach, 1981, 1984). In most other states it does not appear to be in any immediate jeopardy.

Thamnophis rufipunctatus
NARROW-HEADED
GARTER SNAKE
(Plates 10 and 11)

Chilopoma rufipunctatum Cope *in*
  Yarrow 1875
Atomarchus multimaculatus Cope, 1883a
Thamnophis rufipunctatus unilabialis
  Tanner, 1985

Identification

Dorsal scales usually in a maximum of 21 rows; supralabials 8 or 9; maxillary teeth 24 to 29; the dorsum brown

Thamnophis rufipunctatus

241

with 5 or 6 alternating rows of red-dish-brown or very dark brown to black spots; usually 2 nuchal blotches; vertebral and lateral stripes lacking; supralabial bars usually wedge-shaped and brown with a black border anteriorly; ventrals predominantly light, with dark pigment confined to the anterior half of each scute or arranged in 2 to 4 rows of irregular spots; oral peritoneum with black pigment; tongue uniformly black.

Content and Distribution

No subspecies are currently recognized. The narrow-headed garter snake ranges from north-central Arizona southeastward to southwestern New Mexico, and from northern Chihuahua to northern Durango (see Map 22). Elevation ranges from 701 to 2430 m (Rosen and Schwalbe, 1988).

Description

The following is based on Rossman (1995b), Tanner (1985), and Thompson (1957). *Thamnophis rufipunctatus* is a long species of garter snake, reaching a maximum total length of 953 mm (Boundy, 1994). The dorsum is olive-brown or dark brown in living or freshly preserved specimens, and it usually bears 5 or 6 alternating rows

of spots (Thompson, 1957, reported 3 to 9 rows). These spots are either very dark brown or reddish-brown outlined in black. There usually are 2 rounded, more or less distinct nuchal blotches, but in southwestern Chihuahua these blotches may fuse occasionally. The throat is cream-colored, but the venter may possess either 2 to 4 rows (if the latter, one pair usually predominates) of fairly large, irregular spots or a dense reticulum of dark pigment that extends across the anterior portion of each scute. The dark bars preceding the supralabial sutures usually are brown with a narrow black border anteriorly and are wedge-shaped or crescentic. In very large adults the labials and ventrals are covered with a wash of brown pigment. The oral peritoneum (especially along the margins) is heavily invested with melanophores (a phenomenon first reported by Taylor, 1941), a feature this species shares only with *T. nigronuchalis*. The tongue is uniformly black.

There usually are 21-21-17 dorsal scale rows (rarely increasing to 22 or 23 anteriorly). Ventrals in *T. rufipunctatus* range from 155 to 179 in males, 151 to 171 in females; males average 4.8 to 6.3 more ventrals than females. Subcaudals range from 71 to 89 in males, 65 to 79 in females; males average 6.2 to 11.7 more subcaudals

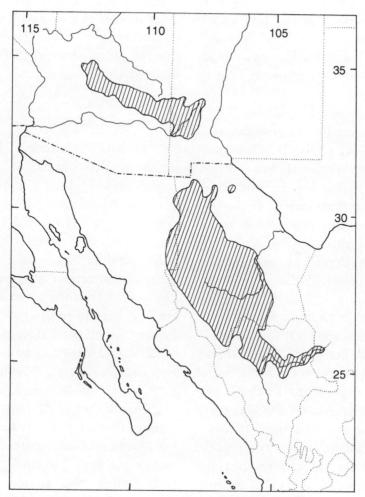

Map 22 Distribution of *Thamnophis rufipunctatus.*

than females. Relative tail length ranges from 22.2 to 25.2% in males, 21.2 to 23.7% in females; it averages 0.9 to 1.6% longer in males than in females.

Preoculars usually number 2 to a side (occasionally 3), postoculars 3 (frequently 4, rarely 2). There normally are 8 supralabials to a side (frequently 9, rarely 7 or 10) and 10 infralabials (occasionally 11 or 9). Maxillary teeth range from 24 to 29; too few of the available skulls are identified as to gender to permit determination of possible sexual dimorphism.

The head of *Thamnophis rufipunctatus* constitutes 5.2% of SVL in the U. S. populations, 5.6% in the Mexican populations—long for a garter snake. The eye is small, ED/FL averaging from 60.5 to 64.2%. The tip of the muzzle is very narrow (when it can be measured; a postrostral scale, which renders the standard measurement impossible, is present in most U.S. specimens), InR/NR averaging 69.6%. The muzzle is long (the postrostral scale also prevents measurement of standard muzzle length), ML/FL averaging 75.3%. The prefrontals are shorter than the internasals (still another character affected by the presence of a postrostral), Prf/In averaging 81.0%. The parietals of *T. rufi-*

punctatus are of moderate length, FL/PL averaging 73.7%. The posterior chin shields are short, ACS/PCS averaging 93.4%.

Taxonomic Comments

On the basis of Ruthven's (1908) assumption that *Eutaenia angustirostris* Kennicott, 1860, is a senior synonym of *Chilopoma rufipunctatum* Cope, 1875, the narrow-headed garter snake was for many years (1908–1940) called *Thamnophis augustirostris*—hence the adjectival descriptor "narrow-headed," although it would be more accurately translated "narrow-snouted" or "narrow-muzzled," which would also fit more closely the biological reality. Taylor and Knobloch (1940) examined the "type" of *E. angustirostris* (USNM 959) and declared that it represented a different species than the narrow-headed garter snake, but they presented no data. H. M. Smith (1942) subsequently re-examined USNM 959 and suggested that it was hybrid between *T. rufipunctatus* and *T. melanogaster*. Finally, Thompson (1957) also studied USNM 959, formally declared it to be the lectotype of *E. angustirostris* (since Kennicott had not actually designated a holotype and apparently had more than one specimen on which he

Species
Accounts

based his new taxon), and concluded that it is a melanistic specimen of *T. marcianus*. D. A. Rossman (unpubl. data) also examined the lectotype of *E. angustirostis* and found that it has too many maxillary teeth (28), too narrow a muzzle tip (InR/NR = 44.9%), too small an eye (ED/FL = 60.2%), and too short posterior chin shields (ACS/PCS = 88.8%) to be a *T. marcianus*. The specimen is too dark for its color pattern to be very useful in determining its identity. Unfortunately, USNM 959 does not agree perfectly with either *T. rufipunctatus* or *T. melanogaster* either, despite exhibiting some similarities to each (it differs from both in having the prefrontals substantially longer than the internasals). It is easy to understand why Smith (1942) chose to treat the animal as a hybrid between the two taxa, but this solution presupposes more biological certainty than actually exists. Treating *E. angustirostris* Kennicott as a *nomen dubium* would seem to be the most easily justified course of action (or inaction) at this time, considering the extent of our knowledge.

Tanner (1985) described the Mexican populations of the narrow-headed garter snake as a distinct subspecies, *T. rufipunctatus unilabialis*, and relegated *T. nigronuchalis* to subspecific status under *T. rufipunctatus*. (The latter situation is discussed in the *T. nigronuchalis* species account.) The subspecific distinctness of *T. r. unilabialis* was based on its having only one supralabial contacting the orbit (usually two in *T. r. rufipunctatus*), fewer ventrals and subcaudals than *T. r. rufipunctatus*, and a different ventral pattern than *T. r. rufipunctatus*. Rossman (1995b) showed that only the differences in ventral and subcaudal numbers are reasonably consistent, and he concluded that this seemed an insufficient basis for taxonomic recognition of the Mexican populations.

Lowe (1955) removed the narrow-headed garter snake from the genus *Thamnophis* and placed it in the genus *Natrix* (now *Nerodia*) because *rufipunctatus* has a divided anal plate, dorsally positioned nostrils, an unstriped dorsal pattern, and aquatic habits. In rejecting this generic assignment, Thompson (1957) correctly pointed out that fewer than 10% of *rufipunctatus* have a divided anal plate; that the nostrils are, in fact, no more dorsally situated than in other semiaquatic garter snakes; that there are other species of *Thamnophis* that lack stripes (as well as a *Nerodia* that has them); and that there are many other species of *Thamnophis* that are

Thamnophis rufipunctatus

245

semiaquatic. Recently, Chiasson and Lowe (1989) suggested that both *rufipunctatus* and *melanogaster* be assigned to *Nerodia* on the basis of scale microdermatoglyphics, those two species having a scale pattern similar to *Nerodia* rather than to the five other species of *Thamnophis* they examined. However, their conclusions are contradicted by the work of Blaney (1977), who examined 18 species of *Thamnophis* and found a gradation of pattern types among the species rather than either/or differences. The generic status of *rufipunctatus*—and its sister-species, *nigronuchalis*—may still be open to question, but available molecular data (de Quieroz and Lawson, 1994) cluster them with the garter snakes rather than with the water snakes.

LIFE HISTORY AND ECOLOGY

Habitat

This species is considered to be one of the most aquatic garter snakes (Conant, 1963). In his study at Wall Lake, New Mexico, Fleharty (1967) found *T. rufipunctatus* preferred rocky areas around the lake, where snakes were typically beneath or very near rock refuges. In Arizona, nearly all individuals were found in the water or on the banks of larger streams in riparian deciduous forests and Sonoran riparian scrub (Rosen and Schwalbe, 1988). These authors also concluded that the occurrence of *T. rufipunctatus* was strongly associated with loose rocks and boulders but that the snakes bask on shrubs and snags in the streams as well. Important species of shrub and saplings on the banks were willows (*Salix* sp.), Arizona alder (*Alnus oblongifolia*), velvet ash (*Fraxinus pennsylvanica*), and canyon grape (*Vitis arizonica*) (Rosen and Schwalbe, 1988). The authors found that the greatest number of snakes were in partially submerged complexes of boulders at the junction of pools and riffles but that more snakes were actually in the pools than in riffles. D. A. Rossman (pers. obs.) found juveniles and subadults under rocks at the edge of a river rapids in Chihuahua, Mexico.

Activity

In Arizona, this species is active from late March to October, but the active season is likely to be longer in Mexico. Animals maintain a body temperature plateau during the day, but this dropped several degrees at night (Rosen, 1993). Body temperature during the active season averaged 25.0 C (range = 19.2 to 31.4 C) in Arizona and

Species
Accounts

24.7 C (20.0 to 29.0 C) in New Mexico (Fleharty, 1967; Rosen 1991). These temperatures were taken opportunistically and may be constrained by the behaviors of the snakes; thus they may not reflect preferred body temperatures (see Chap. 5).

Feeding

This species feeds on aquatic prey, primarily fish (Fleharty, 1967; Hulse, 1973), although ambystomatid salamander larvae have also been reported as prey (Stebbins, 1985). Of 29 individuals examined in New Mexico, 29% had fed recently, and all contained fish (Fleharty, 1967). Arizona specimens (Rosen and Schwalbe, 1988) contained speckled dace (*Rhinichthys osculus*), Gila mountain suckers (*Pantosteus clarki*), and red shiners (*Notropis lutrensis*). Rosen and Schwalbe (1988) observed *T. rufipunctatus* foraging for fish in shallow riffles. Tanner (1985) observed *T. r. unilabialis* in the Sierra Madre Occidental eating minnows and tadpoles.

Reproduction

Courtship in this species has not been reported. The mean clutch size for three Arizona females was 11.3 (8 to 17, Rosen and Schwalbe, 1988) and a Chihuahuan specimen had a clutch of 18 on 8 July 1961 (D. Rossman, per. obs.). Most females were gravid each year in Rosen's study; the snakes apparently ovulate in March and have young in late July. Neonates collected in Arizona in late July and early August ranged from 192 to 254 mm SVL (Rosen and Schwalbe, 1988). Neonates from Chihuahua ranged from 146.5 to 161.5 mm SVL (D. Rossman, pers. obs.).

Population Biology

On the basis of distributions of body sizes, Rosen and Schwalbe (1988) suggested that *T. rufipunctatus* would reach sexual maturity in two years, at least in populations at lower elevations. They developed a preliminary life table for *T. rufipunctatus* and suggested that, except for human predation, adults over 2 years of age had relatively high survivorship (70%). They also suggested some individuals may live 10 years or more and that neonatal mortality was high (about 93%).

Captive maintenance

This species has rarely been kept in captivity, but Fleharty (1967) suggests it is difficult to maintain. As with other fish-eating specialists, *T. rufi-*

Thamnophis rufipunctatus

247

punctatus may require some visual stimuli to encourage feeding, such as waving a dead fish (frozen and thawed) on the end of long forceps. Live minnows in a shallow bowl will often produce the correct sensory cues, but they can transmit endoparasites to the snake. (See Chap. 6). Rossi and Rossi (1995) reported that specimens fed frozen and thawed salamanders developed a heavy infestation of flukes (trematodes) in their oral cavities.

Conservation

This species is considered "threatened" in Arizona and "endangered" in New Mexico due to human-caused mortality and the introduction of predatory game fish and bullfrogs (Rosen and Schwalbe, 1988). Nothing is known about its status in Mexico.

Thamnophis sauritus
EASTERN RIBBON SNAKE
(Plate 11)

Coluber saurita Linnaeus, 1766
    (= *T. s. sauritus*)
Eutaenia sackenii Kennicott, 1859
    (= *T. s. sackenii*)
Prymnomiodon chalceus Cope, 1861b
    (= *T. s. sackenii*)

Thamnophis sauritus septentrionalis Rossman, 1963
    (= *T. s. septentrionalis*)
Thamnophis sauritus nitae Rossman, 1963
    (= *T. s. nitae*)

Identification

Dorsal scales in a maximum of 19 rows; supralabials 7 (rarely 8); maxillary teeth 27 to 34; the dorsum uniformly reddish-brown, brown, or black between the light stripes; the lateral stripe confined to dorsal scale rows 3 and 4; a dark ventrolateral stripe present and relatively broad; labials without dark markings.

Content and Distribution

Four subspecies of the eastern ribbon snake are currently recognized (see Map 23): *T. s. sauritus*, which ranges from southern New England west-southwestward through southern Ohio and southern Indiana to the Mississippi River and southward throughout the rest of the eastern United States except for southeastern Georgia and Peninsular Florida; *T. s. nitae*, which is restricted to northwestern Peninsular Florida; *T. s. sackenii*, which ranges throughout most

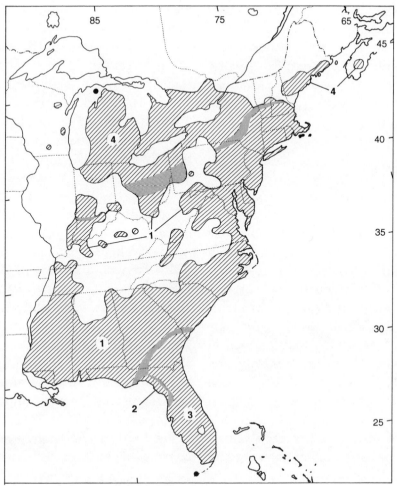

Map 23 Distribution of *Thamnophis sauritus* and its subspecies:
(1) *T. s. sauritus*; (2) *T. s. nitae*; (3) *T. s. sackenii*; (4) *T. s. septentrio-nalis*. Stippling represents zones of intergradation.

of Peninsular Florida and southeastern Georgia to the southern tip of South Carolina; and *T. s. septentrionalis*, which ranges from Nova Scotia westward to Wisconsin. Elevations range from 0 to 610 m (Wright and Wright, 1957).

Description

The following is based on Rossman (1963) and previously unpublished data. *Thamnophis sauritus* is a long species of garter snake, reaching a maximum total length of 1018 mm (UF 12120). The dorsum is tan, reddish-brown, dark brown, or black between the lateral stripes, which are light yellow, white, bluish-white, or light blue. In living or freshly preserved specimens, the dark coloration below the lateral stripes extends far onto the venter, usually covering ⅖ or more of the area of each ventral scute. The vertebral stripe varies geographically and may be golden yellow, yellow with a brown overlay, tan (often metallic), or obscure to lacking altogether. The light parietal spots—if present at all—are small and rarely bright or fused together.

There are 19-19-17 dorsal scale rows. Ventrals in *T. sauritus* range from 145 to 177 in males, 143 to 169 in females; sexual dimorphism ranges from females averaging 0.8 more ventrals than males to males averaging 5.7 more ventrals than females. Subcaudals range from 98 to 136 in males, 94 to 131 in females; males average 3.4 to 10.2 more subcaudals than females. Relative tail length ranges from 29.8 to 38.8% in males, 28.8 to 38.8% in females; it averages 0.7 to 1.4% longer in males than females.

Preoculars number 1 to a side, postoculars usually 3 (occasionally 4, rarely 2). There usually are 7 supralabials in most of the range of *T. sauritus* (8 in the subspecies *sackenii*) and 10 infralabials (occasionally 9, rarely 8 or 11). Maxillary teeth range from 27 to 34 with a mean of 30.4; there appears to be no sexual dimorphism, but a sample from Pennsylvania averages fewer teeth than a sample from Peninsular Florida.

The head in *Thamnophis sauritus* constitutes 3.9% of SVL, which is very short for a garter snake. The eye is of moderate size, ED/FL averaging 64.6%. The tip of the muzzle is of moderate width, InR/NR averaging 89.2%. The muzzle is short, ML/FL averaging 66.4%. The prefrontals are usually longer than the internasals, Prf/In averaging 111.1%. The parietals of *T. sauritus* are short, FL/PL averaging 82.8%. The posterior chin shields are long, ACS/PCS averaging 74.0%.

Taxonomic Comments

Klauber (1948) showed that the original description of *Coluber sirtalis* by Linnaeus (1758) does not fit the common garter snake and that the name probably should be applied to the eastern ribbon snake. For several years some authors followed Klauber in calling the latter *T. sirtalis*, but others did not and the resulting confusion led to a request that the International Commission on Zoological Nomenclature conserve the pre-Klauber arrangement in the interest of nomenclatural stability. The commission complied in 1956, and neotypes were subsequently designated by Schmidt and Conant (1956–1957). Other pertinent taxonomic comments appear in the *T. proximus* account.

LIFE HISTORY AND ECOLOGY

Habitat

Thamnophis sauritus is strongly associated with water sources such as swamps, ponds, streams, roadside ditches, marshes, and bogs (Rossman, 1963). In these habitats it is generally found close to or in brushy vegetation or thickets. In the Everglades National Park in Florida, *T. sauritus* was most common in seasonally flooded prairies and hardwood hammocks (Dalrymple, 1988). In Carpenter's (1952a) study of three species of *Thamnophis* in Michigan, ribbon snakes showed a greater tendency to be found in bushes than either *T. sirtalis* or *T. butleri*. During late summer, Carpenter (1952a) reported that 61% of *T. sauritus* were found in brush above ground, up to 1.8 m high. Rossman (1963) observed more than 30 *T. sauritus sackenii* 0.6 to 1.2 m high in vegetation on one August night in north-central Florida. Bishop and Farrell (1994) found a *T. s. sackenii* foraging for treefrogs 5.7 m above the ground in a hammock in Florida.

Activity

In northern parts of its range *T. sauritus* is one of the first snakes active in the spring (Wright and Wright, 1957). For example, in Indiana, Minton (1972) found them from late March to mid-October. In Michigan, Carpenter (1953) found *T. sauritus* emerging from hibernacula in late March and

Thamnophis sauritus

early April, but indicated that ribbon snakes emerged about two weeks later than either *T. butleri* or *T. sirtalis*. *Thamnophis sauritus* has been found hibernating in crayfish burrows and mammal tunnels (Carpenter, 1953; Ernst and Barbour, 1989). Adults in colder areas may hibernate completely submerged under water. In Michigan, Carpenter (1953) found several juveniles in an ant mound hibernating at depths of 48 cm. In the southern part of its range *T. sauritus* may be encountered during any month of the year (Dalrymple et al., 1991b), although its activity in December, January, and February may be limited to areas near overnight refuges.

The thermal ecology of eastern ribbon snakes has been studied intensively in Michigan by Carpenter (1956) and Rosen (1991). Carpenter (1956) reported mean cloacal temperatures of 26 C with a strong correlation to substrate temperature. Rosen (1991) found that cloacal temperatures of *T. sauritus* averaged 27.5 C. During the spring the snakes raise their temperature by basking in open areas. Snakes moving at this time exhibit lower body temperatures, which may explain why Carpenter reported lower cloacal temperatures than did Rosen. In the summer, females also exhibited less variable body temperatures than did males, presumably to ensure proper embryo development. (See Chap. 5).

Feeding

This species feeds primarily on frogs, although salamanders and fish are also eaten (Carpenter, 1952a; Rossman, 1963). However, as is true of other *Thamnophis*, the diet of *T. sauritus* varies among seasons and among size classes (see Chap. 4). Carpenter (1952a) found that during the spring, small species of frogs (*Hyla*) at breeding sites were the main prey. Later in the year, tadploes of larger species (*Rana*) are taken more frequently. Carpenter (1952a) also found that larger snakes ate larger frogs and took a wider variety of prey than did smaller individuals.

Reproduction

For such a widespread and common snake, surprisingly few detailed studies have been conducted (or at least reported) on the reproductive ecology of individual populations of ribbon snakes. Dalrymple et al. (1991b) recorded gravid females from June to October in southern Florida. Rossman (1963) summarized the parturition dates for this species as being from 2 July to 4 October. Clutch size ranges from 3 (Ditmars, 1896) to 26 (Telford, 1952) with a mean of 11 from 69 clutches (Rossman, 1963). Mean clutch size shows considerable geographic variation, ranging from 6.0 in Michigan (Burt, 1928) to 12.2 in Ontario (Rossman, 1963). (See Table 4-1 for a summary.) Carpenter (1952b) recorded that 65% of the females were gravid each year; only one female was pregnant two years in a row. Because Rossman (1963) found that several Florida specimens had late parturition dates, he suggested that females in southern areas might produce two litters a year, but confirmation of this is lacking (see Chap. 4). Neonate size ranged from 141.1 to 165.3 mm among nine broods from Ontario (Rossman, 1963). Southern populations appear to have larger clutch sizes (Fitch, 1985) and the longest neonates (Rossman, 1963).

Population Biology

Carpenter conservatively estimated that his 19.4 ha study site had about 477 ribbon snakes (24.5/ha). In the Everglades, this species was the third most abundant snake of the 21 taxa represented (Dalrymple et al., 1991a). Carpenter (1952b) reported that females matured at 2 to 3 years of age at SVL of about 420 mm. In other localities females as small as 330 to 340 mm SVL are known to reproduce (McCauley, 1945; Rossman, 1963).

Captive Maintenance

Eastern ribbon snakes are nervous in captivity and rarely take kindly to handling. They eat fish and frogs readily, and, with proper refuges to hide in, they do quite well in captivity. However, they are very susceptible to skin diseases if they are kept in humid conditions (Rossi, 1992; see Chap. 6).

Conservation

This species is listed as "threatened" or "endangered" in several states, usually in areas of peripheral distribution (See Chap. 4). Large numbers of ribbon snakes are killed by automobile traffic. In one of the few quantitative studies done on the impacts of road mortality on snake populations, Dalrymple et al. (1991a) found 336 *T. sauritus* killed over a three-year period in Everglades National Park; only common garter snakes were killed more frequently.

Thamnophis sauritus

Thamnophis scalaris
MEXICAN ALPINE
BLOTCHED
GARTER SNAKE
(Plate 11)

Thamnophis scalaris Cope, 1861a

Identification

Dorsal scales usually in a maximum of 19 rows (but frequently 17); supralabials usually 7 (occasionally 8); maxillary teeth 15 to 19; the dorsum brown with one or two rows of relatively large, black-edged, dark-brown blotches or spots between the stripes; the vertebral stripe involving the vertebral row and the adjacent edge of each paravertebral row; the lateral stripe usually confined to dorsal scale rows 2 and 3 (occasionally indistinct); the posterior supralabials the same color as the other supralabials; tongue uniformly black.

Content and Distribution

No subspecies are currently recognized. The Mexican alpine blotched garter snake occurs at high elevations (2103 to 4273 m) across the Transverse Volcanic Axis of central Mexico from central Jalisco to Veracruz (see Map 24).

Description

The following is based primarily on Rossman and Lara-Gongora (1991). *Thamnophis scalaris* is a moderate-sized species of garter snake, reaching a maximum SVL of 601 mm (the tail is incomplete on this specimen, UTA R-4932). The dorsum is brown with a series of short (up to 2 scales long), black-edged, dark-brown blotches anteriorly; sometimes these blotches are broken up to form 2 alternating rows of black-edged, dark-brown spots. Posteriorly, only fragmentary remnants of the black edging may persist. In some individuals the dorsal pattern is difficult to see. The venter is usually grayish-brown, occasionally with a light peppering, fine reticulum, or dense mottling of black pigment. The chin and throat are white, cream, or yellow, in strong contrast to the color of the venter. The nuchal blotches usually are interrupted by the vertebral stripe, and they may be partially or completely separated from the parietal on each side by a narrow, vertical light line. Another light line often extends anteriorly from the light parietal spots along the

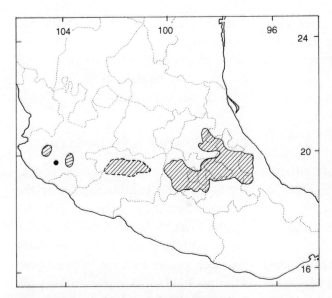

Map 24 Distribution of *Thamnophis scalaris*. Dashed line indicates uncertainty about range limits.

dorsal scale rows 2 and 3, but it may be indistinct and/or involve rows 1 and 2, 2 alone, or 1, 2, and 3. The black spots below the lateral stripe are small to moderate in size. The tongue is uniformly black.

There usually are 19-19-17 dorsal scale rows, occasionally 19-17-17, 17-19-17, 17-17-17, or 17-17-15. Ventrals in *T. scalaris* range from 130 to 147 in males, 134 to 144 in females; females average 1.7 to 3.4 more ventrals than males, which is unusual for a garter snake. Subcaudals range from 66 to 85 in males, 51 to 69 in females; males average 13.2 to 14.1 more subcaudals than females. Subcaudal counts average higher in the Veracruz population than in any other part of the range. Relative tail length ranges from 27.6 to 33.2% in adult males (subadults have a proportionally shorter tail), 19.5 to 25.0% in females; it averages 7.1 to 8.1% longer in males than in females.

Preoculars number 1 to a side, postoculars usually 3 (occasionally 2). There usually are 7 supralabials to a side (occasionally 8) and 10 or 9 in-

interparietal suture to fork at the frontal-parietal sutures and form a Y-shaped figure. All supralabials are yellow suffused with brown, in contrast to the top of the head. Black bars are variably present along the supralabial sutures, but usually they are relatively narrow. In four living specimens from Veracruz the vertebral stripe was gold in 3 and pale yellow suffused with brown in 1. The grayish-white lateral stripe is variable; it usually is distinct and confined to fralabials (occasionally 8, rarely 11). Maxillary teeth range from 15 to 19, averaging 16.9 in males and 16.4 in females.

The head in adult *Thamnophis scalaris* constitutes 5.5% of SVL, which is long for a garter snake. The eye is small, ED/FL averaging 61.8%. The tip of the muzzle is broad, InR/NR averaging 131.2%. The muzzle is short, ML/FL averaging 64.3%. The prefrontals are longer than the internasals, Prf/In averaging 109.6% in Veracruz, 122.3% in the other parts of the range. The parietals of *T. scalaris* are short, FL/PL averaging 85.0% in Veracruz, 79.9% in the other parts of the range. The posterior chin shields are short, ACS/PCS averaging 92.9%.

Taxonomic Comments

The Mexican alpine blotched garter snake is such a distinctive species that it has been continuously recognized as a valid taxon since its description by Cope (1861a). Only its sister-species, *T. scaliger*, has been confused with *T. scalaris*, and for a time *T. godmani* was considered to be one of its subspecies.

The hemipenis of *T. scalaris* is unique among members of the tribe Thamnophiini in being extraordinarily long and slender, the inverted organ extending in length an average of 27.5 subcaudals (Rossman and Lara-Gongora, 1991).

LIFE HISTORY AND ECOLOGY

Thamnophis scalaris occurs in the high-elevation conifer forests of the central Mexican Plateau (H. M. Smith, 1942). Fouquette and Rossman (1963) collected one under loose bark on steep grassy hillside in open pine forest at 3048 m. D. A. Rossman (pers. obs.) found them in bunchgrass near a pine forest, near rock piles, and under logs, lava chunks, and dirt clumps in meadow-pine ecotones. The snakes found in bunchgrass areas were very active and difficult to catch. Lizards are the only prey recorded for this species. Two *Sceloporus* were regurgitated by a *T. scalaris* after it was placed in a bag (Fouquette and Rossman, 1963), and another specimen yielded a partially digested adult anguid lizard, *Barisia imbricata* (Lemos-Espinal and Ballinger 1992). Two recorded broods were born between May 18 and 30; brood sizes were 8 and 15, and neonate total length ranged from 168.5 to 181.5 millimeters.

Thamnophis scaliger
**MESA CENTRAL BLOTCHED
GARTER SNAKE**
(Plate 12)

Tropidonotus (Eutainia) scaliger Jan, 1863

Identification

Dorsal scales usually in a maximum of 19 rows (but occasionally 17); supralabials usually 7 (rarely 6); maxillary teeth 15 to 17; the dorsum brown with one or two rows of relatively large, black-edged, dark-brown

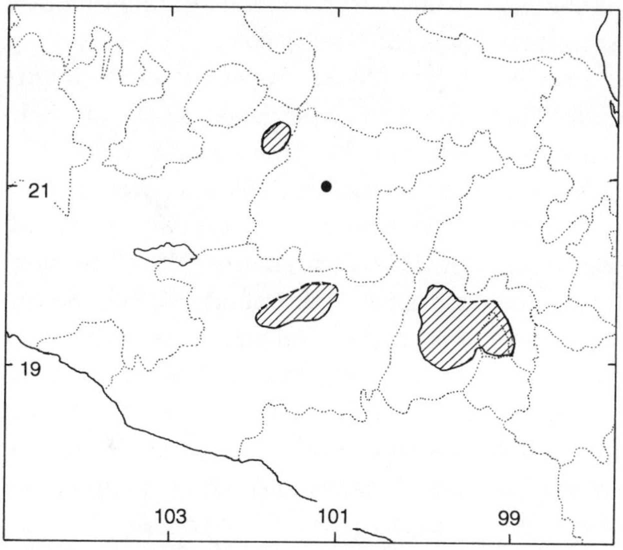

Map 25 Distribution of *Thamnophis scaliger*. Dashed lines indicate uncertainty about range limits.

blotches or spots between the stripes; the vertebral stripe confined to the vertebral row; the lateral stripe usually confined to dorsal scale row 2 or rows 2 and 3 (often indistinct); the posterior supralabial same color as the temporals; tongue uniformly black.

Content and Distribution

No subspecies are currently recognized. The Mesa Central blotched garter snake occurs in the central part of the Mexican Mesa Central, which lies immediately north of the Transverse Volcanic Axis (see Map 25), at elevations ranging from 2288 to 2575 m.

Description

The following is based primarily on Rossman and Lara-Gongora (1991). *Thamnophis scaliger* is a short species of garter snake, reaching a maximum total length of 567 mm (KU 95968). The dorsum is brown with a series of short (up to 2 scales long), black-edged, dark-brown blotches anteriorly; sometimes these blotches are broken

Thamnophis scaliger

257

up to form two alternating rows of black-edged, dark-brown spots. Posteriorly only fragmentary remnants of the black edging may persist. The venter is usually light gray or grayish-white, with prominent black "squiggles" extending across the anterior margin of most ventrals. The color of the chin and throat does not contrast strongly with that of the venter. The nuchal blotches are interrupted by the vertebral stripe; rarely they are also separated from the parietal on each side by a narrow, vertical light line. A light Y-shaped figure is usually present on the interparietal and frontal-parietal sutures. Most supralabials are cream or white, but the posteriormost 1 or 1½ are the same shade of brown as the adjacent temporals. The black supralabial sutures bars are very broad; many have a brown center, and the ones on supralabials 3 and 4 usually connect beneath the orbit. The vertebral stripe is pale yellow, distinct, and confined to the vertebral row. The lateral stripe may be either distinct or indistinct; the stripe is usually confined to row 2 or involves rows 2 and 3 (only rarely is row 1 involved). The black spots below the lateral stripe are large. The tongue is uniformly black.

There usually are 19-19-17 dorsal scale rows, occasionally 19-17-17, 17-19-17, or 17-17-17. Ventrals in *T. scaliger* range from 135 to 151 in males, 130 to 146 in females; males average 7.4 more ventrals than females. Subcaudals range from 49 to 58 in males, 40 to 49 in females; males average 9.5 more subcaudals than females. Relative tail length ranges from 17.6 to 21.3% in males, 15.5 to 18.5% in females; it averages 2.4% longer in males than in females.

Preoculars number 1 to a side, postoculars either 2 or 3 (rarely 1). There usually are 7 supralabials to a side (occasionally 6) and 9 infralabials (occasionally 8). Maxillary teeth range from 15 to 17, averaging 15.9 in males and 15.1 in females.

The head in adult *Thamnophis scaliger* constitutes 5.2% of SVL, which is long for a garter snake. The eye is small, ED/FL averaging 59.5%. The tip of the muzzle is broad, InR/NR averaging 126.9%. The muzzle is extremely short, ML/FL averaging 55.5%. The prefrontals are longer than the internasals, PrF/In averaging 114.4%. The parietals of *T. scaliger* are short, FL/PL averaging 83.9%. The posterior chin shields are of moderate length, ACS/PCS averaging 89.4%.

Taxonomic Comments

With the exception of Boulenger

(1893), all authors after Jan (1863) considered *T. scaliger* to be a synonym or a subspecies of *T. scalaris* until Rossman and Lara-Gongora (1991) demonstrated that these two taxa are distinct species. Their color patterns are remarkably similar—and unique among garter snakes (with the possible exception of *T. exsul*)—but the male hemipenes are dramatically different (see *T. scalaris* account; *T. scaliger* has an organ typical of the genus), and there are numerous, less obvious meristic and mensural distinctions as well.

LIFE HISTORY AND ECOLOGY

Very little is known about the ecology of this species. Most of the available information comes from the unpublished observations of G. Lara-Gongora, whose data are summarized here.

This species inhabits semiarid desert-scrub valleys and oak forests at the lower portions of high mountain ranges. Field observations and data from captive specimens show that *T. scaliger* feeds on the larvae of spadefoot toads, *Spea hammondii*. The species has a seasonal activity period, being most active during the hottest and wettest season of the year, coming out after the first spring rains.

Thamnophis sirtalis
COMMON GARTER SNAKE
(Plates 12, 13, and 14)

Coluber sirtalis Linnaeus, 1758, *sensu* Harlan 1827
    (= *T. s. sirtalis*)
Coluber ordinatus Linnaeus, 1766
    (= *T. s. sirtalis*)
Coluber taenia Schoepf, 1788
    (= *T. s. sirtalis*)
Coluber ibibe Daudin, 1803
    (= *T. s. sirtalis*)
Coluber parietalis Say in James, 1823
    (= *T. s. parietalis*)
Coluber infernalis Blainville, 1835
    (= *T. s. infernalis*)
Tropidonotus bipunctatus Schlegel, 1837
    (= *T. s. sirtalis*)
Tropidonotus concinnus Hallowell, 1852
    (= *T. s. concinnus*)
Eutainia pickeringii Baird and Girard, 1853
    (= *T. s. pickeringii*)
Eutainia dorsalis Baird and Girard, 1853
    (= *T. s. dorsalis*)
Tropidonotus jauresi Duméril, Bibron, and Duméril, 1854
    (= *T. s. sirtalis*)
Eutaenia ornata Baird, 1859
    (= *T. s. dorsalis*)
Eutaenia sirtalis obscura Cope in Yarrow, 1875
    (= *T. s. sirtalis*)
Eutainia sirtalis tetrataenia Cope in Yarrow, 1875
    (= *T. s. infernalis*)
Eutaenia sirtalis melanota Higley, 1889
    (= *T. s. sirtalis*)

Thamnophis sirtalis

259

Eutaenia sirtalis graminea Cope, 1889
    (= *T. s. sirtalis*)
Eutaenia sirtalis semifasciata Cope,
  1892b
    (= *T. s. semifasciatus*)
Eutaenia sirtalis trilineata Cope, 1892b
    (= *T. s. pickeringii*)
Thamnophis sirtalis pallidula Allen, 1899
    (= *T. s. pallidulus*)
Tropidonotus obalskii Mocquard, 1903
    (= *T. s. pallidulus*)
Thamnophis sirtalis annectens Brown,
  1950
    (= *T. s. annectens*)
Thamnophis sirtalis fitchi Fox, 1951b
    (= *T. s. fitchi*)
Thamnophis sirtalis similis Rossman,
  1965b
    (= *T. s. similis*)
Thamnophis sirtalis lowei Tanner, 1988
    (= *T. s. dorsalis*)

Identification

Dorsal scales in a maximum of 19 rows; supralabials usually 7; maxillary teeth 20 to 26; dorsal pattern highly variable—area between the stripes may have two alternating rows of black spots, spots may be fused vertically to form bars, spots may be fused horizontally to form longitudinal lines, or area may be so dark that no pattern is discernible; dorsal ground color—when visible—usually some shade of brown or gray, but often red in western populations; lateral stripe usually confined to dorsal scale rows 2 and 3.

Content and Distribution

Eleven subspecies of the widely distributed common garter snake are currently recognized: *T. s. sirtalis*, which ranges from southern New England and south-central Canada southward to Florida and southeastern Texas; *T. s. pallidulus*, which occurs in northern New England, southern Quebec, and the Canadian Maritime Provinces; *T. s. similis*, which occurs along the northwestern coast of Peninsular Florida; *T. s. semifasciatus*, which occurs in northeastern Illinois and adjacent southeastern Wisconsin and northwestern Indiana; *T. s. annectens*, which ranges from east-central Texas through west-central Oklahoma to the eastern Texas Panhandle and southwestern Kansas; *T. s. parietalis*, which ranges throughout the Great Plains from the Red River Valley separating Texas and Oklahoma northward into Canada as far as the southernmost edge of the Northwest Territories; *T. s. fitchi*, which ranges from southern British Columbia (exclusive of the southwestern coast and Vancouver Island) southward through Idaho and the eastern two-thirds of Washington to north-central Utah on the east, and through the inland portions of Oregon to central California on the west (it reaches the California coast between Monterey and Santa Barbara counties); *T. s. pickeringii*, which occurs on Vancouver Island, the southwestern coast of British Columbia, and in the western third of Washington; *T. s. concinnus*, which ranges along the Pacific Coast from the outer Olympic Peninsula and the Columbia River Valley separating Washington and Oregon southward to the northern side of San Francisco Bay and—south of the San Francisco Peninsula—thence to just north of San Diego (the southernmost populations are isolated by the coastal intrusion of *T. s. fitchi*); *T. s. infernalis*, which is confined to the San Francisco Peninsula; and *T. s. dorsalis*, which occurs in two isolated populations, one along the Rio Grande in southern New Mexico, and the other in northwestern Chihuahua, Mexico (see Map 26). Elevational distribution ranges from 0 to 2540 m (Stebbins, 1985).

Description

The following is based largely on Bleakney (1959), Brown (1950), Fitch (1941a), Fitch and Maslin (1961), Rossman (1965b), P. W. Smith (1961),

Tanner (1988), and Boundy (pers. comm.). *Thamnophis sirtalis* is a very long species of garter snake, reaching a maximum total length of 1372 mm (Froom, 1972). The dorsal color pattern is the most variable of any species of *Thamnophis*, and it is upon this variation—where it is geographically consistent—that the various subspecies are based (see the key, Chap. 3, for details). The widespread eastern subspecies, *T. s. sirtalis*, exhibits a great deal of individual variation related to vertebral stripe distinctness and color, lateral stripe distinctness, size and distinctness of dorsolateral spots, and darkness of ground color. In addition, there are some areas within the range of *T. s. sirtalis* (especially near Lake Erie) where entirely melanistic individuals occur fairly frequently. The vertebral stripe in most subspecies usually is fairly distinct and covers not only the vertebral row but at least half of each paravertebral row; however, the stripe is weakly developed or lacking in ⅔ of *T. s. pallidulus* (Bleakney, 1959), often confined to the vertebral row in *T. s. pickeringii* (Fitch, 1941a), and involves most of the width of each paravertebral row in *T. s. annectens* (Brown, 1950). The lateral stripe usually is confined to dorsal scale rows 2 and 3, but characteristically it

Thamnophis sirtalis

261

also involves row 4 anteriorly in *T. s. annectens*. In some areas (Sacramento and San Joaquin valleys of California, and occasionally in specimens from the Great Lakes region), the stripe appears to be on rows 1, 2, and 3 anteriorly. Red pigment usually occurs in the dorsolateral area of specimens from the Great Plains to the Pacific Coast; it may be confined to the skin between the scales and visible only when the skin is stretched, it may entirely cover the scales as well, or it may exist in almost any condition in between. Even the top and sides of the head are red in *T. s. concinnus* and *T. s. infernalis*. The black spots in the dorsolateral area may fuse vertically to form bars (*T. s. semifasciatus*), or they may fuse transversely to form broad black borders adjoining the vertebral stripe (*T. s. dorsalis*) or adjoining both the vertebral and lateral stripes (*T. s. infernalis*).

There usually are 19-19-17 dorsal scale rows (21-19-17 in northwestern Chihuahua). Ventrals in *T. sirtalis* range from 142 to 178 in males, 134 to 174 in females; males average 3.2 to 9.0 more ventrals than females. Subcaudals range from 61 to 97 in males, 52 to 90 in females; males average 7.0 to 12.3 more subcaudals than females. Relative tail length ranges from 21.6 to 27.7% in males, 18.0 to 26.5% in females; it averages 2.0 to 3.0% longer in males than in females.

Preoculars almost always number 1 to a side, postoculars usually 3 (occasionally 4, rarely 2). There usually are 7 supralabials (frequently 8, especially in western North America; rarely 6 or 9) and 10 infralabials (occasionally 9, rarely 8 or 11), except in Manitoba where 9 is the modal number of infralabials. Maxillary teeth range from 20 to 26, averaging 23.5 in males and 22.3 in females.

The head of *Thamnophis sirtalis* constitutes 4.8% of snout-vent length, which is of moderate size for a garter snake. The eye is variable in size, being moderately small in Texas and California (ED/FL averaging 59.4% and 61.2%, respectively) and moderately large in New York (69.2%). The tip of the muzzle is broad, InR/NR averaging 127.6%. The muzzle is of moderate length in California and New York (ML/FL averaging 67.0% and 69.7%, respectively) and moderately long in Texas (76.7%). The prefrontals are substantially longer than the internasals, Prf/In averaging 123.6%. The parietals of *T. sirtalis* are of moderate length, FL/PL averaging 76.3%. The posterior chin shields are very long, ASC/PCS averaging 74.5%.

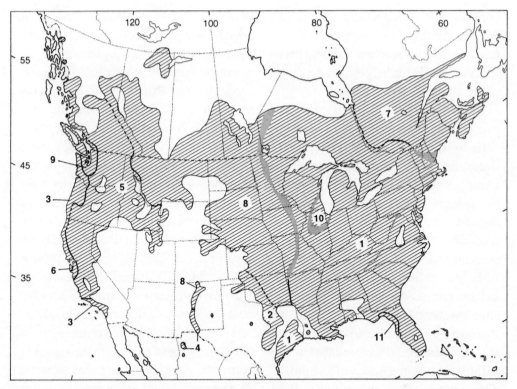

Map 26 Distribution of *Thamnophis sirtalis* and its subspecies: (1) *T. s. sirtalis*; (2) *T. s. annectens*; (3) *T. s. concinnus*; (4) *T. s. dorsalis*; (5) *T. s. fitchi*; (6) *T. s. infernalis*; (7) *T. s. pallidulus*; (8) *T. s. parietalis*; (9) *T. s. pickeringii*; (10) *T. s. semifasciatus*; (11) *T. s. similis*. Stippling represents zones of intergradation; dashed lines indicate uncertainty about range limits.

Taxonomic Comments

Perhaps because of its great individual and geographic variability, *Thamnophis sirtalis* has experienced a confusing taxonomic history. Between 1835 and 1853, five western forms of *T. sirtalis* currently recognized as subspecies (*infernalis, parietalis, concinnus, pickeringii, dorsalis*) were described as distinct species. Cope (1900) and Ruthven (1908) correctly recognized the taxonomic limits of the common garter snake, although the former recognized 11 subspecies and the latter only three. In marked

Thamnophis sirtalis

contrast were Boulenger (1893) and Brown (1901), who included 10 and four additional species, respectively, in their much-inclusive and confused concepts of *T. sirtalis*.

Klauber (1948) showed that the original description of *Coluber sirtalis* by Linnaeus (1758) does not fit the common garter snake and that the name probably should be applied to the eastern ribbon snake. For about a decade some authors followed Klauber in calling the garter snake *T. ordinatus* and the ribbon snake *T. sirtalis*, but others did not and the resulting confusion led to a request that the International Commission on Zoological Nomenclature conserve the pre-Klauber arrangement in the interest of nomenclatural stability. The commission complied (1956), and neotypes were subsequently designated by Schmidt and Conant (1956–1957). Cook (1963, 1964) later requested that the commission set aside both the neotype and associated type locality for *T. sirtalis* and rule that the name and type locality be interpreted from the description of the common garter snake given by Harlan (1827). The commission complied with Cook's request (Evans and China, 1966).

Marked geographic variation in *T. sirtalis* has resulted in the description of a plethora of subspecies, most of which are still recognized (Fitch, 1980b). The Chicago garter snake, *T. s. semifasciatus*, which had not been recognized by Ruthven (1908), was revived by P. W. Smith (1956). Benton (1980a, b) concluded that this is not a valid subspecies, but it is apparent from the discussion in the two papers that Benton's application of the subspecies concept differs so markedly from that of other snake systematists that it cannot be applied usefully to interpret the infraspecific taxonomy of *T. sirtalis*. Tanner (1988) described the northwestern Chihuahua populations as *T. s. lowei*, but his own illustrations show the color pattern to be the same as that of *T. s. dorsalis*; aside from having an extra pair of scale rows on the neck for an average of six more scale lengths than that in *T. s. dorsalis*, there seem to be no other characteristics distinguishing *T. s. lowei*. *T. s. lowei* is herewith relegated to the synonymy of *T. s. dorsalis*.

Many readers undoubtedly are familiar with the San Francisco Peninsula race under the name *T. s. tetrataenia*, which has been applied to that taxon since 1951. Recently, however, Boundy and Rossman (1995) reexamined the holotype of *Coluber infernalis* Blainville, 1835, and discovered that it is a representative of the San

Francisco Peninsula population. Since *infernalis* is the older name, this required changing the scientific name of the population but does not alter its recognition as a distinct subspecies. Boundy and Rossman also concurred with Van Denburgh and Slevin (1918) that the coastal California populations should be called *T. s. concinnus*.

An intensive, rangewide study of variation in *T. sirtalis* by J. Boundy is currently in progress.

LIFE HISTORY AND ECOLOGY

Thamnophis sirtalis has the greatest geographical distribution of any garter snake, extending from the Atlantic to the Pacific Coasts and much farther northward than any other snake in the Western Hemisphere. Although this species is arguably the best-studied snake in the world (*Vipera berus* probably being the closest competitor), the marked plasticity in its ecological traits makes an attempt to generalize aspects of its life history strategies nearly impossible (see Chap. 4). In addition, the number of papers providing limited data on this species is almost overwhelming. We therefore will concentrate our review on those populations whose ecology has been examined in detail.

Habitat

The ranking of the habitats of this species by Wright and Wright (1957) gives an idea of the generalist nature of the common garter snake. Of the 154 categories they listed, the most frequent habitat given was "Everywhere." Throughout much of its geographic range *T. sirtalis* is sympatric with one or two other species of *Thamnophis*. In those situations, *T. sirtalis* is typically the more generalized in habitat preference. Below, we give a brief overview of the habitat associations of this species.

In the southeastern United States, *T. sirtalis* is associated with a variety of mesic habitats. In the Everglades, *T. sirtalis* prefers seasonally flooded prairies over pineland and hardwood hammocks (Dalrymple, 1988). In the Great Plains of Kansas, *T. s. parietalis* is found in every mesic habitat in the summer (Fitch, 1965). Fitch (1965) ranked its habitat preference as follows: margins of ponds with low vegetation, a silt flat with willows and trees, woodland edges and trees in pastures, native prairie, meadows with introduced grasses, a fallow field in a bottomland, hardwood woodlands, upland fallow fields with weedy vegetation, and, finally, disturbed and barren roads and yards.

Thamnophis sirtalis

265

Some of the western subspecies of *T. sirtalis* tend to be more aquatic than those in the east and Great Plains. In Oregon's Willamette Valley, Stewart (1968) always found *T. s. concinnus* to be near marshes, ponds, and sloughs in lowland areas. In the northern Sierras of California, White and Kolb (1974) found that both marshes and streams were utilized by *T. sirtalis*. However, in central California *T. sirtalis* occurs in valley grasslands, oak savannas, marshes, oak woodlands, and montane conifer forests (Hansen and Tremper, *in prep.*).

Activity

Many investigators have reported that *T. sirtalis* has the longest activity season and coldest temperature tolerance of any snake in North America. Even in the extreme environments of northern Canada this species is able to sustain activity for about five months. However, there is marked geographic variation in seasonal activity patterns. In northern Alberta males have been observed on the surface as early as the 2nd week of April (Macartney et al., 1989). In southeastern British Columbia, individuals emerged in mid-March and returned to dens in early October (Farr, 1988).

In Michigan, *T. sirtalis* was the first species of snake active in the spring and the last to enter hibernation in the fall (Carpenter, 1952a). Carpenter calculated it had an activity period of 215 days. In Kansas, *T. sirtalis* has a longer season than any other snake (Fitch, 1965), and was collected as early as late February and as late as mid- to late November.

At some (mainly southern) localities, common garter snakes may be active all year. In the Everglades, *T. sirtalis* were active year-round but had a bimodal activity pattern (Dalrymple et al., 1991b). Adults were found most often in June and July, whereas neonates were common in October. Gibbons and Semlitsch (1987) found some activity in all months of the year except January in South Carolina. In Oregon, males emerged to bask on mild days even in January, whereas females began to be active in mid-February (Stewart, 1968). In lowland California, snakes were active from February to October, but activity declined dramatically after August because of reduction in the availability of aquatic habitats and prey (Hansen and Tremper, *in prep.*).

Common garter snakes (like most *Thamnophis*) are primarily diurnal. However, daily activity periods may show considerable seasonal variation. In Ohio, *T. sirtalis* were active from 0900 to 1800 hours in the spring and fall but became bimodally active (0700–1100 and 1500–1900 hours) in midsummer (Reichenbach and Dalrymple, 1986). Nocturnal activity was reported in lowland California by Hansen and Tremper (*in prep.*), where *T. sirtalis* may be active at night during warm rains.

This species can function at lower temperatures than any other garter snake (Fitch, 1965). Doughty (1994) found that *T. sirtalis* had the lowest critical thermal minimum temperature of any of the five species of garter snakes tested. In extreme northern Alberta, Canada, males emerging from hibernation at a communal den site had cloacal temperatures as low as 0.5° C (Larsen and Gregory, 1988). A snake with an implanted temperature-sensitive transmitter hibernating in this den had a body temperature averaging 3.9 C (a range of 1.8 to 6.5 C; Macartney et al., 1989). On Vancouver Island, British Columbia, active *T. sirtalis* exhibited an overall mean body temperature of 23.4 C (Gregory and McIntosh, 1980). In Ohio, *T. sirtalis* cloacal temperature averaged 26.1 C (Dalrymple and Reichenbach, 1981). Gibson and Falls (1979a) found that this species pre-

cisely regulated its body temperature when a range of environmental temperatures was available, but not early or late in the active season or early or late in the day. Males were also less precise thermoregulators than females. This species apparently has a circadian rhythm in temperature preference, since higher temperatures are selected during daylight than during dark periods (Justy and Mallory, 1985). Differences in thermoregulation may also exist between gravid females and males (see Chap. 4 for review).

Common garter snakes are known to make very long movements in some areas. For example, garter snakes (*T. s. parietalis*) from Manitoba moved from 4.3 to 17.7 km between hibernation sites and summer feeding grounds (Gregory and Stewart 1975) and in Alberta moved up to 9 km one way (Lawson, 1989). Fitch (1965) found a mean activity range of 142,000 m^2 for male *T. s. parietalis* in Kansas compared to 92,000 m^2 for females. Carpenter (1952a) reported an activity range of 8000 m^2 in Michigan. By contrast, Freedman and Catling (1979) found that most recaptured common garter snakes were within 160 m of their original capture site. The variation in movements probably reflects population differ-

Thamnophis sirtalis

ences in distance between suitable hibernation sites and summer foraging areas.

Feeding

As was true for habitat utilization, *T. sirtalis* is a generalist, feeding on a remarkably wide variety of prey, including terrestrial and aquatic invertebrates, fish, amphibians and their larvae, mammals, and even birds. Indeed, because of high seasonal, geographic, and ontogenetic plasticity in diet, broad generalizations are difficult (see Chap. 4 for discussion). In Kansas, adult *T. s. parietalis* ate primarily ranid frogs (50 to 71% of their diet), but neonates ate mostly earthworms (40%) (Fitch, 1965). Adults also occasionally ate voles and mice (*Microtus, Peromyscus,* and *Reithrodontomys;* Fitch, 1982). In Michigan, *T. sirtalis* ate primarily earthworms (80%), but also amphibians (15%), and a few mammals (*Microtus*), birds, and fish (Carpenter, 1952a). In Texas, earthworms also composed the main prey (62%; Fouquette, 1954) with amphibians and birds eaten as well (23% and 8%, respectively). In the interior of Oregon, *T. sirtalis* ate amphibians (including tadpoles of the introduced bullfrog, *Rana catesbeiana*), earthworms, leeches, and fish (Stewart, 1968). In California, *T. sirtalis* fed mainly on amphibians, including yellow-legged and red-legged frogs, bullfrogs, toads, treefrogs, and salamanders. Fitch (1941b) found that the toads *Bufo* and *Scaphiopus* made up 31% of the diet, other terrestrial amphibians 28%, with earthworms contributing 24%; tadpoles were the primary aquatic prey taken (10%). White and Kolb (1974) found that *T. s. fitchi* eats primarily treefrogs (*Hyla*) (55.5%), fish (*Catostomus*, 21.8% and *Rhinichthys*, 11.5%), and some voles (*Microtus*) (5.4%). On Vancouver Island in British Columbia, *T. sirtalis* fed mainly on earthworms and amphibians, with smaller snakes showing a higher proportion of earthworms in their diet (Gregory, 1984b). The young of this population have been tested for their innate preference of prey in terms of tongue-flicking rates (Carr and Gregory, 1976; see Chap. 5). Their responses did not reflect exactly the feeding habits of wild populations since the strongest reaction was to mouse odor, but salamander, frog, and earthworm odors also elicited high tongue-flick rates.

Drummond (1983) observed foraging of *T. sirtalis* both in the field and in artificial ponds. Individuals hunted primarily by open-mouth searching along the margins of the pool. The body of this species was positively buoyant, and fish that were attacked were primarily at the surface of the water or randomly encountered while snakes were briefly submerged. Gillingham and Rowe (1984) describe the terrestrial foraging behavior of common garter snakes (see fig. 5.3). The snake locates earthworm castings, then thrusts its snout into the tunnel below to capture the worm.

Reproduction

Although fall mating was reported in several early studies (Blanchard and Blanchard, 1941, 1942; Fitch, 1965; Fox, 1956), until recently most of the studies of mating behavior and the factors that regulate the timing of reproduction in T. sirtalis have focused primarily (if not exclusively) on spring activities (e.g., Bona-Gallo and Licht, 1983; Crews et al., 1984; Garstka et al., 1982; Whittier et al., 1987; Whittier and Tokarz, 1992). This is perhaps not surprising, considering the more obvious nature of spring mating, best illustrated by the huge mating aggregations of red-sided garter snakes in Manitoba, where large numbers of males actively courted females as they emerged from hibernation in the spring (e.g., Aleksiuk and Gregory, 1974; Crews et al.,

1984; Gregory, 1977a, b; see Fig. 4-1). However, mating in the fall may be much more common then earlier believed, even in Manitoba (see Chap. 4 for details). On the other hand, spring mating does appear to be the rule at other localities; for example, Stewart (1968) observed mating activity from mid-March to early April in the interior valley of Oregon. He noted only subdued courtship in the fall.

Most data suggest that T. sirtalis offspring are born between midsummer and early fall, although the timing of birth is subject to considerable variation both among and within populations. In Manitoba, offspring were born between the end of July and late September (Gregory, 1977b). In the Everglades (the opposite end of the range), females gave birth as early as May and as late as November (Dalrymple et al., 1991b). Snakes were born in August and early September in British Columbia (Farr, 1988) and in late July or early August in Kansas (Fitch, 1965).

The quantity of data available on the fecundity of T. sirtalis is immense and can only be summarized briefly here. Fecundity in T. sirtalis is highly plastic; in addition to both geographic and temporal variation, fecundity is affected by body size, diet, and other environmental factors (Gregory and

Thamnophis sirtalis

Larsen, 1993). (See Table 4-1 for a summary of reproductive data on *T. sirtalis*.)

Overall, mean clutch sizes in *T. sirtalis* range from a low of 7.6 at one site in British Columbia to a high of 32.5 in Maryland (see Table 4-1). Most litters average 10 to 15. In general, larger females produce larger clutch sizes (Gregory and Larsen, 1993; Seigel and Ford, 1987). Geographic variation can be substantial; Gregory and Larsen (1993) found significant differences among several eastern and western populations of *T. sirtalis*, even after accounting for differences in female size. Clutch sizes also vary among years within the same populations; Seigel and Fitch (1985) found that the average clutch size at the Natural History Reservation in Kansas varied from 11 to 23.

More data on offspring size are available for common garter snakes than perhaps for any other snake. Offspring SVLs range from a low of 154.4 mm in Manitoba to a high of 201.3 mm in British Columbia (Table 4-1), suggesting considerable geographic variation. However, offspring size in snakes may be affected by the size of the mother, the mother's clutch size, and the time spent in captivity (Ford and Seigel, 1989b; King, 1993), and this informa-

tion has rarely been taken into account when records for *T. sirtalis* are given. Therefore careful records of reproduction of this species (giving all this data) can still be quite valuable.

Although clear patterns are not yet apparent, evidence is mounting that some females do not reproduce each year, especially in northern areas. Based on the data summarized in Table 4-1, overall reproductive frequency in *T. sirtalis* (% of mature females gravid in a sample) varies from 28.6% to 88%. However, these figures are only estimates and are subject to considerable variation. In Michigan, 65% of adult females were gravid overall, but some individual snakes were known to be gravid in successive years (Carpenter, 1952a). In the Lake Erie area, King (1988) found that the percentage of gravid females increased over the active season, reaching a maximum of 75% in August; the percentage of gravid females also varied among size classes (King, 1988). The percentage of gravid females in Manitoba varied from 23.5 to 88% over two years (Whittier and Crews, 1990). The lowest reproductive frequency was found in the Northwest Territories of Canada, where only 3 of 24 females reproduced in consecutive years (Larsen et al., 1993). Low reproductive frequencies have also been reported by Fitch (1965), Hebard (1951), and Stewart (1968).

Population Biology

Even away from dens, common garter snakes can have impressive population sizes for snakes (see the summary in Table 4-3). The highest reported density for *T. sirtalis* was 45 to 89/ha, at an isolated prairie in Ohio (Dalrymple and Reichenbach, 1984). Other sites also had relatively high numbers of common garter snakes; Carpenter (1952a) reported 24.8/ha for a study site in Michigan, followed closely by 18.7/ha in Illinois (Blaesing, 1979). In Kansas, Fitch (1982) estimated a mean density of 3.7/ha in three areas ranging in size from 71 to 151 ha), but these densities were reduced from earlier estimates of 11.0/ha (Fitch, 1965), apparently as a result of secondary succession (H. Fitch, pers. comm.). In southeastern Manitoba, Farr (1988) indicated densities of 1.7/ha in his 2000-ha tract; much-lower densities occurred in areas of open water, but higher densities were evident closer to overwintering sites.

Adequate data on age and size at maturity are lacking (see Chap. 4). On the basis of growth-rate data, Fitch (1965) and Gregory (1977a, b) suggested that most females matured at 2 and 3 years of age in Kansas and Manitoba, respectively. Conversely, the minimum age at maturity in northern California was 3 to 4 years and possibly older (Jayne and Bennett, 1990). Most females mature at between 426 and 570 mm SVL; males mature at smaller sizes of 360 to 387 mm SVL, but there is likely to be geographical and phenotypic plasticity in this trait (see summary in Table 4-3).

The best data on survival rates for garter snakes comes from populations of *T. sirtalis* in Kansas (Fitch, 1965), northern California (Jayne and Bennett, 1990), and western Canada (Gregory, 1977a, b; Larsen and Gregory, 1989). Annual survival of neonates ranged from about 29 to 43%, although there was variation among and within populations (Fitch, 1965; Jayne and Bennett, 1990; see Chap. 4 for details). Although it is likely that predation on neonates is greater than on adults, in a study in California, yearling *T. sirtalis* had a survival rate of 50.8% (Jayne and Bennett, 1990), whereas snakes > 2 years old in this population had a lower survival rate, 32.7%. In contrast, adult annual survival was estimated at 50% in Kansas (Fitch, 1965; Parker and Plummer,

Thamnophis sirtalis

1987), 34% in Manitoba (Gregory, 1977b), and 67% in the Northwest Territories (Larsen and Gregory, 1989).

Mortality of small snakes in hibernation was documented by Carpenter (1952a) in Michigan and by Gregory (1977b) in Manitoba, where from 33 to 50% of all individuals may die during winter. Common garter snakes are subject to population declines when amphibian populations decrease because *T. sirtalis* lacks the ability to forage effectively on fish (Drummond, 1983; Kephart and Arnold, 1982).

Captive Maintenance

Because of its local availability throughout much of North America, this species is probably one of the most common snakes kept by individuals. If maintained properly, most specimens are hardy, tolerate handling reasonably well, and readily eat in captivity. *Thamnophis sirtalis* can be maintained easily on fish or larval amphibians, and juveniles can be started on earthworms. Colonies of this species have been maintained in several laboratories through many generations and their care is well documented. (See Chap. 6.)

Conservation

One subspecies in California (*T. sirtalis infernalis*) is listed on the U. S. Endangered Species List, mainly the result of habitat loss and overcollecting. No other populations are known to be in serious jeopardy, but populations of common garter snakes in Manitoba were substantially reduced in size by overcollecting for the pet and scientific trade. (See Chap. 4.)

Thamnophis sumichrasti
SUMICHRAST'S
GARTER SNAKE
(Plate 14)

Eutaenia sumichrasti Cope, 1866
Eutaenia phenax Cope, 1868
Thamnophis halophilus Taylor, 1940

Identification

Dorsal scales in a maximum of 19 rows, reducing to 17 (rarely 16) posteriorly; supralabials 8 (rarely 7) and infralabials 10 (occasionally 9, rarely 8 or 11) on at least one side of head; maxillary teeth 24 to 29; the dorsum olive-brown with either a series of very broad, black-edged brown blotches separated by narrow interspaces, or 3 to 5 alternating rows of moderate-sized black—or black-edged brown—spots or bars; light stripes usually lacking; a prominent black postocular stripe; tongue uniformly black.

Content and Distribution

No subspecies are currently recognized. Sumichrast's garter snake occurs in eastern Mexico along the Sierra Madre Oriental from eastern Queretaro and southeastern San Luis Potosí to the vicinity of Cordoba, Veracruz (see Map 27), at elevations between 1365 and 2305 m.

Description

The following is based on Rossman (1992b). *Thamnophis sumichrasti* is a moderate-sized species of garter snake, reaching a maximum total length of 756 mm (AMNH 93131). The dorsal pattern is strongly dimorphic; both a spotted and a blotched morph may occur in the same brood (see Rossman, 1966). In the former, a row of black or black-edged brown lateral spots (½ to 2 scales long) on dorsal scale rows 3 to 5 to 3 to 8 alternate with vertebral bars (½ to 1 scale long, 3 to 7 scales wide—depending on whether the two sides are connected). There also may be an alternating row of small spots on the lowermost row(s) of dorsal scales. The spotted pattern is well developed in juveniles, but it may or may not become indistinct in adults. The skin between the scales in living specimens is yellow, brightest anteriorly. Light stripes usually are lacking, but a faint, irregular, narrow vertebral stripe was visible in a few specimens. The blotched morph has 34 to 49 black-edged brown blotches extending ventrally to the upper half of dorsal scale row 1. The blotches are 3 to 3½ scales long, separated by slightly lighter interspaces 1 to 1½ scales long. Light stripes are always lacking. The dark nuchal blotches are shaped like expanded, inverted commas with the "tails" extending onto the parietals, where they break up into an irregular network of dark pigment that usually involves the frontal, supraoculars, prefrontals, and internasals as well. An irregular, broad, black postocular stripe extends across the middle of the anterior temporal and along the suture between supralabials 7 and 8 to the lip. The tongue is uniformly black.

With but a single known exception, *T. sumichrasti* has a maximum of 19 dorsal scale rows, reducing to 17 pos-

Thamnophis sumichrasti

273

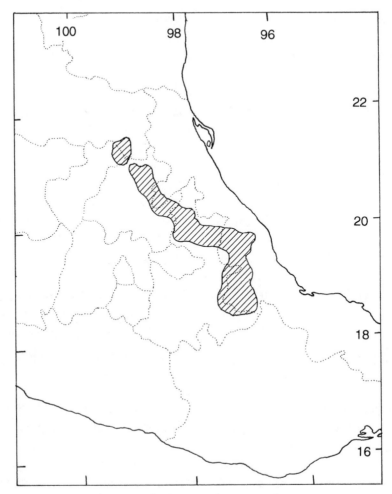

Map 27 Distribution of *Thamnophis sumichrasti*.

teriorly. Ventrals range from 149 to 161 in males, 147 to 158 in females; males average 3.1 more ventrals than females. Subcaudals range from 67 to 80 in males, 57 to 68 in females; males average 8.6 more subcaudals than females. Relative tail length ranges from 21.4 to 24.3% in males, 19.4 to 22.6% in females; it averages 1.7% longer in males than in females.

Preoculars number 1 to a side, postoculars usually 3. There are normally 8 supralabials (rarely 7) and 10 infralabials (frequently 9, rarely 8 or 11) on each side. Maxillary teeth range from 24 to 29, averaging 26.3 in males and 25.4 in females.

The head constitutes 4.9% of SVL in adult males, 5.1% in adult females—of moderate length and long, respectively, for a garter snake. The eye is large, ED/FL averaging 76.4%. The muzzle tip is of moderate width, the combined InR/NR averaging 104.5%. The muzzle is long, ML/PL averaging 75.2%. The prefrontals are shorter than the internasals, Prf/In averaging 89.5%. The parietals of *T. sumichrasti* are short in males and of moderate length in females, Fl/PL averaging 80.3% and 76.6%, respectively. The posterior chin shields are of moderate length, ACS/PCS averaging 81.9%.

Taxonomic Comments

Sumichrast's garter snake (a name coined by Yarrow, 1882) has had a confusing taxonomic history, due in large part to the striking pattern dimorphism exhibited by this species. The two syntypes of *T. sumichrasti* are of the spotted morph; the blotched morph was described two years later as a separate species, *T. phenax* (Cope, 1868). Cope (1892b) recognized that a relationship existed between the two taxa and suggested that *phenax* was ancestral to *sumichrasti.* The following year, both Boulenger (1893) and Bocourt (1893) associated the name *sumichrasti* with what was then thought to be a Guatemalan subspecies of *T. cyrtopsis* but is now recognized to be a distinct species, *T. fulvus.* Although Cope stuck by his earlier conclusions, Ruthven (1908) and most subsequent authors until 1965 followed the notion that *sumichrasti* is a southern race of *T. cyrtopsis* (H. M. Smith, 1942, treated *sumichrasti* as a full species, but he assigned the name to *T. fulvus* and the southern races of *T. marcianus* rather than to the form originally described by Cope). During this period, Taylor (1940) described as a new species, *T. halophilus* from Hidalgo,

Thamnophis sumichrasti

275

which he noted as being similar to *T. phenax*. Rossman (1965a) compared the syntypes of *sumichrasti* with the holotypes of *halophilus* and found them to be conspecific, thus reassociating the name *sumichrasti* with the taxon it represents. A year later, Rossman (1966) demonstrated that *sumichrasti* and *phenax* are simply pattern morphs of a single species.

Meanwhile, Walker (1955) observed that *T. mendax* appears to be morphologically intermediate between *T. scalaris* and *T. phenax* (subsequently *T. sumichrasti*), but he concluded that there was a closer affinity between *T. scalaris* and *T. mendax*. In contrast, Rossman (1992b), while agreeing that the meristic and mensural data are equivocal, argued that the similarities between *T. mendax* and *T. sumichrasti* in head and body patterns strongly suggest that they are sister-species.

LIFE HISTORY AND ECOLOGY

Data on life history and ecology are sparse. Rossman (1992b) found this species in humid montane forests in the immediate vicinity of small streams or narrow irrigation ditches with fast-moving water. The snakes dived into the water to escape capture. Duellman's field notes (University of Kansas) report specimens from streams in cloud forest.

Thamnophis validus
MEXICAN PACIFIC LOWLANDS GARTER SNAKE
(Plate 14)

Regina valida Kennicott, 1860
    (= *T. v. validus*)
Tropidonotus celaeno Cope, 1860
    (= *T. v. celaeno*)
Tropidonotus tephropleura Cope, 1860
    (= *T. v. celaeno*)
Tropidonotus quadriserialis Fischer, 1879
    (= *T. v. validus*)
Natrix valida isabelleae Conant, 1953
    (= *T. v. isabelleae*)
Natrix valida thamnophisoides Conant, 1961
    (= *T. v. thamnophisoides*)

Identification

Anal plate divided; dorsal scales in a maximum of 19 or 21 rows (usually 19 except in female *T. v. celaeno*, which more frequently have 21); supralabials usually 8; maxillary teeth 23 to 27; the dorsum brown, gray, or nearly black, usually with 4 alternating rows of small dark spots (but large spots in many *T. v. celaeno*); a light vertebral stripe present only in *T. v. thamnophisoides*; the lateral stripe, when present, confined to dorsal scale rows 1 and 2 or 1, 2, and 3.

Content and Distribution

Four subspecies of Mexican Pacific lowlands garter snake are currently recognized: *T. v. validus,* which ranges from the Río Yaqui in southern Sonora southward to the vicinity of San Blas, Nayarit; *T. v. thamnophisoides,* which occurs only in the Río San Cayetano near Tepic, Nayarit; *T. v. isabelleae,* which ranges from southwestern Jalisco to the vicinity of Acapulco, Guerrero; and *T. v. celaeno,* which is confined to the Cape Region of Territorio Sur de Baja California (see Map 28). Elevational distribution ranges from 0 to 1200 m (Conant, 1969).

Description

The following is based on Conant (1969) and previously unpublished data. *Thamnophis validus* is a long species of garter snake, reaching a maximum SVL of 867 mm (the tail is incomplete in the largest specimen; Conant, 1969). The dorsum is gray or brown (often with considerable melanism in *T. v. celaeno*), usually with four alternating rows of small dark spots (large in dark-phase *T. v. cel-*

aeno). A light vertebral stripe (confined to the vertebral row, or involving part of each scale in the paravertebral rows) occurs only in *T. v. thamnophisoides.* A gray or olive lateral stripe with irregular edges involves dorsal scale rows 1 and 2 or 1, 2, and 3 in all subspecies except *T. v. validus.* The venter ranges from pale yellow unmarked by black pigment, through having varying amounts of black pigment midventrally, to being uniformly black.

There usually are 19-19-17 dorsal scale rows except in female *T. v. celaeno,* which more frequently have 21-19-17 or 19-21-19-17. Ventrals in *T. validus* range from 130 to 150 in males, 127 to 147 in females; males average 0.3 to 1.7 more ventrals than females. Subcaudals range from 69 to 86 in males, 61 to 78 in females; males average 5.6 to 7.4 more subcaudals than females. Relative tail length averages (extremes not reported) from 26.4 to 27.5% in males, 24.7 to 25.9% in females; it averages 1.3 to 1.6% longer in males than in females.

Preoculars usually number 1 to a side (occasionally 2), postoculars usually 3 (occasionally 2, rarely 4). There usually are 8 supralabials (occasionally 9, rarely 7) and 10 infralabials, rarely 9 or 11. Maxillary teeth range from 23 to 27, averaging 25.2 (no sex-

Thamnophis validus

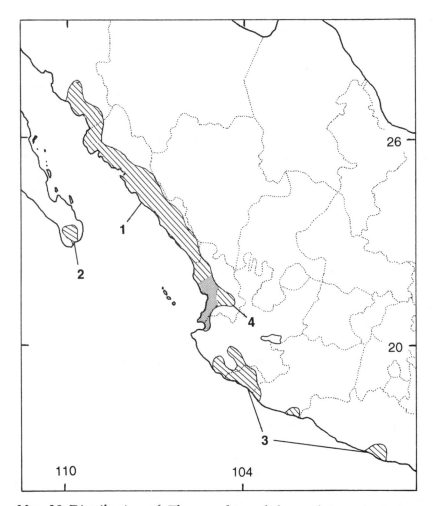

Map 28 Distribution of *Thamnophis validus* and its subspecies: (1) *T. v. validus*; (2) *T. v. celaeno*; (3) *T. v. isabelleae*; (4) *T. v. thamnophisoides*. Stippling represents a zone of intergradation.

ual dimorphism was reported by Conant, 1969).

The head of *Thamnophis validus* constitutes 5.5% of SVL, which is long for a garter snake. The eye is small, ED/FL averaging 62.0%. The tip of the muzzle is narrow, InR/NR averaging 74.8%. The muzzle is long, ML/FL averaging 72.6%. The prefrontals are shorter than the internasals, Prf/In averaging 88.1%. The parietals of *T. validus* are long, FL/PL averaging 71.0%. The posterior chin shields are of moderate length, ACS/PCS averaging 84.1%.

Taxonomic Comments

Save for its original placement in the genus *Regina* (Kennicott, 1860), *T. validus* was considered to be a water snake (first as *Tropidonotus*, then *Natrix*, and subsequently *Nerodia*) until Lawson (1987) presented biochemical evidence that, despite having a divided anal plate, *T. validus* is more closely related to the garter snakes than to the water snakes.

Geographically and taxonomically puzzling is the fact that "many specimens of (*T. v.*) *celaeno* are indistinguishable in coloration and pattern from those of mainland (*T. v.*) *valida*" (Conant, 1969), the sole distinction being a greater average number of dorsal spots in the former. Such individuals of *T. v. celaeno* are representatives of what Conant called the Pale Populations, which coexist with the Dark Populations at three localities (but at only one of the three have intermediates been found). One cannot help but wonder if what we are seeing here is simply a single taxon (*T. v. validus*) that is pattern-polymorphic in only a portion of its range (the Cape Region), a not-unprecedented condition among garter snakes (e.g., *T. atratus hydrophilus*, *T. gigas*).

LIFE HISTORY AND ECOLOGY

Habitat

Thamnophis v. isabelleae occurs in short stretches of narrow coastal plain on the Pacific side of Mexico, in floodplains at the mouths of rivers flowing into the Pacific, and in attenuated lagoons paralleling the coast. It occupies both tropical deciduous forest and thorn forest, characterized by small deciduous trees that are leafless in the dry season. Specimens have been collected in marshes, swamplands, and concrete irrigation canals. The species is usually closely associated with water and is often restricted to gallery forest. Occasionally it may enter the estuarine environment and

Thamnophis validus

be found in the mangroves of brackish-water lagoons (Duellman, 1961). Some forms (*T. v. celaeno*) are found in more-upland habitats, occurring in the foothills of the mountains of extreme southern Baja California in intermittent streams that flow from the mountains to the seas (sea level to 1200 m), and even in volcanic lakes (Conant, 1969). *Thamnophis v. thamnophisoides* has been taken in spring-fed meadows, and *T. v. celaeno* occurs in rocky arroyos with pools and small streams.

Activity

This species is commonly collected on roads at night or in aquatic vegetation or along banks from early in the evening to as late as midnight (Conant, 1969; D. Rossman, pers. obs.). Conant (1969) suggested that *T. v. celaeno* is more diurnal than the other subspecies.

Feeding

Thamnophis validus principally eat small fishes, frogs, and toads (Conant, 1969). Conant (1969) observed these snakes pursuing fish, and several disgorged *Poecilia mexicana* and *Gobiomorus maculatus*. One was seen swallowing an adult *Bufo mazatla-*

nensis, another eating a road-killed *Leptodactylus melanonotus*. *Rana* have also been reported as prey (Conant, 1946). Conant (1969) observed *T. v. thamnophisoides* feeding both in riffles and at the surface at night. One of these specimens had a *Cichlasoma* in its stomach. Conant (1969) also collected a *T. v. celaeno* that disgorged a small *Bufo punctatus*; another individual contained 16 toadlets.

Reproduction

Quantified data on reproduction are not available. Offspring are born from 6 June to 1 August. Newborns vary from 165 to 223 mm in total length. (Dixon and Webb, 1965).

Captive Maintenance

Conant (1946) kept a number of *T. validus* in captivity for several years. His snakes ate leopard frogs and fishes. *Thamnophis validus* is an aggressive species and bites repeatedly when captured. Some individuals tame down, but some remain aggressive. Conant noted lumpy swellings that were likely nematodes, which are commonly found in *Thamnophis* that eat fish and frogs (Lichtenfels and Lavies, 1976).

GLOSSARY

Acclimation. To physiologically adjust to new environmental conditions over time.

Allometric growth. Growth of one part of the body at a rate different from that of another part.

Allopatric. Descriptive of two or more taxa having geographic ranges that are completely separated.

Allotopic. Occurring separately; when two organisms are allotopic, their habitat usage does not overlap. The opposite of syntopic.

Allozyme. One of several forms of an enzyme that is coded for by different alleles at a single locus.

Artenkreis. A German term referring to a group of closely related species.

Biological species concept. A concept in which recognition of species is based primarily on the criterion of reproductive isolation.

Caudocephalic waves. Ripples of muscle contractions moving from the posterior to the anterior end of a snake.

Character. A category of features (e.g., number of ventral scales, position of lateral stripe, width of vertebral stripe) that can be used to distinguish between populations or taxa.

Character-state (or characteristic). The specific expression of a particular character (e.g., having more than 135 ventral scales, a lateral stripe on 2nd and 3rd dorsal scale rows, or a vertebral stripe one scale row wide).

Circadian. Exhibiting a 24-hour periodicity.

Cladistic analysis. A method of estimating phylogenetic relationships that focuses on evolutionary changes in character-states.

Clinal variation. A geographic character gradient (e.g., *Thamnophis couchii* has considerably more black pigment on the venter at the northern end of its range than at the southern end).

Concordant variation. Clinal variation in which two or more characters exhibit changes in the same geographic region.

Conspecific. Belonging to the same species.

Crypsis. Concealing or camouflaging behavior.

Defecation. The voiding of waste products from the bowels.

Discordant variation. Clinal variation in which the changes in two or more characters occur in different geographic regions.

Diurnal. Occurring or active during the daytime rather than at night.

Endogenous. Produced from internal sources.

Evolutionary species concept. A concept in which recognition of species is based primarily on ancestor-descendant relationships rather than reproductive isolation.

Fecundity. The number of offspring produced by an organism, usually expressed as the number of eggs or neonates produced by a female.

Fitness. The evolutionary success of an organism in terms of passing its genes to the next generation; mathematically, the combination of fecundity times survival.

Habituation. A simple form of learning in which responses decline after repetitive exposure to a stimulus.

Heterospecific. Belonging to another species.

Immunological distance. A measure of the similarity of the immune systems of two organisms based on the degree of identity of antibodies from one organism with antigens from the other.

Incomplete penetrance. A manifestation of genes in the phenotype of individuals at a lower frequency than mathematically expected.

Interspecific. Between two (or more) species.

Intraspecific (or infraspecific). Within a species.

Mast crop. The production of young at one time to reduce effective predation.

Melanism. A dark coloration of the skin because of a high concentration of the pigment melanin.

Mensural. Descriptive of a feature that is measured.

Meristic. Descriptive of a feature that is counted.

Microcomplement fixation. A technique used to estimate immunological distances.

Mycotic. Referring to a disease caused by fungi.

Neonate. A newborn organism.

Nomen dubium. Literally, "doubtful

name"; a taxonomic name that cannot be assigned with confidence to any known species.

Nomen nudum. Literally, "naked name"; a taxonomic name that does not meet the International Code of Zoological Nomenclature's criteria for adequately describing, defining, or otherwise indicating the identity of a new taxon.

Ontogenetic. Refers to changes occurring during the developmental history of an individual organism; for example, changes in body color from the time of birth to maturity.

Ophiophagous. Feeding on snakes.

Oxytocin. A posterior pituitary hormone involved in smooth muscle contraction.

Parapatric. Descriptive of two or more taxa having geographic ranges that meet but do not overlap to any substantial degree.

Paraphyletic. Referring to a higher taxon that does not contain all the descendants of the most recent common ancestor of its members.

Penultimate. Next to the last.

Phenogram. A branching diagram that links taxa on the basis of overall similarity of characters.

Phenotypic. The outward (physical) expression of the genes of an individual.

Pheromone. A chemical secreted by an animal that influences the behavior or physiology of others of the same species.

Pineal gland. A small endocrine organ in the brain of vertebrates that is involved in rhythmic activity.

Polygenic. A trait that is controlled from more than one source.

Polymorphism. The condition of having more than one form or appearance.

Polyphyletic. Referring to a higher taxon that does not contain its most recent common ancestor.

Speciose. Having many species.

Stochastic. A random or unpredictable process; the opposite of deterministic.

SVL. Snout-vent length.

Sympatric. Descriptive of two or more taxa having geographic ranges that overlap to a substantial degree.

Syntopic. Occurring together; when two organisms are syntopic, their habitat usage overlaps. The opposite of allotopic.

Taxon (pl. taxa). A specific taxonomic entity, e.g., a particular species or genus.

Thamnophiine. A member of the tribe Thamnophiini in the subfamily Natricinae of the family Colubridae.

Trinomial. A three-part name applied to subspecies (e.g., *Thamnophis sauritus septentrionalis*).

Type-species. The species on which the generic name is based.

Type specimens. The specific specimens on which the scientist who first names a new taxon bases the original description. One individual is designated as the holotype, the name bearer, in order to permanently attach the name to a single taxon in the event that later research reveals that the type series was composed of more than one species.

Typological thinking. Descriptive of the logic that considers type specimens to be "typical" of the species, allowing for very little in the way of variation.

Vas deferens. The duct through which semen is carried from storage in the epididymis to be ejaculated.

Vitellogenesis. The process of producing and storing yolk in eggs.

Volatile. A chemical that vaporizes readily at normal temperatures and pressures.

LITERATURE CITED

Aldridge, R. D. 1979. Female reproductive cycles of the snakes *Arizona elegans* and *Crotalus viridis*. *Herpetologica* 35:256–261.

Aleksiuk, M. 1976. Reptilian hibernation: Evidence of adaptive strategies in *Thamnophis sirtalis parietalis*. *Copeia* 1976:170–178.

—— and P. T. Gregory. 1974. Regulation of seasonal mating behavior in *Thamnophis sirtalis parietalis*. *Copeia* 1974:681–723.

Allen, G. M. 1899. Notes on the reptiles and amphibians of Intervale, New Hampshire. *Proc. Boston Soc. Nat. Hist.* 29:63–75.

Allen, W. B. 1988. *State Lists of Endangered and Threatened Species of Reptiles and Amphibians and Laws and Regulations Covering Collecting of Reptiles and Amphibians in Each State.* Chicago Herpetol. Soc., Chicago, Illinois.

Andrew, E. W. 1937. Notes on snakes from the Yucatan Peninsula. *Zool. Series Field Mus. Nat. Hist.* 20:355–359.

Andrews, R. M. 1982. Patterns of growth in reptiles. *In* C. Gans and F. H. Pough (eds.), *Biology of the Reptilia*, Vol. 13, pp. 273–320. Academic Press, New York.

Arnold, S. J. 1977. Polymorphism and geographic variation in the feeding behavior of the garter snake *Thamnophis elegans*. *Science* 197:676–678.

——. 1978. Some effects of early experience on feeding responses in the common garter snake, *Tham-*

nophis sirtalis. *Anim. Behav.* 26:455–462.

————. 1980. The microevolution of feeding behavior. *In* A. Kamil and T. Sargent (eds.), *Foraging Ecology: Ecological, Ethological, and Psychological Approaches*, pp. 409–455. Garland Press, New York.

————. 1981a. Behavioral variation in natural populations. I. Phenotypic, genetic, and environmental correlations between chemoreceptive responses to prey in the garter snake, *Thamnophis elegans. Evolution* 35:489–509.

————. 1981b. Behavioral variation in natural populations. II. The inheritance of a feeding response in crosses between geographic races of the garter snake, *Thamnophis elegans. Evolution* 35:510–515.

————. 1993. Foraging theory and prey-size–predator-size relations in snakes. *In* R. A. Seigel and J. T. Collins (eds.), *Snakes: Ecology and Behavior*, pp. 87–115. McGraw-Hill, New York.

———— and A. F. Bennett. 1984. Behavioral variation in natural populations. III: antipredator displays in the garter snake *Thamnophis radix. Anim. Behav.* 32:1108–1118.

———— and ————. 1988. Behavioral variation in natural populations. V. Morphological correlates of locomotion in the garter snake *Thamnophis radix. Biol. J. Linnean Soc.* 34:175–190.

———— and R. J. Wassersug. 1978. Differential predation on metamorphic anurans by garter snakes (*Thamnophis*): Social behavior as a possible defense. *Ecology* 59:1014–1022.

Asplund, K. K. 1963. Ecological factors in the distribution of *Thamnophis brachystoma* (Cope). *Herpetologica* 19:128–132.

Avery, R. A. 1982. Field studies of body temperatures. *In* C. Gans and F. H. Pough (eds.), *Biology of the Reptilia*, Vol. 12, pp. 25–91. Academic Press, New York.

Ayres, F. A., and S. J. Arnold. 1983. Behavioural variation in natural populations. IV. Mendelian models and heritability of a feeding response in the garter snake, *Thamnophis elegans. Heredity* 51:405–413.

Baird, S. F. 1854. *On the serpents of New York; with a notice of species not hitherto included in the fauna of the state.* C. Van Benthuysen, Albany, New York. 28 pp.

————. 1859. Reptiles of the boundary. *U.S. and Mex. Boundary Surv.* 2:1–35.

———— and C. Girard. 1852. Descriptions of new species of reptiles, collected by the U.S. Exploring Expedition under the command of Capt. Charles Wilkes, U.S.N.

Literature
Cited

286

First part.—Including the species from the western coast of America. *Proc. Acad. Nat. Sci. Philadelphia* 6:174–177.

———— and ————. 1853. *Catalogue of North American Reptiles in the Museum of the Smithsonian Institution. Part I. Serpents.* Smithsonian Inst., Washington, D.C. 172 pp.

Ball, R. L. 1978. The courtship and mating behavior of a Mexican garter snake *Thamnophis melanogaster*. Master's Thesis, Univ. of Oklahoma, Norman.

Ballinger, R. E., J. D. Lynch, and P. H. Cole. 1979. Distribution and natural history of amphibians and reptiles in western Nebraska with ecological notes on the herptiles of Arapaho Prairie. *Prairie Natur.* 11:65–74.

Barton, A. J. 1956. A statistical study of *Thamnophis brachystoma* (Cope) with comments on the kinship of *T. butleri* (Cope). *Proc. Biol. Soc. Washington* 69:71–82.

Bauerle, B. 1972. *Biological productivity of snakes of the Pawnee Site 1970–1971.* U.S. IBP Grassland Biome Tech. Rep. No. 207. Colorado State Univ., Fort Collins.

Bellemin, J. M., and G. R. Stewart. 1977. Diagnostic characters and color convergence of the garter snakes *Thamnophis elegans terrestris* and *Thamnophis couchii atratus*

along the central California coast. *Bull. So. California Acad. Sci.* 76:73–84.

Benton, M. J. 1980a. Geographic variation in the garter snakes (*Thamnophis sirtalis*) of the north-central United States: A multivariate study. *Zool. J. Linnean Soc.* 68:307–323.

————. 1980b. Geographic variation and the validity of subspecies names for the eastern garter snake, *Thamnophis sirtalis. Bull. Chicago Herpetol. Soc.* 15:57–69.

Bernardino, F. S., Jr., and G. H. Dalrymple. 1992. Seasonal activity and road mortality of the snakes of the Pa-hay-okee wetlands of Everglades National Park, USA. *Biol. Conserv.* 62:71–75.

Berner, N. J., and R. L. Ingermann. 1988. Molecular basis of the difference in oxygen affinity between maternal and foetal red blood cells in the viviparous garter snake *Thamnophis elegans. J. Exp. Biol.* 140:437–453.

Bishop, L. A., and T. M. Farrell. 1994. *Thamnophis sauritus sackenii.* Behavior. *Herpetol. Rev.* 25:127.

Blaesing, M. E. 1979. Some aspects of the ecology of the eastern garter snake, *Thamnophis sirtalis sirtalis* (Reptilia, Serpentes, Colubridae), in a semi-disturbed habitat in west-central Illinois. *J. Herpetol.* 13:177–181.

Literature
Cited

Blainville, H. D. de. 1835. Description de quelques espèces de reptiles de la California. *Nouv. Ann. Mus. Hist. Paris* 4:1–64.

Blanchard, F. C. 1943. A test of fecundity of the garter snake *Thamnophis sirtalis sirtalis* (Linnaeus) in the year following insemination. *Papers Michigan Acad. Sci. Arts Letters* 28:313–316.

Blanchard, F. N. 1925. A key to the snakes of the United States, Canada, and Lower California. *Papers Michigan Acad. Sci. Arts Letters* 4:1–65.

—— and F. C. Blanchard. 1941. Factors determining the time of birth in the garter snake, *Thamnophis sirtalis sirtalis* (Linnaeus). *Papers Michigan Acad. Sci. Arts Letters* 26:161–176.

—— and ——. 1942. Mating of the garter snake *Thamnophis sirtalis sirtalis* (Linnaeus). *Papers Michigan Acad. Sci. Arts Letters* 27:215–234.

Blaney, P. K. 1977. A survey of the microornamentation of snake scales. Master's thesis, Louisiana St. Univ., Baton Rouge.

Bleakney, S. 1959. *Thamnophis sirtalis sirtalis* (Linnaeus) in eastern Canada, redescription of *T. s. pallidula* Allen. *Copeia* 1959:52–56.

Bocourt, M.-F. 1892. Note sur un Ophidien appartenant au genre *Eutae-*

nia. Le Naturaliste 14:278.

——. 1893. Mission scientifique au Mexique et dans L'Amérique Centrale—Recherches Zoologiques. Part 3, Sect. 1. *Livr.* 13:733–780.

Bogert, C. M., and J. A. Oliver. 1945. A preliminary analysis of the herpetofauna of Sonora. *Bull. Amer. Mus. Nat. Hist.* 83:301–425.

Bona-Gallo, A., and P. Licht. 1983. Effects of temperature on sexual receptivity and ovarian recrudescence in the garter snake, *Thamnophis sirtalis parietalis. Herpetologica* 39:173–182.

Bothner, R. C. 1963. A hibernaculum of the short-headed garter snake, *Thamnophis brachystoma* Cope. *Copeia* 1963:572–573.

——. 1976. *Thamnophis brachystoma. Cat. Amer. Amphib. Reptiles* (190):1–2.

——. 1986. A survey of New York populations of the short-headed garter snake, *Thamnophis brachystoma* (Cope) (Reptilia: Colubridae). Unpubl. report for NYSDEC Endangered Species Unit.

Boulenger, G. A. 1893. *Catalogue of the Snakes in the British Museum (Natural History).* Vol. 1. London.

Boundy, J. 1990. Biogeography and variation in southern populations of the garter snake *Thamnophis*

Literature
Cited

288

atratus, with a synopsis of the *T. couchii* complex. Master's thesis, San Jose State University, San Jose, California.

———. 1994. *Thamnophis rufipunctatus* (narrow-headed garter snake). Color and size. Herpetol. Rev. 25:126–127.

——— and D. A. Rossman. 1995. Allocation and status of the garter snake names *Coluber infernalis* Blainville, *Eutaenia sirtalis tetrataenia* Cope, and *Eutaenia imperialis* Coues and Yarrow. *Copeia* 1995:236–240.

Bowers, B. B., A. E. Bledsoe, and G. M. Burghardt. 1993. Responses to escalating predatory threat in garter and ribbon snakes. *J. Comp. Psychol.* 107:25–33.

Boyer, D. 1992. The use of trichlorfon spray for mites in snakes. *Bull. Assoc. Rept. Amphib. Vet.* 2:2–3.

Brattstrom, B. H. 1965. Body temperatures of reptiles. *Amer. Midl. Natur.* 73:376–422.

———. 1974. The evolution of reptilian social behavior. *Amer. Zool.* 14:35–39.

Breder, C. M. 1946. Amphibians and reptiles of the Rio Chucunaque drainage, Darien, Panama, with notes on their life histories and habits. *Bull. Amer. Mus. Nat. Hist.* 86:381–435.

Brill, E. J. 1990. Ontogeny of fish capture and ingestion in four species of garter snakes (*Thamnophis*). *Behaviour* 112:299–318.

Brodie, E. D., III. 1989a. Behavioral modification as a means of reducing the cost of reproduction. *Amer. Natur.* 134:225–238.

———. 1989b. Genetic correlations between morphology and antipredator behaviour in natural populations of the garter snake *Thamnophis ordinoides. Nature* 342:542–543.

———. 1990. Genetics of the garter's getaway. *Natural History* July 1990:45–51.

———. 1991. Functional and genetic integration of color pattern and antipredator behavior in the garter snake *Thamnophis ordinoides.* Ph.D. Diss., Univ. Chicago, Chicago, Illinois.

———. 1992. Correlation selection for color pattern and antipredator behavior in the garter snake *Thamnophis ordinoides. Evolution* 46:1284–1298.

———. 1993a. Consistency of individual differences in anti-predator behavior and color patterns in the garter snake, *Thamnophis ordinoides. Anim. Behav.* 45:851–861.

———. 1993b. Homogeneity of the genetic variance-covariance matrix for antipredator traits in two nat-

Literature
Cited

ural populations of the garter snake *Thamnophis ordinoides* *Evolution* 47:844–854.

——— and E. D. Brodie, Jr. 1990. Tetrodotoxin resistance in garter snakes: An evolutionary response of predators to dangerous prey. *Evolution* 44:651–659.

Brown, A. E. 1889. Description of a new species of *Eutaenia*. *Proc. Acad. Nat. Sci. Philadelphia* 41:421–422.

———. 1901. A review of the genera and species of American snakes, north of Mexico. *Proc. Acad. Nat. Sci. Philadelphia* 53:10–110.

———. 1904. Post-glacial Nearctic centres of dispersal for reptiles. *Proc. Acad. Nat. Sci. Philadelphia* 56:464–474.

Brown, B. C. 1950. *An Annotated Check List of the Reptiles and Amphibians of Texas*. Baylor Univ. Studies, Baylor Univ. Press, Waco, Texas.

Brown, T. W. 1980. The present status of the garter snake on Santa Catalina Island, California. *In* D. M. Power (ed.), *The California Islands: Proceedings of a Multidisciplinary Symposium*, pp. 585–595. Santa Barbara Mus. Nat. Hist., Santa Barbara, California.

Brown, W. L., and E. O. Wilson. 1954. The case against the trinomen. *Syst. Zool.* 3:174–176.

Brown, W. S., W. S. Parker, and J. A. Elder. 1974. Thermal and spatial relationships of two species of colubrid snakes during hibernation. *Herpetologica* 30:32–38.

Brumwell, M. J. 1939. Variation in the snake, *Thamnophis macrostemma* Kennicott. *Trans. Kansas Acad. Sci.* 42:423–429.

Bull, J. J. 1987: Evolution of phenotypic variance. *Evolution* 41:303–315.

Burghardt, G. M. 1966. Stimulus control of the prey attack response in naive garter snakes. *Psychon. Sci.* 4:37–38.

———. 1969. Comparative prey-attack studies in newborn snakes of the genus *Thamnophis*. *Behaviour* 33:77–113.

———. 1970. Intraspecific geographical variation in chemical food cue preferences of newborn garter snakes (*Thamnophis sirtalis*). *Behaviour* 36:246–257.

———. 1975. Chemical prey preference polymorphism in newborn garter snakes *Thamnophis sirtalis*. *Behaviour* 52:202–225.

———. 1978. Behavioral ontogeny in reptiles: Whence, whither, and why? *In* G. M. Burghardt and M. Bekoff (eds.), *The Development of Behavior: Comparative and Evolutionary Aspects*, pp. 149–174. Garland Press, New York.

———. 1983. Aggregation and species discrimination in newborn

Literature
Cited

snakes. *Z. Tierpsychol.* 61:89–101.

———. 1990. Chemically mediated predation in vertebrates: Diversity, ontogeny, and information. *In* D. McDonald, D. Muller-Schwarze, and S. Natynozuk (eds.), *Chemical Signals in Vertebrates*, Vol. 5, pp. 475–499. Oxford University Press, Oxford.

———. 1992. Prior exposure to prey cues influences chemical prey preferences and prey choice in neonatal garter snakes. *Anim. Behav.* 44:787–789.

——— and P. J. Chmura. 1993. Strike-induced chemosensory searching by ingestive naive garter snakes (*Thamnophis sirtalis*). *Copeia* 1993:1–6.

——— and D. Denny. 1983. Effects of prey movement and prey odor on feeding in garter snakes. *Z. Tierpsychol.* 62:329–347.

——— and D. Layne. 1995. Effects of ontogenetic processes and rearing conditions. *In* C. Warwick, F. L. Frye, and J. B. Murphy. *Health and Welfare of Captive Reptiles*, pp. 165–185. Chapman and Hall, London.

Burt, M. D. 1928. The relationship of size to maturity in the garter snakes, *Thamnophis sirtalis sirtalis* (L.) and *T. sauritus sauritus. Copeia* 1928:8–12.

Carpenter, C. C. 1951. Young goldfinches eaten by garter snakes. *Wilson Bull.* 63:117–118.

———. 1952a. Comparative ecology of the common garter snake (*Thamnophis s. sirtalis*), the ribbon snake (*Thamnophis s. sauritus*), and Butler's garter snake (*Thamnophis butleri*) in mixed populations. *Ecol. Monogr.* 22:235–258.

———. 1952b. Growth and maturity of the three species of *Thamnophis* in Michigan. *Copeia* 1952:237–243.

———. 1953. A study of hibernacula and hibernating associations of snakes and amphibians in Michigan. *Ecology* 34:74–80.

———. 1955. The garter snake. *Scientific Monthly* 81:249–251.

———. 1956. Body temperatures of three species of *Thamnophis. Ecology* 37:732–735.

———. 1958. Reproduction, young, eggs, and food of Oklahoma snakes. *Herpetologica* 14:113–114.

———. 1977. Communication and displays of snakes. *Amer. Zool.* 17:217–223.

Carr, C. M., and P. T. Gregory. 1976. Can tongue flicks be used to measure niche sizes? *Can. J. Zool.* 54:1389–1394.

Catling, P. M., and B. Freedman. 1980a. Food and feeding behavior of sympatric snakes at Amherstburg, Ontario. *Can. Field-Natur.* 94:28–33.

—— and —— 1980b. Variation in distribution and abundance of four sympatric species of snakes at Amherstburg, Ontario. *Can. Field-Natur.* 94:19–27.

—— and W. Freedman. 1977. Melanistic Butler's garter snakes (*Thamnophis butleri*) at Amherstburg, Ontario. *Can. Field-Natur.* 91:397–399.

Chan, J. 1993. Evaluation of methods to reduce road mortality of red-sided garter snakes at Narcisse Wildlife Management Area. Master's Thesis, Univ. of Manitoba, Winnipeg.

Charland, M. B. *In press.* Thermal consequences of reptilian viviparity: Thermoregulation in gravid and nongravid garter snakes (*Thamnophis*) *J. Herpetol.*

Chiasson, R. B., and C. H. Lowe. 1989. Ultrastructural scale patterns in *Nerodia* and *Thamnophis. J. Herpetol.* 23:109–118.

Chiszar, D., S. V. Taylor, C. W. Radcliffe, H. M. Smith, and B. O'Connell. 1981. Effects of chemical and visual stimuli upon chemosensory searching by garter snakes and rattlesnakes. *J. Herpetol.* 15:415–424.

——, W. T. Tomlinson, H. M. Smith, J. B. Murphy, and C. W. Radcliffe. 1995. Behavioural consequences of husbandry manipulations: Indicators of arousal, quiescence, and awareness in reptiles. *In* C. Warrick, F. L. Frye, and J. B. Murphy (eds.), *Health and Welfare in Captive Reptiles*, pp. 186–204. Chapman and Hall, London.

Cieslak, E. S. 1945. Relations between the reproductive cycle and the pituitary gland in the snake *Thamnophis radix. Physiol. Zool.* 18:299–329.

Clark, D. R., Jr. 1974. The western ribbon snake (*Thamnophis proximus*): Ecology of a western population. *Herpetologica* 30:372–379.

Cole, L. C. 1954. The population consequences of life history phenomena. *Q. Rev. Biol.* 29:103–137.

Collins, J. T. 1991. Viewpoint: A new taxonomic arrangement for some North American amphibians and reptiles. *Herpetol. Rev.* 22:42–43.

Conant, R. 1938. On the seasonal occurrence of reptiles in Lucas County, Ohio. *Herpetologica* 1:137–144.

——. 1946. Studies on North American water snakes—II, the subspecies of *Natrix valida. Amer. Midl. Natur.* 35:250–275.

——. 1950. On the taxonomic status of *Thamnophis butleri* (Cope). *Bull. Chicago Acad. Sci.* 9:71–77.

——. 1951. *The Reptiles of Ohio.* 2nd ed. Univ. Notre Dame Press, Notre Dame, Indiana.

Literature
Cited

292

———. 1953. Three new water snakes of the genus *Natrix* from Mexico. *Nat. Hist. Misc.* (126):1–9.

———. 1958. *A Field Guide to Reptiles and Amphibians of the United States and Canada East of the 100th Meridian.* Houghton Mifflin, Boston.

———. 1961. A new water snake from Mexico, with notes on anal plates and apical pits in *Natrix* and *Thamnophis. Amer. Mus. Novitates* (2060):1–22.

———. 1963. Semiaquatic snakes of the genus *Thamnophis* from the isolated drainage system of the Rio Nazas and adjacent areas in Mexico. *Copeia* 1963:473–499.

———. 1965. Notes on reproduction in two natricine snakes from Mexico. *Herpetologica* 21:140–144.

———. 1969. A review of the water snakes of the genus *Natrix* in Mexico. *Bull. Amer. Mus. Nat. Hist.* 142:1–140.

———. 1975. *A Field Guide to Reptiles and Amphibians of Eastern and Central North America.* 2nd ed. Houghton Mifflin, Boston.

Conant, R., and J. T. Collins. 1991. *A Field Guide to Reptiles and Amphibians of Eastern and Central North America.* 3rd ed. Houghton Mifflin, Boston.

———, E. S. Thomas, and R. L. Rausch. 1945. The plains garter snake, *Thamnophis radix,* in Ohio. *Copeia* 1945:61–68.

Cook, F. 1963. Proposed rejection of the neotype and type-locality of *Thamnophis sirtalis* (Linnaeus, 1758) (Reptilia). *Bull. Zool. Nomencl.* 20:397–400.

———. 1964. Further comments on the proposed rejection of the neotype and type-locality of *Thamnophis sirtalis* (Linnaeus, 1758) (Reptilia). *Bull. Zool. Nomencl.* 21:327–328.

Cooper, J. E., and O. F. Jackson. 1981. *Diseases of Reptiles.* Academic Press, New York.

Cooper, J. G. 1860. Report upon the reptiles collected on the survey. *U.S. and Pacific R.R. Exploration and Survey, 47th Parallel (2),* 12:292–306.

———. 1870. The fauna of California and its geographical distribution. *Proc. California Acad. Sci.* 4:61–81.

Cooper, W. E., Jr. 1992. Post-bite elevation in tongue-flick rate by neonatal garter snakes (*Thamnophis radix*). *Ethology* 91:339–345.

——— and G. M. Burghardt. 1990a. A comparative analysis of scoring methods for chemical discrimination of prey by squamate reptiles. *J. Chem. Ecol.* 16:45–65.

——— and ———. 1990b. Vomerolfaction and vomodor. *J. Chem. Ecol.* 16:103–105.

———, S. G. McDowell, and J. Ruffer. 1989. Strike-induced chemosensory searching in the colubrid snakes *Elaphe g. guttata* and *Thamnophis sirtalis*. *Ethology* 81:19–28.

Cope, E. D. 1860. Notes and descriptions of new and little known species of American reptiles. Ophidia. *Proc. Acad. Nat. Sci. Philadelphia* 12:339–345.

———. 1861a [dated 1860]. Descriptions of reptiles from tropical America and Asia. *Proc. Acad. Nat. Sci. Philadelphia* 12:368–374.

———. 1861b [dated 1860]. Catalogue of the Colubridae in the museum of the Academy of Natural Sciences of Philadelphia. Part 3. *Proc. Acad. Nat. Sci. Philadelphia* 12:553–566.

———. 1861c. Contributions to the ophiology of Lower California, Mexico and Central America. *Proc. Acad. Nat. Sci. Philadelphia* 13:292–306.

———. 1866. On the Reptilia and Batrachia of the Sonoran Province of the Nearctic Region. *Proc. Acad. Nat. Sci. Philadelphia* 18:300–314.

———. 1868. Additional descriptions of Neotropical Reptilia and Batrachia not previously known. *Proc. Acad. Nat. Sci. Philadelphia* 20:119–140.

———. 1880. On the zoological position of Texas. *Bull. U.S. Natl. Mus.* (17):1–51.

———. 1883a. A new snake from New Mexico. *Amer. Natur.* 17:1300–1301.

———. 1883b. Notes on the geographical distribution of Batrachia and Reptilia in western North America. *Proc. Acad. Nat. Sci. Philadelphia* 35:10–35.

———. 1885a [dated 1884]. Twelfth contribution to the herpetology of tropical America. *Proc. Amer. Philos. Soc.* 22:167–194.

———. 1885b. A contribution to the herpetology of Mexico. *Proc. Amer. Philos. Soc.* 22:379–404.

———. 1889. On the Eutaeniae of southeastern Indiana. *Proc. U.S. Natl. Mus.* 11:399–401.

———. 1892a. A new species of *Eutaenia* from western Pennsylvania. *Amer. Natur.* 26:964–965.

———. 1892b. A critical review of the characters and variations of the snakes of North America. *Proc. U.S. Natl. Mus.* 14:589–694.

———. 1900. The crocodilians, lizards and snakes of North America. *Ann. Rept. U.S. Natl. Mus. for 1898*:153–1270.

Costanzo, J. P. 1985. The bioenergetics of hibernation in the eastern garter snake *Thamnophis sirtalis sirtalis*. *Physiol. Zool.* 58:682–692.

Literature
Cited

294

———. 1988. Recovery from ice-entombment in garter snakes. *Herpetol. Rev.* 19:76–77.

———. 1989a. Conspecific scent trailing by garter snakes (*Thamnophis sirtalis*) during autumn: Further evidence for use of pheromones in den location. *J. Chem. Ecol.* 15:2531–2538.

———. 1989b. Effects of humidity, temperature, and submergence behavior on survivorship and energy use in hibernating garter snakes, *Thamnophis sirtalis. Can J. Zool.* 67:2486–2492.

———. 1989c. A physiological basis for prolonged submergence in hibernating garter snakes *Thamnophis sirtalis:* Evidence for an energy-sparing adaptation. *Physiol. Zool.* 62:580–592.

Coues, E. 1875. Synopsis; with critical and field notes, and an extensive synonymy of the reptiles and batrachians of Arizona. In *Report upon Geographical and Geological Explorations and Surveys West of the One-Hundredth Meridian, in Charge of First Lieut. Geo. M. Wheeler. U.S. Army, Washington, D.C.* Vol. 5:587–633.

——— and H. C. Yarrow. 1878. Notes on the herpetology of Dakota and Montana. *Bull. U.S. Geological and Geographical Survey Terr.* 4:259–291.

Cracraft, J. 1992. Species concepts and speciation analysis. *In* M. Ereshefsky (ed.), *The Units of Evolution: Essays on the Nature of Species*, pp. 93–120. MIT Press, Cambridge, Massachusetts.

Crews, D. 1984. Gamete production, sex hormone secretion, and mating behavior uncoupled. *Horm. Behav.* 18:22–28.

———, M. Diamond, R. Tokarz, B. Camazine, and W. Garstka. 1984. Hormone independence of male sexual behavior in a garter snake. *Horm. Behav.* 18:29–41.

——— and W. R. Garstka. 1982. The ecological physiology of a garter snake. *Sci. Amer.* 247:158–171.

———, V. Hingorani, and R. J. Nelson. 1988. Role of the pineal gland in the control of annual reproduction behavioral and physiological cycles in the redsided garter snake (*Thamnophis sirtalis parietalis*). *J. Biol. Rhythms* 3:293–302.

Cunningham, J. D. 1959. Reproduction and food in some California snakes. *Herpetologica* 15:17–19.

Dalrymple, G. H. 1988. The herpetofauna of Long Pine Key, Everglades National Park, in relation to vegetation and hydrology. *In* R. C. Szaro, K. E. Severson, and D. R. Patton (eds.), *Management of*

Amphibians, Reptiles, and Small Mammals in North America, pp. 72–86. USDA Forest Service General Tech. Rep. RM-166.

———, F. S. Bernardino, Jr., T. M. Steiner, and R. J. Nodell. 1991. Patterns of species diversity of snake community assemblages with data on two Everglades snake assemblages. *Copeia* 1991:517–521.

——— and N. G. Reichenbach. 1981. Interactions between the prairie garter snake (*Thamnophis radix*) and the common garter snake (*T. sirtalis*) in Killdeer Plains, Wyandot County, Ohio. *Ohio Biol. Surv. Biol. Notes.* 15:244–250.

——— and ———. 1984. Management of an endangered species of snake in Ohio, U.S.A. *Biol. Conserv.* 30:195–200.

———, T. M. Steiner, R. J. Nodell, and F. S. Bernardino, Jr. 1991b. Seasonal activity of the snakes of Long Pine Key, Everglades National Park. *Copeia* 1991:294–302.

Daudin, F. 1803. *Histoire naturelle générale et particulière des reptiles.* Vol. 7. F. Dufart, Paris.

Davenport, J. W. 1943. *Field Book of the Snakes of Bexar County, Texas, and Vicinity.* Witte Mem. Mus., San Antonio, Texas.

Davis, D. D. 1932. On the occurrence of *Thamnophis butleri* Cope in Wisconsin. *Copeia* 1932:113–118.

———. 1936. Courtship and mating behavior in snakes. *Zool. Ser. Field Mus. Nat. Hist.* 20:257–290.

Deppe, W. 1830. *Preis-Verzeichniss der Saugethiere, Vogel, Amphibien, Fische und Krebse, welche von den Herren Deppe und Schiede in Mexico gesammelt worden, und bei dem unterzeichneten bevollmachtigten in Berlin gegen baare Zahlung in Preuss. Courant zu erhalten sind.* Privately printed, Berlin.

de Queiroz, A., and R. Lawson. 1994. Phylogenetic relationships of the garter snakes based on DNA sequence and allozyme variation. *Biol. J. Linnean Soc.* 53:209–229.

Devine, M. C. 1975. Copulatory plugs in snakes: Enforced chastity. *Science* 187:844–845.

———. 1984. Potential for sperm competition in reptiles: Behavioral and physiological consequences. *In* R. L. Smith (ed.), *Sperm Competition and the Evolution of Animal Mating Systems,* pp. 509–521. Academic Press, New York.

Ditmars, R. L. 1896. The snakes found within fifty miles of New York City. *Proc. Linnean Soc. New York* 8:9–24.

Dixon, J. R., and R. G. Webb. 1965. Variation in a large brood of the Mexi-

Literature
Cited

can water snake, *Natrix valida valida* (Kennicott), in Sinaloa. *Southwest. Natur.* 10:140–141.

Dodd, C. K. 1987. Status, conservation, and management. *In* R. A. Seigel, J. T. Collins, and S. S. Novak (eds.), *Snakes: Ecology and Evolutionary Biology*, pp. 478–513. McGraw-Hill, New York.

Doughty, P. 1994. Critical thermal minima of garter snakes (*Thamnophis*) depends on species and body size. *Copeia* 1994:537–540.

Dowling, H. G. 1951. A proposed standard system of counting ventrals in snakes. *Brit. J. Herpetol.* 1:97–99.

———, R. Highton, G. C. Maha, and L. R. Maxson. 1983. Biochemical evaluation of colubrid snake phylogeny. *J. Zool. London* 201:309–329.

——— and L. R. Maxson. 1990. Genetic and taxonomic relations of the short-tailed snakes, genus *Stilosoma. J. Zool. London* 221:77–85.

Drummond, H. 1983. Aquatic foraging in garter snakes: A comparison of specialists and generalists. *Behaviour* 86:1–30.

———. 1985. The role of vision in the predatory behaviour of natricine snakes. *Anim. Behav.* 33:206–215.

——— and G. M. Burghardt. 1983. Geographic variation in the foraging behavior of the garter snake,

Thamnophis elegans. Behav. Ecol. Sociobiol. 12:43–48.

Duellman, W. E. 1961. The amphibians and reptiles of Michoacán, Mexico. *Univ. Kansas Publ. Mus. Nat. Hist.* 15:1–148.

Duellman, W. E. 1965. A biogeographic account of the herpetofauna of Michoacán, Mexico. *Univ. Kansas Publ. Mus. Nat. Hist.* 15:627–709.

Duméril, A.M.C., G. Bibron, and A.H.A. Duméril. 1854. *Erpetologie générale ou histoire naturelle complète des reptiles.* Vol. 7, Pt. 1. pp. 1–780. Librairie Encyclopedique de Roret, Paris.

Dundee, H. A. 1989. Inconsistencies, inaccuracies, and inadequacies in herpetological methodology and terminology, with suggestions for conformity. *Herpetol. Rev.* 20:62–65.

Dunham, A. E., D. B. Miles, and D. N. Reznick. 1988. Life history patterns in squamate reptiles. *In* C. Gans and R. B. Huey (eds.), *Biology of the Reptilia*, Vol. 16, pp. 441–451. Alan R. Liss, New York.

Dunlap, K. D., and J. W. Lang. 1990. Offspring sex ratio varies with maternal size in the common garter snake, *Thamnophis sirtalis. Copeia* 1990:568–570.

Dunn, E. R. 1940. Notes on some American lizards and snakes in the museum at Goteborg. *Herpetologica* 1:189–194.

Duvall, D., L. J. Guillette, Jr., and R. E. Jones. 1982. Environmental control of reptilian reproductive cycles. *In* C. Gans and F. H. Pough (eds.) *Biology of the Reptilia,* Vol. 13, pp. 201–231. Academic Press, New York.

Ernst, C. H., and R. W. Barbour. 1989. *Snakes of Eastern North America.* George Mason Univ. Press, Fairfax, Virginia.

——— and S. W. Gotte. 1986. Notes on the reproduction of the shorthead garter snake, *Thamnophis brachystoma. Bull. Maryland Herpetol. Soc.* 22:6–9.

Evans, G., and W. China. 1966. Opinion 771. *Thamnophis sirtalis* (Linnaeus), 1758 (Reptilia): Rejection under the plenary powers of the neotype specimen designated for that species by Opinion 385. *Bull. Zool. Nomencl.* 23:38–40.

Farr, D. R. 1988. The ecology of garter snakes, *Thamnophis sirtalis* and *T. elegans* in southeastern British Columbia. Master's Thesis, Univ. of Victoria, British Columbia.

——— and P. T. Gregory. 1991. Sources of variation in estimating litter characteristics of snakes. *J. Herpetol.* 25:261–267.

Feder, M. E., and S. J. Arnold. 1982. Anaer-obic metabolism and behavior during predatory encounters between snakes (*Thamnophis elegans*) and salamanders (*Plethodon jordani. Oecologia (Berlin)*) 53:93–97.

Fetterolf, P. M. 1989. Common garter snake predation on ring-billed gull chicks. *Can. Field-Natur.* 93:317–318.

Finneran, L. C. 1949. A sexual aggregation of the garter snake *Thamnophis butleri* (Cope). *Copeia* 1949: 141–144.

Fischer, J. G. 1879. Neue oder wenig bekannte Reptilien. *Verhandl. Naturwiss. Ver. Hamburg-Altona* (new series 3) 1878:78–103.

Fitch, H. S. 1936. Amphibians and reptiles of the Rogue River basin, Oregon. *Amer. Midl. Natur.* 17:634–652.

———. 1940. A biogeographical study of the ordinoides artenkreis of garter snakes (genus *Thamnophis*). *Univ. California Publ. Zool.* 44:1–150.

———. 1941a. Geographic variation in garter snakes of the species *Thamnophis sirtalis* in the Pacific Coast region of North America. *Amer. Midl. Natur.* 26:570–592.

———. 1941b. The feeding habits of California garter snakes. *California Fish and Game* 27:2–32.

———. 1948. Further remarks concern-

Literature Cited

298

ing *Thamnophis ordinoides* and its relatives. *Copeia* 1948:121–126.

————. 1949. Study of snake populations in central California. *Amer. Midl. Natur.* 41:513–579.

————. 1965. An ecological study of the garter snake, *Thamnophis sirtalis. Univ. Kansas Publ. Mus. Nat. Hist.* 15:493–564.

————. 1970. Reproductive cycles in lizards and snakes. *Univ. Kansas Mus. Nat. Hist. Misc. Publ.* (52):1–247.

————. 1980a. Remarks concerning certain western garter snakes of the *Thamnophis elegans* complex. *Trans. Kansas Acad. Sci.* 83:106–113.

————. 1980b. *Thamnophis sirtalis. Cat. Amer. Amphib. Reptiles* (270):1–4.

————. 1982. Resources of a snake community in prairie-woodland habitat of northeastern Kansas. *In* N. J. Scott (ed.), *Herpetological Communities*, pp. 83–97. U.S. Fish Wildl. Serv. Wildl. Res. Rep. 13, Washington, D.C.

————. 1983. *Thamnophis elegans. Cat. Amer. Amphib. Reptiles* (320):1–4.

————. 1984. *Thamnophis couchii. Cat. Amer. Amphib. Reptiles* (351):1–3.

————. 1985. Variation in clutch and litter size in New World reptiles. *Univ. Kansas Mus. Nat. Hist., Misc. Publ.* (76):1–76.

————. 1987. Collecting and life-history techniques. *In* R. A. Seigel, J. T. Collins, and S. S. Novak (eds.), *Snakes: Ecology and Evolutionary Biology*, pp. 143–164. McGraw-Hill, New York.

————. 1993. Relative abundance of snakes in Kansas. *Trans. Kansas Acad. Sci.* 96:213–224.

———— and T. P. Maslin. 1961. Occurrence of the garter snake, *Thamnophis sirtalis*, in the Great Plains and Rocky Mountains. *Univ. Kansas Publ. Mus. Nat. Hist.* 13:289–308.

———— and W. W. Milstead. 1961. An older name for *Thamnophis cyrtopsis* (Kennicott). *Copeia* 1961:112.

Fitzinger, L. 1843. *Systema reptilium. Fasciculus primus. Amblyglossae.* Braumuller and Seidel Bibliopolas, Vindobonae.

Fleharty, E. D. 1967. Comparative ecology of *Thamnophis elegans, T. cyrtopsis*, and *T. rufipunctatus* in New Mexico. *Southwestern Natur.* 12:207–230.

Ford, N. B. 1978. Evidence for species specificity of pheromone trails in two sympatric garter snakes, *Thamnophis. Herpetol. Rev.* 9:10.

———. 1981. Seasonality of pheromone trailing behavior in two species of garter snake, *Thamnophis* (Colubridae). *Southwestern. Natur.* 26:385–388.

———. 1982. Species specificity of sex pheromone trails of sympatric and allopatric garter snakes (*Thamnophis*). *Copeia* 1982:10–13.

———. 1986. The role of pheromone trails in the sociobiology of snakes. *In* D. Duvall, D. Muller-Schwarze, and R. M. Silverstein (eds.), *Chemical Signals in Vertebrates*, Vol. 4, pp. 261–278. Plenum, New York.

———. 1992. Captive care and handling of snakes. *In* D. O. Schaeffer, K. M. Klewow, and L. Krulisch (eds.), *The Care and Use of Amphibians, Reptiles, and Fish in Research*, pp. 67–71. Scientists Center for Animal Welfare, Bethesda, Maryland.

——— and R. Ball. 1977. Clutch size and size of young in the Mexican garter snake, *Thamnophis melanogaster* (Reptilia, Serpentes, Colubridae). *Herpetol. Rev.* 8:118.

——— and G. M. Burghardt. 1993. Perceptual mechanisms and the behavioral ecology of snakes. *In* R. A. Seigel and J. T. Collins (eds.), *Snakes: Ecology and Behavior*, pp. 117–164. McGraw-Hill, New York.

——— and V. A. Cobb. 1992. Timing of courtship in two colubrid snakes of the southern United States. *Copeia* 1992:573–577.

———, ———, and W. W. Lamar. 1990. Reproductive data on snakes from northeastern Texas. *Texas J. Sci.* 42:355–368.

———, ———, and J. Stout. 1991. Species diversity and seasonal abundance of snakes in a mixed pine-hardwood forest of eastern Texas. *Southwestern Natur.* 36:171–177.

——— and D. Holland. 1990. The role of pheromones in the spacing behaviour of snakes. *In* D. Duvall, D. Muller-Schwarze, and S. E. Natynczuk (eds.), *Chemical Signals in Vertebrates*, Vol. 5, pp. 466–472. Oxford Univ. Press, Oxford.

——— and J. P. Karges. 1987. Reproduction in the checkered garter snake, *Thamnophis marcianus*, from southern Texas and northeastern Mexico: Seasonality and evidence for multiple clutches. *Southwestern Natur.* 32:93–101.

——— and D. W. Killebrew. 1983. Reproductive tactics and female body size in Butler's garter snake, *Thamnophis butleri. J. Herpetol.* 17:271–275.

——— and J. R. Low, Jr. 1984. Sex pheromone source location by garter snakes: A mechanism for detection of direction in non-volatile trails. *J. Chem. Ecol.* 10:1193–1199.

—— and M. L. O'bleness. 1986. Species and sexual specificity of pheromone trails of the garter snake *Thamnophis marcianus. J. Herpetol.* 20:259–262.

—— and C. W. Schofield. 1984. Species specificity of sex pheromone trails in the plains garter snake, *Thamnophis radix. Herpetologica* 40:51–55.

—— and R. A. Seigel. 1989a. Phenotypic plasticity in reproductive traits: Evidence from a viviparous snake. *Ecology* 70:1768–1774.

—— and ——. 1989b. Relationships among body size, clutch size, and egg size in three species of oviparous snakes. *Herpetologica* 45:75–83.

—— and ——. 1994. Phenotypic plasticity: Implications for captive-breeding and conservation programs. *In* J. B. Murphy, J. T. Collins, and K. Adler (eds.), *Captive Management and Conservation of Amphibians and Reptiles,* pp. 175–182. SSAR Publ.

Fouquette, M. J., Jr. 1954. Food competition among four sympatric species of garter snakes, genus *Thamnophis. Texas J. Sci.* 6:172–188.

—— and D. A. Rossman. 1963. Noteworthy records of Mexican amphibians and reptiles in the Florida State Museum and Texas Natural History Collection. *Herpetologica* 19:185–201.

Fox, W. 1948. The relationships of the garter snake *Thamnophis ordinoides. Copeia* 1948:113–120.

——. 1951a. Relationships among the garter snakes of the *Thamnophis elegans* rassenkreis. *Univ. California Publ. Zool.* 50:485–530.

——. 1951b. The status of the garter snake, *Thamnophis sirtalis tetrataenia. Copeia* 1951:257–267.

——. 1952. Notes on the feeding habits of Pacific coast garter snakes. *Herpetologica* 8:4–8.

——. 1954. Genetic and environmental variation in the timing of the reproductive cycles of male garter snakes. *J. Morphol.* 95:415–450.

——. 1956. Seminal receptacles of snakes. *Anat. Rec.* 124:519–540.

—— and H. C. Dessauer. 1965. Collection of garter snakes for blood studies. *Amer. Philos. Soc. Year Book* 1964:263–266.

——, C. Gordon, and M. H. Fox. 1961. Morphological effects of low temperatures during the embryonic development of the garter snake, *Thamnophis elegans. Zoologica* 46:57–71.

Freedman, B., and P. M. Catling. 1979. Movements of sympatric species of snakes at Amherstburg, Ontario. *Can. Field-Natur.* 93:399–404.

Freedman, W., and P. M. Catling. 1978. Population size and structure of four sympatric species of snakes at Amherstburg, Ontario. *Can. Field-Natur.* 92:167–173.

Froom, B. 1972. *The Snakes of Canada.* McClelland and Stewart, Toronto.

Frost, D. R., and D. M. Hillis. 1990. Species in concept and practice: Herpetological applications. *Herpetologica* 46:87–104.

———, A. G. Kluge, and D. M. Hillis. 1992. Species in contemporary herpetology: Comments on phylogenetic inference and taxonomy. *Herpetol. Rev.* 23:46–54.

Frye, F. L. 1991. *Biomedical and Surgical Aspects of Captive Reptile Husbandry.* 2nd ed. Krieger, Macabar, Florida.

Fuchs, J., and G. M. Burghardt. 1971. Effects of early feeding experience on the responses of garter snakes to food chemicals. *Learn. Motiv.* 2:271–279.

Fuenzalida, C. E., and G. Ulrich. 1975. Escape learning in the plains garter snake, *Thamnophis radix. Bull. Psychonomic Soc.* 6:134–136.

———, ———, and B. T. Ichikawa. 1975. Response decrement to repeated shadow stimuli in the garter snake, *Thamnophis radix.*

Bull. Psychonomic Soc. 5:221–222.

Gans, C., and D. Crews (eds.). 1992. *Biology of the Reptilia,* Vol. 18, *Hormones, Brain, and Behavior.* Univ. Chicago Press, Chicago, Illinois.

Gardner, J. B. 1955. A ball of gartersnakes. *Copeia* 1955:310.

Garland, T., Jr. 1988. Genetic basis of activity metabolism. I. Inheritance of speed, stamina, and antipredator displays in the garter snake *Thamnophis sirtalis. Evolution* 42:335–350.

——— and S. J. Arnold. 1983. Effects of a full stomach on locomotory performance of juvenile garter snakes (*Thamnophis elegans*). *Copeia* 1983:1092–1096.

———, A. F. Bennett, and C. B. Daniels. 1990. Heritability of locomotor performance and its correlates in a natural population. *Experientia* 46: 530–533.

Garstka, W. R., B. Camazine, and D. Crews. 1982. Interactions of behavior and physiology during the annual reproductive cycle of the red-sided garter snake (*Thamnophis sirtalis parietalis*). *Herpetologica* 38:104–123.

——— and D. Crews. 1981. Female sex pheromone in the skin and circulation of a garter snake. *Science* 214:681–683.

—— and ——. 1982. Female control of male reproductive function in a Mexican snake. *Science* 217:1159–1160.

—— and ——. 1985. Mate preference in garter snakes. *Herpetologica* 41:9–19.

Gartside, D. F., J. S. Rogers, and H. C. Dessauer. 1977. Speciation with little genic and morphological differentiation in the ribbon snakes *Thamnophis proximus* and *T. sauritus* (Colubridae). *Copeia* 1977:697–705.

Gibbons, J. W., and R. D. Semlitsch. 1987. Activity patterns. *In* R. A. Seigel, J. T. Collins, and S. S. Novak (eds.), *Snakes: Ecology and Evolutionary Biology*, pp. 396–421. McGraw-Hill, New York.

Gibson, A. R., and J. B. Falls. 1975. Evidence for multiple insemination in the common garter snake, *Thamnophis sirtalis. Can. J. Zool.* 53:1362–1368.

—— and ——. 1979a. Thermal biology of the common garter snake *Thamnophis sirtalis* (L.), I. Temporal variations, environmental effects and sex differences. *Oecologia (Berlin)* 43:79–93.

—— and ——. 1979b. Thermal biology of the common garter snake *Thamnophis sirtalis* (L.), II. The effects of melanism. *Oecologia (Berlin)* 43:99–109.

——, D. A. Smucny, and J. Kollar. 1989. The effects of feeding and ecdysis on temperature selection by young garter snakes in a simple thermal mosaic. *Can. J. Zool.* 67:19–23.

Gillingham, J. C. 1976. Reproductive behavior of the rat snakes in eastern North America, genus *Elaphe.* Ph.D. Diss., Univ. Oklahoma, Norman.

—— and J. Rowe. 1984. Daily foraging behavior of the eastern garter snake, *Thamnophis sirtalis. Amer. Zool.* 24:17A.

——, ——, and M. A. Weins. 1990. Chemosensory orientation and earthworm location by foraging eastern garter snakes, *Thamnophis s. sirtalis. In* D. McDonald, D. Muller-Schwarze, and S. Natynczuk (eds.), *Chemical Signals in Vertebrates*, Vol. 5, pp. 522–532. Oxford Univ. Press, New York.

—— and M. A. Weins. 1985. Earthworm location by foraging garter snakes, *Thamnophis sirtalis. Amer. Zool.* 25:2A.

Gordon, M. B., and F. R. Cook. 1980. An aggregation of gravid snakes in the Quebec Laurentians. *Can. Field-Natur.* 94:456–457.

Graves, B. M., and D. Duvall. 1990. Spring emergence patterns of wandering garter snakes and prairie rattlesnakes in Wyoming. *J. Herpetol.* 27:33–41.

—— and M. Halpern. 1988. Neonate plains garter snakes (*Thamnophis radix*) are attracted to conspecific skin extracts. *J. Comp. Psychol.* 102:251–253.

——, ——, and J. L. Friesen. 1991. Snake aggregation pheromones: Source and chemosensory mediation in western ribbon snakes (*Thamnophis proximus*). *J. Comp. Psychol.* 105:140–144.

Greenwell, M. G., M. Hall, and O. J. Sexton. 1984. Phenotypic basis for a feeding change in an insular population of garter snake. *Develop. Psychol.* 17:457–463.

Gregory, P. T. 1974. Patterns of spring emergence of the red-sided garter snake (*Thamnophis sirtalis parietalis*) in the Interlake region of Manitoba. *Can. J. Zool.* 52:1063–1069.

——. 1975. Aggregations of gravid snakes in Manitoba. *Copeia* 1975:185–186.

——. 1977a. Life history observations of three species of snakes in Manitoba. *Can. Field-Natur.* 91:19–27.

——. 1977b. Life-history parameters of the red-sided garter snake (*Thamnophis sirtalis parietalis*) in an extreme environment, the Interlake region of Manitoba. *Natl. Mus. Canada Publ. Zool.* 13:1–44.

——. 1978. Feeding habits and diet overlap of three species of garter snakes (*Thamnophis*) on Vancouver Island. *Can. J. Zool.* 56:1967–1974.

——. 1980. Thermal niche overlap in garter snakes (*Thamnophis*) on Vancouver Island. *Can. J. Zool.* 58:351–355.

——. 1982. Reptilian hibernation. *In* C. Gans and F. H. Pough (eds.), *Biology of the Reptilia*, Vol. 13D, pp. 53–154. Academic Press, London.

——. 1984a. Correlations between body temperature and environmental factors and their variations with activity in garter snakes (*Thamnophis*). *Can. J. Zool.* 62:2244–2249.

——. 1984b. Habitat, diet, and composition of assemblages of garter snakes (*Thamnophis*) at eight sites on Vancouver Island. *Can. J. Zool.* 62:2013–2022.

——. 1990. Temperature differences between head and body in garter snakes (*Thamnophis*) at a den in central British Columbia. *J. Herpetol.* 24:241–245.

——, R. J. Douwens, and A. G. D. McIntosh. 1982. A versatile thermal gradient apparatus for studying the thermal biology of snakes in the laboratory. *Can. J. Zool.* 60:3456–3459.

——, L. A. Gregory, and J. M. Macartney, 1983. Color-pattern variation in *Thamnophis melanogaster*. *Copeia* 1983:530–534.

——— and K. W. Larsen. 1993. Geographic variation in reproductive characteristics among Canadian populations of the common garter snake (*Thamnophis sirtalis*). *Copeia* 1993:946–958.

———, J. M. Macartney, and K. W. Larsen. 1987. Spatial patterns and movements. *In* R. A. Seigel, J. T. Collins, and S. S. Novak (eds.), *Snakes: Ecology and Evolutionary Biology*, pp. 366–395. McGraw-Hill, New York.

———, ———, and D. H. Rivard. 1980. Small mammal predation and prey handling by the garter snake *Thamnophis elegans*. *Herpetologica* 36:87–93.

——— and A. G. D. McIntosh. 1980. Thermal niche overlap in garter snakes (*Thamnophis*) on Vancouver Island. *Can. J. Zool.* 58:351–355.

——— and K. J. Nelson. 1991. Predation on fish and intersite variation in the diet of common garter snakes, *Thamnophis sirtalis*, on Vancouver Island. *Can. J. Zool.* 69:988–994.

——— and C. J. Prelypchan. 1994. Analysis of first-year growth in captive garter snakes (*Thamnophis elegans*) by family and sex. *J. Zool.* (London) 232:313–332.

——— and K. W. Stewart. 1975. Long-distance dispersal and feeding strategy of the red-sided garter snake (*Thamnophis sirtalis parietalis*) in the Interlake District of Manitoba. *Can. J. Zool.* 53:238–245.

Griffin, D. R. 1952. Bird navigation. *Biol. Rev. Cambridge Philos. Soc.* 27:359–400.

Grinnell, J., and C. L. Camp. 1917. A distributional list of the amphibians and reptiles of California. *Univ. California Publ. Zool.* 17:127–208.

Guillette, L. J., Jr., A. Cree, and A. A. Rooney. 1995. Biology of stress: Interaction with reproduction, immunology, and intermediary metabolism. *In* C. Warwick, F. L. Frye, and J. B. Murphy. *Health and Welfare of Captive Reptiles*, pp. 32–81. Chapman and Hall, London.

Günther, A. C. L. G. 1894 (1885–1902). Vol. 7 *in Biologia Centrali-Americana Reptilia and Batrachia*. Taylor and Frances, London.

Hallowell, E. 1852. Descriptions of new species of reptiles from Oregon. *Proc. Acad. Nat Sci. Philadelphia* 6:182–183.

———. 1853. On some new reptiles from California. *Proc. Acad. Nat. Sci, Philadelphia* 6:236–238.

Halloy, M., and G. M. Burghardt. 1990.

Ontogeny of fish capture and ingestion in four species of garter snakes (*Thamnophis*). *Behaviour* 112:299–318.

Halpern, M. 1983. Nasal chemical senses in snakes. *In* J. P. Ewert, R. R. Capranica, and D. J. Ingle (eds.), *Advances in Neurobiology*, pp. 141–176. Plenum, New York.

———. 1992. Nasal chemical senses in reptiles: Structure and function. *In* C. Gans and D. Crews (eds.), *Biology of the Reptilia*, Vol. 18, pp. 423–523. Univ. Chicago Press, Chicago, Illinois.

Halpert, A. P., W. R. Garstka, and D. Crews. 1982. Sperm transport and storage and its relation to the annual cycle of the female red-sided garter snake, *Thamnophis sirtalis parietalis*. *J. Morphol.* 174:149–159.

Halpin, Z. T. 1990. Responses of juvenile eastern garter snakes (*Thamnophis sirtalis sirtalis*) to own, conspecific, and clean odors. *Copeia* 1990:1157–1160.

Hampton, R. E., and J. C. Gillingham. 1989. Habituation of the alarm reaction in neonatal eastern garter snakes, *Thamnophis sirtalis*. *J. Herpetol.* 23:433–435.

Hansen, G. E., and J. M. Brode. 1980. Status of the giant garter snake *Thamnophis couchii gigas* Fitch. *Inland Fisheries Endangered Species Program Spec. Publ.* 80-5:1–14.

Hansen, R. W. 1980. Western aquatic garter snakes in central California: An ecological and evolutionary perspective. Master's Thesis, California State Univ., Fresno.

——— and G. E. Hansen. 1990. *Thamnophis gigas*. Reproduction. *Herpetol. Rev.* 21:93–94.

——— and R. L. Tremper. *In prep. Amphibians and Reptiles of Central California*. Univ. California Press, Berkeley.

Harlan, R. 1827. Genera of North American Reptilia and a synopsis of the species. *J. Acad. Nat. Sci. Philadelphia* 5:317–372.

Hart, D. R. 1979. Niche relationships of *Thamnophis radix haydeni* and *Thamnophis sirtalis parietalis* in the Interlake District of Manitoba. *Tulane Stud. Zool. Bot.* 21:125–140.

Hartweg, N., and J. A. Oliver. 1938. A contribution to the herpetology of the Isthmus of Tehuantepec. III. Three new snakes from the Pacific slope. *Occ. Papers Mus. Zool. Univ. Michigan* (390):1–8.

Hebard, W. B. 1950. Relationships and variation in the garter snakes, genus *Thamnophis*, of the Puget Sound region of Washington State. *Herpetologica* 6:97–101.

———. 1951. Notes on the life history

of the Puget Sound garter snake, *Thamnophis ordinoides. Herpetologica* 7:177–179.

Heckrotte, C. 1975. Temperature and light effects on the circadian rhythm and locomotory activity of the plains garter snake (*Thamnophis radix haydenii*). *J. Interdiscipl. Cycle Res.* 6:279–290.

Heller, S. B., and M. Halpern. 1981. Laboratory observations on conspecific and congeneric scent trailing in garter snakes (*Thamnophis*). *Behav. Neural. Biol.* 33:372–377.

——— and ———. 1982. Laboratory observations of aggressive behavior of garter snakes, *Thamnophis sirtalis:* Roles of the visual, olfactory, and vomeronasal senses. *J. Comp. Psychol.* 96:984–999.

Herzog, H. A., Jr. 1990. Experiential modification of defensive behaviors in garter snakes *Thamnophis sirtalis. J. Comp. Psychol.* 104:334–339.

——— and C. Bern. 1992. Do garter snakes strike at the eyes of predators? *Animal Behav.* 44:771–773.

———, B. B. Bowers, and G. M. Burghardt. 1989. Stimulus control of antipredator behavior in newborn and juvenile garter snakes *Thamnophis. J. Comp. Psychol.* 100:372–379.

———, ———, and ———. 1992.

Development of antipredator responses in snakes: V. Species differences in ontogenetic trajectories. *Dev. Psychobiol.* 25:199–211.

——— and G. M. Burghardt. 1986. Development of antipredator responses in snakes. I. Defensive and open-field behaviors in newborns and adults of three species of garter snakes (*Thamnophis melanogaster, T. sirtalis, T. butleri*). *Devel. Psychobio.* 22:489–508.

——— and ———. 1988. Development of antipredator responses in snakes. III. Stability of individual and litter differences over the first year of life. *Ethology* 77:250–258.

Highfill, D. R., and R. A. Mead. 1975. Sources and levels of progesterone during pregnancy in the garter snake, *Thamnophis elegans. Gen. Comp. Endocrinol.* 27:389–400.

Higley, W. 1889. Reptilia and Batrachia of Wisconsin. *Trans. Wisconsin Acad. Arts Sci. Letters* 7:155–176.

Hoff, G. L., F. L. Frye, and E. R. Jacobson. 1984. *Diseases of Amphibians and Reptiles.* Plenum, New York.

Holtzman, D. A., G. R. Ten Eyck, and D. Begun. 1989. Artificial hibernation of garter (*Thamnophis* sp.)

and corn (*Elaphe guttata guttata*) snakes. *Herpetol. Rev.* 20:67–69.

Huey, R. B., C. R. Peterson, S. J. Arnold, and W. P. Porter. 1989. Hot rocks and not-so-hot rocks: Retreat-site selection by garter snakes and its thermal consequences. *Ecology* 70:931–944.

Hulse, A. C. 1973. Herpetofauna of the Fort Apache Indian Reservation, east-central Arizona. *J. Herpetol.* 7:275–282.

Ingermann, R. L., N. J. Berner, and F. R. Ragsdale. 1991. Effect of pregnancy and temperature on red cell oxygen-affinity in the viviparous snake *Thamnophis elegans*. *J. Exper. Biol.* 1991:1–8.

——, ——, and ——. *In press.* Changes in red cell ATP concentration and oxygen affinity following birth in the neonatal garter snake, *Thamnophis elegans*. *J. Exper. Biol.*

Jacobson, E. R. 1980. Mycotic diseases of reptiles. *In* J. B. Murphy and J. T. Collins (eds.), *Reproductive Biology and Diseases of Captive Reptiles*, SSAR Contrib. Herpetol. 1:235–241.

Jaksic, F. M., and H. W. Greene. 1984. Empirical evidence of non-correlation between tail loss frequency and predation intensity on lizards. *Oikos* 42:407–411.

James, E. 1823. *Account of an Expedition from Pittsburgh to the Rocky Mountains, Performed in the Years 1819, 1820.* Vol. 1. Longman, Hurst, Rees, Orme, and Brown, London.

Jan, G. 1863. *Elenco sistematico degli ofidi.* A. Lombardi, Milan.

—— and F. Sordelli. 1868 [actually published 1866–1870]. *Iconographie générale des ophidiens.* Vol. 2. Milan.

Jansen, D. W. 1987. The myonecrotic effect of Duvernoy's gland secretion of the snake *Thamnophis elegans vagrans. J. Herpetol.* 21:81–83.

Jayne, B. C., and A. F. Bennett. 1990. Selection of locomotor performance capacity in a natural population of garter snakes. *Evolution* 44:1204–1229.

Jennings, W. B., D. F. Bradford, and D. F. Johnson. 1992. Dependence of the garter snake *Thamnophis elegans* on amphibians in the Sierra Nevada of California. *J. Herpetol.* 26:503–505.

Johnson, J. L. 1947. The status of the *elegans* subspecies of *Thamnophis*, with description of a new subspecies from Washington state. *Herpetologica* 3:159–165.

Jones, K. B. 1990. Habitat use and predatory behavior of *Thamnophis cyrtopsis* (Serpentes: Colubridae) in a seasonally variable aquatic environment. *Southwest. Natur.* 35:115–122.

Literature
Cited

Jordan, O. R. 1967. The occurrence of *Thamnophis sirtalis* and *T. radix* in the prairie-forest ecotone west of Itasca State Park, Minnesota. *Herpetologica* 23:303–308.

Joy, J. E., and D. Crews. 1985. Social dynamics of group courtship behavior in male red-sided garter snakes (*Thamnophis sirtalis parietalis*). *J. Comp. Psychol.* 99:145–149.

——— and ———. 1988. Male mating success in red-sided garter snakes: Size is not important. *Anim. Behav.* 36:1839–1841.

Justy, G. M., and F. F. Mallory. 1985. Thermoregulatory behavior in the northern water snake, *Nerodia s. sipedon*, and the eastern garter snake, *Thamnophis s. sirtalis*. *Can. Field-Nat.* 99:246–249.

Karges, J. P. 1983. Reproductive biology and seasonal activity of the checkered gartersnake (*Thamnophis marcianus*). Master's Thesis, Univ. of Texas—Arlington, Arlington, Texas.

Kennicott, R. 1859. Notes on *Coluber calligaster* of Say, and a description of new species of serpents in the collection of the North Western University of Evanston, Ill. *Proc. Acad. Nat. Sci. Philadelphia* 11:98–100.

———. 1860. Descriptions of new species of North American serpents in the museum of the Smithsonian Institution, Washington. *Proc. Acad. Nat. Sci. Philadelphia* 12:328–338.

Kephart, D. G. 1981. Population ecology and population structure of *Thamnophis elegans* and *Thamnophis sirtalis*. Ph.D. Diss., Univ. of Chicago, Illinois.

———. 1982. Microgeographic variation in the diets of garter snakes. *Oecologia (Berlin)* 52:287–291.

——— and S. J. Arnold. 1982. Garter snake diets in a fluctuating environment: A seven year study. *Ecology.* 63:1232–1236.

King, R. B. 1988. Polymorphic populations of the garter snake *Thamnophis sirtalis* near Lake Erie. *Herpetologica* 44:451–458.

———. 1989. Body size variation among island and mainland snake populations. *Herpetologica* 45:84–88.

———. 1993. Determinants of offspring number and size in the brown snake, *Storeria dekayi*. *J. Herpetol.* 27:175–185.

Kirk, J. J. 1979. *Thamnophis ordinoides*. *Cat. Amer. Amphib. Reptiles* (233):1–2.

———. 1983. Life history notes: *Thamnophis ordinoides* behavior. *Herpetol. Rev.* 14:22.

Kitchell, J. F. 1969. Thermophilic and thermophobic responses of snakes in a thermal gradient. *Copeia* 1969:189–191.

Klauber, L. M. 1924. Notes on the distribution of snakes in San Diego County, California. *Bull. Zool. Soc. San Diego* 1:1–23.

Klauber, L. M. 1948. Some misapplications of the Linnaean names applied to American snakes. *Copeia* 1948:1–14.

Klingenberg, R. J. 1993. *Understanding Reptile Parasites*. Advanced Vivarium Systems, Lakeside, California.

Klingener, D. 1957. A marking study of the short-headed garter snake in Pennsylvania. *Herpetologica* 13:100.

Kubie, J. L., J. Cohen, and M. Halpern. 1978. Shedding enhances the sexual attractiveness of oestradiol treated garter snakes and their untreated penmates. *Anim. Behav.* 26:562–570.

—— and M. Halpern. 1978. Garter snake trailing behavior: Effects of varying prey-extract concentration and mode of prey-extract presentation. *J. Comp. Physiol. Psychol.* 92:362–373.

——, A. Vagvolgyi, and M. Halpern. 1978. The roles of the vomeronasal and olfactory systems in the courtship behavior of male garter snakes. *J. Comp. Physiol. Psychol.* 92:627–641.

Kupferberg, S. J. 1994. Exotic larval bullfrogs (*Rana catesbeiana*) as prey for native garter snakes: Func-

tional and conservation implications. *Herpetol. Rev.* 25:95–97.

Larsen, K. W., and P. T. Gregory. 1988. Amphibians and reptiles in the Northwest Territories. *Occ. Pap. Prince of Wales Northern Heritage Centre* 1988:31–51.

—— and ——. 1989. Population size and survivorship of the common garter snake, *Thamnophis sirtalis*, near the northern limit of its distribution. *Holarctic Ecol.* 12:81–86.

——, ——, and R. Antoniak. 1993. Reproductive ecology of the common garter snake *Thamnophis sirtalis* at the northern limit of its range. *Amer. Midl. Natur.* 129:336–345.

Lawson, P. A. 1989. Orientation abilities and mechanisms in a northern migratory population of the common garter snake (*Thamnophis sirtalis*). *Musk-Ox* 37:110–115.

——. 1991. Movement patterns and orientation mechanisms in garter snakes. Ph.D. Diss., Univ. Victoria, British Columbia.

——. 1994. Orientation abilities and mechanisms in nonmigratory populations of garter snakes (*Thamnophis sirtalis* and *T. ordinoides*). *Copeia* 1994:263–274.

—— and D. M. Secoy. 1991. The use of solar cues as migratory orientation guides by the plains garter snake, *Thamnophis radix. Can. J. Zool.* 69:2700–2702.

Lawson, R. 1987. Molecular studies of thamnophiine snakes: 1. The phylogeny of the genus *Nerodia. J. Herpetol.* 21:140–157.

——— and H. C. Dessauer. 1979. Biochemical genetics and systematics of garter snakes of the *Thamnophis elegans-couchii-ordinoides* complex. *Occ. Papers Mus. Zool. Louisiana State Univ.* (56):1–24.

Lemos-Espinal, J. A., and Ballinger, R. E. 1992. Life history notes *Barisia imbricata imbricata:* Predation. *Herpetol. Rev.* 23:117.

Leviton, A. E., R. H. Gibbs, Jr., E. Heal, and C. E. Downs. 1985. Standards in herpetology and ichthyology: Part I. Standard symbolic codes for institutional research collections in herpetology and ichthyology. *Copeia* 1985:802–832.

Licht, P. 1984. Reptiles. *In* G. E. Lamming (ed.), *Marshall's Physiology of Reproduction,* pp. 206–282. Churchill Livingston, Edinburgh.

Lichtenfels, J. R., and B. Lavies. 1976. Mortality in red-sided garter snakes. *Thamnophis sirtalis parietalis,* due to larval nematode, *Eustrobglyides* sp. *Lab. Animal Sci.* 26:465–467.

Lillywhite, H. B. 1987. Temperature, energetics, and physiological ecol-

ogy. *In* R. A. Seigel, J. T. Collins, and S. S. Novak (eds.), *Snakes: Ecology and Evolutionary Biology,* pp. 422–477. McGraw-Hill, New York.

Lind, A. J., and H. W. Welsh, Jr. 1990. Predation by *Thamnophis couchii* on *Dicamptodon ensatus. J. Herpetol.* 24:104–106.

——— and ———. 1994. Ontogenetic changes in foraging behaviour and habitat use by the Oregon garter snake, *Thamnophis atratus hydrophilus. Behaviour* 48:1261–1273.

Linnaeus, C. 1758. *Systema naturae per regna tria naturae, secundum classes, ordines, genera, species cum characteribus, differentiis, synonymis, locis.* 10th ed. L. Salvius, Stockholm.

———. 1766. *Systema naturae per regna tria naturae, secundum classes, ordines, genera, species cum characteribus, differentiis, synonymis, locis.* 12th ed. L. Salvius, Stockholm.

List, J. C., Jr. 1950. Observation on the courtship behavior of *Thamnophis sirtalis sirtalis. Herpetologica* 6:71–74.

Logier, E. B. S. 1939. Butler's garter-snake, *Thamnophis butleri,* in Ontario. *Copeia* 1939:20–23.

Lowe, C. H., Jr. 1955. Generic status of the aquatic snake *Thamnophis* angustirostris. *Copeia* 1955: 307–309.

Lysenko, S., and J. E. Gillis. 1980. The effect of ingestive status on the thermoregulatory behavior of *Thamnophis sirtalis sirtalis* and *Thamnophis sirtalis parietalis. J. Herpetol.* 14:155–159.

Macartney, J. M., P. T. Gregory, and K. W. Larsen. 1988. A tabular survey of data on movements and home ranges of snakes. *J. Herpetol.* 22:61–73.

——, K. W. Larsen, and P. T. Gregory. 1989. Body temperatures and movements of hibernating snakes (*Crotalus* and *Thamnophis*) and thermal gradients of natural hibernacula. *Can. J. Zool.* 67:108–114.

Macias Garcia, C., and H. Drummond. 1988a. Seasonal and ontogenetic variation in the diet of the Mexican garter snake, *Thamnophis eques*, in Lake Tecocomulco, Hidalgo. *J. Herpetol.* 22:129–134.

—— and ——. 1988b. The use of frozen fish to test chemoreceptive preferences of garter snakes. *Copeia* 1988:785–787.

Malnate, E. V. 1960. Systematic division and evolution of the colubrid snake genus *Natrix*, with comments on the subfamily Natricinae. *Proc. Acad. Nat. Sci. Philadelphia* 112:41–71.

Marcus, L. C. 1980. Bacterial infection in reptiles. *In* J. B. Murphy and J. T. Collins (eds.), *Reproductive Biology and Diseases of Captive Reptiles*, SSAR Contrib. Herpetol. 1:211–226.

——. 1981. *Veterinary Biology and Medicine of Captive Amphibians and Reptiles*. Lea and Febiger, Philadelphia, Pennsylvania.

Martin, P. S. 1958. A biogeography of reptiles and amphibians in the Gomez Farias region, Tamaulipas, Mexico. *Misc. Publ. Mus. Zool. Univ. Michigan* (101):1–102.

Mason, R. T., H. M. Fales, T. H. Jones, J. W. Chinn, L. K. Pannell, and D. Crews. 1989. Sex pheromones in snakes. *Science* 245:290–293.

Mayr, E. 1942. *Systematics and the Origin of Species*. Columbia Univ. Press, New York.

——. 1963. *Animal Species and Evolution*. Harvard Univ. Press, Cambridge, Massachusetts.

——. 1969. *Principles of Systematic Zoology*. Harvard Univ. Press, Cambridge, Massachusetts.

McCauley, R. H., Jr. 1945. *The Reptiles of Maryland*. Privately printed, Hagerstown, Maryland.

McGuire, J. A., and L. A. Grismer. 1993. The taxonomy and biogeography of *Thamnophis hammondii* and *T. digueti* (Reptilia: Squamata: Colubridae) in Baja California,

Mexico. *Herpetologica* 49:354–365.

McKitrick, M. C., and R. M. Zink. 1988. Species concepts in ornithology. *Condor* 90:1–14.

McLain, R. B. 1899. *Contributions to Neotropical Herpetology.* Privately printed, Wheeling, West Virginia.

Meek, S. E. 1899. Notes on a collection of cold-blooded vertebrates from the Olympia Mountains. *Field Mus. Nat. Hist. Zool. Ser.* 1:225–236.

Mendonca, M. T., and D. Crews. 1989. Effect of fall mating on ovarian development in the red-sided garter snake. *Amer. J. Physiol.* 257:R1548–R1550.

Milstead, W. W. 1953. Geographic variation in the garter snake, *Thamnophis cyrtopsis. Texas J. Sci.* 5:348–379.

Minton, S. A., Jr. 1972. Amphibians and reptiles of Indiana. *Indiana Acad. Sci. Monogr.* (3):1–346.

———. 1980. *Thamnophis butleri. Cat. Amer. Amphib. and Reptiles* (258):1–2.

Mittleman, M. B. 1949. Geographic variation in Marcy's garter snake, *Thamnophis marcianus* (Baird and Girard). *Bull. Chicago Acad. Sci.* 8:235–249.

Mocquard, M. F. 1899. Contribution a la faune herpetologique de la Basse-Californie. *Nouv. Arch. Mus. d'Hist. Naturelle, ser. 4,* 1:297–344.

———. 1903. Notes herpetologiques. *Bull. Mus. Hist. Natur., Paris* 9:209–221.

Moore, M., and J. Lindzey. 1992. The physiological basis of sexual behavior in male reptiles. *In* C. Gans and D. Crews (eds.), *Biology of the Reptilia,* Vol. 18, pp. 70–113. Univ. Chicago Press, Chicago, Illinois.

Müller, J. W. 1865. *Reisen in den Vereinigten Staaten, Canada und Mexiko. III. Beitrage zur Geschicte, Statistik und Zoologie von Mexiko. Dritte Abtheilung. Die Wirbelthiere Mexikos. III. Amphibia.* Brockhaus, Leipzig.

Munro, D. F. 1948. Mating behavior and seasonal cloacal discharge of female *Thamnophis sirtalis parietalis. Herpetologica* 4:185–188.

Murphy, J. B., and J. T. Collins (eds.). 1980. *Reproductive Biology and Diseases of Captive Reptiles.* SSAR Contrib. Herpetol. (1):1–277.

Murray, A. 1867. List of Coleoptera received from Old Calabar, on the west coast of Africa. *Ann. Mag. Nat. Hist.* 20 (3rd. ser.):20–30.

Mushinsky, H. R. 1987. Foraging ecology. *In* R. A. Seigel, J. T. Collins, and S. S. Novak (eds.), *Snakes: Ecology and Evolutionary Biology,* pp. 302–334. McGraw-Hill, New York.

———, J. J. Hebrard, and D. S. Vodopich. 1982. Ontogeny of water snake foraging. *Ecology* 63:1624–1629.

Neill, W. T., and R. Allen. 1959. Studies on the amphibians and reptiles of British Honduras. *Publ. Res. Div. Ross Allen's Reptile Inst.* (2):1–76.

Nelson, R. J., R. T. Mason, R. W. Krohmer, and D. Crews. 1987. Pinealectomy blocks vernal courtship behavior in red-sided garter snakes. *Physiol. Behav.* 39:231–233.

Nero, R. W. 1957. Observations at a garter snake hibernaculum. *Blue Jay* 15:116–118.

———. 1960. Large plains garter snake found. *Blue Jay* 18:184.

Noble, G. K. 1937. The sense organs involved in the courtship of *Storeria, Thamnophis,* and other snakes. *Bull. Amer. Mus. Nat. Hist.* 73:673–725.

Novotny, R. J. 1990. Geographic distribution. *Thamnophis brachystoma. Herpetol. Rev.* 21:42.

Nussbaum, R. A., E. D. Brodie, Jr., and R. M. Storm. 1983. *Amphibians and Reptiles of the Pacific Northwest.* Univ. Idaho Press, Moscow.

Osgood, D. W. 1970. Thermoregulation in water snakes studied by telemetry. *Copeia* 1970:568–571.

Parker, W. S., and M. V. Plummer. 1987. Population ecology. *In* R. A. Seigel, J. T. Collins, and S. S. Novak (eds.), *Snakes: Ecology and Evolutionary Biology,* pp. 253–301. McGraw-Hill, New York.

Perry-Richardson, J. J. 1987. Female selection of male fitness in checkered garter snakes, *Thamnophis marcianus.* Master's Thesis, Univ. of Texas—Tyler, Tyler, Texas.

———, C. W. Schofield, and N. B. Ford. 1990. Courtship of the garter snake, *Thamnophis marcianus,* with a description of a female behavior for coitus interruption. *J. Herpetol.* 24:76–78.

Peters, W. C. H. 1864. Ueber einige neue Saugethiere (*Mormops, Macrotus, Vesperus, Molossus, Capromys*), Amphibien (*Platydactylus, Otocryptis, Euprepres, Dromicus, Tropidonotus, Xenodon, Hylodes*) und Fische (*Sillago, Sebastes, Channa, Mycotophum, Carassius, Barbus, Capoeta, Poecilia, Saurenchelys, Leptocephalus*). *Monatsb. dt. Akad. Wissen, Berlin* 1864:381–399.

Peterson, C. R. 1987. Daily variation in the body temperatures of free-ranging garter snakes. *Ecology* 68:160–169.

———, A. R. Gibson, and M. E. Dorcas.

1993. Snake thermal ecology: The causes and consequences of body-temperature variation. *In* R. A. Seigel and J. T. Collins (eds.), *Snakes: Ecology and Behavior*, pp. 241–314. McGraw-Hill, New York.

Pisani, G. R. 1967. Notes on the courtship and mating behavior of *Thamnophis brachystoma* (Cope). *Herpetologica* 23:112–115.

——— and R. C. Bothner. 1970. The annual reproductive cycle of *Thamnophis brachystoma*. *Science Studies* 26:15–34.

Plummer, M. V., and J. M. Goy. 1984. Ontogenetic dietary shifts of water snakes (*Nerodia rhombifera*) in a fish hatchery. *Copeia* 1984:550–552.

Pope, C. G. 1944. *Amphibians and Reptiles of the Chicago Area*. Chicago Nat. Hist. Mus., Chicago, Illinois.

Porter, R. H., and J. A. Czaplicki. 1974. Responses of water snakes (*Natrix r. rhombifera*) and garter snakes (*Thamnophis sirtalis*) to chemical cues. *Anim. Learning Behav.* 2:129–132.

Powell, R. 1982. Life history notes: *Thamnophis proximus* reproduction. *Herpetol. Rev.* 13:48.

Pough, F. H. 1980. The advantages of ectothermy for tetrapods. *Amer. Natur.* 115:92–112.

———. 1991. Recommendations for the care of amphibians and reptiles in academic institutions. *I. L. A. R. News* 33(4):1–21.

——— and C. Gans. 1982. The vocabulary of reptilian thermoregulation. *In* C. Gans and F. H. Pough (eds.), *Biology of the Reptilia*, Vol. 12, pp. 17–23. Academic Press, New York.

——— and J. D. Groves. 1983. Specializations of the body form and food habits of snakes. *Amer. Zool.* 23:443–454.

Price, A. H. 1978. New locality records and range extensions for *Thamnophis brachystoma* (Reptilia: Serpentes) in Pennsylvania. *Bull. Maryland Herpetol. Soc.* 14:260–263.

Rafinesque, C. S. 1818. A journal of the progress of vegetation near Philadelphia, between the 20th of February and the 20th of May, 1816, with occasional zoological remarks. *Amer. J. Sci. Arts* 1:77–82.

———. 1820. *Annals of nature or annual synopsis of new genera and species of animals, plants, & c. discovered in North America*. Privately published, Lexington, Kentucky.

Rahn, H. 1940. Sperm viability in the uterus of the garter snake, *Thamnophis*. *Copeia* 1940:109–115.

Rayburn, L. A. 1990. Geographic variation in prey preference of neonate checkered garter snakes (*Thamnophis marcianus*). Master's Thesis, Southeastern Louisiana Univ., Hammond, Louisiana.

Reichenbach, N. G., and G. H. Dalrymple. 1986. Energy use, life histories, and the evaluation of potential competition in two species of garter snake. *J. Herpetol.* 20:133–153.

Reuss, A. 1834. Zoologische miscellen, reptilien, ophidier. *Abhandlung. Senckenberg. Mus.* 1:130–162.

Richardson, J., et al. 1839. *The Zoology of Captain Beechey's Voyage to the Pacific and Behring's Straits Performed in His Majesty's Ship Blossom.* Henry G. Bohn, London.

Riches, R. J. 1976. *Breeding Snakes in Captivity.* Palmetto Pub. Co. St. Petersburg, Fl.

Rosen, P. C. 1991. Comparative field study of thermal preferenda in garter snakes (*Thamnophis*). *J. Herpetol.* 25:301–312.

—— and C. R. Schwalbe. 1988. Status of the Mexican and narrow-headed garter snakes (*Thamnophis eques megalops* and *Thamnophis rufipunctatus*) in Arizona. Unpubl. report U.S. Fish & Wildlife Service.

Rosenberg, H. I. 1973. Functional anatomy of pulmonary ventilation in the garter snake, *Thamnophis elegans. J. Morphol.* 140:171–184.

Ross, P., Jr., and D. Crews. 1977. Influence of the seminal plug on mating behaviour in the garter snake. *Nature* 267:344–345.

—— and ——. 1978. Stimuli influencing mating behavior in the garter snake, *Thamnophis radix. Behav. Ecol. Sociobiol.* 4:133–142.

Ross, R. A., and G. Marzec. 1984. *The Bacterial Diseases of Reptiles.* Inst. for Herpetol. Research, Stanford, California.

Rossi, J. V. 1992. *Snakes of the United States and Canada: Keeping Them Healthy in Captivity.* Vol. 1: *Eastern Area.* Krieger, Malabar, Florida.

—— and R. Rossi. 1995. *Snakes of the United States and Canada: Keeping Them Healthy.* Vol. 2: *Western Area.* Krieger, Malabar, Florida.

Rossman, C. E. 1980. Ontogenetic changes in skull proportions of the diamondback water snake, *Nerodia rhombifera. Herpetologica* 36:42–46.

Rossman, D. A. 1962a. *Thamnophis proximus* (Say), a valid species of garter snake. *Copeia* 1962:741–748.

——. 1962b. Nomenclatural status of the black-necked garter snake, *Thamnophis cyrtopsis. Ab-*

stracts Ann. Meet. Amer. Soc. Ichthy. Herpetol., Washington, D.C.

———. 1963. The colubrid snake genus *Thamnophis:* A revision of the *sauritus* group. *Bull. Florida St. Mus.* 7:99–178.

———. 1964. Relationships of the *elegans* complex of the garter snakes, genus *Thamnophis. Amer. Philos. Soc. Year Book,* 1963:347–348.

———. 1965a. Identity and relationships of the Mexican garter snake *Thamnophis sumichrasti* (Cope). *Copeia* 1965:242–244.

———. 1965b. A new subspecies of the common garter snake, *Thamnophis sirtalis,* from the Florida Gulf Coast. *Proc. Louisiana Acad. Sci.* 27:67–73.

———. 1966. Evidence for conspecificity of the Mexican garter snakes *Thamnophis phenax* (Cope) and *Thamnophis sumichrasti* (Cope). *Herpetologica* 22:303–305.

———. 1969. A new natricine snake of the genus *Thamnophis* from northern Mexico. *Occ. Papers Mus. Zool. Louisiana St. Univ.* (39):1–4.

———. 1971. Systematics of the Neotropical populations of *Thamnophis marcianus* (Serpentes: Colubridae). *Occ. Papers Mus. Zool. Louisiana St. Univ.* (41):1–13.

———. 1972. An unusual specimen of *Thamnophis marcianus* from Veracruz, Mexico. *Herpetol. Rev.* 4:169.

———. 1979. Morphological evidence for taxonomic partitioning of the *Thamnophis elegans* complex (Serpentes, Colubridae). *Occ. Papers Mus. Zool. Louisiana St. Univ.* (55):1–12.

———. 1991. Identity of the garter snake *Thamnophis sumichrasti cerebrosus* Smith. *Herpetol. Rev.* 22:80–81.

———. 1992a. The black-necked garter snake (*Thamnophis cyrtopsis*): Polytypic species or cryptic species complex? *Abstracts Ann. Meet. Amer. Soc. Ichthy. Herpetol., Urbana, Illinois.*

———. 1992b. Taxonomic status and relationships of the Tamaulipan montane garter snake, *Thamnophis mendax* Walker, 1955. *Proc. Louisiana Acad. Sci.* 55:1–14.

———. 1995a. A second external character for distinguishing garter snakes (*Thamnophis*) from water snakes (*Nerodia*). *Herpetol. Rev.* 26, in press.

———. 1995b. Taxonomic status of the southern Durango spotted garter snake *Thamnophis nigronuchalis. Proc. Louisiana Acad. Sci.* 58, in press.

———. 1996. Identity and taxonomic status of the Mexican garter snake *Thamnophis vicinus* Smith (Reptilia: Serpentes: Natricidae). *Proc. Biol. Soc. Washington* 109, in press.

—— and G. Lara-Gongora. 1991. Taxonomic status of the Mexican garter snake *Thamnophis scaliger* (Jan). *Abstracts Ann. Meet. Herpetol. League, Soc. Study Amphib. Reptiles*, State College, Pennsylvania.

——, E. A. Liner, C. H. Treviño, and A. H. Chaney. 1989. Redescription of the garter snake *Thamnophis exsul* Rossman, 1969. (Serpentes: Colubridae). *Proc. Biol. Soc. Washington* 102:507–514.

—— and G. R. Stewart. 1987. Taxonomic reevaluation of *Thamnophis couchii* (Serpentes: Colubridae). *Occ. Papers Mus. Zool. Louisiana State Univ.* (63):1–25.

Rossman, N. J., D. A. Rossman, and N. K. Keith. 1982. Comparative visceral topography of the New World snake tribe Thamnophiini (Colubridae, Natricinae). *Tulane Studies Zool. Bot.* 23:123–164.

Ruthven, A. G. 1908. Variations and genetic relationships of the gartersnakes. *Bull. U.S. Natl. Mus.* (61):1–201.

——. 1912. On the breeding habits of Butler's garter-snake. *Biol. Bull.* 24:18–20.

Savage, J. M. 1960. Evolution of a peninsular herpetofauna. *Syst. Zool.* 9:184–212.

Schaeffel, F., and A. de Queiroz. 1990. Alternative mechanisms of enhanced underwater vision in the garter snakes *Thamnophis melanogaster* and *T. couchii. Copeia* 1990:50–58.

Schieffelin, C. D., and A. de Queiroz. 1991. Temperature and defense in the common garter snake: Warm snakes are more aggressive than cold snakes. *Herpetologica* 47:230–237.

Schlegel, H. 1837. *Essai sur la physionomie des serpens*, Vol. 2. Arnz and Co., Leide.

Schmidt, K. P., and R. Conant. 1956–57. Appendix 385. Request that the International Commission on Zoological Nomenclature should direct that the nominal species "Coluber sirtalis" Linnaeus, 1758, and "Coluber saurita" Linnaeus, 1766, should be interpreted by the neotypes here designated by the present authors instead of as hitherto proposed, by reference to specified previously published figures and descriptions, pp. 224–230. Opinion 385. *Opinions and Declarations Rendered by the International Commission on Zoological Nomenclature* 12(6):191–230. London.

Schoepf, J. 1788. *Reise durch der mittlern*

und südlichen vereinigten nordamerikanischen Staaten. J. J. Palm, Erlangen.

Schwartz, J. M., G. F. McCracken, and G. M. Burghardt. 1989. Multiple paternity in wild populations of the garter snake, *Thamnophis sirtalis*. *Behav. Ecol. Sociobiol.* 25:269–273.

Scott, J. R., and Pettus, D. 1979. Effects of seasonal acclimation on the preferred body temperature of *Thamnophis elegans vagrans*. *J. Therm. Biol.* 4:307–309.

——, C. R. Tracy, and D. Pettus. 1982. A biophysical analysis of daily and seasonal utilization of climate space by a montane snake. *Ecology* 63:482–493.

Scudder-Davis, R. M., and G. M. Burghardt. 1987. Diet and growth in juveniles of the garter snakes *Thamnophis sirtalis infernalis* and *Thamnophis radix radix*. *Growth* 51:74–85.

Seibert, H. C. 1950. Population density of snakes in an area near Chicago. *Copeia* 1950:229–230.

Seigel, R. A. 1984. The foraging ecology and resource partitioning patterns of two species of garter snakes. Ph.D. diss., Univ. of Kansas, Lawrence.

——. 1986. Ecology and conservation of an endangered rattlesnake, *Sistrurus catenatus*, in Missouri, USA. *Biol. Conserv.* 35:333–346.

——. 1993. Summary: Future research on snakes, or how to combat "lizard envy." *In* R. A. Seigel and J. T. Collins (eds.), *Snakes: Ecology and Behavior*, pp. 395–402. McGraw-Hill, New York.

—— and H. S. Fitch. 1985. Annual variation in reproduction in snakes in a fluctuating environment. *J. Anim. Ecol.* 54:497–505.

—— and N. B. Ford. 1987. Reproductive ecology. *In* R. A. Seigel, J. T. Collins, and S. S. Novak (eds.), *Snakes: Ecology and Evolutionary Biology*, pp. 210–253. McGraw-Hill, New York.

——, M. M. Huggins, and N. B. Ford. 1987. Reduction in locomotor ability as a cost of reproduction in snakes. *Oecologia (Berlin)*. 73:481–485.

Shine, R. 1977. Reproduction in Australian elapid snakes. II. Female reproductive cycles. *Austral. J. Zool.* 25:655–666.

Shreve, B., and C. Gans. 1958. *Thamnophis bovallii* Dunn rediscovered (Reptilia, Serpentes). *Breviora* (83):1–8.

Simpson, G. G. 1961. *Principles of Animal Taxonomy*. Columbia Univ. Press, New York.

Slevin, J. R. 1939. Notes on a collection of reptiles and amphibians from Guatemala. I. Snakes. *Proc. California Acad. Sci.*, 4th Ser., 23:393–414.

Smith, A. G. 1945. The status of *Thamnophis butleri* Cope, and a redescription of *Thamnophis brachystoma* (Cope). *Proc. Biol. Soc. Washington* 58:147–154.

———. 1949. The subspecies of the plains garter snake, *Thamnophis radix*. *Bull. Chicago Acad. Sci.* 8:285–300.

Smith, H. M. 1940. Descriptions of new lizards and snakes from Mexico and Guatemala. *Proc. Biol. Soc. Washington* 53:55–64.

———. 1942. The synonymy of the garter snakes (*Thamnophis*), with notes on Mexican and Central American species. *Zoologica* 27:97–123.

———. 1946. Hybridization between two species of garter snakes. *Univ. Kansas Publ. Mus. Nat. Hist.* 1:97–100.

———. 1949. The identity of *Coluber subcarinata* Gray. *Herpetologica* 5:63–64.

———. 1951. The identity of the ophidian name *Coluber eques* Reuss. *Copeia* 1951:138–140.

———. 1990. The universal species concept. *Herpetologica* 46:122–124.

———, C. W. Nixon, and P. W. Smith. 1950. Mexican and Central American garter snakes (*Thamnophis*) in the British Museum (Natural History). *Linnean Soc. J. Zool.* 41:571–584.

Smith, P. W. 1956. The geographical distribution and constancy of the *semifasciata* pattern in the eastern garter snake. *Herpetologica* 12:81–84.

———. 1961. The amphibians and reptiles of Illinois. *Illinois Nat. Hist. Surv. Bull.* 28:1–298.

Smucny, D. A., and A. R. Gibson. *In press.* Patterns of heat use by female common garter snakes in a laboratory thermal mosaic. *J. Herpetol.*

Stebbins, R. C. 1985. *A Field Guide to Western Amphibians and Reptiles.* 2nd ed. Houghton Mifflin, Boston, Massachusetts.

Stejneger, L. 1894. Notes on Butler's garter-snake. *Proc. U.S. Natl. Mus.* 17:593–594.

Stevenson, R. D., C. R. Peterson, and J. S. Tsuji. 1985. The thermal dependence of locomotion, tongue flicking, digestion, and oxygen consumption in the wandering garter snake. *Physiol. Zool.* 58:46–57.

Stewart, G. R. 1965. Thermal ecology of the garter snakes *Thamnophis sirtalis concinnus* (Hallowell) and *Thamnophis ordinoides* (Baird and Girard). *Herpetologica* 21:81–102.

———. 1968. Some observations on the natural history of two Oregon garter snakes (genus *Thamnophis*). *J. Herpetol.* 2:71–86.

Literature
Cited

———. 1972. An unusual record of sperm storage in a female garter snake (genus *Thamnophis*). *Herpetologica* 28:346–347.

Stewart, J. R., D. G. Blackburn, D. C. Baxter, and L. H. Hoffman. 1990. Nutritional provision to embryos in a predominantly lecithotrophic placental reptile, *Thamnophis ordinoides* (Squamata: Serpentes). *Physiol. Zool.* 63:722–734.

Stone, W. 1906. Notes on reptiles and batrachians of Pennsylvania, New Jersey, and Delaware. *Amer. Natur.* 40:159–170.

Stuart, L. C. 1948. The amphibians and reptiles of Alta Verapaz, Guatemala. *Misc. Publ. Mus. Zool. Univ. Michigan* (69):1–109.

———. 1951. The herpetofauna of the Guatemalan Plateau, with special reference to its distribution on the southwestern highlands. *Contrib. Lab. Vert. Biol. Univ. Michigan* (49):1–71.

———. 1954. Herpetofauna of the southeastern highlands of Guatemala. *Contri. Lab. Vert. Biol. Univ. Michigan* (68):1–65.

Swanson, P. L. 1952. The reptiles of Venango County, Pennsylvania. *Amer. Midl. Natur.* 47:161–182.

Sweeney, R. 1992. *Garter Snakes: Their Natural History and Care in Captivity.* Blandford, London.

Tanner, W. W. 1950. Variation in the scale and color pattern of the wandering garter snake in Utah and southern Idaho. *Herpetologica* 6:194–196.

———. 1959. A new *Thamnophis* from western Chihuahua with notes on four other species. *Herpetologica* 15:165–172.

———. 1986 [dated 1985]. Snake of western Chihuahua. *Great Basin Natur.* 45:615–676.

———. 1988. Status of *Thamnophis sirtalis* in Chihuahua, Mexico (Reptilia: Colubridae). *Great Basin Natur.* 48:499–507.

———. 1990. *Thamnophis rufipunctatus. Cat. Amer. Amphib. Reptiles* (505):1–2.

——— and C. H. Lowe. 1989. Variations in *Thamnophis elegans* with descriptions of new subspecies. *Great Basin Natur.* 49:511–516.

Taylor, E. H. 1940. Two new snakes of the genus *Thamnophis* from Mexico. *Herpetologica* 1:183–189.

———. 1941. Herpetological miscellany, no. II. *Univ. Kansas Sci. Bull.* 27, Pt. 1 (7):105–139.

——— and I. W. Knobloch. 1940. Report on a herpetological collection from the Sierra Madre mountains of Chihuahua. *Proc. Biol. Soc. Washington* 53:125–130.

Teather, K. L. 1991. The relative importance of visual and chemical cues for foraging in newborn blue-striped garter snakes (*Tham-*

nophis sirtalis similis). *Behaviour* 117:255–261.

Telford, S. R., Jr. 1952. A herpetological survey in the vicinity of Lake Shipp, Polk Co., Florida. *Quart. J. Florida Acad. Sci.* 15:175–185.

Tennant, A. 1984. *The Snakes of Texas.* Texas Monthly Press, Austin.

Thompson, F. G. 1957. A new Mexican garter snake (genus *Thamnophis*) with notes on related forms. *Occ. Papers Mus. Zool. Univ. Michigan* (584):1–10.

Thorpe, R. S. 1975. Quantitative handling of characters useful in snake systematics with particular reference to intraspecific variation in the ringed snake *Natrix natrix* (L.). *Biol. J. Linnean Soc.* 7:27–43.

Tinkle, D. W. 1957. Ecology, maturation and reproduction of *Thamnophis sauritus proximus. Ecology* 38:69–77.

Turner, F. B. 1977. The dynamics of populations of squamates and crocodilians. *In* C. Gans and D. W. Tinkle (eds.), *Biology of the Reptilia*, Vol. 7, pp. 157–264. Academic Press, New York.

United States Fish & Wildlife Service. 1991. Proposed endangered status for the giant garter snake. *Federal Register* 56:67046–67052.

Van Denburgh, J. 1897. The reptiles of the Pacific Coast and Great Basin. *Occ. Papers California Acad. Sci.* (5):1–236.

—— and J. R. Slevin. 1918. The garter snakes of western North America. *Proc. California Acad. Sci.* Ser. 4, 8:181–270.

—— and ——. 1923. Preliminary diagnoses of four new snakes from Lower California, Mexico. *Proc. California Acad. Sci.*, Ser. 4, 13:1–2.

Van Devender, T. R., and C. H. Lowe. 1977. Amphibians and reptiles of Yepomera, Chihuahua, Mexico. *J. Herpetol.* 11:41–50.

——, ——, H. McCrystal, and H. Lawler. 1992. Viewpoint: Reconsider suggested systematic arrangements for some North American amphibians and reptiles. *Herpetol. Rev.* 23:10–14.

Varkey, A. 1979. Comparative cranial myology of North American natricine snakes. *Milwaukee Public Mus. Publ. Biol. and Geol.* (4):1–70.

Vial, J. 1957. A new size record for *Thamnophis marcianus*, Baird and Girard. *Copeia* 1957:143.

Vincent, T. 1975. Body temperatures of *Thamnophis sirtalis parietalis* at the den site. *J. Herpetol.* 9:252–254.

Vitt, L. J. 1974. Body temperatures of high latitude reptiles. *Copeia* 1974:255–256.

——. 1983. Ecology of an anuran-eating guild of terrestrial tropical snakes. *Herpetologica* 39:52–66.

—— and R. A. Seigel. 1985. Life history traits of lizards and snakes. *Amer. Natur.* 125:480–484.

Voris, H. K., and M. W. Moffett. 1981. Size and proportion relationship between the beaked sea snake and its prey. *Biotropica* 13:15–19.

Walker, C. F. 1955. A new garter snake (*Thamnophis*) from Tamaulipas. *Copeia* 1955:110–113.

Warwick, C., F. L. Frye, and J. B. Murphy. 1995. *Health and Welfare of Captive Reptiles.* Chapman and Hall, London.

—— and C. Steedman. 1995. Naturalistic versus clinical environments in husbandry and research. *In* C. Warwick, F. L. Frye, and J. B. Murphy (eds.), *Health and Welfare of Captive Reptiles*, pp. 113–130. Chapman and Hall, London.

Waye, H. L., and P. T. Gregory. 1993. Choices of neonate *Thamnophis elegans vagrans* between conspecific, congeneric, and heterogeneric odors. *J. Herpetol.* 27:435–441.

Webb, R. G. 1966. Resurrected names for Mexican populations of black-necked garter snakes, *Thamnophis cyrtopsis* (Kennicott). *Tulane Studies Zool. Bot.* 13:55–70.

——. 1976. A review of the garter snake *Thamnophis elegans* in Mexico. *Nat. Hist. Mus. Los Angeles Co., Contrib. Sci.* (284):1–13.

——. 1978. A review of the Mexican garter snake *Thamnophis cyrtopsis postremus* Smith with comments on *Thamnophis vicinus* Smith. *Milwaukee Public Mus. Contrib. Biol. Geol.* (19):1–13.

——. 1982. Taxonomic status of some Neotropical garter snakes (genus *Thamnophis*). *Bull. Southern California Acad. Sci.* 81:26–40.

Weil, M. R. 1985. Comparison of plasma and testicular testosterone levels during the active season in the common garter snake, *Thamnophis sirtalis. Comp. Biochem. Physiol.* 81A:585–587.

Weldon, P. J. 1982. Responses to ophiophagous snakes by snakes of the genus *Thamnophis. Copeia* 1982:788–794.

Wendelken, P. W. 1978. On prey-specific hunting behavior in the western ribbon snake, *Thamnophis proximus* (Reptilia, Serpentes, Colubridae). *J. Herpetol.* 12:577–578.

White, M., and J. Kolb. 1974. A preliminary study of *Thamnophis* near Sagehen Creek, California. *Copeia* 1974:126–136.

Whittier, J. M., and D. Crews. 1986. Ovarian development in red-sided garter snakes, *Thamnophis sirtalis parietalis:* Relationship to mating. *Gen. Comp. Physiol.* 61:5–12.

——— and ———. 1990. Body mass and reproduction in female red-sided garter snakes (*Thamnophis sirtalis parietalis*). *Herpetologica* 46:219–226.

———, R. T. Mason, and D. Crews. 1985. Mating in the red-sided garter snake, *Thamnophis sirtalis parietalis:* Differential effects on male and female sexual behavior. *Behav. Ecol. Sociobiol.* 16:257–261.

———, ———, and ———. 1987. Plasma steroid hormone levels of female red-sided garter snakes, *Thamnophis sirtalis parietalis:* Relationship to mating and gestation. *Gen. Comp. Physiol.* 67:33–43.

———, ———, ———, and P. Licht. 1985. Role of light and temperature in the regulation of reproduction in the red-sided snake, *Thamnophis sirtalis parietalis.* *Can. J. Zool.* 65:2090–2096.

——— and R. R. Tokarz. 1992. Physiological regulation of sexual behavior in female reptiles. *In* C. Gans and D. Crews (eds.), *Biology of the Reptilia,* Vol. 18, pp. 24–69. Univ. of Chicago Press, Chicago.

Wiley, E. O. 1978. The evolutionary species concept reconsidered. *Syst. Zool.* 27:17–26.

———. 1981. *Phylogenetics: The Theory and Practice of Phylogenetic Systematics.* Wiley, New York.

Willis, L., S. T. Threlkeld, and C. C. Carpenter. 1982. Tail loss patterns in *Thamnophis* (Reptilia: Colubridae) and the probable fate of injured individuals. *Copeia* 1982:98–101.

Wilson, E. O., and W. L. Brown. 1953. The subspecies concept and its taxonomic application. *Syst. Zool.* 2:97–111.

Woodin, W. H. 1950. Notes on Arizona species of *Thamnophis. Herpetologica* 6:39–40.

Woodward, B. D., and S. Mitchell, 1990. Predation on frogs in breeding choruses. *Southwestern Natur.* 35:449–450.

Wozniak, E. M., and R. C. Bothner. 1966. Some ecological comparisons between *Thamnophis brachystoma* and *Thamnophis sirtalis sirtalis* on the Allegheny High Plateau. *J. Ohio Herpetol. Soc.* 5:164–165.

Wright, A. H., and A. A. Wright. 1957. *Handbook of Snakes of the United States and Canada.* Comstock, Ithaca, New York.

Yarrow, H. C. 1875. Report upon the collections of batrachians and reptiles made in portions of Nevada, Utah, California, Colorado, New Mexico, and Arizona, during the years 1871, 1872, 1873, and 1874. *Report upon Geographical and*

Literature
Cited

Geological Explorations and Surveys West of the One Hundredth Meridian. Vol. 5, Chap. 4:509–633.

———. 1882. Check list of North American Reptilia and Batrachia, with catalogue of specimens in U.S. National Museum. *Bull. U.S. Natl. Mus.* (24):1–249.

———. 1883. Description of new species of reptiles in the United States National Museum. *Proc. U.S. Natl. Mus.* 6:152–154.

Zehr, D. R. 1962. Stages in the normal development of the common garter snake, *Thamnophis sirtalis sirtalis. Copeia* 1962:322–329.

INDEX TO SCIENTIFIC NAMES

Index

327

Index

Index

Index

Index